Second Edition

INFORMATION VISUALIZATION

Perception for Design

The Morgan Kaufmann Series in Interactive Technologies

Series Editors: Stuart Card, PARC; Jonathan Grudin, Microsoft; Jakob Nielsen, Nielsen Norman Group

Second Edition

INFORMATION VISUALIZATION

Perception for Design

Colin Ware

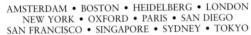
AMSTERDAM • BOSTON • HEIDELBERG • LONDON
NEW YORK • OXFORD • PARIS • SAN DIEGO
SAN FRANCISCO • SINGAPORE • SYDNEY • TOKYO

ELSEVIER

Morgan Kaufmann is an imprint of Elsevier

MORGAN KAUFMANN PUBLISHERS

Publishing Director	Diane Cerra
Publishing Services Manager	Simon Crump
Project Manager	Justin Palmeiro
Editorial Coordinator	Mona Buehler
Marketing Manager	Brian Grimm
Production Coordinator	Graphic World Publishing Services
Cover Design	Ross Carron Design
Text Design	Frances Baca, Frances Baca Design
Composition	SNP Best-set Typesetter, Ltd., Hong Kong
Technical Illustration	SNP Best-set Typesetter, Ltd., Hong Kong
Copyeditor	Graphic World Publishing Services
Proofreader	Graphic World Publishing Services
Indexer	Ty Koontz

Morgan Kaufmann Publishers is an imprint of Elsevier.
500 Sansome Street, Suite 400, San Francisco, CA 94111

This book is printed on acid-free paper.

Library of Congress Cataloging-in-Publication Data
Application submitted.

ISBN: 1-55860-819-2

For information on all Morgan Kaufmann publications, visit our website at *www.mkp.com*.

Printed in China
09 08 07 06 05   5 4 3 2

CONTENTS

CHAPTER 2

The Environment, Optics, Resolution, and the Display   29

CHAPTER 3

Lightness, Brightness, Contrast, and Constancy   69

CHAPTER 4

Color   97

CHAPTER 5

Visual Attention and Information that Pops Out   145

CHAPTER 6

Static and Moving Patterns   187

CHAPTER 9

Images, Words, and Gestures   297

FIGURE CREDITS

The following figures are reprinted with permission:

2.11   State et al. (1996). Copyright © 1996 Association for Computing Machinery, Inc.

3.11   "Bathers at Asnières" by Georges-Pierre Seurat, 1884. Copyright © The National Gallery, London. All rights reserved.

4.29   Courtesy of SmartMoney.com.

6.22   Turk and Banks (1996). Copyright © 1996 Association for Computing Machinery, Inc.

7.18   Interrante et al. (1997). Copyright © 1997 IEEE.

7.19 and 7.20   Norman et al. (1995). Copyright © 1995 Psychonomic Society.

8.6   Serra et al. (1997). Copyright © 1997 Association for Computing Machinery, Inc.

8.27   Robertson et al. (1993). Copyright © 1993 Association for Computing Machinery, Inc.

8.29   Li (1997). (1996). Copyright © 1997 Yanchao Li, University of New Brunswick.

9.2   Bellugi and Klima (1976). Copyright © 1976 Annals of New York Academy of Sciences.

9.5   Parker et al. (1998). Copyright © 1998 Academic Press.

9.7   Chandler and Sweller (1991). Copyright © 1991 Lawrence Erlbaum.

9.8   Kahn (1996). Copyright © 1996 Association for Computing Machinery, Inc.

9.9   Cypher and Smyth (1995). Copyright © 1995 Association for Computing Machinery, Inc.

10.3   T. Bray (1996). Copyright © 1996 Elsevier Science.

FOREWORD

I see what you mean. This common expression illustrates the deeply-held intuition that vision and artful images are an alternate and seemingly direct route to *insight*, which is itself another of the many words or phrases relating to vision and understanding. *A picture is worth 10,000 words*, to quote another example. Over history, visual abstractions have been developed to aid thinking: pictures from antiquity, maps from ancient Egypt, the geometry diagrams of Euclid, and the statistical diagrams of Playfair. In fact, disciplines of practice have grown up around how to do these: cartography; mechanical drawing; electrical schematics; information design for signs, labeling, and books; and statistical data graphics.

Information visualization, which is the use of interactive visual representations of abstract data to amplify cognition, is the latest of these disciplines. Because of the computer, information diagrams or visualizations can be prepared automatically at time of use, can be made dynamic and interactive, and can be integrated into a larger process of sensemaking and creation. The potential for information visualization is vast. Staggering advances in interactive computer graphics over the last two decades potentially enable building systems that give rapid insight into information-intensive problems in medicine, finance, business, and scholarship. But the design of information visualization systems is also very subtle, and there needs to be a supporting science for how to do it.

New disciplines or areas tend to go through phases. First there is the phase of exploratory design—point designs that explore the space of what can be done with the new capabilities. This has already been completed for information visualization. Then there is the characterization phase, taxonomizing or otherwise organizing the methods that have been developed and developing theories of what works. This is the current frontier of information visualization and the one most directly attacked in this book. It is necessary to progress to the future stages of validating that the theories can be used to form new designs and, finally, the codification into handbooks of engineering principles.

What information visualization is really about is external cognition, that is, how resources outside the mind can be used to boost the cognitive capabilities of the mind. Hence the study of information visualization involves analysis of both the machine side and the human side. Almost any interesting task is too difficult to be done purely mentally. Information visualization enables mental operations with rapid access to large amounts of data outside the mind, enables substituting of perceptual relation detection for some cognitive inferencing, reduces demands on user working memory, and enables the machine to become a co-participant in a joint task, changing the visualizations dynamically as the work proceeds.

Successful design of information visualization systems depends on adequately characterizing the task, the human visual system, visual displays, and the dynamic interaction among all of these. The apparent simplicity of seeing belies the complex mechanisms to achieve it. Colin Ware has written a book that brings together what is know about information visualization and its connection to vision, perception, and visual cognition. He is the perfect person to do it, with a long history of prominent contributions to the visual interaction with machines and to information visualization directly. This book starts with the visual system and moves out to its interaction with displays, visual forms, and tasks. It fills in and makes accessible much of the supporting science needed for the progress of this field beyond intuitions of what makes a useful picture. tithes book goes a long way toward joining science to the practical design of information visualization systems.

Stuart Card

PREFACE

The problem of visual thinking provided the motivation for another edition of this book. From the moment I finished the first edition, I felt the need to explore further the broader issues of how we use visualizations as cognitive tools in problem solving. The initial inspiration for the account that has emerged came from an essay by Kevin O'Regan (1992), wherein he argued that we do not have a detailed image of the world in our heads. As he put it, the world is "its own memory." He maintained that the reason we see a coherent world is that we can sample it any time we need to with a rapid eye movement or a redirection of attention within a single fixation. O'Regan was not the first to make this point, and I had already argued something similar with respect to space perception in the first edition. However, after reading O'Regan's eloquent essay I started to think more seriously about the implications of the detailed representations of the visual world.

This fact—that most of what we see is actually "out there," not in our heads—has profound implications. It explains why one's ability to think is extremely limited without external props and tools. Most cognition can be regarded as a distributed process that includes cognitive components, such as the visual system, verbal processing systems, and memory structures traditionally studied by psychologists, plus cognitive tools such as paper and pencil, diagrams, books, and the manipulation of external symbols on paper. Very rapid problem solving can be done with the right interactive display, as we pull out patterns through rapid visual searches. Increasingly, cognitive tools are computer-based, and an interactive visualization is a critical interface between the human and machine. The much-debated issue of whether or not computers can be intelligent is beside the point—people are not very intelligent without external cognitive tools. Intellectual products, such as books, pictures, theories, designs, and plans are, with few exceptions, the products of cognitive systems made up of human brains acting in concert with cognitive tools. Thus, productive intelligence can be said to reside in the system as a whole.

The process of visual thinking is the subject of an entirely new final chapter. This provides an account of visual thinking that has visual queries as a central component. Visual queries are acts of attention, pulling out patterns from the display, to meet the requirements of the task at hand. The other key components of this account of visual thinking are the data representation and the cost of acquiring knowledge—a function of both the cognitive overhead of using the computer interface and various navigation costs. Eye movements, zooming, and hyperlinks can all be treated as navigation devices whose various tradeoffs must be considered carefully in cognitive systems design.

In addition to the new chapter on visual thinking, this edition is expanded and updated throughout. It contains new sections on topics including color sequences, flow visualization, and face perception. It has many new references and figures. A new appendix deals with how to evaluate visualization techniques.

I wish to acknowledge two individuals for their contributions to the visual thinking chapter. The work of my graduate student, Matt Plumlee, has been especially helpful in showing how useful, practical guidelines for interface design can come from a relatively simple cognitive systems model. Conversations with Ron Rensink, of the University of British Columbia, also substantially influenced my thinking.

I very much appreciate the continuing support of Diane Cerra and Mona Buehler at Morgan Kaufmann. Credit for improved grammar and many corrections in references is due to the patient and polite assistance of production editor Denise DeLancey and her team. Also, my wife Dianne Ramey read the whole manuscript once again and made countless suggestions for improvement, most of which I adopted. The remaining errors, both grammatical and factual, are all mine.

PREFACE TO THE FIRST EDITION

In 1973, after I had completed my master's degree in the psychology of vision, I was frustrated with the overly focused academic way of studying perception. Inspired by the legacy of freedom that seemed to be in the air in the late sixties and early seventies, I decided to become an artist and explore perception in a different way. But after three years with only small success, I returned, chastened, to the academic fold, though with a broader outlook, a great respect for artists, and a growing interest in the relationship between the way we present information and the way we see. After obtaining a Ph.D. in the psychology of perception at the University of Toronto, I took a position at the National Research Council of Canada to work on color perception. Three years later I moved on to computer science, via the University of Waterloo and another degree, and have been working on data visualization, in one way or another, ever since. In a way, this book is a direct result of my ongoing attempt to reconcile the scientific study of perception with the need to convey meaningful information. It is about art in the sense that "form should follow function," and it is about science because the science of perception can tell us what kinds of patterns are most readily perceived.

Why should we be interested in visualization? Because the human visual system is a pattern seeker of enormous power and subtlety. The eye and the visual cortex of the brain form a massively parallel processor that provides the highest-bandwidth channel into human cognitive centers. At higher levels of processing, perception and cognition are closely interrelated, which is why the words *understanding* and *seeing* are synonymous. We know that the visual system has its own rules. We can easily see patterns presented in certain ways, but if they are presented in other ways, they become invisible. Thus, for example, the word *DATA*, shown in Figure 1, is much more visible in the bottom version than in the one at the top. This is despite the fact that identical parts of the letters are visible in each case and in the lower figure there is more irrelevant "noise" than in the upper figure. The rule that applies here, apparently, is that when the missing pieces are interpreted as foreground objects, continuity between the background letter fragments is easier to infer. The more general point is that when data is presented in certain ways, the patterns can be readily perceived. If we can understand how perception works, our knowledge can be translated into rules for displaying information. Following perception-based rules, we can present data in such a way that the important and informative patterns stand out. If we disobey these rules, our data will be incomprehensible or misleading.

This is a book about what the science of perception can tell us about visualization. There is a gold mine of information about how we see, to be found in more than a century of work by vision researchers. The purpose of this book is to extract from that large body of research literature those design principles that apply to displaying information effectively.

Figure 1   The word *DATA* is easier to read when the overlapping bars are visible. *Adapted from Nakayama et al. (1989).*

Visualization can be approached in many ways. It can be studied in the art-school tradition of graphic design. It can be studied within computer graphics as an area concerned with the algorithms needed to display data. It can be studied as part of semiotics, the constructivist approach to symbol systems. These are valid approaches, but a scientific approach based on perception uniquely promises design rules that transcend the vagaries of design fashion, being based on the relatively stable structure of the human visual system.

The study of perception by psychologists and neuroscientists has advanced enormously over the past three decades, and it is possible to say a great deal about how we see that is relevant to data visualization. Unfortunately, much of this information is stored in highly specialized journals and couched in language that is accessible only to the specialist. The research literature concerning human perception is voluminous. Several hundred new papers are published every month, and a surprising number of them have some application in information display. This information can be extremely useful in helping us design better displays, both by avoiding mistakes and by coming up with original solutions. *Information Visualization: Perception for Design* is intended to make this science and its applications available to the nonspecialist. It should be of interest to anyone concerned with displaying data effectively. It is designed with a number of audiences in mind: multimedia designers specializing in visualization, researchers in both industry and academia, and anyone who has a deep interest in effective information display. The book presents extensive technical information about various visual acuities, thresholds, and other basic properties of human vision. It also contains, where possible, specific guidelines and recommendations.

The book is organized according to bottom-up perceptual principles. The first chapter provides a general conceptual framework and discusses the theoretical context for a vision science–based approach. The next four chapters discuss what can be considered the low-level perceptual elements of vision, color, texture, motion, and elements of form. These primitives of vision tell us about the design of attention-grabbing features and the best ways of coding data so that one object will be distinct from another. The later chapters move on to discussing what it takes to perceive patterns in data: first 2D pattern perception and later 3D space perception. Visualization design, data space navigation, interaction techniques, and visual problem solving are all discussed.

Here is a road map to the book: the pattern for each chapter is first to describe some aspect of human vision and then to apply this information to some problem in visualization. The first chapters provide a foundation of knowledge on which the later chapters are built. Nevertheless, it is perfectly reasonable to access the book randomly to learn about specific topics. When it is needed, missing background information can be obtained by consulting the index.

Chapter 1: Foundation for a Science of Data Visualization A conceptual framework for visualization design is based on human perception. The nature of claims about sensory representations is articulated, with special attention paid to the work of perception theorist J.J. Gibson. This analysis is used to define the differences between a design-based approach and a science of perception–based approach. A classification of abstract data classes is provided as the basis for mapping data to visual representations.

Chapter 2: The Environment, Optics, Resolution, and the Display This chapter deals with the basic inputs to perception. It begins with the physics of light and the way light interacts with objects in the environment. Central concepts include the structure of light as it arrives at a viewpoint and the information carried by that light array about surfaces and objects available for interaction. The chapter goes on to discuss the basics of visual optics and issues, such as how much detail we can resolve. Human acuity measurements are described and applied to display design.

The applications discussed include design of 3D environments, how many pixels are needed for visual display systems and how fast they should be updated, requirements for virtual-reality display systems, how much detail can be displayed using graphics and text, and detection of faint targets.

Chapter 3: Lightness, Brightness, Contrast, and Constancy The visual system does not measure the amount of light in the environment; instead, it measures *changes* in light and color. The way the brain uses this information to discover properties of the surfaces of objects in the environment is presented. This is related to issues in data coding and setting up display systems.

The applications discussed include integrating the display into a viewing environment, minimal conditions under which targets will be detected, methods for creating gray scales to code data, and errors that occur because of contrast effects.

Chapter 4: Color   This chapter introduces the science of color vision, starting with receptors and trichromacy theory. Color measurement systems and color standards are presented. The standard equations for the CIE standard and the *CIEluv* uniform color space are given. Opponent process theory is introduced and related to the way data should be displayed using luminance and chrominance.

The applications discussed include color measurement and specification, color selection interfaces, color coding, pseudocolor sequences for mapping, color reproduction, and color for multidimensional discrete data.

Chapter 5: Visual Attention and Information That Pops Out   A "searchlight" model of visual attention is introduced to describe the way eye movements are used to sweep for information. The bulk of the chapter is taken up with a description of the massively parallel processes whereby the visual image is broken into elements of color, form, and motion. Preattentive processing theory is applied to critical issues of making one data object distinct from another. Methods for coding data so that it can be perceptually integrated or separated are discussed.

The applications discussed include display for rapid comprehension, information coding, the use of texture for data coding, the design of symbology, and multidimensional discrete data display.

Chapter 6: Static and Moving Patterns   This chapter looks at the process whereby the brain segments the world into regions and finds links, structure, and prototypical objects. These are converted into a set of design guidelines for information display.

The applications discussed include display of data so that patterns can be perceived, information layout, node–link diagrams, and layered displays.

Chapter 7: Visual Objects and Data Objects   Both image-based and 3D structure–based theories of object perception are reviewed. The concept of the object display is introduced as a method for using visual objects to organize information.

The applications discussed include presenting image data, using 3D structures to organize information, and the object display.

Chapter 8: Space Perception and the Display of Data in Space   Increasingly, information display is being done in 3D virtual spaces as opposed to 2D, screen-based layouts. The different kinds of spatial cues and the ways we perceive them are introduced. The latter half of the chapter is taken up with a set of seven spatial tasks and the perceptual issues associated with each.

The applications discussed include 3D information displays, stereo displays, the choice of 2D vs. 3D visualization, 3D graph viewing, and virtual environments.

Chapter 9: Images, Words, and Gestures Visual information and verbal information are processed in different ways and by different parts of the brain. Each has its own strengths, and often both should be combined in a presentation. This chapter addresses when visual and verbal presentation should be used and how the two kinds of information should be linked.

The applications discussed include integrating images and words, visual programming languages, and effective diagrams.

Chapter 10: Interacting with Visualizations Major interaction cycles are defined. Within this framework, low-level data manipulation, dynamic control over data views, and navigation through data spaces are discussed.

The applications discussed include interacting with data, selection, scrolling, zooming interfaces, and navigation.

Chapter 11: Thinking with Visualization The process whereby a visualization is used as part of a decision-making process is outlined. Central to this is a description of how visual queries are formed to guide attention and determine what is loaded into visual working memory. This model provides insights into how to balance the tradeoffs between navigation costs and screen layout in the design of visual information systems.

The applications discussed include problem solving with visualization, design of interactive systems, and creativity.

These are exciting times for visualization design. The computer technology used to produce visualizations has reached a stage at which sophisticated, interactive 3D views of data can be produced on ordinary desktop computers. The trend toward more and more visual information is accelerating, and there is an explosion of new visualization techniques being invented to help us cope with our need to analyze huge and complex bodies of information. This creative phase will not last long. With the dawn of a new technology, there is often only a short burst of creative design before the forces of standardization make what is new into what is conventional. Undoubtedly, many of the visualization techniques that are now emerging will become routine tools in the near future. Even badly designed things can become industry standards. Designing for perception can help us to avoid such mistakes. If we can harness the knowledge that has been accumulated about how perception works, we can make visualizations into more transparent windows into the world of information.

I wish to thank the many people who have helped me with this book. The people who most influenced the way I think about perception and visualization are Donald Mitchell, John Kennedy, and William Cowan. I have gained enormously by working with Larry Mayer in developing new tools to map the oceans, as well as with colleagues Kelly Booth, Dave Wells, Tim Dudely, Scott Mackenzie, and Eric Neufeld. It has been my good fortune to work with many talented graduate students and research assistants on visualization-related projects: Daniel Jessome, Richard Guitard, Timothy Lethbridge, Siew Hong Yang, Sean Riley, Serge Limoges, David Fowler, Stephen Osborne, K. Wing Wong, Dale Chapman, Pat Cavanaugh, Ravin Balakrishnan, Mark Paton, Monica Sardesai, Cyril Gobrecht, Suryan Stalin, Justine Hickey, Yanchao Li, Rohan Parkhi, Kathy Lowther, Li Wang, Greg Parker, Daniel Fleet, Jun Yang, Graham Sweet, Roland Arsenault, Natalie Webber, Poorang Irani, Jordan Lutes, Nhu Le, Irina Padioukova, Glenn Franck, Lyn Bartram, and Matthew Plumlee. Many of the ideas presented here have been refined through their efforts.

Peter Pirolli, Doug Gillan, and Nahum Gershon made numerous suggestions that helped me improve the manuscript. As a result, the last two chapters, especially, underwent radical revision. I also wish to thank the editorial staff at Morgan Kaufmann: Diane Cerra, Belinda Breyer, and Heather Collins. Finally, my wife, Dianne Ramey, read every word, made it readable, and kept me going.

CHAPTER 1

Foundation for a Science of Data Visualization

In his book *The End of Science*, science writer John Horgan (1997) argues that science is finished except for the mopping up of details. He makes a good case where physics is concerned. In that discipline, the remaining deep problems may involve generating so much energy as to require the harnessing of entire stars. Similarly, biology has its foundations in DNA and genetics and is now faced with the infinite but often tedious complexity of mapping genes into proteins through intricate pathways.

What Horgan fails to recognize is that cognitive science has fundamental problems that are still to be solved. In particular, the mechanisms of the construction and storage of knowledge remain open questions. He implicitly adopts the physics-centric view of science, which holds that physics is the queen of sciences, and in descending order come chemistry, then biology, with psychology barely acknowledged as a science at all. In this pantheon, sociology is regarded as somewhere on a par with astrology. This attitude is short-sighted. Chemistry builds on physics, enabling our understanding of materials; biology builds on chemistry, enabling us to understand the much greater complexity of living organisms; and psychology builds on neurophysiology, enabling us to understand the processes of cognition. At each level is a separate discipline greater in complexity and level of difficulty than those beneath. It is difficult to conceive of a value scale for which the mechanisms of thought are not of fundamentally greater interest and importance than the interaction of subatomic particles.

Those who dismiss psychology as a pseudo-science have not being paying attention. Over the past few decades, enormous strides have been made in identifying the brain structures and cognitive mechanisms that have enabled humans to create the huge body of knowledge that now exists. But we need to go one step further and recognize that people with machines, and in groups, are much more cognitively powerful than a single person alone with his or her thoughts. This has been true for a long time. *Artifacts* such as paper, writing, and geometry instruments have been cognitive tools for centuries. It is not necessary to take the cultural relativists' view to see that sciences are built using socially constructed symbol systems. The review process employed

1

by scientific journals is an obvious example of a social process critical to the construction of knowledge.

As Hutchins (1995) so effectively pointed out, thinking is not something that goes on entirely, or even mostly, inside people's heads. Little intellectual work is accomplished with our eyes and ears closed. Most cognition is done as a kind of interaction with cognitive tools, pencils and paper, calculators, and increasingly, computer-based intellectual supports and information systems. Neither is cognition mostly accomplished alone with a computer. It occurs as a process in systems containing many people and many cognitive tools. Since the beginning of science, diagrams, mathematical notations, and writing have been essential tools of the scientist. Now we have powerful interactive analytic tools, such as MATLAB, Maple, Mathematica, and S-PLUS, together with databases. The entire fields of genomics and proteomics are built on computer storage and analytic tools. The social apparatus of the school system, the university, the academic journal, and the conference are obviously designed to support cognitive activity.

But we should not consider classical science only. Cognition in engineering, banking, business, and the arts is similarly carried out through distributed cognitive systems. In each case, "thinking" occurs through interaction between individuals, using cognitive tools, and operating within social networks. Hence, cognitive systems theory is a much broader discipline than psychology. This is emerging as the most interesting, difficult, complex, yet fundamentally the most important, of sciences.

Visualizations have a small but crucial and expanding role in cognitive systems. Visual displays provide the highest bandwidth channel from the computer to the human. We acquire more information through vision than through all of the other senses combined. The 20 billion or so neurons of the brain devoted to analyzing visual information provide a pattern-finding mechanism that is a fundamental component in much of our cognitive activity. Improving cognitive systems often means tightening the loop between a person, computer-based tools, and other individuals. On the one hand, we have the human visual system, a flexible pattern finder, coupled with an adaptive decision-making mechanism. On the other hand are the computational power and vast information resources of the computer and the World Wide Web. Interactive visualizations are increasingly the interface between the two. Improving these interfaces can substantially improve the performance of the entire system.

Until recently, the term *visualization* meant *constructing a visual image in the mind (Shorter Oxford English Dictionary, 1972)* It has now come to mean something more like *a graphical representation of data or concepts*. Thus, from being an internal construct of the mind, a visualization has become an external artifact supporting decision making. The way visualization functions as cognitive tools is the subject of this book.

One of the greatest benefits of data visualization is the sheer quantity of information that can be rapidly interpreted if it is presented well. Figure 1.1 shows a visualization derived from a multibeam echo sounder scanning part of Passamoquoddy Bay, between Maine, in the United States, and New Brunswick, Canada, where the tides are the highest in the world. Approximately one million measurements were made. Traditionally, this kind of data is presented in the form of a nautical chart with contours and spot soundings. However, when the data is converted to a

Figure 1.1   Passamoquoddy Bay visualization. *Data courtesy of the Canadian Hydrographic Service.*

height field and displayed using standard computer graphics techniques, many things become visible that were previously invisible on the chart. A pattern of features called *pockmarks* can immediately be seen, and it is easy to see how they form lines. Also visible are various problems with the data. The linear ripples (not aligned with the pockmarks) are errors in the data because the roll of the ship that took the measurements was not properly taken into account.

The Passamoquoddy Bay image highlights a number of the advantages of visualization:

- Visualization provides an ability to comprehend huge amounts of data. The important information from more than a million measurements is immediately available.

- Visualization allows the perception of emergent properties that were not anticipated. In this visualization, the fact that the pockmarks appear in lines is immediately evident. The perception of a pattern can often be the basis of a new insight. In this case, the pockmarks align with the direction of geological faults, suggesting a cause. They may be due to the release of gas.

- Visualization often enables problems with the data itself to become immediately apparent. A visualization commonly reveals things not only about the data itself, but about the way it is collected. With an appropriate visualization, errors and artifacts in the data often jump out at you. For this reason, visualizations can be invaluable in quality control.

- Visualization facilitates understanding of both large-scale and small-scale features of the data. It can be especially valuable in allowing the perception of patterns linking local features.

• Visualization facilitates hypothesis formation. For example, the visualization in Figure 1.1 was directly responsible for a research paper concerning the geological significance of the pockmark features (Gray et al., 1997).

This first chapter has the general goal of defining the scope of a science of visualization based on perceptual principles. Much of it is devoted to outlining the intellectual basis of the endeavor and providing an overview of the kinds of experimental techniques appropriate to visualization research. In the latter half of the chapter, a brief overview of human visual processing is introduced to provide a kind of road map to the more detailed analysis of later chapters. The chapter concludes with a categorization of data. It is important to have a conception of the kinds of data we may wish to visualize so that we can talk in general terms about the ways in which whole classes of data should be represented.

Visualization Stages

The process of data visualization includes four basic stages, combined in a number of feedback loops. These are illustrated in Figure 1.2.

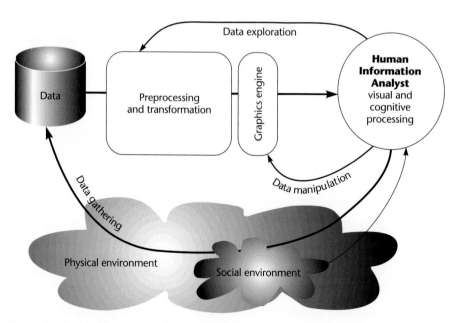

Figure 1.2   A schematic diagram of the visualization process.

The four stages consist of:

- The collection and storage of data itself

- The preprocessing designed to transform the data into something we can understand

- The display hardware and the graphics algorithms that produce an image on the screen

- The human perceptual and cognitive system (the perceiver)

The longest feedback loop involves gathering data. A data seeker, such as a scientist or a stock-market analyst, may choose to gather more data to follow up on an interesting lead. Another loop controls the computational preprocessing that takes place prior to visualization. The analyst may feel that if the data is subjected to a certain transformation prior to visualization, it can be persuaded to give up its meaning. Finally, the visualization process itself may be highly interactive. For example, in 3D data visualization, the scientist may fly to a different vantage point to better understand the emerging structures. Alternatively, a computer mouse may be used interactively, to select the parameter ranges that are most interesting. Both the physical environment and the social environment are involved in the data-gathering loop. The physical environment is a source of data, while the social environment determines in subtle and complex ways what is collected and how it is interpreted.

In this book, the emphasis is on data, perception, and the various tasks to which visualization may be applied. In general, algorithms are discussed only insofar as they are related to perception. The computer is treated, with some reservations, as a universal tool for producing interactive graphics. This means that once we figure out the best way to visualize data for a particular task, we assume that we can construct algorithms to create the appropriate images. The critical question is how best to transform the data into something that people can understand for optimal decision making. Before plunging into a detailed analysis of human perception and how it applies in practice, however, we must establish the conceptual basis for the endeavor.

The purpose of this discussion is to stake out a theoretical framework wherein claims about visualizations being "visually efficient" or "natural" can be pinned down in the form of testable predictions.

Experimental Semiotics Based on Perception

This book is about the science of visualization, as opposed to the craft or art of visualization. But the claim that visualization can be treated as a science may be disputed. Let's look at the alternative view. Some scholars argue that visualization is best understood as a kind of learned language and not as a science at all. In essence, their argument is that visualization is about diagrams and how they can convey meaning. Generally, diagrams are held to be made up of symbols, and symbols are based on social interaction. The meaning of a symbol is normally understood to be created by convention, which is established in the course of person-to-person communication. Diagrams are arbitrary and are effective in much the same way as the written words on this page are effective—we must learn the conventions of the language, and the better we learn them, the clearer that language will be. Thus, one diagram may ultimately be as good as another; it is just a matter of learning the code, and the laws of perception are largely irrelevant. This view has strong philosophical proponents from the field of semiotics. Although it is not the position adopted here, the debate can help us define where vision research can assist us in designing better visualizations, and where we would be wise to consult a graphic designer trained in an art college.

Semiotics of Graphics

The study of symbols and how they convey meaning is called *semiotics*. This discipline was originated in the United States by C.S. Peirce and later developed in Europe by the French philosopher and linguist Ferdinand de Saussure (1959). Semiotics has been dominated mostly by philosophers and by those who construct arguments based on example rather than on formal experiment. In his great masterwork, *Semiology of Graphics*, Jacques Bertin (1983) attempted to classify all graphic marks in terms of how they could express data. For the most part, this work is based on his own judgment, although it is a highly trained and sensitive judgment. There are few, if any, references to theories of perception or scientific studies.

It is often claimed that visual languages are easy to learn and use. But what do we mean by the term *visual language*—clearly not the writing on this page. Reading and writing take years of education to master, and it can take almost as long to master some diagrams. Figure 1.3 shows three examples of languages that have some claim to being visual. The first example of visual language is based on a cave painting. We can readily interpret human figures and infer that the people are using bows and arrows to hunt deer. The second example is a schematic diagram showing the interaction between a person and a computer in a virtual environment system; the brain in the diagram is a simplified picture, but it is a part of the anatomy that few have directly perceived. The arrows show data flows and are arbitrary conventions, as are the printed words. The third example is the expression of a mathematical equation that is utterly obscure to all but the initiated. These examples clearly show that some visual languages are easier to "read" than others. But why? Perhaps it is simply that we have more experience with the kind of pictorial image shown in the cave painting and less with the mathematical notation. Perhaps the concepts expressed in the cave painting are more familiar than those in the equation.

The most profound threat to the idea that there can be a science of visualization originates with Saussure. He defined a principle of *arbitrariness* as applying to the relationship between the symbol and the thing that is signified. Saussure was also a founding member of a group of structuralist philosophers and anthropologists who, although they disagreed on many fundamental issues, were unified in their general insistence that truth is relative to its social context. Meaning in one culture may be nonsense in another. A trash can as a visual symbol for deletion is meaningful only to those who know how trash cans are used. Thinkers such as Lévi-Strauss, Barthes,

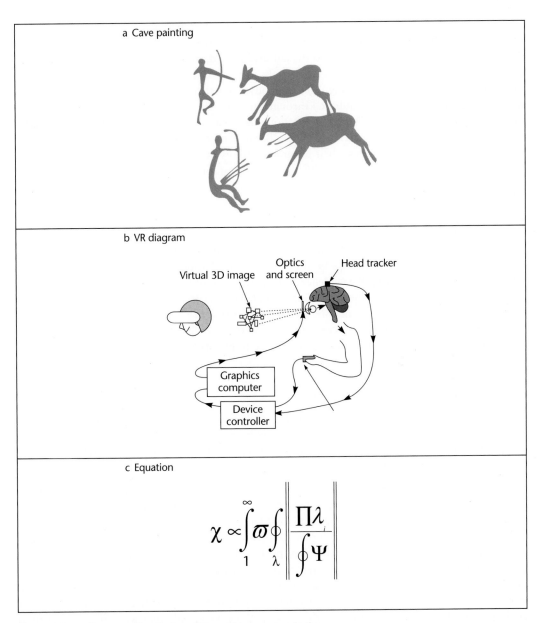

Figure 1.3   Three graphics. Each could be said to be a visualization.

and Lacan have condemned the cultural imperialism and intellectual arrogance implicit in applying our intellects to characterizing other cultures as "primitive." As a result, they have developed
the theory that all meaning is relative to the culture. Indeed, meaning is created by society. They
claim that we can interpret another culture only in the context of our own culture and using
the tools of our own language. Languages are conventional means of communication in which
the meanings of symbols are established through custom. Their point is that no one representation is "better" than another. All representations have value. All are meaningful to those who
understand them and agree to their meanings. Because it seems entirely reasonable to consider
visualizations as communications, their argument strikes at the root of the idea that there can
be a natural science of visualization with the goal of establishing specific guidelines for better
representations.

Pictures as Sensory Languages

The question of whether pictures and diagrams are purely conventional, or are perceptual
symbols with special properties, has been the subject of considerable scientific investigation. A
good place to begin reviewing the evidence is the perception of pictures. There has been a debate
over the last century between those who claim that pictures are every bit as arbitrary as words
and those who believe that there may be a measure of *similarity* between pictures and the things
that they represent. This debate is crucial to the theory presented here; if even "realistic" pictures do not embody a sensory language, it will be impossible to make claims that certain diagrams and other visualizations are better designed perceptually.

The nominalist philosopher Nelson Goodman has delivered some of the more forceful attacks
on the notion of similarity in pictures (1968):

> *Realistic representation, in brief, depends not upon imitation or illusion or information
> but upon inculcation. Almost any picture may represent almost anything; that is, given
> picture and object there is usually a system of representation—a plan of correlation—
> under which the picture represents the object.*

For Goodman, realistic representation is a matter of convention; it "depends on how stereotyped
the model of representation is, how commonplace the labels and their uses have become."
Bieusheuvel (1947) expresses the same opinion: "The picture, particularly one printed on paper,
is a highly conventional symbol, which the child reared in Western culture has learned to interpret." These statements, taken at face value, invalidate any meaningful basis for saying that a
certain visualization is fundamentally better or more natural than another. This would mean that
all languages are equally valid and that all are learned. If we accept this position, the best
approach to designing visual languages would be to establish graphical conventions early and
stick to them. It would not matter what the conventions were, only that we adhered to them in
order to reduce the labor of learning new conventions.

In support of the nominalist argument, a number of anthropologists have reported expressions of puzzlement from people who encounter pictures for the first time. "A Bush Negro woman

turned a photograph this way and that, in attempting to make sense out of the shadings of gray on the piece of paper she held" (Herskovits, 1948). The evidence related to whether or not we must learn to see pictures has been carefully reviewed and analyzed by Kennedy (1974). He rejects the strong position that pictures and other visual representations are entirely arbitrary. In the case of the reported puzzlement of people who are seeing pictures for the first time, Kennedy argues that these people are amazed by the technology rather than unable to interpret the picture. After all, a photograph is a remarkable artifact. What curious person would not turn it over to see if, perhaps, the reverse side contains some additional interesting information?

Here are two of the many studies that contradict the nominalist position and suggest that people can interpret pictures without training. Deregowski (1968) reported studies of adults and children, in a remote area of Zambia, who had very little graphic art. Despite this, these people could easily match photographs of toy animals with the actual toys. In an extraordinary but very different kind of experiment, Hochberg and Brooks (1962) raised their daughter nearly to the age of two in a house with no pictures. She was never read to from a picture book and there were no pictures on the walls in the house. Although her parents could not completely block the child's exposure to pictures on trips outside the house, they were careful never to indicate a picture and tell the child that it was a representation of something. Thus, she had no social input telling her that pictures had any kind of meaning. When the child was finally tested, she had a reasonably large vocabulary, and she was asked to identify objects in line drawings and in black-and-white photographs. Despite her lack of instruction in the interpretation of pictures, she was almost always correct in her answers.

However, the issue of how pictures, and especially line drawings, are able to unambiguously represent things is still not fully understood. Clearly, a portrait is a pattern of marks on a page; in a physical sense, it is utterly unlike the flesh-and-blood person it depicts. The most probable explanation is that at some stage in visual processing, the pictorial outline of an object and the object itself excite similar neural processes (Pearson et al., 1990). This view is made plausible by the ample evidence that one of the most important products of early visual processing is the extraction of linear features in the visual array. These may be either the visual boundaries of objects or the lines in a line drawing. The nature of these mechanisms is discussed further in Chapter 6.

Although we may be able to understand certain pictures without learning, it would be a mistake to underestimate the role of convention in representation. Even with the most realistic picture or sculpture, it is very rare for the artifact to be mistaken for the thing that is represented. *Trompe l'oeil* art is designed to "fool the eye" into the illusion that a painting is real. Artists are paid to paint pictures of niches containing statues that look real, and sometimes, for an instant, the viewer will be fooled. On a more mundane level, a plastic laminate on furniture may contain a photograph of wood grain that is very difficult to tell from the real thing. But in general, a picture is intended to represent an object or a scene; it is not intended to be mistaken for it. Many pictures are highly stylized—they violate the laws of perspective and develop particular methods of representation that no one would call realistic.

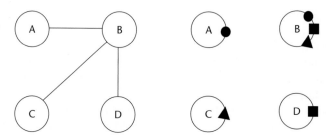

Figure 1.4   Two different graphical methods for showing relationships between entities.

When we turn to diagrams and nonpictorial visualizations, it is clear that convention must play a greater role. Figure 1.3(b) is not remotely "like" any scene in the real world under any system of measurement. Nevertheless, we can argue that many elements in it are constructed in ways that for perceptual reasons make the diagram easy to interpret. The lines that connect the various components, for example, are a notation that is easy to read, because the visual cortex of the brain contains mechanisms specifically designed to seek out continuous contours. Other possible graphical notations for showing connectivity would be far less effective. Figure 1.4 shows two different conventions for demonstrating relationships between entities. The connecting lines on the left are much more effective than the symbols on the right.

Sensory versus Arbitrary Symbols

In this book, the word *sensory* is used to refer to symbols and aspects of visualizations that derive their expressive power from their ability to use the perceptual processing power of the brain without learning. The word *arbitrary* is used to define aspects of representation that must be learned, because the representations have no perceptual basis. For example, the written word *dog* bears no perceptual relationship to any actual animal. Probably very few graphical languages consist of entirely arbitrary conventions, and probably none is entirely sensory. However, the sensory-versus-arbitrary distinction is important. Sensory representations are effective (or misleading) because they are well matched to the early stages of neural processing. They tend to be stable across individuals, cultures, and time. A cave drawing of a hunt still conveys much of its meaning across several millennia. Conversely, arbitrary conventions derive their power from culture and are therefore dependent on the particular cultural milieu of an individual.

The theory of sensory languages is based on the idea that the human visual system has evolved as an instrument to perceive the physical world. It rejects the idea that the visual system is a truly universal machine. It was once widely held that the brain at birth was an undifferentiated neural net, capable of configuring itself to perceive in any world, no matter how strange. According to this theory, if a newborn human infant were to be born into a world with entirely different rules for the propagation of light, that infant would nevertheless learn to see. Partly, this view came from the fact that all cortical brain tissue looks more or less the same, a uniform pinkish gray, so it was thought to be functionally undifferentiated. This *tabula rasa* view has been overthrown as neurologists have come to understand that the brain has a great many specialized regions. Figure 1.5 shows the major neural pathways between different parts of the brain involved in visual processing (Distler et al., 1993). Although much of the functionality remains unclear, this diagram represents an amazing achievement and summarizes the work of dozens of researchers. These structures are present both in higher primates and in humans. The brain is clearly not an undifferentiated mass; it is more like a collection of highly specialized parallel-processing machines with high-bandwidth interconnections. The entire system is designed to

Figure 1.5   The major visual pathways of the Macaque monkey. This diagram is included to illustrate the structural complexity of the visual system and because a number of these areas are referenced in different sections of this book. *Adapted from Distler et al. (1993); notes added. V1–V4, visual areas 1–4; PO, parieto-occipital area; MT, middle temporal area (also called V5); DP, dorsal prestiate area; PP, posterior parietal complex; STS, superiotemporal sulcus complex; IT, inferotemporal cortex.*

extract information from the world in which we live, not from some other environment with entirely different physical properties.

Certain basic elements are necessary for the visual system to develop normally. For example, cats reared in a world consisting only of vertical stripes develop distorted visual cortices, with an unusual preponderance of vertical-edge detectors. Nevertheless, the basic elements for the development of normal vision are present in all but the most abnormal circumstances. The interaction of the growing nervous system with everyday reality leads to a more or less standard visual system. This should not surprise us; the everyday world has ubiquitous properties that are common to all environments. All earthly environments consist of objects with well-defined surfaces, surface textures, surface colors, and a variety of shapes. Objects exhibit temporal persistence—they do not randomly appear and vanish, except when there are specific causes. At a more fundamental level, light travels in straight lines and reflects off surfaces in certain ways. The law of gravity continues to operate. Given these ubiquitous properties of the everyday world, the evidence suggests that we all develop essentially the same visual systems, irrespective of cultural milieu. Monkeys and even cats have visual structures very similar to those of humans.

For example, although Figure 1.5 is based on the visual pathways of the Macaque monkey, a number of lines of evidence show that the same structures exist in humans. First, the same areas can be identified anatomically in humans and animals. Second, specific patterns of blindness occur that point to the same areas having the same functions in humans and animals. For example, if the brain is injured in area V4, patients suffer from achromatopsia (Zeki, 1992; Milner and Goodale, 1995). These patients perceive only shades of gray. Also, they cannot recall colors from times before the lesion was formed. Color processing occurs in the same region of the monkey cortex. Third, new research imaging technologies, such as positron emission tomography (PET) and functional magnetic resonance imaging (fMRI), show that in response to colored or moving patterns, the same areas are active in people as in the Macaque monkey (Zeki, 1992; Beardsley, 1997). The key implication of this is that because we all have the same visual system, it is likely that we all see in the same way, at least as a first approximation. Hence, the same visual designs will be effective for all of us.

Sensory aspects of visualizations derive their expressive power from being well designed to stimulate the visual sensory system. In contrast, arbitrary, conventional aspects of visualizations derive their power from how well they are learned. Sensory and arbitrary representations differ radically in the ways they should be studied. In the former case, we can apply the full rigor of the experimental techniques developed by sensory neuroscience, while in the latter case visualizations and visual symbols can best be studied with the very different interpretive methodology, derived from the structuralist social sciences. With sensory representations, we can also make claims that transcend cultural and racial boundaries. Claims based on a generalized perceptual processing system will apply to all humans, with obvious exceptions such as color blindness.

This distinction between the sensory and social aspects of the symbols used in visualization also has practical consequences for research methodology. It is not worth expending a huge effort carrying out intricate and highly focused experiments to study something that is only this year's fashion. However, if we can develop generalizations that apply to large classes of visual representations, and for a long time, the effort is worthwhile.

If we accept the distinction between sensory and arbitrary codes, we nevertheless must recognize that most visualizations are hybrids. In the obvious case, they may contain both pictures and words. But in many cases, the sensory and arbitrary aspects of a representation are much more difficult to tease apart. There is an intricate interweaving of learned conventions and hard-wired processing. The distinction is not as clean as we would like, but there are ways of distinguishing the different kinds of codes.

Properties of Sensory and Arbitrary Representation

The following paragraphs summarize some of the important properties of sensory representations.

Understanding without training: A sensory code is one for which the meaning is perceived without additional training. Usually, all that is necessary is for the audience to understand that *some* communication is intended. For example, it is immediately clear that the image in Figure 1.6 has an unusual spiral structure. Even though this visually represents a physical process that cannot actually be seen, the detailed shape can be understood because it has been expressed using an artificial shading technique to make it look like a 3D solid object. Our visual systems are built to perceive the shapes of 3D surfaces.

Figure 1.6   The expanding wavefront of a chemical reaction is visualized (Cross et al., 1997). Even though this process is alien to most of us, the shape of the structure can be readily perceived.

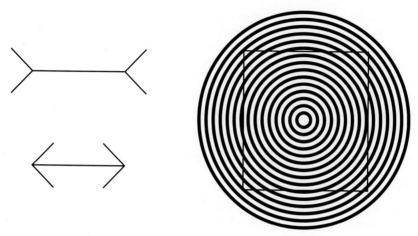

Figure 1.7   In the Muller-Lyer illusion, on the left, the horizontal line in the upper figure appears longer than the same line in the lower figure. On the right, the rectangle is distorted into a "pincushion" shape.

Resistance to instructional bias: Many sensory phenomena, such as the illusions shown in Figure 1.7, persist despite the knowledge that they are illusory. When such illusions occur in diagrams, they are likely to be misleading. But what is important to the present argument is that some aspects of perception can be taken as bottom-line facts that we ignore at our peril. In general, perceptual phenomena that persist and are highly resistant to change are likely to be hard-wired into the brain.

Sensory immediacy: The processing of certain kinds of sensory information is hard-wired and fast. We can represent information in certain ways that are neurally processed in parallel. This point is illustrated in Figure 1.8, which shows five different textured regions. The two regions on the left are almost impossible to separate. The upright Ts and inverted Ts appear to be a single patch. The region of oblique Ts is easy to differentiate from the neighboring region of inverted Ts. The circles are the easiest to distinguish (Beck, 1966). The way in which the visual system divides the visual world into regions is called *segmentation*. The evidence suggests that this is a function of early rapid-processing systems. (Chapter 5 presents a theory of texture discrimination.)

Cross-cultural validity: A sensory code will, in general, be understood across cultural boundaries. These may be national boundaries or the boundaries between different user groups. Instances in which a sensory code is misunderstood occur when some group has dictated that a sensory code be used arbitrarily in contradiction to the natural interpretation. In this case, the natural response to a particular pattern will, in fact, be wrong.

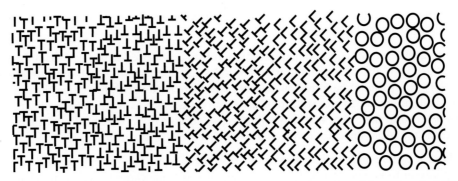

Figure 1.8   Five regions of texture. Some are easier to distinguish visually than others. *Adapted from Beck (1966).*

Testing Claims about Sensory Representations

Entirely different methodologies are appropriate to the study of representations of the sensory and arbitrary types. In general, the study of sensory representations can employ the scientific methods of vision researchers and biologists. The study of arbitrary conventional representations is best done using the techniques of the social sciences, such as sociology and anthropology; philosophers and cultural critics have much to contribute. Appendix C provides a brief summary of the research methodologies that apply to the study of sensory representations. All are based on the concept of the controlled experiment. For more detailed information on techniques used in vision research and human-factors engineering, see Sekuler and Blake (1990) and Wickens (1992).

Arbitrary Conventional Representations

Arbitrary codes are by definition socially constructed. The word *dog* is meaningful because we all agree on its meaning and we teach our children the meaning. The word *carrot* would do just as well, except we have already agreed on a different meaning for that word. In this sense, words are arbitrary; they could be swapped and it would make no difference, so long as they are used consistently from the first time we encounter them. Arbitrary visual codes are often adopted when groups of scientists and engineers construct diagramming conventions for new problems that arise. Examples include circuit diagrams used in electronics, diagrams used to represent molecules in chemistry, and the unified modeling language used in software engineering. Of course, many designers will intuitively use perceptually valid forms in the codes, but many aspects of these diagrams are entirely conventional. Arbitrary codes have the following characteristics:

Hard to learn: It takes a child hundreds of hours to learn to read and write, even if the child has already acquired spoken language. The graphical codes of the alphabet and their rules of combination must be laboriously learned. The Chinese character set is reputed to be even harder to work with than the Roman.

Easy to forget: Arbitrary conventional information that is not overlearned can easily be forgotten. It is also the case that arbitrary codes can interfere with each other. In contrast, sensory codes cannot be forgotten. Sensory codes are hard-wired; forgetting them would be like learning not to see. Still, some arbitrary codes, such as written numbers, are overlearned to the extent that they will never be forgotten. We are stuck with them because the social upheaval involved in replacing them is too great.

Embedded in culture and applications: An Asian student in my laboratory was working on an application to visualize changes in computer software. She chose to represent deleted entities with the color green and new entities with red. I suggested to her that red is normally used for a warning, while green symbolizes renewal, so perhaps the reverse coding would be more appropriate. She protested, explaining that green symbolizes death in China, while red symbolizes luck and good fortune. The use of color codes to indicate meaning is highly culture-specific.

Many graphical symbols are transient and tied to a local culture or application. Think of the graffiti of street culture, or the hundreds of new graphical icons that are being created on the Internet. These tend to stand alone, conveying meaning; there is little or no syntax to bind the symbols into a formal structure. On the other hand, in some cases, arbitrary representations can be almost universal. The Arabic numerals shown in Figure 1.9 are used widely throughout the world. Even if a more perceptually valid code could be constructed, the effort would be wasted. The designer of a new symbology for Air Force or Navy charts must live within the confines of existing symbols because of the huge amount of effort invested in the standards. We have many standardized visualization techniques that work well and are solidly embedded in work practices, and attempts to change them would be foolish. In many applications, good design is standardized design.

Culturally embedded aspects of visualizations persist because they have become embedded in ways in which we think about problems. For many geologists, the topographic contour map is the ideal way to understand relevant features of the earth's surface. They often resist shaded computer graphics representations, even though these appear to be much more intuitively understandable to most people. Contour maps are embedded in cartographic culture and training.

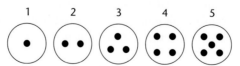

Figure 1.9   Two methods for representing the first five digits. The code given below is probably easier to learn. However, it is not easily extended.

Formally powerful: Arbitrary graphical notations can be constructed that embody formally defined, powerful languages. Mathematicians have created hundreds of graphical languages to express and communicate their concepts. The expressive power of mathematics to convey abstract concepts in a formal, rigorous way is unparalleled. However, the languages of mathematics are extremely hard to learn (at least for most people). Clearly, the fact that something is expressed in a visual code does not mean that it is easy to understand.

Capable of rapid change: One way of looking at the sensory/arbitrary distinction is in terms of the time the two modes have taken to develop. Sensory codes are the products of the millions of years it has taken for our visual systems to evolve. Although the time frames for the evolution of arbitrary conventional representations are much shorter, they can still have lasted for thousands of years (e.g., the number system). But many more have had only a few decades of development. High-performance interactive computer graphics have greatly enhanced our capability to create new codes. We can now control motion and color with great flexibility and precision. For this reason, we are currently witnessing an explosive growth in the invention of new graphical codes.

The Study of Arbitrary Conventional Symbols

The appropriate methodology for studying arbitrary symbols is very different from that used to study sensory symbols. The tightly focused, narrow questions addressed by psychophysics are wholly inappropriate to investigating visualization in a cultural context. A more appropriate methodology for the researcher of arbitrary symbols may derive from the work of anthropologists such as Clifford Geertz (1973), who advocated "thick description." This approach is based on careful observation, immersion in culture, and an effort to keep "the analysis of social forms closely tied . . . to concrete social events and occasions." Also borrowing from the social sciences, Carroll and coworkers have developed an approach to understanding complex user interfaces that they call *artifact analysis* (Carroll, 1989). In this approach, user interfaces (and presumably visualization techniques) are best viewed as artifacts and studied much as an anthropologist studies cultural artifacts of a religious or practical nature. Formal experiments are out of the question in such circumstances, and if they were actually carried out, they would undoubtedly change the very symbols being studied.

Unfortunately for researchers, sensory and arbitrary aspects of symbols are closely intertwined in many representations, and although they have been presented here as distinct categories, the boundary between them is very fuzzy. There is no doubt that culture influences cognition; it is also true that the more we know, the more we may perceive. Pure instances of sensory or arbitrary coding may not exist, but this does not mean that the analysis is invalid. It simply means that for any given example we must be careful to determine which aspects of the visual coding belong in each category.

In general, the science of visualization is still in its infancy. There is much about visualization and visual communication that is more craft than science. For the visualization designer, training in art and design is at least as useful as training in perceptual psychology. For those who wish to do good design, the study of design by example is generally most appropriate. But the science of visualization can inform the process by providing a scientific basis for design rules, and it can suggest entirely new design ideas and methods for displaying data that have not been thought of before. Ultimately, our goal should be to create a new set of conventions for information visualization, based on sound perceptual principles.

Gibson's Affordance Theory

The great perception theorist J.J. Gibson brought about radical changes in how we think about perception with his theories of *ecological optics, affordances,* and *direct perception.* Aspects of each of these theoretical concepts are discussed throughout this book. We begin with affordance theory (Gibson, 1979).

Gibson assumed that we perceive in order to operate on the environment. Perception is designed for action. Gibson called the perceivable possibilities for action *affordances;* he claimed that we perceive these properties of the environment in a direct and immediate way. This theory is clearly attractive from the perspective of visualization, because the goal of most visualization is decision making. Thinking about perception in terms of action is likely to be much more useful than thinking about how two adjacent spots of light influence each other's appearance (which is the typical approach of classical psychophysicists).

Much of Gibson's work was in direct opposition to the approach of theorists who reasoned that we must deal with perception from the bottom up, as with geometry. The pre-Gibsonian theorists tended to have an atomistic view of the world. They thought we should first understand how single points of light were perceived, and then we could work on understanding how pairs of lights interacted and gradually build up to understanding the vibrant, dynamic visual world in which we live.

Gibson took a radically different, top-down approach. He claimed that we do not perceive points of light; rather, we perceive possibilities for action. We perceive surfaces for walking, handles for pulling, space for navigating, tools for manipulating, and so on. In general, our whole evolution has been geared toward perceiving useful possibilities for action. In an experiment that supports this view, Warren (1984) showed that subjects were capable of accurate judgments of the "climbability" of staircases. These judgments depended on their own leg lengths. Gibson's affordance theory is tied to a theory of direct perception. He claimed that we perceive affordances of the environment *directly,* not indirectly by piecing together evidence from our senses.

Translating the affordance concept into the interface domain, we might construct the following principle: to create a good interface, we must create it with the appropriate affordances to make the user's task easy. Thus, if we have a task of moving an object in 3D space, it should have clear handles to use in rotating and lifting the object. Figure 1.10 shows a design for a 3D object-manipulation interface from Houde (1992). When an object is selected, "handles" appear that allow the object to be lifted or rotated. The function of these handles is made more explicit by illustrations of gripping hands that show the affordances.

Figure 1.10   Small drawings of hands pop up to show the user what interactions are possible in the prototype interface. *Reproduced, with permission, from Houde (1992).*

However, Gibson's theory presents problems if it is taken literally. According to Gibson, affordances are *physical* properties of the environment that we *directly* perceive. Many theorists, unlike Gibson, think of perception as a very active process: the brain deduces certain things about the environment based on the available sensory evidence. Gibson rejected this view in favor of the idea that our visual system is tuned to perceiving the visual world and that we perceive it accurately except under extraordinary circumstances. He preferred to concentrate on the visual system as a whole and not to break perceptual processing down into components and operations. He used the term *resonating* to describe the way the visual system responds to properties of the environment. This view has been remarkably influential and has radically changed the way vision researchers think about perception. Nevertheless, few would accept it today in its pure form.

There are three problems with Gibson's direct perception in developing a theory of visualization. The first problem is that even if perception of the environment is direct, it is clear that visualization of data through computer graphics is very indirect. Typically, there are many layers of processing between the data and its representation. In some cases, the source of the data may be microscopic or otherwise invisible. The source of the data may be quite abstract, such as company statistics in a stock-market database. Direct perception is not a meaningful concept in these cases.

Second, there are no clear *physical* affordances in *any* graphical user interface. To say that a screen button "affords" pressing in the same way as a flat surface affords walking is to stretch the theory beyond reasonable limits. In the first place, it is not even clear that a real-world button affords pressing. In another culture, these little bumps might be perceived as rather dull architectural decorations. Clearly, the use of buttons is arbitrary; we must learn that buttons, when pressed, do interesting things in the real world. Things are even more indirect in the computer world; we must learn that a *picture* of a button can be "pressed" using a mouse, a cursor, or yet another button. This is hardly a direct interaction with the physical world.

Third, Gibson's rejection of visual mechanisms is a problem. To take but one example, much that we know about color is based on years of experimentation, analysis, and modeling of the perceptual mechanisms. Color television and many other display technologies are based on an understanding of these mechanisms. To reject the importance of understanding visual mechanisms would be to reject a tremendous proportion of vision research as irrelevant. This entire book is based on the premise that an understanding of perceptual mechanisms is basic to a science of visualization.

Despite these reservations, Gibson's theories color much of this book. The concept of affordances, loosely construed, can be extremely useful from a design perspective. The idea suggests that we build interfaces that beg to be operated in appropriate and useful ways. We should make virtual handles for turning, virtual buttons for pressing. If components are designed to work together, this should be made perceptually evident, perhaps by creating shaped sockets that afford the attachment of one object to another. This is the kind of design approach advocated by Norman in his famous book, *The Psychology of Everyday Things* (1988). Nevertheless, on-screen widgets present affordances only in an indirect sense. They borrow their power from our ability to represent pictorially, or otherwise, the affordances of the everyday world. Therefore, we can be inspired by affordance theory to produce good designs, but we cannot expect much help from that theory in building a science of visualization.

A Model of Perceptual Processing

In this section, we introduce a simplified information-processing model of human visual perception. As Figure 1.5 shows, there are many subsystems in vision and we should always be wary of overgeneralization. Still, an overall conceptual framework is often useful in providing a starting point for more detailed analysis. Figure 1.11 gives a broad schematic overview of a three-stage model of perception. In Stage 1, information is processed in parallel to extract basic features of the environment. In Stage 2, active processes of pattern perception pull out structures and segment the visual scene into regions of different color, texture, and motion patterns. In Stage 3, the information is reduced to only a few objects held in visual working memory by active mechanisms of attention to form the basis of visual thinking.

Stage 1: Parallel Processing to Extract Low-Level Properties of the Visual Scene

Visual information is first processed by large arrays of neurons in the eye and in the primary visual cortex at the back of the brain. Individual neurons are selectively tuned to certain kinds of information, such as the orientation of edges or the color of a patch of light. In Stage 1 processing, billions of neurons work in parallel, extracting features from every part of the visual

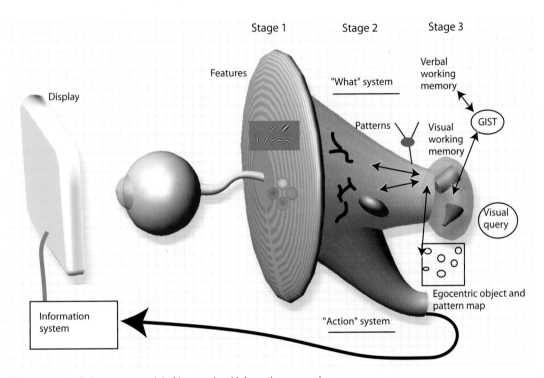

Figure 1.11   A three-stage model of human visual information processing.

field simultaneously. This parallel processing proceeds whether we like it or not, and it is largely independent of what we choose to attend to (although not of where we look). It is also rapid. If we want people to understand information quickly, we should present it in such a way that it could easily be detected by these large, fast computational systems in the brain.

Important characteristics of Stage 1 processing include:

- Rapid parallel processing

- Extraction of features, orientation, color, texture, and movement patterns

- Transitory nature of information, which is briefly held in an iconic store

- Bottom-up, data-driven model of processing

Stage 2: Pattern Perception

At the second stage, rapid active processes divide the visual field into regions and simple patterns, such as continuous contours, regions of the same color, and regions of the same texture.

Patterns of motion are also extremely important, although the use of motion as an information code is relatively neglected in visualization. The pattern-finding stage of visual processing is extremely flexible, influenced both by the massive amount of information available from Stage 1 parallel processing and by the top-down action of attention driven by visual queries. Marr (1982) called this stage of processing the 2-1/2D sketch. Triesman (1985) called it a feature map. Rensink (2002) called it a proto-object flux to emphasize its dynamic nature.

There is increasing evidence that tasks involving eye–hand coordination and locomotion may be processed in pathways distinct from those involved in object recognition. This is the two–visual system hypothesis: one system for locomotion and action, called the "action system," and another for symbolic object manipulation, called the "what system." A detailed and convincing account of it can be found in Milner and Goodale (1995).

Important characteristics of Stage 2 processing include:

- Slow serial processing

- Involvement of both working memory and long-term memory

- More emphasis on arbitrary aspects of symbols

- In a state of flux, a combination of bottom-up feature processing and top-down attentional mechanisms

- Different pathways for object recognition and visually guided motion

Stage 3: Sequential Goal-Directed Processing

At the highest level of perception are the objects held in visual working memory by the demands of active attention. In order to use an external visualization, we construct a sequence of visual queries that are answered through visual search strategies. At this level, only a few objects can be held at a time; they are constructed from the available patterns providing answers to the visual queries. For example, if we use a road map to look for a route, the visual query will trigger a search for connected red contours (representing major highways) between two visual symbols (representing cities).

Beyond the visual processing stages shown in Figure 1.11 are interfaces to other subsystems. The visual object identification process interfaces with the verbal linguistic subsystems of the brain so that words can be connected to images. The perception-for-action subsystem interfaces with the motor systems that control muscle movements.

The three-stage model of perceptions is the basis for the structure of this book. Chapters 2, 3, 4, and some of 5 deal mainly with Stage 1 issues. Chapters 5, 6, 7, and 8 deal mainly with Stage 2 issues. Chapters 9, 10, and 11 deal with Stage 3 issues. The final three chapters also discuss the interfaces between perceptual and other cognitive processes, such as those involved in language and decision making.

Types of Data

If the goal of visualization research is to transform data into a perceptually efficient visual format, and if we are to make statements with some generality, we must be able to say something about the types of data that can exist for us to visualize. It is useful, but less than satisfying, to be able to say that color coding is good for stock-market symbols but texture coding is good for geological maps. It is far more useful to be able to define broader categories of information, such as continuous-height maps (scalar fields), continuous-flow fields (vector maps), and category data, and then to make general statements such as "Color coding is good for category information" and "Motion coding is good for highlighting selected data." If we can give perceptual reasons for these generalities, we have a true science of visualization.

Unfortunately, the classification of data is a *big* issue. It is closely related to the classification of knowledge, and it is with great trepidation that we approach the subject. What follows is an informal classification of data classes using a number of concepts that we will find helpful in later chapters. We make no claims that this classification is especially profound or all-encompassing.

Bertin (1977) has suggested that there are two fundamental forms of data: data values and data structures. A similar idea is to divide data into entities and relationships (often called *relations*). Entities are the objects we wish to visualize; relations define the structures and patterns that relate entities to one another. Sometimes the relationships are provided explicitly; sometimes discovering relationships is the very purpose of visualization. We also can talk about the attributes of an entity or a relationship. Thus, for example, an apple can have color as one of its attributes. The concepts of entity, relationship, and attribute have a long history in database design and have been adopted more recently in systems modeling. However, we shall extend these concepts beyond the kinds of data that are traditionally stored in a relational database. In visualization, it is necessary to deal with entities that are more complex and we are also interested in seeing complex structured relationships—data structures—not captured by the entity relationship model.

Entities

Entities are generally the objects of interest. People can be entities; hurricanes can be entities. Both fish and fishponds can be entities. A group of things can be considered a single entity if it is convenient—for example, a school of fish.

Relationships

Relationships form the structures that relate entities. There can be many kinds of relationships. A wheel has a "part-of" relationship to a car. One employee of a firm may have a supervisory relationship to another. Relationships can be structural and physical, as in defining the way a house is made of its many component parts, or they can be conceptual, as in defining the relationship between a store and its customers. Relationships can be causal, as when one event causes another, and they can be purely temporal, defining an interval between two events.

Attributes of Entities or Relationships

Both entities and relationships can have attributes. In general, something should be called an attribute (as opposed to an entity itself) when it is a property of some entity and cannot be thought of independently. Thus, the color of an apple is an attribute of the apple. The temperature of water is an attribute of the water. Duration is an attribute of a journey. However, defining what should be an entity and what should be an attribute is not always straightforward. For example, the salary of an employee could be thought of as an attribute of the employee, but we can also think of an amount of money as an entity unto itself, in which case we would have to define a relationship between the employee entity and the sum-of-money entity.

Attribute Quality

It is often desirable to describe data visualization methods in light of the quality of attributes they are capable of conveying. A useful way to consider the quality of data is the taxonomy of number scales defined by the statistician S.S. Stevens (1946). According to Stevens, there are four levels of measurement: nominal, ordinal, interval, and ratio scales.

1. **Nominal:** This is the labeling function. Fruit can be classified into apples, oranges, bananas, and so on. There is no sense in which the fruit can be placed in an ordered sequence. Sometimes numbers are used in this way. Thus, the number on the front of a bus generally has a purely nominal value. It identifies the route on which the bus travels.

2. **Ordinal:** The ordinal category encompasses numbers used for ordering things in a sequence. It is possible to say that a certain item comes before or after another item. The position of an item in a queue or list is an ordinal quality. When we ask people to rank some group of things (films, political candidates, computers) in order of preference, we are requiring them to create an ordinal scale.

3. **Interval:** When we have an interval scale of measurement, it becomes possible to derive the gap between data values. The time of departure and the time of arrival of an aircraft are defined on an interval scale.

4. **Ratio:** With a ratio scale, we have the full expressive power of a real number. We can make statements such as "Object A is twice as large as object B." The mass of an object is defined on a ratio scale. Money is defined on a ratio scale. The use of a ratio scale implies a zero value used as a reference.

In practice, only three of Stevens's levels of measurement are widely used, and these in somewhat different form. The typical basic data classes most often considered in visualization have been greatly influenced by the demands of computer programming. They are the following:

Category data: This is like Stevens's nominal class.

Integer data: This is like his ordinal class in that it is discrete and ordered.

Real-number data: This combines the properties of interval and ratio scales.

These classes of data can be very useful in discussing visualization techniques. For example, here are two generalizations: (1) Using graphic size (as in a bar chart) to display category information is likely to be misleading, because we tend to interpret size as representing quantity. (2) If we map measurements to color, we can perceive nominal or, at best, ordinal values, with a few discrete steps. Perceiving metric intervals using color is not very effective. Many visualization techniques are capable of conveying only nominal or ordinal data qualities.

Attribute Dimensions: 1D, 2D, 3D, . . .

An attribute of an entity can have multiple dimensions. We can have a single *scalar* quantity, such as the weight of a person. We can have a *vector* quantity, such as the direction in which that person is traveling. *Tensors* are higher-order quantities that describe both direction and shear forces, such as occur in materials that are being stressed.

We can have a *field* of scalars, vectors, or tensors. The gravitational field of the earth is a three-dimensional attribute of the earth. In fact, it is a three-dimensional vector field attribute. If we are interested only in the strength of gravity at the earth's surface, it is a two-dimensional scalar attribute. Often the term *map* is used to describe this kind of field. Thus, we talk about a gravity map or a temperature map.

Operations Considered as Data

An entity relationship model can be used to describe most kinds of data. However, it does not capture the operations that may be performed on entities and relationships. We tend to think of operations as somehow different from the data itself, neither entities nor relationships nor attributes. The following are but a few common operations:

- Mathematical operations on numbers—multiplication, division, and so on

- Merging two lists to create a longer list

- Inverting a value to create its opposite

- Bringing an entity or relationship into existence (such as the mean of a set of numbers)

- Deleting an entity or relationship (a marriage breaks up)

- Transforming an entity in some way (the chrysalis turns into a butterfly)

- Forming a new object out of other objects (a pie is baked from apples and pastry)

- Splitting a single entity into its component parts (a machine is disassembled)

In some cases, these operations can themselves form a kind of data that we may wish to capture. Chemistry contains a huge catalog of the compounds that result when certain operations are applied to combinations of other compounds. These operations may form part of the data that is stored. Certain operations are easy to visualize: For example, the merging of two entities can easily be represented by showing two visual objects that combine (visually merge) into a single entity. Other operations are not at all easy to represent in any visualization. For example, the detailed logical structure of a computer program may be better represented using a written code that has its basis in natural language than using any kind of diagram. What should and should not be visualized is a major topic in Chapter 9.

Operations and procedures often present a particularly difficult challenge for visualization. It is difficult to express operations effectively in a static diagram, and this is especially a problem in the creation of visual languages. On the other hand, the use of animation opens up the possibility of expressing at least certain operations in an immediately accessible visual manner. We shall deal with the issue of animation and visual languages in Chapter 9.

Metadata

When we are striving to understand data, certain products are sure to emerge as we proceed. We may discover correlations between variables or clusters of data values. We may postulate certain underlying mechanisms that are not immediately visible. The result is that theoretical entities come into being. Atoms, photons, black holes, and all the basic constructs of physics are like this. As more evidence accumulates, the theoretical entities seem more and more real, but they are nonetheless only observable in the most indirect ways. These theoretical constructs that emerge from data analysis have sometimes been called *metadata* (Tweedie, 1997). They are generally called *derived data* in the database modeling community. Metadata can be of any kind. It can consist of new entities, such as identified classes of objects, or new relationships, such as postulated interactions between different entities, or new rules. We may impose complex structural relationships on the data, such as tree structures or directed acyclic graphs, or we may find that they already exist in the data.

The problem with the view that metadata and primary data are somehow essentially different is that all data is interpreted to some extent—there is no such thing as raw data. Every data-gathering instrument embodies some particular interpretation in the way it is built. Also, from the practical viewpoint of the visualization designer, the problems of representation are the same for metadata as for primary data. In both cases, there are entities, relationships, and their attributes to be represented, although some are more abstract than others. Thus the metadata concept is not discussed further in this book.

Conclusion

Visualization applies vision research to practical problems of data analysis in much the same way as engineering applies physics to practical problems of building manufacturing plants. Just as engineering has influenced physicists to become more concerned with areas such as semiconductor technology, so we may hope that the development of an applied science of data visualization can encourage vision researchers to intensify their efforts in addressing such problems as 3D space and task-oriented perception. There is considerable practical benefit in understanding these things. As the importance of visualization grows, so do the benefits of a scientific approach. But there is no time left to lose. New symbol systems are being developed constantly to meet the needs of a society increasingly dependent on data. Once developed, they may stay with us for a very long time, so we should try to get them right.

We have introduced a key distinction between the ideas of sensory and arbitrary conventional symbols. This is a difficult and sometimes artificial distinction. Readers can doubtless come up with counterexamples and reasons why it is impossible to separate the two. Nonetheless, the distinction is essential. With no basic model of visual processing on which we can support the idea of a good data representation, ultimately the problem of visualization comes down to establishing a consistent notation. If the best representation is simply the one we know best because it is embedded in our culture, then standardization is everything—there is no good representation, only widely shared conventions.

In opposition to the view that everything is arbitrary, this book takes the view that all humans do have more or less the same visual system. This visual system has evolved over tens of millions of years to enable creatures to perceive and act within the natural environment. Although very flexible, the visual system is tuned to receiving data presented in certain ways, but not in others. If we can understand how the mechanism works, we can produce better displays and better thinking tools.

The Environment, Optics, Resolution, and the Display

We can think of the world itself as an information display. Objects may be used as tools or as construction materials, or they may be obstacles to be avoided. Every intricate surface reveals the properties of the material from which it is made. Creatures signal their intentions inadvertently or deliberately through movement. There are almost infinite levels of detail in nature, and we must be responsive to both small and large things, but in different ways: large things, such as boulders, are obstacles; smaller things, such as rocks, can be used as tools; still smaller things, such as grains of sand, are useful by the handful. If our extraordinary skill in perceiving the information inherent in the environment can be applied to data visualization, we will have gained a truly powerful tool.

The visual display of a computer is only a single rectangular planar surface, divided into a regular grid of small colored dots. It is astonishing how successful it is as an information display, given how little it resembles the world we live in. This chapter concerns the lessons we can learn about information display by appreciating the environment in broad terms and how the same kind of information can be picked up from a flat screen. It begins with a discussion of the most general properties of the visual environment, then considers the lens-and-receptor system of the eye as the principal instrument of vision. The basic abilities of the eye are related to the problem of creating an optimal display device.

This level of analysis bears on a number of display problems. If we want to make virtual objects seem real, how should we simulate the interaction of light with their surfaces? What is the optimal display device, and how do current display devices measure up? How much detail can we see? How faint a target can we see? How good is the lens system of the human eye? This is a foundation chapter, introducing much of the basic vocabulary of vision research.

The Environment

A strategy for designing a visualization is to transform the data so that it appears like a common environment—a kind of data landscape. We should then be able to transfer skills obtained in interpreting the real environment to understanding our data. This is not to say that we should represent data by means of synthetic trees, flowers, and undulating lawns—that would be quaint and ludicrous. It seems less ludicrous to create synthetic offices, with desks, filing cabinets, phones, books, and Rolodexes, and this is already being done in a number of computer interfaces.

Understanding the general properties of the environment is important for a more basic reason. When trying to understand perception, it is always useful to think about what perception is *for*. The theory of evolution tells us that the visual system must have survival value, and adopting this perspective allows us to understand visual mechanisms in the broader context of useful skills, such as navigation, food seeking (which is like information seeking), and tool use (which depends on object-shape perception).

What follows is a short tour of the visual environment, beginning with light.

Visible Light

Perception is about understanding patterns of light. Visible light constitutes a very small part of the electromagnetic spectrum, as is shown in Figure 2.1. Some animals, such as snakes, can see in the infrared, while certain insects can see in the ultraviolet. Humans can perceive light only in the range of 400 to 700 nanometers. (In vision research, wavelength is generally expressed in units of 10^{-9} meters, called *nanometers*). At wavelengths shorter than 400 nm are ultraviolet light and X-rays. At wavelengths longer than 700 nm are infrared light, microwaves, and radio waves.

Ecological Optics

The most useful broad framework for describing the visual environment is given by ecological optics, a discipline developed by J.J. Gibson. Gibson radically changed the way we think about perception of the visual world. Instead of concentrating on the image on the retina, as did other vision researchers, Gibson emphasized perception of *surfaces in the environment*. The following quotations strikingly illustrate how he broke with a traditional approach to space perception that was grounded in the classical geometry of points, lines, and planes (Gibson, 1979):

A surface is substantial; a plane is not. A surface is textured; a plane is not. A surface is never perfectly transparent; a plane is. A surface can be seen; a plane can only be visualized.

A fiber is an elongated object of small diameter, such as a wire or thread. A fiber should not be confused with a geometrical line.

In surface geometry the junction of two flat surfaces is either an edge or a corner; in abstract geometry the intersection of two planes is a line.

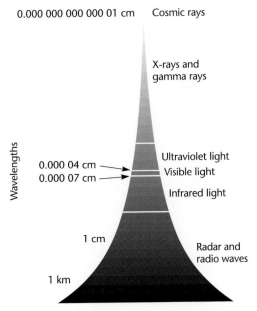

Figure 2.1   The visible light spectrum is a tiny part of a much larger spectrum of electromagnetic radiation.

Much of human visual processing becomes more understandable if we assume that a key function of the visual system is to extract properties of surfaces. As our primary interface with objects, surfaces are essential to understanding the potential for interaction and manipulation in the environment that Gibson called *affordances*.

A second key concept in Gibson's ecological optics is the ambient optical array (Gibson, 1986). To understand the ambient optical array, consider what happens to light entering the environment from some source such as the sun. It is absorbed, reflected, refracted, and diffracted as it interacts with various objects such as stones, grass, trees, and water. The environment, considered in this way, is a hugely complex matrix with photons traveling in all directions, consisting of different mixtures of wavelengths and polarized in various ways. This complexity is quite impossible to simulate. However, from any particular stationary point in the environment, critical information is contained in the structure of the light arriving at that point. This vast simplification is what Gibson called the *ambient optical array*. This array encompasses all the rays arriving at a particular point as they are structured in both space and time. Figure 2.2 is intended to capture the flavor of the concept.

Much of the effort of computer graphics can be characterized as an attempt to model the ambient optical array. Because the interactions of light with surfaces are vastly complex, it is not possible to directly model entire environments. But the ambient array provides the basis for simplifications such as those used in ray tracing, so that approximations can be computed.

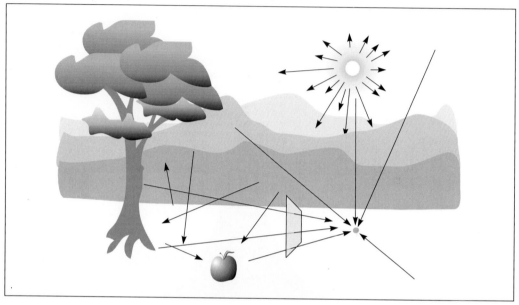

Figure 2.2 *Ambient optical array* is a term that describes the array of light that arrives from all directions at some designated point in the environment. Simulating the appearance of the bundle of rays that would pass through a glass rectangle is one of the goals of computer graphics.

If we can capture the structure of a bundle of rays passing through a glass rectangle on their way to the stationary point, we have something that we may be able to reproduce on a screen (see Figure 2.2).

Optical Flow

The ambient optical array is dynamic, changing over time both as the viewpoint moves and as objects move. As we advance into a static environment, a characteristic visual flow field develops. Figure 2.3 illustrates the visual field expanding outward as a result of forward motion. There is evidence that the visual system contains processes to interpret such flow patterns and that they are important in understanding how animals (including humans) navigate through space, avoid obstacles, and generally perceive the layout of objects in the world. The flow pattern in Figure 2.3 is only a very simple case; if we follow something with our eyes while we move forward, the pattern becomes more complex. The perceptual mechanisms to interpret flow patterns must therefore be sophisticated. The key point here is that visual images of the world are dynamic, so that the perception of motion patterns may be as important as the perception of the

Figure 2.3   An expanding flow pattern of visual information is created as an observer moves forward through the environment.

static world, albeit less well understood. Chapter 8 deals with motion perception in the context of space perception and 3D information display.

Textured Surfaces and Texture Gradients

Gibson pointed out that surface texture is one of the fundamental visual properties of an object. In visual terms, a surface is merely an unformed patch of light unless it is textured. Texture is critical to perception in a number of ways. The texture of an object helps us see where an object is and what shape it has. On a larger scale, the texture of the ground plane on which we walk, run, and crawl is important in judging distances and other aspects of space. Figure 2.4 shows that the texture of the ground plane produces a characteristic texture gradient that is important in space perception. Of course, surfaces themselves are infinitely varied. The surface of a wooden table is very different from the surface of an ocelot. Generally speaking, most surfaces have clearly defined boundaries; diffuse, cloudlike objects are exceptional. Perhaps because of this, we have great difficulty in visualizing uncertain data as fuzzy clouds of points.

At present, most computerized visualizations present objects as smooth and untextured. This may be partly because texturing is not yet easy to do in most visualization software packages.

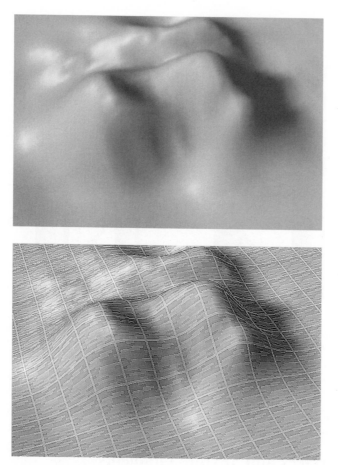

Figure 2.4   An undulating surface with and without surface texture.

Perhaps visualization designers have avoided texturing surfaces by applying the general esthetic principle that we should avoid irrelevant decoration in displays—"chart junk," to use Tufte's memorable phrase (Tufte, 1983). But texturing surfaces is not chart junk, especially in 3D visualizations. Even if we texture all objects in exactly the same way, this can help us perceive the orientation, shape, and spatial layout of a surface. Textures need not be garish or obtrusive, but when we want something to appear to be a 3D surface, it should have at least a subtle texture. As we shall see in Chapter 5, texture can also be used to code information, but using unobtrusive textures will require better pixel resolution than is available on most displays.

The Paint Model of Surfaces

Surfaces in nature are endlessly varied and complex. Microtextures give irregular patterns of reflection, so the amount and color of reflected light can vary with both the illumination angle and the viewing angle. However, there is a simple model that approximates many common materials. This model can be understood by considering a glossy paint. The paint has pigment particles embedded in a more or less clear medium, as shown in Figure 2.5. Some of the light is reflected from the surface of the glossy medium and is unchanged in color. Most of the light penetrates the medium and is selectively absorbed by the pigment particles, altering its color. According to this model, there are three important direct interactions of light with surfaces, as described in the following paragraphs. An additional fourth property is related to the fact that parts of objects cast shadows, revealing more information about their shapes. (See Figure 2.6.)

- *Lambertian shading.* With most materials, light penetrates the surface and interacts with the pigment in the medium. This light is selectively absorbed and reflected depending on the color of the pigment, and some of it is scattered back through the surface out into the environment. If we have a perfectly matte surface, how bright the surface appears depends only on the cosine of the angle between the incident light and the surface normal. This is called the Lambertian model, and although few real-world materials have exactly this property it is computationally very simple. A patch of a Lambertian surface can be viewed from any angle and the surface color will seem the same. Figure 2.6(a) shows a surface with only Lambertian shading. Lambertian shading is the simplest method for representing surface shape from shading. It can also be highly effective.

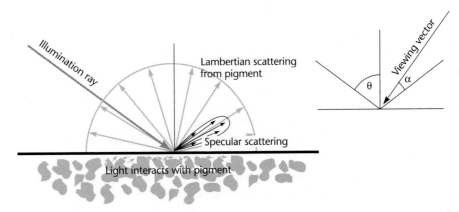

Figure 2.5   This simplified model of light interacting with surfaces is used in most computer graphics. Specular reflection is light that is reflected directly from the surface without penetrating to the underlying pigment.

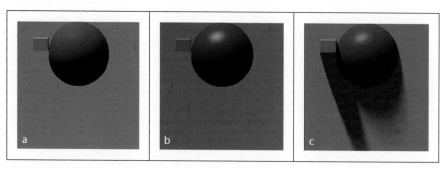

Figure 2.6   (a) Lambertian shading only. (b) Lambertian shading with specular and ambient shading. (c) Lambertian shading with specular, ambient, and cast shadows.

- *Specular shading.* The light that is reflected directly from a surface is called specular light. This is what we see as the highlights on glossy objects. Specular reflection obeys the optical principle of mirror reflection: the angle of reflection equals the angle of incidence. It is possible to simulate high-gloss, semigloss, or eggshell finishes by causing the specular light to spread out somewhat, simulating different degrees of roughness at a microscopic level. Specular light reflected from a surface retains the color of the illuminant; it is not affected by the color of the underlying pigment. Hence, we see white highlights gleaming from the surface of a red automobile. Both the viewing direction and the positions of the light sources affect the locations where highlights appear. Figure 2.6(b) shows a surface with both Lambertian and specular shading.

- *Ambient shading.* Ambient light is the light that illuminates a surface from everywhere in the environment, except for the actual light sources. In reality, ambient light is as complex as the scene itself. However, in computer graphics, ambient light is often grossly simplified by treating it as a constant, which is like assuming that an object is situated in a uniformly gray room. The radiosity technique (Cohen and Greenberg, 1985) properly models the complexity of ambient light, but it is rarely used for visualization. One of the consequences of modeling ambient light as a constant is that no shape-from-shading information is available in areas of cast shadow. In Figures 2.6(b) and 2.6(c), ambient light is simulated by the assumption that a constant amount of light is reflected from all points on the surface. Ambient light is reflected both specularly and nonspecularly.

- *Cast shadows.* An object can cast shadows either on itself or on other objects. As shown in Figure 2.6(c), cast shadows can greatly influence the perceived height of an object.

The mathematical expression for the amount of light reflected, *R,* according to this simplified model, is as follows:

$$R = a + b\cos\theta + c\cos^k(\alpha) \qquad\qquad \textbf{(2.1)}$$

where θ is the angle between the incident ray and the surface normal and α is the angle between the reflected ray and the view vector. a, b, and c represent the relative amounts of ambient, Lambertian, and specular light, respectively. The exponent k is used to control the degree of glossiness. A high value of k, such as 50, models a very shiny surface, while a lower value, such as 6, results in a semigloss appearance. Note that this is a simplified treatment, providing only the crudest approximation of the way light interacts with surfaces, but nevertheless it is so effective in creating real-looking scenes that it is widely used in computer graphics with only a small modification to simulate color. It is sufficient for most visualization purposes. This surface/light interaction model and others are covered extensively by computer graphics texts concerned with realistic image synthesis. The reader is referred to Foley et al. (1990) for more information.

What is interesting is that these simplifying assumptions may, in effect, be embedded in our visual systems. The brain may assume a model similar to this when we estimate the shape of a surface defined by shading information. Arguably, using more sophisticated modeling of light in the environment might actually be detrimental to our understanding of the shapes of surfaces. Chapter 7 discusses the way we perceive this shape-from-shading information.

Figures 2.7 and 2.8 illustrate some consequences of the simplified lighting model. Figure 2.7 shows glossy leaves to make the point that the simplified model is representative of at least some nonsynthetic objects. In this picture, the specular highlights from the shiny surface are white because the illuminant is white. The nonspecular light from the leaf pigmentation is green. As a

Figure 2.7   Glossy leaves. Note that the highlights are the color of the illuminant.

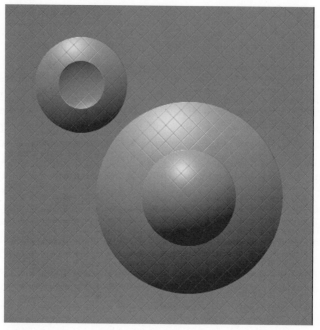

Figure 2.8   Specular light reveals fine details of surface structure. However, it depends on the viewpoint.

tool in data visualization, specular reflection is useful in visualization of fine surface features, such as scratches on glass. The effect is illustrated in Figure 2.8, in which the line grid lines are most distant in the region of specular reflection. Specular highlights can be similarly useful in revealing subtle differences in surface microroughness. The nonspecular Lambertian reflection is more effective in giving an overall impression of the shape of the surface.

To summarize this brief introduction to the visual environment, we have seen that much of what is useful to organisms is related to objects, to their layout in space, and to the properties of their surfaces. As Gibson so effectively argued, in understanding how surfaces are perceived, we must understand how light becomes structured when it arrives at the eye. We have covered two important kinds of structuring thus far. One is the structure that is present in the ambient array of light that arrives at a viewpoint. This structure has both static pattern components and dynamic pattern flows as we move through the world. The second is the more detailed structuring of light that results from the interaction of light with surfaces.

The Eye

We now consider the instrument of sight. The human eye, like a camera, contains the equivalents of a lens, an aperture (the pupil), and a film (the retina). Figure 2.9 illustrates these parts.

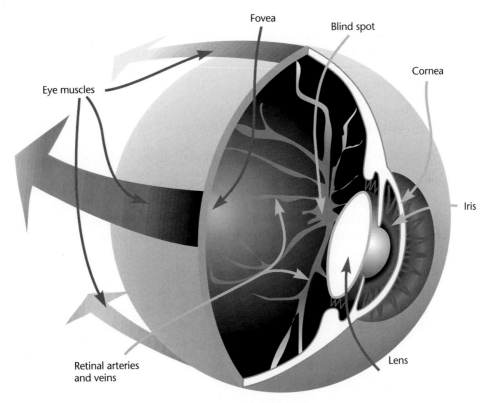

Fovea

Blind spot

Cornea

Eye muscles

Iris

Retinal arteries
and veins

Lens

Figure 2.9   The human eye. Important features include the fovea, where vision is sharpest; the iris, which determines the amount of light that enters the eye; and the large eye muscles that enable eye movements. The blind spot is caused by the absence of receptors where the retinal arteries enter the eyeball and in the two principal optical elements, the lens and the cornea.

The lens focuses a small, inverted picture of the world onto the retina. The iris performs the function of a variable aperture, helping the eye to adjust to different lighting conditions. Some people find it difficult to understand how we can see the world properly when the image is upside down. The right way to think about this is to adopt a computational perspective. We do not perceive what is on the retina; instead, our brains compute a percept based on sensory information. Inversion of the images is the least of the brain's computational problems.

We should not take the eye/camera analogy too far. If seeing were like photography, you would only have to copy the image on the back of the eye to produce a perfect likeness of a friend; anyone could be a great portrait painter. Yet artists spend years studying perspective geometry and anatomy, and constantly practicing their skills. Early cave artists represented human figures with spindly lines for arms and legs. Children still do this. It took thousands of years, culminating in the golden age of Greek art, for artists to develop the skills to draw natural figures, properly shaded and foreshortened. Following this, the skill was largely lost again until the Renaissance, in the fifteenth century. Yet in the image on the back of the eye, everything is in perfect proportion and in perspective. Clearly, we do not "see" what is on the retina. The locus of conscious perception is farther up the chain of processing, and at this later stage most of the simple properties of the retinal image have been lost. The world that we perceive is not at all what is imaged on the retina.

The Visual Angle Defined

The visual angle is a key concept in defining the properties of the eye and early vision. As Figure 2.10 illustrates, a visual angle is the angle subtended by an object at the eye of an observer. Visual angles are generally defined in degrees, minutes, and seconds of arc. (A minute is 1/60 degree and a second is 1/60 minute). As a general rule, a thumbnail held at arm's length subtends about 1 degree of visual angle. Another useful fact is that a 1-cm object viewed at 57 cm has a visual angle of approximately 1 degree. This is useful because 57 cm is a reasonable approximation to the distance at which we view a computer monitor.

To calculate visual angle, use this equation:

$$\tan\left(\frac{\theta}{2}\right) = \frac{h}{2}$$

(2.2)

or

$$\theta = 2 \arctan\left(\frac{h}{2d}\right)$$

(2.3)

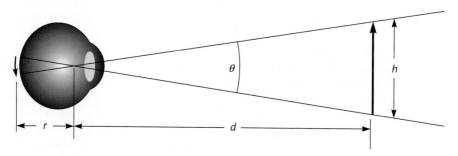

Figure 2.10   The visual angle of an object is measured from the optical center of the eye.

The Lens

The human eye contains a compound lens. This lens has two key elements: the curved front surface of the cornea and the crystalline lens. The nodal point is the optical center of the compound lens; it is positioned approximately 17 mm from the retina. The distance from the eye to an object is usually measured from the cornea, but in terms of optics it is better to estimate the distance from the first nodal point. (See Figure 2.10.)

The following equation describes the imaging properties of a simple lens:

$$\frac{1}{f} = \frac{1}{d} + \frac{1}{r} \tag{2.4}$$

where f is the focal length of the lens, d is the distance to the object that is imaged, and r is the distance to the image that is formed. If the units are meters, the *power* of a lens is given by the reciprocal of the focal length ($1/f$) in units of *diopters*. Thus, a 1-diopter lens has a focal length of 1 m. The 17 mm focal length of the human lens system corresponds to a power of 59 diopters. To get this from Equation 2.3, consider viewing an object at infinity ($d = \infty$).

To a first approximation the power of a compound lens can be computed by adding the powers of the components. We obtain the focal length of a two-part compound lens by using the following equation:

$$\frac{1}{f_3} = \frac{1}{f_1} + \frac{1}{f_2} \tag{2.5}$$

f_3 is the result of combining lenses f_1 and f_2.

In the compound lens of the human eye, most of this power, about 40 diopters, comes from the front surface of the cornea; the remainder comes from the variable-focus lens. When the cillary muscle that surrounds the lens contracts, the lens assumes a more convex and more powerful shape, and nearby objects come into focus. Young children have very flexible lenses, capable of adjusting over a range of 12 diopters or more, which means that they can focus on an object as close as 8 cm. However, the eye becomes less flexible with age, at roughly the rate of 2 diopters per decade, so that by the age of 60, the lens is almost completely rigid (Sun et al., 1988). Hence the need for reading glasses at about the age of 48, when only a few diopters of accommodation are left.

The *depth of focus* of a lens is the range over which objects are in focus when the eye is adjusted for a particular distance. The depth of focus of the human eye varies with the size of the pupil (Smith and Atchison, 1997), but assuming a 3-mm pupil and a human eye focused at infinity, objects between about 3 m and infinity are in focus. Depth of focus can usefully be described in terms of the power change that takes place without the image becoming significantly blurred. This is about 1/3 diopter, assuming a 3-mm pupil.

Assuming the 1/3-diopter depth-of-focus value and an eye focused at distance d (in meters), objects in the range

$$\left[\frac{3d}{d+3}, \frac{-3d}{d-3} \right] \tag{2.6}$$

will be in focus.

To illustrate, for an observer focusing at 50 cm, roughly the normal monitor-viewing distance, an object can be about 7 cm in front of the screen or 10 cm behind the screen before it appears to be out of focus. In helmet-mounted displays, it is common to use lenses that set the screen at a virtual focal distance of 2 m. This means that in the range 1.2 m to 6.0 m, it is not necessary to worry about simulating depth-of-focus effects, something that is difficult and computationally expensive to do. However, the large pixels in typical virtual-reality displays prevent us from modeling image blur to anywhere near this resolution.

Table 2.1 gives the range that is in focus for a number of viewing distances, given a 3-mm pupil. For more detailed modeling of depth of focus as it varies with pupil diameter, consult Smith and Atchison (1997).

Optics and Augmented-Reality Systems

Augmented-reality systems involve superimposing visual imagery on the real world so that people can see a computer graphics–enhanced view of the world. For this blending of real and virtual imagery to be achieved, the viewpoint of the observer must be accurately known and the objects' positions and shapes in the local environment must also be stored in the controlling computer. With this information, it is a straightforward application of standard computer graphics techniques to draw 3D images that are superimposed on the real-world images. However, the tech-

Viewing Distance	Near	Far
50 cm	43 cm	60 cm
1 m	75 cm	1.5 m
2 m	1.2 m	6.0 m
3 m	1.5 m	infinity

Table 2.1   Depth of Focus at Various Viewing Distances

nical difficulties in getting precise registration information and in designing optical systems that are light and portable should not be underestimated.

Figure 2.11 illustrates an experimental augmented-reality system in which a radiologist can see within a woman's breast to guide a biopsy needle in taking a tissue sample (from State et al., 1996). Given how difficult it is for the surgeon to accomplish this task with a gland that is easily deformed, such a development would have very large benefits. Other applications for augmented displays include automobile servicing machines in which the mechanic sees instructions and structural diagrams superimposed on the actual machinery; tactical military displays in which the pilot or tank driver sees indicators of friendly or hostile targets superimposed on a view of the landscape; and medical technology in which the surgeon sees an internal object, such as a brain tumor, highlighted within the brain during surgical planning or actual surgery. In each case, visual data is superimposed on real objects to supplement the information available to the user and enable better or more rapid decision making. This data may take the form of written text labels or sophisticated symbology.

In many augmented-reality systems, computer graphics imagery is superimposed on the environment using a device called a beam-splitter. The splitter is actually used not to split but to *combine* the images coming from the real world with those presented on a small computer monitor. The result is like a double-exposed photograph. A typical beam-splitter allows approximately half the light to pass through and half the light to be reflected. Figure 2.12 illustrates the essential optical components of this type of augmented-reality display.

Because the optics are typically fixed in augmented-reality systems, there is only one depth at which both the computer-generated imagery and the real-world imagery are in focus. This can be both good and bad. If both real-world and virtual-world scenes are simultaneously in focus, it will be easier to perceive them together. If this is desirable, care should be taken to set the focal plane of the virtual imagery at the typical depth of the real imagery. However, it is sometimes desirable that the computer imagery remain perceptually distinct from the real-world image. For example, a transparent layer of text from an instruction manual might be presented on a

Left eye ↖ ↗ Right eye ↖ ↗ Left eye
Fuse wall-eyed   Fuse cross-eyed

Figure 2.11 Augmented system for assisting in breast biopsies. This is a simulation of a system that is under development. The inside of the breast has been imaged using ultrasound, allowing the surgeon to guide the biopsy needle to the suspicious-looking tissue. Reprinted with permission (State et al., 1996).

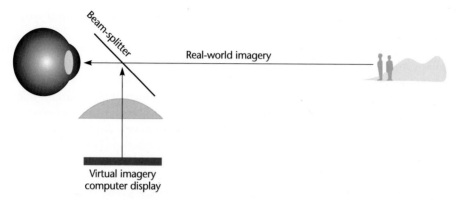

Figure 2.12 In augmented-reality displays, computer graphics imagery is superimposed on the real-world environment using a beam-splitter. The effect is like a transparent overlay on the environment. The focal distance of the computer imagery depends on the power of the lenses used.

see-through display (Feiner et al., 1993). If the focal distances are different, the user can choose to focus either on the text or on the imagery, and in this way selectively attend to one or the other.

There is evidence that focus can cause problems with distance estimation in aircraft heads-up displays (HUDs). In these displays, the virtual image is set at optical infinity, because only distant objects are normally seen through a cockpit screen. Despite this, experiments have shown that observers tend to focus at a distance closer than infinity with HUDs, and this can cause over-estimation of distances to objects in the environment (Roscoe, 1991). This may be a serious problem; according to Roscoe, it has been at least partially responsible for large numbers (one per month) of generally fatal "controlled flight into the terrain" accidents in the United States Air force.

Roscoe's theory of what occurs is that the average apparent size of objects is almost per-fectly correlated with the distance at which the eyes are focused (Iavecchia et al., 1988). But with HUDs, the eyes are focused closer (for reasons that are not fully understood), leading to an under-estimation of size and an overestimation of distance. Roscoe suggests that this can also partially account for the fact that when virtual imaging is used, either in simulators or in real aircraft with HUDs, pilots make fast approaches and land hard.

There are a number of other optical and perceptual problems with head-mounted displays (HMDs). Progressive eyeglass lenses are not compatible with these displays because they require a single focal distance. People use coordinated movements of both the eyes and the head to conduct visual searches of the environment, and HMDs do not allow for the redirection of the gaze with head movements. Ordinarily, when the angular movement of the eyes to the side is large, head movements actually begin first. Peli (1999) suggested that looking sideways more than 10 degrees off the center line is very uncomfortable to maintain. With an HMD the viewed image moves with the head, so compensatory head movements will fail to eliminate the discomfort. Another problem is that see-through HMDs are typically only worn over one eye, and the effect of binocular rivalry means that parts of the visual world and HMD imagery are likely to spontaneously appear and disappear (Laramee and Ware, 2002). Thus, someone wearing such a display while walking along a sidewalk would be likely to walk into lampposts!

Optics in Virtual-Reality Displays

Virtual-reality (VR) displays block out the real world, unlike the see-through augmented-reality displays discussed previously. Thus the VR system designer need only be concerned with computer-generated imagery. However, it is still highly desirable that correct depth-of-focus information be presented to the user. Ideally, objects on which the user fixates should be in sharp focus, while objects farther away or nearer should be blurred to the appropriate extents. Focus is important in helping us to differentiate objects that we wish to attend to from other objects in the environment.

Unfortunately, simulating depth of focus using a flat-screen display is a major technical problem. It has two parts: simulating optical blur and simulating the optical distance of the virtual object. There is also the problem of knowing what the user is looking at so that the object of attention can be made sharp while other objects are displayed as though out of focus. Figure 2.13 illustrates one way that correct depth-of-focus information could be presented on a flat-screen VR display. An eye tracker is used to determine where in the scene the eye is fixated. If binocular eye trackers were used in a stereoscopic display, this information would be even more accurate, because eye convergence information can be used to estimate the distance to the fixated object. Once the object of attention is identified, an image is computed in such a way that the fixated object is in sharp focus and other objects are appropriately out of focus. A sophisticated system might measure pupil diameter and take this information into account. At the same time, other system components change the focal lengths of the lenses in the display system so that the attended virtual object is placed at the correct focal distance. All virtual objects are actually displayed on the screen in the conventional way, but with simulated depth of focus. Neveau and Stark (1998) describe the optical and control requirements of such a system.

Chromatic Aberration

The human eye is not corrected for chromatic aberration. *Chromatic aberration* means that different wavelengths of light are focused at different distances within the eye. Short-wavelength blue light is refracted more than long-wavelength red light. A typical monitor has a blue phosphor peak wavelength at about 480 nm and a red peak at about 640 nm, and a lens with a power of 1.5 diopters is needed to make blue and red focus at the same depth. This is the kind of blur that causes people to reach for their reading glasses. If we focus on a patch of light produced by the red phosphor, an adjacent blue patch will be significantly out of focus. Because of chromatic aberration, it is inadvisable to make fine patterns that use undiluted blue phosphor. Also, pure blue text on a black background can be almost unreadable if there is white or red text nearby

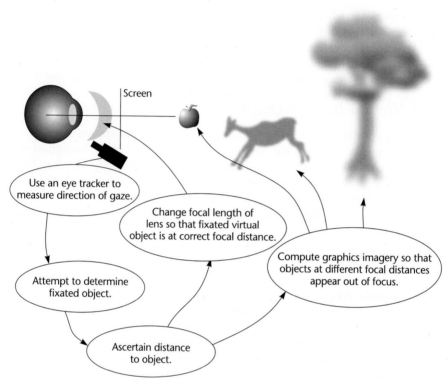

Figure 2.13   A possible solution to the problem of how correct depth-of-focus information might be displayed in a virtual-reality (VR) display. The apple is the fixated object and is drawn in sharp focus. The other objects are drawn out of focus, depending on their relative depths.

to attract the focusing mechanism. The addition of even a small amount of red and green will alleviate the problem, because these colors will provide luminance edges to perceptually define the color boundary.

The chromatic aberration of the eye can give rise to strong illusory depth effects (Jackson et al., 1994). This is illustrated in Figure 2.14, where both blue text and red text are superimposed on a black background. For about 60% of observers, the red appears closer. But 30% see the reverse, and the remaining 10% see the colors lying in the same plane. It is common to take advantage of this in slide presentations by making the background a deep blue, which makes white or red lettering appear to stand out for most people.

Receptors

The lens focuses an image on a mosaic of photoreceptor cells that line the back of the eye in a layer called the retina. There are two types of such cells: rods, which are extremely sensitive at

Figure 2.14   Chromostereopsis. For most people, the red advances and the blue recedes.

low light levels, and cones, which are sensitive under normal working light levels. There are about 100 million rods and only 6 million cones. Rods contribute far less to normal daytime vision than cones do. The input from rods is pooled over large areas, with thousands of rods contributing to the signal that passes up through a single fiber in the optic nerve. Rods are so sensitive that they are overloaded in daylight and effectively shut down; therefore, most vision researchers ignore their very slight contribution to normal daylight vision.

The fovea is a small area in the center of the retina that is densely packed only with cones, and it is here that vision is sharpest. Cones at the fovea are packed about 20–30 sec of arc apart (180 per degree). There are more than 100,000 cones packed into this central small area, subtending a visual angle of 1.5 to 2 degrees. Although it is usual to speak of the fovea as a 2-degree field, the greatest resolution of detail is obtained only in the central 1/2 degree of this region. Remember that one degree is about the size of your thumbnail held at arm's length. Figure 2.15 is an image of the receptor mosaic in the fovea. The receptors are arranged in an irregular but roughly hexagonal pattern.

Simple Acuities

Visual acuities are measurements of our ability to see detail. Acuities are important in display technologies because they give us an idea of the ultimate limits on the information densities that we can perceive. Some of the basic acuities are summarized in Figure 2.16.

Most of the acuity measurements in Figure 2.16 suggest that we can resolve things, such as the presence of two distinct lines, down to about 1 minute. This is in rough agreement with the spacing of receptors in the center of the fovea. For us to see that two lines are distinct, the blank space between them should lie on a receptor; therefore, we should only be able to perceive lines separated by roughly twice the receptor spacing. However, there are a number of *superacuities*, of which vernier acuity and stereo acuity are examples. A superacuity is the ability to perceive visual properties of the world to a greater precision than could be achieved based on a simple receptor model. Superacuities can be achieved only because postreceptor mechanisms are capable of integrating the input from many receptors to obtain better than single-receptor resolution. A good example of this is vernier acuity, the ability to judge the colinearity of two fine line segments. This can be done with amazing accuracy to better than 10 seconds of arc. To give

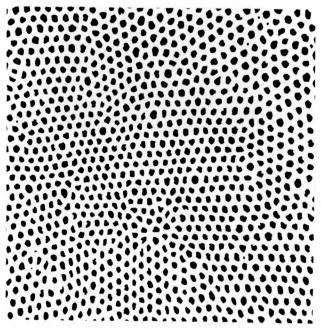

Figure 2.15   The receptor mosaic in the fovea. From Frisby (1979). *Used by permission.*

an idea of just how accurate this is, a normal computer monitor has about 40 pixels (picture elements) per centimeter. We can perform vernier acuity tasks that are accurate to about 1/10 of a pixel.

Neural postprocessing can efficiently combine input from two eyes. Campbell and Green (1965) found that binocular viewing improves acuity by 7% as compared with monocular viewing. They also found a $\sqrt{2}$ improvement in contrast sensitivity. This latter finding is remarkable because it supports the theory that the brain is able to perfectly pool information from the two eyes, despite the three or four synaptic connections that lie between the receptors and the first point at which the information from the two eyes can be combined.

Interestingly, Campbell and Green's findings suggest that we should be able to use the ability of the eye to integrate information over space and time to allow perception of higher-resolution information than is actually available on our display device. One technique for achieving higher-than-device resolution is antialiasing, which is discussed later in this chapter. There is also an intriguing possibility that the temporal-integration capability of the human eye could be used to advantage. This is why a sequence of video frames seems of higher quality than any single frame.

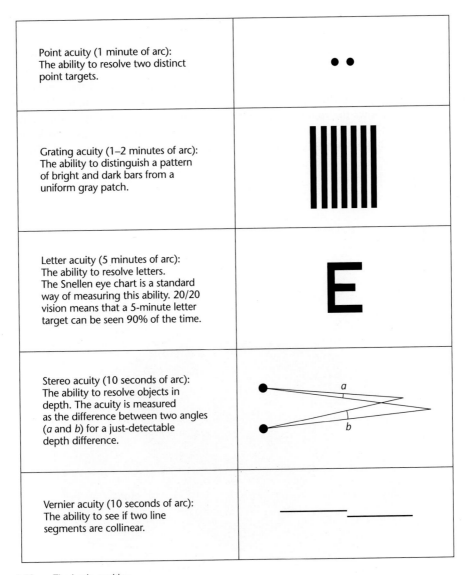

Point acuity (1 minute of arc): The ability to resolve two distinct point targets.	
Grating acuity (1–2 minutes of arc): The ability to distinguish a pattern of bright and dark bars from a uniform gray patch.	
Letter acuity (5 minutes of arc): The ability to resolve letters. The Snellen eye chart is a standard way of measuring this ability. 20/20 vision means that a 5-minute letter target can be seen 90% of the time.	
Stereo acuity (10 seconds of arc): The ability to resolve objects in depth. The acuity is measured as the difference between two angles (*a* and *b*) for a just-detectable depth difference.	
Vernier acuity (10 seconds of arc): The ability to see if two line segments are collinear.	

Figure 2.16 The basic acuities.

Acuity Distribution and the Visual Field

If we look directly ahead and hold our arms straight out to either side, then we can just see both hands when we wiggle our fingers. This tells us that both eyes together provide a visual field of a bit more than 180 degrees. The fact that we cannot see our fingers until they move also tells us that motion sensitivity in the periphery is better than static sensitivity. Figure 2.17 illustrates the visual field and shows the roughly triangular region of binocular overlap within which both eyes receive input. The reason that there is not more overlap is that the nose blocks the view. Visual acuity is distributed over this field in a very nonuniform manner. As shown in Figure 2.18, acuity outside of the fovea drops rapidly, so that we can only resolve about one-tenth the detail at 10 degrees from the fovea.

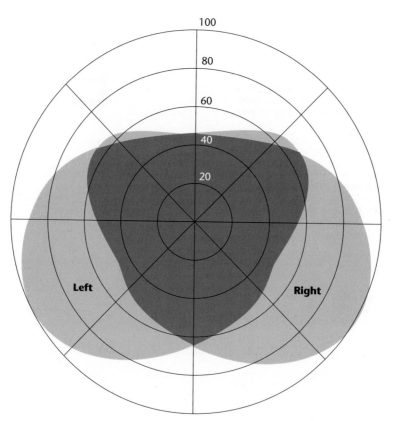

Figure 2.17   The visual field of view for a person gazing straight ahead. The irregular boundaries of the left and right fields are caused by facial features such as the nose. The darker-gray area shows the region of binocular overlap.

Figure 2.18   The acuity of the eye falls off rapidly with distance from the fovea.

Normal acuity measures are one-dimensional; they measure our ability to resolve two points or two parallel lines as a function of the distance between them. But if we consider the total number of points that can be perceived per unit area, this measure falls according to an inverse square law. We can actually only see one hundredth the number of points in an area at 10 degrees of eccentricity from the fovea. To put it another way, in the middle of the visual field, at the fovea, we can resolve about 100 points on the head of a pin. At the edge of the visual field, we can only discriminate objects the size of a fist.

The variation in acuity has been vividly expressed in an eye chart developed by Stuart Anstis (1974). The chart is shown in Figure 2.19. If you look at the center of the chart, each of the characters is equally distinct. To make this chart Anstis took measurements of the smallest letter that could be seen at many angles of eccentricity from the fovea. In this version, each letter is about 5 times the smallest resolvable size for people with 20/20 vision. Anstis found that the size of the smallest distinct characters could be approximated by the simple function

$$Character\ Size = 0.046e \hspace{3cm} \textbf{(2.7)}$$

where *e* is the eccentricity from the fovea measured in degrees of visual angle.

This variation in processing power with eccentricity is revealed in the structure of the brain at many levels of visual processing. For example, area V1 is the primary cortical reception area for signals from the eye. Half of area V1 represents the central 10 degrees of vision and this, in turn, represents only about 3% of the visual field.

Figure 2.19   An eye chart developed by Anstis (1974). Each character is about five times the smallest perceivable size when the center is fixated. This is the case for any viewing distance.

Since space in the brain is carved up very differently than the uniform pixels of a computer screen, we need a new term to talk about the image units used by the brain to process space. Let's call them *brain pixels*. Although there are many areas in the brain with nonuniform image maps, retinal ganglion cells best capture the brain pixel idea. Retinal ganglion cells are neurons that send information from the eyeball up the optic nerve to the cortex. Each one pools information from many rod and cone receptors, as illustrated in Figure 2.20. In the fovea, a single ganglion cell may be devoted to a single cone; whereas in the far periphery each ganglion cell receives information from thousands of rods and cones. There is one nerve fiber called an *axon,* which carries the signal from each ganglion cell, and there are about a million axons in each optic nerve. The visual area that feeds into a ganglion cell is called its *receptive field*. Drasdo (1977) found that retinal ganglion cell size could be approximated by the function

$$Receptive\,Field\,Size = 0.0006(e + 1.0)$$ (2.8)

where *e* is the eccentricity from the fovea measured in degrees of visual angle.

Figure 2.20   The retina is comprised of receptors and several layers of neurons. The big octopuslike neurons at the top of this drawing are retinal ganglion cells. These transmit retinal information to the brain. *Illustration by Tartufieri.*

Note that Equation 2.6 is very similar to Anstis's equation (2.5) when we take into account that many brain pixels are needed to resolve something as complex as a letter of the alphabet. Assuming that a 7 × 7 matrix of brain pixels is needed to represent a character brings the two functions into close agreement.

Brain Pixels and the Optimal Screen

In light of the extreme nonuniformity of brain pixels, we can talk about the visual efficiency of a display screen by asking what screen size provides the best match of screen pixels to brain pixels. What happens when we look at the very wide-angle screen provided by some head-mounted virtual reality displays? Are we getting more information into the brain, or less? What happens when we look at the small screen of a personal digital assistant, or even a wristwatch-sized screen? One way to answer these questions is to model how many brain pixels are stimulated by different screens having different sizes but the same number of pixels. To make the comparison fair, we should keep the viewing distance constant.

There are two types of inefficiency that occur when we view flat displays. These are illustrated in Figure 2.21. At the fovea there are many brain pixels for each screen pixel. To have higher-resolution screens would definitely help foveal vision. However, off to the side, the situation is reversed; there are many more screen pixels than brain pixels. We are, in a sense, wasting information, because the brain cannot appreciate the detail and we could easily get away with fewer pixels.

In modeling the visual efficiency of different screen sizes, we can compute the total number of brain pixels (TBP) stimulated by the display.

$$TPB = total\ number\ of\ brain\ pixels\ stimulated\ by\ a\ display \qquad (2.9)$$

We can also compute the number of *uniquely stimulated brain pixels (USBP)*. Many brain pixels get the same signal when we look at a low-resolution screen and are therefore redundant, pro-

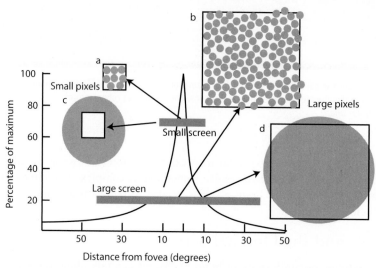

Figure 2.21   The acuity graph illustrates how computer screens of different sizes but the same number of pixels match human visual acuity. Brain pixels are illustrated as circles, screen pixels as squares. (a) In the center of vision, for the small screen, there are 10 or more brain pixels per screen pixel. (b) With the big screen, there are over a hundred brain pixels getting information from the same screen pixel. (c) In the periphery of the visual field, for the small screen, screen pixels are smaller than brain pixels. (d) In the periphery of the visual field, there is a better match for the big screen.

viding no extra information. Therefore, to count uniquely stimulated brain pixels, we use the following formula:

$$USBP = TPB - redundant\ brain\ pixels \tag{2.10}$$

To obtain a measure of how efficiently a display is being used, we take the ratio of USBP to screen pixels (SP). This measure is called *display efficiency (DE)*. Note that if there were a perfect match, with one screen pixel for every brain pixel, we would have a display efficiency of 1.0 or 100%.

$$DE = USPB/SP \tag{2.11}$$

Finally, we might be interested in the ratio between USBP and the brain pixels covered by a display. This measure of *visual efficiency (VE)* tells us the proportion of brain pixels in the screen area that are getting unique information.

$$VE = USPB/TBP \tag{2.12}$$

Figure 2.22 illustrates a numerical simulation of what happens to *TBP* and *USBP* as we change the size of the screen. It is based on Drasdo's (1977) model and assumes a million square pixels at a constant viewing distance of 50 cm. It takes into account that pixels near the edge of a large screen are both farther away and viewed obliquely—and are therefore visually smaller than pixels in the center. In fact, their visual area declines by $cos^2(\theta)$ where θ is the angle of eccentricity. For illustrative purposes, the display widths equivalent to a conventional monitor and a single wall of a Cave Automatic Virtual Environment (CAVE) display are shown. A CAVE is a virtual reality display where the participant stands in the center of a cube, each wall of which is a display screen. In Figure 2.22 the sizes have been normalized to a standard viewing distance by using equivalent visual angles. Thus a CAVE wall of 2 meters at a viewing distance of 1 meter is equivalent to a 1-meter display at 50 centimeters, given that both have the same number of pixels.

The simulation of the one-million pixel display reveals a number of interesting things. For a start, even though a conventional monitor covers only about 5–10% of our visual field when viewed normally, it stimulates almost 50% of brain pixels. Thus even if we could have very high–resolution, large screens, we would not be getting very much more information into the brain. Figure 2.22 shows that USBPs peak at a width close to the normal monitor viewing with a display efficiency of 30% and declines somewhat as the screen gets larger. If we consider that

Figure 2.22 Results from a numerical simulation with a one-million pixel screen to show how many brain pixels are stimulated as a display increases in size. Display efficiency (right-hand scale) gives the percentage of screen pixels that uniquely influence the visual system (unique brain pixels) and only applies to the lower curve.

our visual field is a precious resource and there are other things besides computer graphics that we may wish to see, this confirms that computer screens are currently about the right size for most tasks. However, larger screens certainly have their uses in supporting many viewers.

There is an argument that the center of the visual field is even more important for many tasks than its huge brain pixel concentration would suggest. A natural way of seeking information (discussed in Chapter 11) is to use eye movements to bring the information to the fovea. The parafovea may be optimal for pattern perception; it is an area that is about 6 degrees in diameter, centered on the fovea. Most charts and diagrams in this book are presented to be roughly parafoveal size. The periphery is undoubtedly important in situation awareness and alerting, but when visual pattern finding for decision making is required, this relatively small region may be the most critical.

Of course, one conclusion to be drawn from this analysis is that we need more pixels in our displays. A display recently developed by IBM (T221) is only slightly larger than a normal desktop monitor, but it has 3840 × 2600 pixels, providing a visual quality close to that of high-quality printing. Large field displays become much more effective if they have a similarly large number of pixels, so that when we move our eyes to a new spot we actually gain more information. Another conclusion is that we should have small, high-resolution screens on devices such as personal digital assistants. In terms of the valuable real estate of the human visual field, a small, high-resolution device uses a small part of visual space but does so very efficiently. Figure 2.23 shows that VE is greatest for small screens; a one-million pixel screen that is only 10 cm wide,

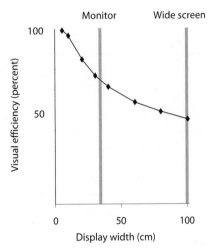

Figure 2.23   Visual efficiency is defined as the percentage of brain pixels that are uniquely stimulated within the retinal image of the screen. This shows the results from a numerical simulation with one million pixels.

held at arm's length, has a resolution equal to the resolution in the fovea and is therefore close to 100% efficient by this measure.

One way to increase the visual efficiency of a display is to have more than one resolution. The CAE fiber-optic helmet-mounted display (FOHMD) is one of the widest-field displays made (Shenker, 1987). Designed for helicopter simulators, it has a 127 × 66–degree low-resolution field of view, with a high-resolution 25 × 19–degree insert that is coupled to the user's eye position via an eye-tracking system (see Figure 2.24). It has 5 arc minutes per pixel in the background and 1.5 arc minutes per pixel in the insert. However, even this advanced system provides computer graphics imagery to less than half the total visual field. The region of binocular overlap is even more impoverished—less than 15% of that available under real-world viewing conditions.

Spatial Contrast Sensitivity Function

The rather simple pattern shown in Figure 2.25 has become one of the most useful tools in measuring basic properties of the human visual system. This pattern is called a *sine wave grating,* because its brightness varies sinusoidally in one direction. There are five ways in which this pattern can be varied:

1.   Spatial frequency (the number of bars of the grating per degree of visual angle)

2.   Orientation

3.   Contrast (the amplitude of the sine wave)

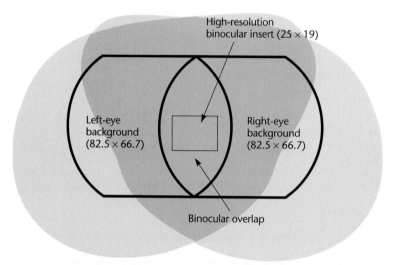

Figure 2.24   The CAE FOHMD has a low-resolution background display for each eye and a high-resolution inset slaved to the user's direction of gaze. The gray region illustrates the human visual field of view for comparison. The high-resolution inset is approximately the size of a computer monitor at a normal viewing distance.

Figure 2.25   A sine wave grating.

4. Phase angle (the lateral displacement of the pattern)

5. Visual area covered by the grating pattern

The grating luminance is defined by the following equation:

$$L = 0.5 + \frac{a}{2}\sin\left(\frac{2\pi x}{\omega} + \frac{\phi}{\omega}\right)$$

(2.13)

where *a* is the contrast (amplitude), ω is the wavelength, ϕ is the phase angle, and *x* is the position on the screen. *L* denotes the resulting output light level in the range [0, 1], assuming that the monitor is linear (see the discussion of gamma correction in Chapter 3).

One way to use a sine wave grating is to measure the sensitivity of the eye/brain system to the lowest contrast that can be detected and to see how this varies with spatial frequency.

Contrast is defined by

$$C = \frac{L_{max} - L_{min}}{L_{max} + L_{min}} \tag{2.14}$$

where L_{max} is the peak luminance and L_{min} is the minimum luminance.

The result is called a *spatial modulation sensitivity function*.

Figure 2.26 is a pattern designed to allow you to see directly the high-frequency fall-off in the sensitivity of your own visual system. It is a sinusoidally modulated pattern of stripes that varies from left to right in terms of spatial frequency and from top to bottom in terms of

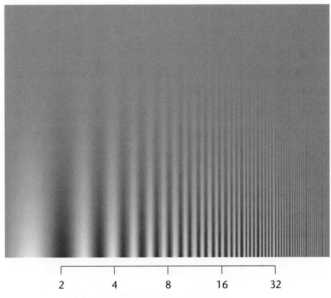

Figure 2.26   This grating pattern changes frequency exponentially from left to right and varies in contrast in a vertical direction. The highest frequency you can resolve depends on the distance from which you view the pattern. The scale gives the spatial frequency if it is viewed from 2.3 m.

contrast. If you view this from 2 m, you can see how your sensitivity to high-frequency patterns is reduced.

The human spatial contrast sensitivity function varies dramatically with spatial frequency, falling off at both high and low values. We are most sensitive to patterns of bright and dark bars occurring at about 2 or 3 cycles per degree. Figure 2.27 shows typical functions for three different age groups. Sensitivity falls off to zero for fine gratings of about 60 cycles per degree for younger people. As we age, we become less and less sensitive to higher spatial frequencies (Owlsley et al., 1983). It is not just that the finest detail we can resolve declines with age. We actually become less sensitive to any pattern components above 1 cycle per degree.

What is perhaps surprising about Figure 2.27 is that there is also a fall-off at low spatial frequencies. We are insensitive both to gradual changes and very rapid changes in light patterns. One of the practical implications of the low-frequency fall-off in sensitivity is that many monitors are very nonuniform, yet this goes unremarked. A typical monitor or television display may vary by as much as 30% or more over its face (it is usually brightest in the center), even if it is displaying a supposedly uniform field. Because we are insensitive to this very gradual (low-frequency) variation, however, we fail to notice the poor quality. Low spatial frequency acuity may also be critical for our perception of large spatial patterns as they are presented in large field displays.

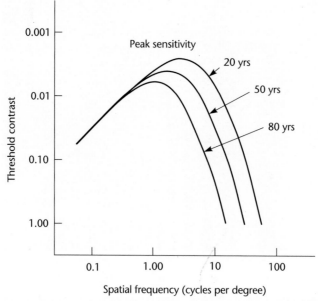

Figure 2.27   Contrast sensitivity varies with spatial frequency. The function is illustrated for three age groups. As we age, our sensitivity to higher spatial frequencies is reduced. *Redrawn from Owlsley et al. (1983).*

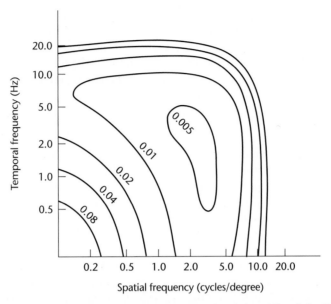

Figure 2.28   Contour map of the human spatiotemporal threshold surface (adapted from Kelly, 1979). Each contour represents the contrast at which a particular combination of spatial and temporal frequencies can be detected.

Most tests of visual acuity, such as letter or point acuity, are really tests of high-frequency resolution, but this may not always be the most useful thing to measure. In tests of pilots' performance, it has been shown that low-frequency contrast sensitivity is actually more important than simple acuity in measuring their performance in flight simulators (Ginsburg et al., 1982).

Visual images on the retina vary in time as well as in space. We can measure the temporal sensitivity of the visual system in much the same way that we measure the spatial sensitivity. This involves taking a pattern, such as that shown in Figure 2.25, and causing it to oscillate in contrast from high to low and back again over time. This oscillation in contrast is normally done using a sinusoidal function. Over time, the dark bars become bright bars and then darken again. When this technique is used, both the spatial and the temporal sensitivity of human vision can be mapped out. Once this is done, it becomes evident that spatial-frequency sensitivity and temporal-frequency sensitivity are interdependent.

Figure 2.28 shows the contrast threshold for a flickering grating as a function of its temporal frequency and its spatial frequency (Kelly, 1979). This shows that optimal sensitivity is obtained for a grating flickering at between 2 and 10 cycles per second (Hz). It is interesting to note that the low-frequency fall-off in sensitivity is much less when a pattern is flickering at between 5 and 10 Hz. If we were interested only in being able to detect the presence of patterns in data, making those patterns flicker at 7 or 8 Hz would be the best way to present them. There are many other reasons, however, why this is not a good idea; in particular, it would undoubtedly be extremely irritating. The limit of human sensitivity to flicker is about 50 Hz.

When the spatial- and temporal-frequency analysis of the visual system is extended to color, we find that chromatic spatial sensitivity is much lower, especially for rapidly changing patterns. In Chapter 4, the spatial and temporal characteristics of color vision are compared to those of the black-and-white vision we have been discussing.

Visual Stress

On December 17, 1997, a Japanese television network canceled broadcasts of an action-packed cartoon because its brightly flashing scenes caused convulsions, and even vomiting of blood, in more than 700 children. The primary cause was determined to be the repetitive flashing lights produced by the computer-generated graphics. The harmful effects were exacerbated by the tendency of children to sit very close to the screen. Vivid, repetitive, large-field flashes are known to be extremely stressful to some people.

The disorder known as pattern-induced epilepsy has been reported and investigated for decades. Some of the earliest reported cases were caused by the flicker from helicopter rotor blades; this resulted in prescreening of pilots for the disorder. In an extensive study of the phenomenon, Wilkins (1995) concludes that a particular combination of spatial and temporal frequencies is especially potent: striped patterns of about 3 cycles per degree and flicker rates of about 20 Hz are most likely to induce seizures in susceptible individuals. Figure 2.29 illustrates a static pattern likely to cause visual stress. The ill effects also increase with the overall size of the pattern. But visual stress may not be confined to individuals with a particular disorder. Wilkins argues that striped patterns can cause visual stress in most people. He gives normal text as an example of a pattern that may cause problems because it is laid out in horizontal stripes, and shows that certain fonts may be worse than others.

The Optimal Display

Acuity information is useful in determining what is needed to produce an adequate or optimal visual display. A modern high-resolution monitor has about 35 pixels per cm. This translates to 40 cycles per degree at normal viewing distances. Given that the human eye has receptors packed into the fovea at roughly 180 per degree of visual angle, we can claim that in linear resolution, we are about a factor of four from having monitors that match the resolving power of the human retina in each direction. A 4000 × 4000–pixel resolution monitor should be adequate for any conceivable visual task, leaving aside, for the moment, the problem of superacuities. Such a monitor would require 16 million pixels. The highest-resolution monitor currently available is an IBM LCD display with 3840 × 2400 pixels, more than nine million. However, at the time of writing there are no consumer graphics cards capable of delivering smooth animation on this display.

We come to a similar conclusion about the ultimate display from the spatial modulation transfer function. Humans can resolve a grating of approximately 50 cycles per degree. If we

Warning! This pattern can cause seizures in some individuals.
If it causes you to feel ill effects, avoid looking at it.

Figure 2.29   A pattern that is designed to be visually stressful. If it is viewed from 40 cm, the spacing of the stripes is about 3 cycles per degree.

take into account the sampling theory that states that we must sample at more than twice the highest frequency we wish to detect, this suggests that we need more than 100 pixels per degree. Perhaps 150 pixels per degree would be reasonable.

If 150 pixels per degree is sufficient, we must ask why manufacturers produce laser printers capable of 1200 dots per inch (460 dots per centimeter). There are three reasons: aliasing, gray levels, and superacuities. The first two of reasons are essentially technical, not perceptual, but they are worth discussing because they have significant implications in perception. The problems are significant for most display devices, not just for printers.

Aliasing

A fundamental theorem of signal transmission tells us that a signal can be reconstructed from its samples only if the samples are obtained at a frequency at least twice the highest frequency contained in the source. This is called the Nyquist limit (Gonzalez and Woods, 1993). Aliasing effects occur when a regular pattern is sampled by another regular pattern at a different frequency. Figure 2.30 illustrates what happens when a pattern of black and white stripes is sampled

Input pattern

Pixel matrix

Output pattern

Figure 2.30   A striped pattern is sampled by pixels. The result is shown in the lower diagram.

Figure 2.31   Aliasing artifacts, with antialiasing as a solution.

by an array of pixels whose spacing is slightly greater than the wavelength. We assume that the pattern of input stripes is sampled at the center of each pixel. The resulting pattern has a much wider spacing.

Aliasing can cause all kinds of unwanted effects. Patterns that should be invisible because they are beyond the resolving power of the human eye can become all too visible. Patterns that are unrelated to the original data can occur in moiré fringes. Aliasing effects are especially bad when some regular pattern is sampled by another regular pattern. This is surely the reason that the retinal mosaic of receptor cells is not regular except in small patches (Figure 2.15).

Another aliasing effect is illustrated in Figure 2.31. The line shown in the top part of the figure becomes a staircase pattern when it is drawn using large pixels. The problem is that each pixel samples the line at a single point. Either the point is on the line, in which case the pixel is colored black, or it is not, in which case the pixel is colored white. A set of techniques known as *antialias-*

Figure 2.32   An aliased line that is not quite horizontal.

ing can help with this. Antialiasing consists of computing the *average* of the light pattern that is represented by each pixel. The result is shown in the lower part of Figure 2.31. Proper antialiasing can be a more cost-effective solution than simply increasing the number of pixels in the display. With it, a low-resolution display can be made as effective as a much higher-resolution display, but it does require extra computation. In addition to antialiasing, a full-color image requires properly averaging the three color components, not just the brightness levels.

In data visualization, aliasing effects can sometimes actually be useful. For example, it is much easier to judge whether a line is perfectly horizontal on the screen with aliasing than without (Figure 2.32). Because of our ability to see very small line displacements (vernier acuity), aliasing makes small misalignments completely obvious. It is also possible that the spatial-frequency amplification illustrated in Figure 2.30 can be used as a deliberate technique to magnify certain kinds of regular patterns, to make invisibly fine variations visible.

Number of Dots

The main reason we need 1200 dots per inch on a laser printer is that the dots of a laser printer are either black or white; to represent gray, many dots must be used. Essentially, one pixel is made up of many dots. Thus, for example, a 16×16 matrix of dots can be used to generate 257 levels of gray because from 0 to 256 of the dots can be colored black. In practice, square patches are not used, because these cause aliasing problems. To correct aliasing effects, randomness is used in distributing the dots, and errors are propagated from one patch to neighboring patches. Most graphics textbooks provide an introduction to these techniques (e.g., Foley et al., 1990). The fact that grays are made from patterns of black and white dots means that the resolution of a laser printer actually is 1200 dots per inch only for black-and-white patterns. For gray patterns, the resolution is at least ten times lower than this.

Superacuities and Displays

Superacuities provide a reason why we might wish to have very high-resolution monitors. As discussed earlier, superacuities occur because the human visual system can integrate information from a number of receptors to give better-than-receptor resolution. For example, in vernier acuity, better than 10-arc-second resolution is achievable.

However, in my laboratory, we have obtained experimental evidence that antialiasing can result in superacuity performance on vernier acuity tasks. This involves making judgments to see differences in the alignment of fine lines that are actually smaller than individual pixels. Figure 2.33 shows data from an experiment that my research assistant, Tim Millar, and I carried out to determine whether vernier acuity performance can be achieved to higher-than-pixel resolution if the lines are antialiased.

Figure 2.33   Results from an experiment measuring vernier acuity. The threshold is defined as half the horizontal difference between the 25% threshold and the 75% threshold.

In the standard vernier acuity task, subjects judge whether one vertical line is above or below another (as in Figure 2.16). The lines are placed end to end with a small lateral displacement between them. The purpose of the experiment is to determine how small a displacement can be perceived more than 50% of the time (Berry, 1948). In our study, one line was displaced horizontally by an amount that varied randomly in a range between 1 pixel and −1 pixel, corresponding to ±30 seconds of arc at the viewing distance we chose. The question asked was "Is the lower line to the right of the upper line?" The percentage correct was computed based on the answers given over a large number of trials. By convention, vernier acuity is defined as half the difference between 25% correct performance and 75% correct performance. In Figure 2.33, two of our results are shown for aliased and antialiased lines. The actual threshold is half of each range on the *x*-axis. Thus, Figure 2.33 shows a 15-sec vernier acuity threshold (30 sec × 0.5) for aliased lines and a 7.5-sec threshold (15 sec × 0.5) for antialiased lines. This data shows that given proper antialiasing, superacuity performance to better-than-pixel resolution can be achieved.

Temporal Requirements of the Perfect Display

Just as we can evaluate the spatial requirements for a perfect monitor, so can we evaluate the temporal requirements. Fifty-Hz flicker is about the limit of resolution that most of us can perceive. Hence the 50–75-Hz refresh rate of the typical monitor would seem to be adequate. However, temporal aliasing artifacts are common in computer graphics and movies. The "reversing wagon wheel" effect is the one most often noticed (the wheel of a wagon in a western movie appears to rotate in the wrong direction). Temporal aliasing effects are especially pronounced when the image update rate is low, and it is common in data visualization systems to have animated images that are updated only about 10 times per second even though the screen is refreshed at 60 Hz or better. An obvious result is the breaking up of a moving object into a series of discrete objects. If the data contains a repetitive temporal pattern, aliasing and sampling effects can occur that are the analogs of the spatial-aliasing effects. Sometimes a single object can appear to be multiple objects.

To correct these problems, temporal antialiasing can be employed. Part of a moving image may pass through several pixels over the course of a single animation frame. The correct antialiasing solution is to color each pixel according to the percentage contributions of all the different objects as they pass through it for the duration of the animation frame. Thus, if the refresh rate is 60 Hz, a program must calculate the *average* color for each pixel that is affected by the moving pattern for each 1/60-second interval. This technique is often called *motion blur*. It can be computationally expensive in practice and is rarely done except in the case of high-quality animations created for the movie industry. As computers become faster, we can expect antialiasing to be more widely used in data visualization, because there is no doubt that aliasing effects can be visually disturbing and occasionally misleading.

Conclusion

In comparison with the richness of the visual world, the cathode ray tube (CRT) computer screen is simple indeed. It is remarkable that we can achieve so much with such a limited device. In the world, we perceive subtly textured, visually rich surfaces, differentiated by shading, depth-of-focus effects, and texture gradients. The CRT screen merely produces a two-dimensional array of colors. Gibson's concept of the ambient optical array, introduced at the beginning of this chapter, provides a context for understanding the success of this device, despite its shortcomings. Given a particular direction and a viewing angle of 20 degrees or so, the CRT is capable of reproducing many (but not all) of those aspects of the ambient array that are most important to perception. As we shall see in Chapter 4, this is especially true in the realm of color, where a mere three colors are used to effectively reproduce much of the gamut to which humans are sensitive. Spatial information, in the form of texture gradients and other spatial cues, is also reproducible to some extent on a CRT. However, there are problems in the reproduction of fine texture. The actual pixel pattern, or phosphor-dot pattern, of a CRT may provide a texture that visually competes with the texture designed for display.

A typical monitor only stimulates perhaps 5–10% of the visual field at normal viewing distances, as shown in Figure 2.24. However, this is not as serious a shortcoming as it might seem, because the central field of view is heavily overweighted in human visual processing. In fact, looking at the center of a typical monitor screen from a normal viewing distance stimulates considerably more than 50% of the visual processing mechanisms in the brain (Wilkins, 1995). A monitor is also deficient in that it has limited dynamic range compared to the huge range of light levels that can occur in the environment. But this is not so bad, because the eye neglects the absolute light level and adapts to the prevailing conditions. At any given time, the range over which the eye functions is no more than two orders of magnitude, and the dynamic range of a CRT is not much worse than this.

Nevertheless, the CRT has some serious deficiencies as a device for presenting visual data. One of these is its lack of ability to provide focal depth-of-focus information. In the real world, the eye must refocus on objects at different distances. Because this is not the case for computer graphics presented on the screen, it can confuse our spatial processing systems. This problem will be discussed further in Chapter 8 under the heading "The Vergence-Focus Problem."

A second major problem with the CRT is perhaps more profound. Although we may be able to fool the eye into thinking that the abstractions displayed on a CRT are in some ways like objects in the real world, the illusion becomes painfully evident when it comes to interacting with these objects. To use Gibson's terminology, we may be able to fool the eye into believing that a certain set of affordances exists, but when users wish to take advantage of these affordances and reach out and touch the artificial objects, the artifice is revealed. There are no haptic affordances on a CRT screen, and interaction is necessarily indirect and more or less artificial.

The idea of virtual reality is to get around these problems by providing natural interaction. With the addition of force feedback devices, it is now possible to simulate a sense of contact with objects. Such haptic devices are now expensive, difficult to program, and have a limited range, but we may hope that displays will eventually offer both high-quality visual information and natural interaction with graphical objects.

CHAPTER 3

Lightness, Brightness, Contrast, and Constancy

It would be dull to live in a gray world, but we would actually get along just fine 99% of the time. Technically, we can divide color space into one luminance (gray scale) dimension and two chromatic dimensions. It is the luminance dimension that is most basic to vision and understanding. It can help us answer practical questions: How do we map data to a gray scale? How much information can we display per unit area? How much data can we display per unit time? Can gray scales be misleading? (The answer is yes.)

However, to understand the applications of gray scales we need to address other, more fundamental questions: How bright is a patch of light? What is white? What is black? What is a middle gray? These are simple-sounding questions, but the answers are complex and lead us to many of the basic mechanisms of perception. The fact that we have light-sensing receptors in our eyes might seem like a good starting point. But individual receptor signals tell us very little. The nerves that transmit information from the eyes to the brain transmit nothing about the amount of light falling on the retina. Instead, they signal the *relative* amount of light: how a particular patch differs from a neighboring patch, or how a particular patch of light has changed in the past instant. Neurons in the early stages of the visual system do not behave like light meters; they behave like change meters.

The signaling of differences is not special to lightness and brightness. This is a general property of many early sensory systems, and we will come across it again and again throughout this book. The implications of this are fundamental to the way we perceive information. The fact that differences, not absolute values, are transmitted to the brain accounts for contrast illusions that can cause substantial errors in the way data is "read" from a visualization. The signaling of differences also means that the perception of lightness is nonlinear, and this has implications for the gray-scale coding of information. But to belabor the occasional inaccuracies of perception does not do justice to millions of years of evolution. The fact that the early stages of vision are nonlinear does not mean that all perception is inaccurate. On the contrary, we usually can make quite sophisticated judgments about the lightness of surfaces in our environments. This chapter shows how simple, early visual mechanisms can help our brains do sophisticated things, such as see objects correctly no matter what the illumination level.

This chapter is also the first part of a presentation of color vision. Luminance can be regarded as one of three color dimensions, albeit the most important one. Discussing this dimension in isolation gives us an opportunity to examine many of the basic concepts of color with a simpler model. (This is expanded, in Chapter 4, into a full three color–channel model.) We start by introducing neurons and the concept of the visual receptive field; a number of display distortion effects that can be explained by these simple mechanisms. The bulk of this chapter is taken up with a discussion of the concepts of luminance, lightness, and brightness and the implications of these for data display.

The practical lessons of this chapter are related to the way data values can be mapped to gray values using gray-scale coding. The kinds of perceptual errors that can occur owing to simultaneous contrast are discussed at length. More fundamentally, the reasons the visual system makes these errors provide a general lesson. The nervous system works by computing difference signals at almost every level. The lesson is that visualization is not good for representing precise absolute numerical values, but rather for displaying patterns of differences or changes over time, to which the eye and brain are extremely sensitive.

Neurons, Receptive Fields, and Brightness Illusions

Neurons are the basic circuits of information processing in the brain. In some respects they are like transistors, only much more complex. Like the digital circuits of a computer, neurons respond with discrete pulses of electricity. However, unlike transistors, neurons are connected to hundreds and sometimes thousands of other neurons. Much of our knowledge about the behavior of neurons comes from single-cell recording techniques whereby a tiny microelectrode is actually inserted into a cell and the cell's electrical activity is monitored. Most neurons are constantly active, emitting pulses of electricity through connections with other cells. Depending on the input, the rate of firing can be increased or decreased as the neuron is excited or inhibited. Neuroscientists often set up amplifiers and loudspeakers in their laboratories so that they can hear the activity of cells that are being probed. The result is like the clicking of a Geiger counter, becoming rapid when the cell is excited and slowing when it is inhibited.

There is considerable neural processing of information in the eye itself. Several layers of cells in the eye culminate in retinal ganglion cells. These ganglion cells send information through the optic nerve via a way station called the *lateral geniculate nucleus*, on to the primary visual processing areas at the back of the brain, as shown in Figure 3.1.

The *receptive field* of a cell is the visual area over which a cell responds to light. This means that patterns of light falling on the retina influence the way the neuron responds, even though it may be many synapses removed from receptors. Retinal ganglion cells are organized with circular receptive fields, and they can be either on-center or off-center. The activity of an on-center cell is illustrated in Figure 3.2. When this cell is stimulated in the center of its receptive field, it

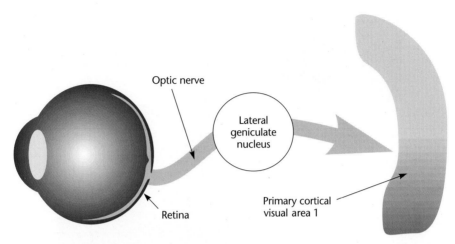

Figure 3.1 Signals from the retina are transmitted along the optic nerve to the lateral geniculate nucleus. From there, they are distributed to a number of areas, but mostly to Visual Area 1 of the cortex, located at the back of the head.

emits pulses at a greater rate. When the cell is stimulated outside of the center of its field, it emits pulses at a lower-than-normal rate and is said to be *inhibited*. Figure 3.2 also shows the output of an array of such neurons being stimulated by a bright edge. The output of this system is an enhanced response on the bright side of the edge and a depressed response on the dark side of the edge, with an intermediate response to the uniform areas on either side. The cell fires more on the bright side because there is less light in the inhibitory region; hence, it is less inhibited.

A widely used mathematical description of the concentric receptive field is the *Difference of Gaussians* model (often called the DOG function):

$$f(x) = \alpha_1 e^{-\left(\frac{x}{w_1}\right)^2} - \alpha_2 e^{-\left(\frac{x}{w_2}\right)^2}$$

(3.1)

In this model, the firing rate of the cell is the difference between two Gaussians. One Gaussian represents the center and the other represents the surround, as illustrated in Figure 3.3. The variable x represents the distance from the center of the field, w_1 defines the width of the center, and w_2 defines the width of the surround. The amount of excitation or inhibition is given by the amplitude parameters α_1 and α_2.

We can easily calculate the effect of the DOG-type receptor on various patterns. We can either think of the pattern passing over the receptive field of the cell, or think of the output of a

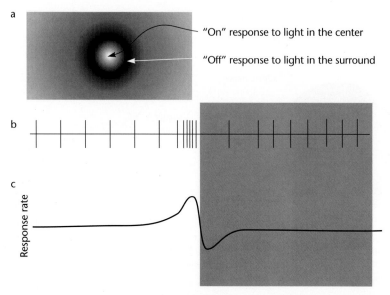

Figure 3.2   (a) The receptive field structure of an on-center simple lateral geniculate cell. (b) As the cell passes over from a light region to a dark region, the rate of neural firing increases just to the bright side of the edge and decreases on the dark side. (c) A smoothed plot of the cell activity level.

Figure 3.3   Difference of Gaussians (DOG) model of a receptive field.

whole array of DOG cells arranged in a line across the pattern. When we use a computer to simulate either operation, we discover that the DOG receptive field can be used to explain a variety of brightness contrast effects.

In the Hermann grid illusion, shown in Figure 3.4, black spots appear at the intersections of the bright lines. The explanation is that there is *more inhibition* at the spaces between two squares, so they seem brighter than the points at the intersections.

Simultaneous Brightness Contrast

The term *simultaneous brightness contrast* is used to explain the general effect whereby a gray patch placed on a dark background looks lighter than the same gray patch on a light background. Figure 3.5 illustrates this effect and the way it is predicted by the DOG model of concentric opponent receptive fields.

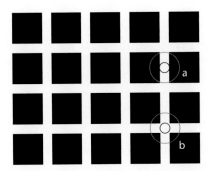

Figure 3.4   Hermann grid illusion. The black spots that are seen at the intersections of the lines are thought to result from the fact that there is less inhibition when a receptive field is at position (a) than at position (b).

Figure 3.5   Illustration of simultaneous brightness contrast. The upper row contains rectangles of an identical gray. The lower rectangles are a lighter gray, but are also all identical. The graph below illustrates the effect of a DOG filter applied to this pattern.

Mach Bands

Figure 3.6 shows a Mach band effect. At the point where a uniform area meets a luminance ramp, a bright band is seen. In general, Mach bands appear where there is an abrupt change in the first derivative of a brightness profile. The lower plot on the right shows how this is simulated by the DOG model.

The Chevreul Illusion

When a sequence of gray bands is generated as shown in Figure 3.7, the bands appear darker at one edge than at the other, even though they are uniform. The diagram to the right in Figure 3.7 shows that this visual illusion can be simulated by the application of a DOG model of the neural receptive field.

Figure 3.6   Illustration of Mach banding. (a) Bright Mach bands are evident at the boundaries between the internal triangles. (b) At the top, the actual brightness profile is shown between the two arrows. The curve below shows how the application of a DOG filter models the bright bands that are seen.

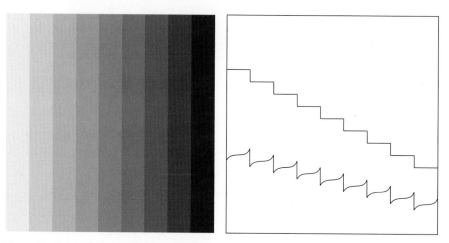

Figure 3.7   The Chevreul illusion. The measured lightness pattern is shown by the staircase pattern on the right. What is perceived can be closely approximated by a DOG model. The lower plot on the right shows the application of a DOG filter to the staircase pattern shown above.

Simultaneous Contrast and Errors in Reading Maps

Simultaneous contrast effects can result in large errors of judgment when reading quantitative (value) information displayed using a gray scale (Cleveland and McGill, 1983). For example, Figure 3.8 shows a gravity map of part of the North Atlantic where the local strength of the gravitational field is encoded in shades of gray. In an experiment to measure the effects of contrast on data encoded in this way, we found substantial errors averaging 20% of the entire scale (Ware, 1988). The contrast in this case comes from the background of the gray scale itself and the regions surrounding any designated sampling point.

Contrast Effects and Artifacts in Computer Graphics

One of the consequences of Mach bands, and of contrast effects in general, is that they tend to highlight the deficiencies in the common shading algorithms used in computer graphics. Smooth surfaces are often displayed using polygons, both for simplicity and to speed the computer graphics rendering process; this leads to visual artifacts because of the way the visual system enhances the boundaries at the edges of polygons.

Figure 3.9 illustrates the effects of the DOG model on three surface-shading methods. In this example, a cylinder has been broken into a series of rectangular facets.

Figure 3.8   A gravity map of the North Atlantic (Ware, 1988). Large errors can occur when values are read using the key.

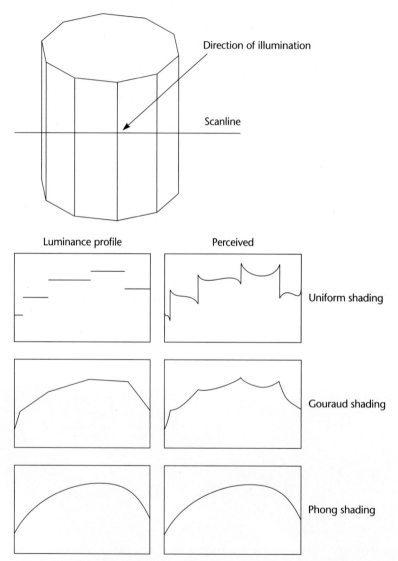

Figure 3.9   The contrast mechanisms of the early visual system enhance a number of artifacts that occur in computer graphics shading algorithms. The illustration at the top shows a single line of pixels through a rendering of a cylinder approximated by a set of rectangular panels. The plots in the left-hand column illustrate the actual light-level distributions that result from three common techniques used in computer graphics. The plots in the right-hand column show how the lack of smoothness in the result is increased by the application of the DOG model.

1. Uniform shading: The light reflected from each rectangular facet is computed by taking into account the incident illumination and the orientation of the surface with respect to the light. Then the entire facet is filled uniformly with the resulting color. Scanning across an object modeled in this way reveals stepwise changes in color. The steps are exaggerated, producing the Chevreul illusion. What was intended to be a smooth cylinder may appear as a fluted column.

2. Gouraud shading: A shading value is calculated not for the facets, but for the edges between the facets. This is done by averaging the surface normals at the boundaries where facets meet. As each facet is painted during the rendering process, the color is linearly interpolated between the facet boundaries. Scanning across the object, we see linear changes in color across polygons, with abrupt transitions in gradient where the facets meet. Mach banding occurs at these facet boundaries, enhancing the discontinuities.

3. Phong shading: As with Gouraud shading, surface normals are calculated at the facet boundaries. However, in this case, the surface normal is interpolated between the edges. The result is smooth changes in lightness with no appreciable Mach banding.

Edge Enhancement

Lateral inhibition can be considered the first stage of an edge detection process that signals the positions and contrasts of edges in the environment. One of the consequences is that pseudo-edges can be created; two areas that physically have the same lightness can be made to look different by having an edge between them that shades off gradually to the two sides (Figure 3.10). The brain does perceptual interpolation so that the entire central region appears lighter than surrounding regions. This is called the *Cornsweet effect*, after the researcher who first described it (Cornsweet, 1970).

Figure 3.10   The Cornsweet effect. The areas in the centers of the circles tend to look lighter than the surrounding area, even though they are actually the same shade. This provides evidence that the brain constructs surface color based largely on edge contrast information.

Figure 3.11   Seurat deliberately enhanced edge contrast to make his figures stand out.

The enhancement of edges is also an important part of some artists' techniques. It is a way to make objects more clearly distinct, given the limited dynamic range of paint. The example given in Figure 3.11 is from Seurat's painting of bathers. The same idea can be used in visualization to make areas of interest stand out. Figure 3.12 is a representation of a flow field without (Figure 3.12a) and with (Figure 3.12b) an adjustment of the background designed to make the central region more clearly distinct.

Figure 3.12   Low spatial frequency adjustment of the background luminance can be used to enhance a flow-field visualization. (a) Shows a flow pattern without enhancement. (b) Shows the same pattern enhanced in the central region.

Luminance, Brightness, Lightness, and Gamma

Contrast effects may cause annoying problems in the presentation of data, but a deeper analysis shows that they can also be used to reveal the mechanisms underlying normal perception. How the contrast mechanism works to enable us to perceive our environment accurately, under all but unusual circumstances, is the main subject of the discussion that follows. The severe illusory contrast effects in computer displays are a consequence of the impoverished nature of those displays, not of any inadequacy of the visual system.

It should now be evident that the perceived brightness of a particular patch of light has almost nothing to do with the amount of light coming from that patch as we might measure it with a photometer. Thus, what might seem like a simple question—How bright is that patch of light?—is not at all straightforward. We start with an ecological perspective, then consider perceptual mechanisms, and finally discuss applications in visualization.

In order to survive, we need to be able to manipulate objects in the environment and determine their properties. Generally, information about the quantity of illumination is of very little use to us. Illumination is a prerequisite for sight, but otherwise we do not need to know whether the light we are seeing by is dim because it is late on a cloudy day, or brilliant because of the noonday sun. What we do need to know about are objects—food, tools, plants, animals, other people, and so on—and we can find out a lot about objects from their surface properties. In particular, we can obtain knowledge of the spectral reflectance characteristics of objects—what we call their color and lightness. The human vision system evolved to extract information about surface properties of objects, often at the expense of losing information about the quality and quantity of light entering the eye. This phenomenon, the fact that we experience colored surfaces and not colored light, is called *color constancy*. When we are talking about the apparent overall reflectance of a surface, it is called *lightness constancy*. Three terms are commonly used to describe the general concept of quantity of light: *luminance*, *brightness*, and *lightness*. The following brief definitions precede more extensive descriptions.

Luminance is the easiest to define; it refers to the *measured amount of light* coming from some region of space. It is measured in units such as candelas per square meter. Of the three terms, only luminance refers to something that can be physically measured. The other two terms refer to psychological variables.

Brightness generally refers to the *perceived amount of light* coming from a source. In the following discussion, it is used to refer only to things that are perceived as self-luminous. Sometimes people talk about bright colors, but *vivid* and *saturated* are better terms.

Lightness generally refers to the *perceived reflectance of a surface*. A white surface is light. A black surface is dark. The shade of paint is another concept of lightness.

Luminance

Luminance is not a perceptual quantity at all. It is a physical measure used to define an amount of light in the visible region of the electromagnetic spectrum. Unlike lightness and brightness, luminance can be read out directly from a scientific measuring instrument. Luminance is a measurement of light energy weighted by the spectral sensitivity function of the human visual system. We are about 100 times less sensitive to light at 450 nanometers than we are to light at 510 nanometers, and it is clearly important to take this difference into account when we are measuring light levels with human observers in mind. The human spectral sensitivity function is illustrated in Figure 3.13 and given at 10-nm intervals in Table 3.1. This function is called the $V(\lambda)$ function. It is an international standard maintained by the Commission Internationale de l'Éclairage (CIE). The $V(\lambda)$ function represents the spectral sensitivity curve of an ideal standard human observer. To find the luminance of a light, we integrate the light distribution $E(\lambda)$ with the CIE estimate of the human sensitivity function $V(\lambda)$. λ represents wavelength.

$$L = \int_{400}^{700} V_\lambda E_\lambda \delta\lambda \qquad (3.2)$$

When multiplied by the appropriate constant, the result is luminance L in units of candelas per square meter. Note that a great many technical issues must be considered when we are measuring light, such as the configuration of the measuring instrument and the sample. Wyszecki and Stiles (1982) have written an excellent reference.

It is directly relevant to data display that the blue phosphor of a monitor has a peak at about 450 nm. Table 3.1 shows that at this wavelength, human sensitivity is only 4% of the maximum in the green range. In Chapter 2, we noted that the chromatic aberration of the human eye means that a monitor's blue light is typically out of focus. The fact that we are also insensitive to this part of the spectrum is another reason why representing text and other detailed information using the pure blue of a monitor is not a good idea, particularly against a black background.

The $V(\lambda)$ function is extremely useful because it provides a close match to the combined sensitivities of the individual cone receptor sensitivity functions. It is reasonable to think of the $V(\lambda)$ function as measuring the luminance efficiency of the first stage of an extended process that ultimately allows us to perceive useful information such as surface lightness and the shapes of surfaces. Technically, it defines how the sensitivity of the so-called *luminance channel* varies with wavelength. The luminance channel is an important theoretical concept in vision research; it is held to be the basis for most pattern perception, depth perception, and motion perception. In Chapter 4, the properties of the luminance channel are discussed in more detail in comparison to the color-processing *chrominance* channels.

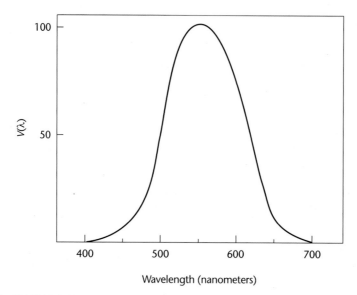

Figure 3.13   The CIE $V(\lambda)$ function representing the relative sensitivity of the human eye to light of different wavelengths.

Wavelength (nanometers)	Relative Sensitivity	Wavelength (nanometers)	Relative Sensitivity	Wavelength (nanometers)	Relative Sensitivity
400	.0004	510	.5030	620	.3810
410	.0012	520	.7100	630	.2650
420	.0040	530	.8620	640	.1750
430	.0116	540	.9540	650	.1070
440	.0230	550	.9950	660	.0610
450	.0380	560	.9950	670	.0320
460	.0600	570	.9520	680	.0170
470	.0910	580	.8700	690	.0082
480	.1390	590	.7570	700	.0041
490	.4652	600	.6310	710	.0010
500	.3230	610	.5030	720	.0005

Table 3.1   Values Show the Sensitivity of the Eye to Light of Different Wavelengths Relative to the Maximum Sensitivity at 555 Nanometers

Text Contrast

For ease of reading, it is essential that text have a reasonable luminance difference from its background. The International Standards Organization (ISO 9241, part 3) recommends a minimum 3:1 luminance ratio of text and background; 10:1 is preferred. This recommendation can be generalized to the display of any kind of information where fine-detail resolution is desirable. In fact, as the spatial modulation sensitivity function shows (Figure 2.27, Chapter 2), the finer the detail, the greater the contrast required.

Brightness

The term *brightness* usually refers to the perceived amount of light coming from self-luminous sources. Thus, it is relevant to the perception of the brightness of indicator lights in an otherwise darkened display—for example, nighttime instrument displays in the cockpits of aircraft and on the darkened bridges of ships.

Perceived brightness is a very nonlinear function of the amount of light emitted by a lamp. Stevens (1961) popularized a technique known as *magnitude estimation* to provide a way of measuring the perceptual impact of simple sensations. In magnitude estimation, subjects are given a stimulus, such as a patch of light viewed in isolation. They are told to assign this stimulus a standard value—for example, 10, to denote its brightness. Subsequently, they are shown other patches of light, also in isolation, and asked to assign them values relative to the standard that they have set. If a patch seems twice as bright as the reference sample, it is assigned the number 20; if it seems half as bright, it is assigned the number 5, and so on. Applying this technique, Stevens discovered that a wide range of sensations could be described by a simple *power law*:

$$S = aI^n \qquad (3.3)$$

This law states that perceived sensation S is proportional to the stimulus intensity I raised to a power n. The power law has been found to apply to many types of sensations, including loudness, smell, taste, heaviness, force, and touch. The power law applies to the perceived brightness of lights viewed in the dark.

$$\text{Brightness} = \text{Luminance}^n \qquad (3.4)$$

However, the value of n depends on the size of the patch of light. For circular patches of light subtending 5 degrees of visual angle, n is 0.333, whereas for point sources of light, n is close to 0.5.

These findings are really only applicable to lights viewed in relative isolation in the dark. Thus, although they have some practical relevance to the design of control panels to be viewed in dark rooms, many other factors must be taken into account in more complex displays. Before we go on to consider these perceptual issues, it is useful to know something about the way computer monitors are designed.

Monitor Gamma

Most visualizations are produced on monitor screens. Anyone who is serious about producing such a thing as a uniform gray scale, or color reproductions in general, must come to grips with the properties of computer monitors. The relationship of physical luminance to voltage on a monitor is approximated by a gamma function:

$$L = V^{\lambda}$$ (3.5)

V is the voltage driving one of the electron guns in the monitor, L is the luminance, and γ is an empirical constant that varies widely from monitor to monitor (values can range from 1.4 to 3.0). See Cowan (1983) for a thorough treatise on monitor calibration.

Monitor nonlinearity is not accidental; it was created by early television engineers to make the most of the available signal bandwidth. They made television screens nonlinear precisely because the human visual system is nonlinear in the opposite direction. For example, a gamma value of 3 will exactly cancel a brightness power function exponent of 0.333, resulting in a display that produces a linear relationship between voltage and perceived brightness. Most monitors have a gamma value much less than 3.0, for reasons that will be explained later.

Adaptation, Contrast, and Lightness Constancy

A major task of the visual system is to extract information about the lightness and color and of objects despite a great variation in illumination and viewing conditions. It cannot be emphasized enough that luminance is completely unrelated to perceived lightness or brightness. If we lay out a piece of black paper in full sunlight on a bright day and point a photometer at it, we may easily measure a value of 1000 candelas per square meter. A typical "black" surface reflects about 10% of the available light, 100 candelas per square meter. If we now take our photometer into a typical office and point it at a white piece of paper, we will probably measure a value of about 50 candelas per square meter. Thus, a black object on a bright day in a beach environment may reflect 20 times more light than white paper in an office. Even in the same environment, white paper lying under the boardwalk may reflect less light (be darker) than black paper lying in the sun. Nevertheless, we can distinguish black from white from gray (achieve lightness constancy) with ease.

Figure 3.14   The eye/brain system is capable of functioning over a huge range of light levels. The amount of light available on a bright day at the beach is 10,000 times greater than the light available in a dimly lit room.

Figure 3.14 illustrates the range of light levels we encounter, from bright sunlight to starlight. A normal interior will have an artificial illumination level of approximately 50 lux. (*Lux* is a measure of incident illumination that incorporates the $V(\lambda)$ function.) On a bright day in summer, the light level can easily be 50,000 lux. Except for the brief period of adaptation that occurs when we come indoors on a bright day, we are generally almost totally oblivious to this huge variation. A change in overall light level of a factor of 2 is barely noticed. Remarkably, our visual systems can achieve lightness constancy over virtually this entire range; in bright sunlight or moonlight, we can tell whether a surface is black, white, or gray.

The first-stage mechanism of lightness constancy is *adaptation*. The second stage of level invariance is *lateral inhibition*. Both mechanisms help the visual system to factor out the effects of the amount and color of the illumination.

The role of adaptation in lightness constancy is straightforward. The changing sensitivity of the receptors and neurons in the eye helps factor out the overall level of illumination. One mechanism is the bleaching of photopigment in the receptors themselves. At high light levels, more photopigment is bleached and the receptors become less sensitive. At low light levels, photopigment is regenerated and the eyes regain their sensitivity. This regeneration can take some time, and this is why we are briefly blinded when coming into a darkened room out of bright sunlight. It can take up to half an hour to develop maximum sensitivity to very dim light, such as moonlight. In addition to the change in receptor sensitivity, the iris of the eye opens and closes. This modulates the amount of light entering the pupil, but is a much less significant factor than is the change in receptor sensitivity. In general, adaptation allows the visual system to adjust overall sensitivity to the ambient light level.

Contrast and Constancy

Contrast mechanisms, such as the concentric opponent receptive fields discussed previously, help us achieve constancy by signaling differences in light levels, especially at the edges of objects. Consider the simple desktop environment illustrated in Figure 3.15. A desk lamp, just to the right of the picture, has created nonuniform illumination over a wooden desk that has two pieces of paper lying on it. The piece nearer the lamp is a medium gray. Because it is receiving more light, it reflects about the same amount of light as the white paper, which is farther from the light. In the original environment, it is easy for people to tell which piece of paper is gray and which is white. Simultaneous contrast can help to explain this. Because the white paper is lighter *relative to its background* than the gray paper is, relative to *its* background, the same mechanism that caused contrast in Figure 3.5 is responsible for enabling an accurate judgment to be made here. The illumination profile across the desk and the pieces of paper is similar to that illustrated in Figure 3.5, except in this case, contrast does not result in an illusion; instead, it helps us to achieve lightness constancy.

Contrast on Paper and on Screen

There is a subtlety here that is worth exploring. Paper reproductions of contrast and constancy effects are often less convincing than these effects are in the laboratory. Looking at Figure 3.15, the reader may well be excused for being less than convinced. The two pieces of paper may not

Figure 3.15   These two pieces of paper are illuminated by a desk lamp just to the right of the picture. This makes the amount of light reflected roughly equal. But the brain achieves lightness constancy in allowing us to differentiate the gray and the white paper.

look very different. But try the experiment with your own desk lamp and paper. Two holes punched in a piece of opaque cardboard can be used as a mask, enabling you to compare the brightness of the gray and white pieces of paper. Under these real-world viewing conditions, it is usually impossible to perceive the true relative *brightness*; instead, the surface *lightness* is perceived. But take a photograph of the scene, like Figure 3.15, and the effect is less strong, although we are better at perceiving the gray levels in the higher-quality color plate. Why is this? The answer lies in the dual nature of pictures. The photograph itself has a surface, and to some extent we perceive the actual gray levels of the photographic pigment, as opposed to the gray levels of what is depicted. The poorer the reproduction, the more we see the actual color printed on the paper. A related effect occurs with depth perception and perspective pictures; to some extent we can see both the surface flatness and the 3D layout of a depicted environment.

Contrast illusions are generally much worse in CRT displays. On a CRT screen there is no texture, except for the uniform pattern of pixels and phosphor dots. Moreover, the screen is self-luminous, which may also confound our lightness constancy mechanisms. Scientists studying simultaneous contrast in the laboratory generally use perfectly uniform textureless fields and obtain extreme contrast effects—after all, under these circumstances, the only information is the differences between patches of light. Computer-generated virtual-reality images lie somewhere between real-world surfaces and the artificial featureless patches of light used in the laboratory. How lightness is judged will depend on exactly how images are designed and presented. On the one hand, a CRT can be set up in a dark room and made to display featureless gray patches of light; in this case, simple contrast effects will dominate. However, if the CRT is used to simulate a very realistic 3D model of the environment, surface lightness constancies can be obtained, depending on the degree of realism, the quality of the display, and the overall setup. To obtain true virtual reality, the screen surface should disappear; to this end some head-mounted displays contain diffusing screens that blur out the pixels and the dot matrix of the screen.

Perception of Surface Lightness

Although both adaptation and contrast can be seen as mechanisms that act in the service of lightness constancy, they are not sufficient. Ultimately, the solution to this perceptual problem can involve every level of perception. Three additional factors seem especially important. The first is that the brain must somehow take the direction of illumination and surface orientation into account in lightness judgments. A flat white surface turned away from the light will reflect less light than one turned toward the light. Figure 3.16 illustrates two surfaces being viewed, one turned away from the light and one turned toward it. Under these circumstances, people can still make reasonably accurate lightness judgments, showing that our brains can take into account both the direction of illumination and the spatial layout (Gilchrist, 1980).

The second important factor is that the brain seems to use the lightest object in the scene as a kind of *reference white* to determine the gray values of all other objects (Cataliotti and Gilchrist, 1995). This is discussed in the following section in the context of lightness-scaling formulas.

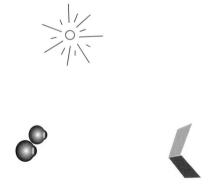

Figure 3.16   When making surface lightness judgments, the brain can take into account the fact that a surface turned away from the light receives less light than a surface turned toward the light.

The third factor is that the ratio of specular and nonspecular reflection can be important under certain circumstances. Figure 3.17(a) is a picture of a world where everything is black, while Figure 3.17(b) shows a world in which everything is white. If we consider these images as slides projected in a darkened room, it is obvious that every point on the black image is brighter than the surroundings. How can we perceive something to be black when it is a bright image? In this case, the most important factor differentiating black from white is the ratio between the specular and the nonspecular reflected light. In the all-black world, the ratio between specular and nonspecular is much larger than in the all-white world.

Lightness Differences and the Gray Scale

Suppose that we wish to display map information using a gray scale. We might, for example, wish to illustrate the variability in population density within a geographical region, or a gravity map as shown in Figure 3.8. For this kind of application, we ideally would like a gray scale such that equal differences in data values are displayed as perceptually equally spaced gray steps (an interval scale). Although the gray scale is probably not the best way of coding this kind of information because of contrast effects (chromatic scales are generally better), the problem does merit some attention because it allows us to discuss some fundamental and quite general issues related to perceptual scales.

Leaving aside contrast effects, the perception of brightness differences depends on whether those differences are small or large. At one extreme, we can consider the smallest difference that can be distinguished between two gray values. In this case, one of the fundamental laws of psychophysics applies. This is called Weber's law, after the nineteenth-century physicist Max Weber (Wyszecki and Stiles, 1982). Weber's law states that if we have a background with luminance L, and superimposed on it is a patch that is a little bit brighter ($L ++ \delta L$), the value of δ that makes this small increment just visible is independent of the overall luminance. Thus, $\delta L/L$ is constant.

Figure 3.17   These two photographs show scenes in which (a) everything is black and (b) everything is white.

Typically, under optimal viewing conditions, we can detect the brighter patch if δ is greater than about 0.005. In other words, we can just detect about a 0.5% change in brightness.

Weber's law applies only to small differences. When large differences between gray samples are judged, many other factors become significant, such as those listed in the previous section. A typical experimental procedure used to study large differences involves asking subjects to select a gray value midway between two other values. The CIE has produced a uniform gray-scale standard based on a synthesis of the results from large numbers of experiments of this kind. This formula includes the concept of a reference white, although many other factors are still neglected.

$$L* = 116(Y/Y_n)^{\frac{1}{3}} - 16 \qquad Y/Y_n > 0.01 \qquad\qquad \textbf{(3.6)}$$

Y_n is a reference white in the environment, normally the surface that reflects most light to the eye. The result $L*$ is a value in a uniform lightness scale. Equal measured differences on this scale approximate equal perceptual differences. It is reasonable to assume that $Y/Y_n > 0.01$ because even the blackest inks and fabrics still reflect more than 1% of incident illumination. This standard is used by the paint and lighting industries to specify such things as color tolerances. Equation 3.5 is part of the *CIEluv* uniform color space standard, which is described more fully in Chapter 4.

Uniform lightness and color scales should always be regarded as providing only rough approximations. Because the visual field is changed radically by many factors that are not taken into account by formulas such as Equation 3.5—perceived illumination, specular reflection from glossy surfaces, and local contrast effects—the goal of obtaining a perfect gray scale is not attainable. Such formulae should be taken as no more than useful approximations.

Contrast Crispening

Another perceptual factor that distorts gray values is called contrast *crispening* (see Wyszecki and Stiles, 1982). Generally, differences are perceived as larger when samples are similar to the background color. Figure 3.18 shows a set of identical gray scales on a range of different gray backgrounds. Notice how the scales appear to divide perceptually at the value of the background. The term *crispening* refers to the way more subtle gray values can be distinguished at the point of crossover. Crispening is not taken into account by uniform gray-scale formulas.

Monitor Illumination and Monitor Surrounds

In some visualization applications, the accurate perception of surface lightness and color is critical. One example is the use of a computer monitor to display wallpaper or fabric samples for customer selection. It is also important for graphic designers that colors be accurately perceived.

Figure 3.18   All the gray strips are the same. Perceived differences between gray-scale values are enhanced where the values are close to the background gray value. The effect is known as crispening.

In these cases, not only is it necessary to calibrate the monitor so that it actually displays the specified color range, but other factors affecting the state of adaptation of the user's eyes must also be taken into account. The color and the brightness of the *surround* of the monitor can be very important in determining how screen objects appear. The adaptation effect produced by room lighting can be equally important.

How should the lighting surrounding a monitor be set up? A monitor used for visual displays engages only the central part of the visual field, so the overall state of adaptation of the eye is maintained at least as much by the ambient room illumination. There are good reasons for maintaining a reasonably high level of illumination in a viewing room, such as the ability to take notes and see other people. However, a side effect of a high level of room illumination is that some light falls on the monitor screen and is scattered back to the eye, degrading the image. In fact, under normal office conditions, between 15% and 40% of the illumination coming to the eye from the monitor screen will come indirectly from the room light, not from the luminous phosphors. Figure 3.19 shows a monitor display with a shadow lying across its face. Although this is a rather extreme example, the effects are clear. Overall contrast is much reduced where the room light falls on the display.

We can model the effects of illumination on a monitor by adding a constant to Equation 3.5.

$$L = V^{\gamma} + A \tag{3.7}$$

where A is the ambient room illumination reflected from the screen, V is the voltage to the monitor, and L is the luminance output for a given gamma.

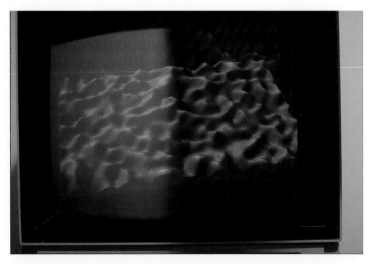

Figure 3.19   A monitor with a shadow falling across its face. Under normal viewing conditions, a significant proportion of the light coming from the screen is reflected ambient room illumination.

If we wish to create a monitor for which equal voltage steps result in equal perceptual steps under conditions where ambient light is reflected, a lower gamma value is needed. Figure 3.20 shows the effects of different gamma values, assuming that 15% of the light coming from the screen is reflected ambient light. The CIE equation (3.5) has been used to model lightness scaling. As you can see, under these assumptions, a monitor is a perceptually more linear device with a gamma of only 1.5 than with a gamma of 2.5 (although under dark viewing conditions, a higher gamma is needed).

If you cover part of your monitor screen with a sheet of white paper, under normal working conditions (when there are lights on in the room), you will probably find that the white of the paper is very different from the white of the monitor screen. The paper may look relatively blue, or yellow, and it may appear darker or lighter. There are often large discrepancies between monitor colors and colors of objects in the surrounding environment. For the creation of an environment where computer-generated colors are comparable to colors in a room, the room should have a standard light level and illuminant color. The monitor should be carefully calibrated and balanced so that the monitor's white matches that of a sheet of white paper held up beside the

Figure 3.20   The three curves show how monitor gun voltage is transformed into lightness, according to the CIE model, with different ambient light conditions and gamma values.

Figure 3.21   A projector was set up containing a mask specially designed so that no light actually fell on the portion of the monitor screen containing the image. In this way, the illumination in the virtual environment displayed on the monitor was made to match closely the illumination falling on the monitor and surrounding region.

screen. In addition, only a minimal amount of light should be allowed to fall on the monitor screen.

Figure 3.21 shows a computer display set up so that the lighting in the virtual environment shown on the monitor is matched with the lighting in the real environment surrounding the monitor. This is achieved by illuminating the region surrounding the monitor with a projector that contains a special mask. This mask was custom-designed so that light was cast on the monitor casing and the desktop surrounding the computer, but no light at all fell on the part of the screen containing the picture. In addition, the direction and color of the light in the virtual environment were adjusted to exactly match the light from the projector. Simulated cast shadows were also created to match the cast shadows from the projector. Using this setup, it is possible to create a virtual environment whose simulated colors and other material properties can be directly compared to the colors and material properties of objects in the room. (This work was done by Justin Hickey and the author.)

Conclusion

As a general observation, the use of gray-scale colors is not a particularly good method for coding data, and not just because contrast effects reduce accuracy. The luminance channel of the visual system is fundamental to so much of perception; it is therefore generally a waste of perceptual resources to use gray-scale encoding. Nevertheless, it is important to understand the problems of brightness and lightness perception because they point to issues that are fundamental to all perceptual systems. One of these basic problems is how perception functions effectively in visual environments where the light level can vary by six orders of magnitude. The solution, arrived at over the course of evolution, is a system that essentially ignores the level of illumination. This may seem like an exaggeration—after all, we can certainly tell the difference between bright sunlight and dim room illumination—but we are barely aware of a change of light level on the order of a factor of 2. For example, in a room lit with a two-bulb fixture, if one bulb burns out, it often goes unnoticed, especially if the bulbs are hidden within a diffusing surround.

A fundamental point made in this chapter is the relative nature of low-level visual processing. As a general rule, nerve cells situated early in the visual pathway do not respond to absolute signals. Rather, they respond to differences in both space and time. At later stages in the visual system, more stable percepts such as the perception of surface lightness can emerge, but this is only because of sophisticated image analysis that takes into account such factors as the position of the light, cast shadows, and the orientation of the object. The relative nature of lightness perception sometimes causes errors. But these errors are due mostly to a simplified graphical environment that confounds the brain's attempt to achieve surface lightness constancy. The mechanism that causes contrast errors is also the reason that we can perceive subtle changes in data values, and can pick out patterns despite changes in the background light level.

Luminance contrast is an especially important consideration for choosing backgrounds and surrounds for a visualization. The way a background is chosen depends on what is important. If the outline shapes of objects are critical, the background should be chosen for maximum luminance contrast with foreground objects. If it is important to see subtle gradations in gray level, the crispening effect suggests that choosing a background in the midrange of gray levels will help us to see more of the important details.

Figure 3.22 provides a summary of the contrast-related effects discussed in this chapter and listed as follows.

- The small two-tone gray squiggles appear lighter on a dark background than on a white background. This is a simple contrast effect.

- The fact that there are two different grays in each squiggle is most clear on the mid-gray background. This is called *sharpening*.

- Mach bands enhance abrupt changes in luminance gradients.

- Gray scales are perceptually altered by background lightness. The light gray background makes differences between light grays clearest. The dark gray background emphasizes differences between dark grays. This is illustrated by the two gray step scales on the left and is another instance of sharpening.

- Text and other detailed visual information requires at least 3 : 1 luminance contrast for clarity. More is better.

- Gray scales are very unreliable as a method for conveying quantitative information.

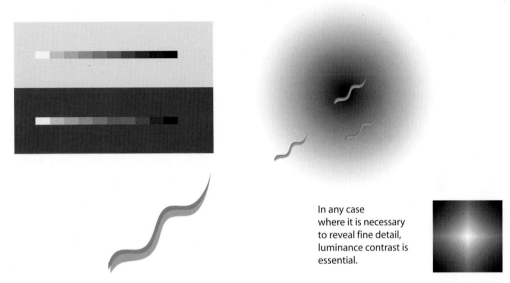

In any case where it is necessary to reveal fine detail, luminance contrast is essential.

Figure 3.22   A summary of the most significant luminance contrast effects.

When people care about image quality on a computer display, they typically reduce the room illumination as much as possible. The main reason for doing this is to reduce the amount of ambient room light that falls on the viewing screen, degrading the image. But this can have unfortunate side effects. Low room illumination causes a kind of visual shock in looking at the screen and away from it. In addition, it is difficult for observers to take notes. When people spend lots of time in dimly lit work environments, it can cause depression and reduced job satisfaction (Rosenthal, 1993). For these reasons, the optimal visualization viewing environment is one that is carefully engineered so that there is a high level of ambient light in the room, with the lights arranged so that minimal illumination falls on the viewing screen.

Luminance is but one dimension of color space. In Chapter 4, this one-dimensional model is expanded to a three-dimensional color perception model. The luminance channel, however, is special. We could not get by without luminance perception, but we can certainly get by without color perception. This is demonstrated by the historic success of black-and-white movies and television. Later chapters describe how information encoded in the luminance channel is fundamental to perception of fine detail, discrimination of the shapes of objects through shading, stereoscopic depth perception, motion perception, and many aspects of pattern perception.

CHAPTER 4

Color

In the summer of 1997, I designed an experiment to measure human ability to trace paths between connected parts in a 3D diagram. Then, as is my normal practice, I ran a pilot study in order to see whether the experiment was well constructed. By ill luck, the first person tested was a research assistant who worked in my lab. He had far more difficulty with the task than anticipated—so much so that I put the experiment back on the drawing board to reconsider, without trying any more pilot subjects. Some months later, my assistant told me he had just had an eye test and the optometrist had determined that he was color blind. This explained the problems with the experiment. Although it was not about color perception, I had marked the targets red in my experiment. He therefore had had great difficulty in finding them, which rendered the rest of the task meaningless.

The remarkable aspect of this story is that my assistant had gone through 21 years of his life without knowing that he was blind to many color differences. This is not uncommon, and it strongly suggests that color vision cannot be all that important to everyday life. In fact, color vision is irrelevant to much of normal vision. It does not help us determine the layout of objects in space, how they are moving, or what their shapes are. It is not much of an overstatement to say that color vision is largely superfluous in modern life. Nevertheless, color is extremely useful in data visualization.

Color vision does have a critical function, which is hardly surprising because this sophisticated ability must surely provide some evolutionary advantage. Color helps us break camouflage. Some things differ visually from their surroundings only by their color. An especially important example is illustrated in Figure 4.1. If we have color vision, we can easily see the cherries hidden in the leaves. If we do not, this becomes much harder. Color also tells us much that is useful about the material properties of objects. This is crucial in judging the condition of our food. Is this fruit ripe or not? It this meat fresh or putrid? What kind of mushroom is this? It is also useful if we are making tools. What kind of stone is this? Clearly, these can be life-or-death decisions. In modern hunter–gatherer societies, men are the hunters and women are the gatherers.

Figure 4.1   Finding the cherries among the leaves is much easier if we have color vision.

This may have been true for long periods of human evolution, which could explain why it is mostly men who are color blind. If they had been gatherers, they would have been more than likely to bring home poison berries—a selective disadvantage. In the modern age of supermarkets, these skills are much less valuable; this is perhaps why color deficiencies so often go unnoticed.

The role that color plays ecologically suggests ways that it can be used in information display. It is useful to think of color as an attribute of an object rather than as its primary characteristic. It is excellent for labeling and categorization, but poor for displaying shape, detail, or space. These points are elaborated in this chapter. We begin with an introduction to the basic theory of color vision to provide a foundation for the applications. The latter half of the chapter consists of a set of five visualization problems requiring the effective use of color; these have to do with color selection interfaces, color labeling, pseudocolor sequences for mapping, color reproduction, and color for multidimensional discrete data. Each has its own special set of requirements. Some readers may wish to skip directly to the applications, sampling the more technical introduction only as needed.

Trichromacy Theory

The most important fact about color vision is that we have three distinct color receptors, called cones, in our retinas that are active at normal light levels—hence *trichromacy*. We also have rods, sensitive at low light levels, but they are so overstimulated in all but the dimmest light that their influence on color perception can be ignored. Thus, in order to understand color vision, we need only consider the cones. The fact that there are only three receptors is the reason for the basic three-dimensionality of human color vision.

The term *color space* means an arrangement of colors in a three-dimensional space. In this chapter, a number of color spaces, designed for different purposes, are discussed. Complex transformations are sometimes required to convert from one color space to another, but they are all three-dimensional, and this three-dimensionality derives ultimately from the three cone types. This is the reason that there are three differently colored phosphors in a television tube—red,

Figure 4.2   Cone sensitivity functions.

green, and blue—and this is the reason that we learn in school that there are three primary paint colors—red, yellow, and blue. It is also the reason that printers have a minimum of three colored inks for color printing—cyan, magenta, and yellow. Engineers should be grateful that humans have only three color receptors. Some birds, such as chickens, have as many as 12 different kinds of color-sensitive cells. A television set for chickens would require 12 electron beams and 12 differently colored phosphors!

Figure 4.2 shows the human cone sensitivity functions. The plots show how light of different wavelengths is absorbed by the different receptors. It is evident that two of the functions, L and M, which peak at 540 nanometers and 580 nanometers, overlap considerably; the third, S, is much more distinct, with peak sensitivity at 450 nanometers. The short-wavelength S receptor absorbs light in the blue part of the spectrum and is much less sensitive, which is another reason (besides chromatic aberration, discussed in Chapter 2) why we should not show detailed information such as text in pure blue on a black background.

Because only three different receptor types are involved in color vision, it is possible to match a particular patch of colored light with a mixture of just three colored lights, usually called *primaries*. It does not matter that the target patch may have a completely different spectral composition. The only thing that matters is that the matching primaries are balanced to produce the same response from the receptors as the patch of light to be matched. Figure 4.3(a) illustrates the three-dimensional space formed by the responses of the three cones.

Color Blindness

About 10% of the male population and about 1% of the female population have some form of color vision deficiency. The most common deficiencies are explained by lack of either the long-wavelength-sensitive cones (protanopia) or the medium-wavelength-sensitive cones

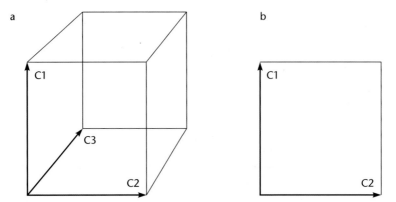

Figure 4.3   (a) Cone response space, defined by the response of each of the three cone types. (b) The space becomes two-dimensional in the case of the common color deficiencies.

(deuteranopia). Both protanopia and deuteranopia result in an inability to distinguish red and green, meaning that the cherries in Figure 4.1 are difficult for people with these deficiencies to see. One way to describe color vision deficiency is by pointing out that the three-dimensional color space of normal color vision collapses to a two-dimensional space, as shown in Figure 4.3(b). An unfortunate result of using color for information coding, is the creation of a new class of people with a disability. Color blindness already disqualifies applicants for some jobs such as those of telephone linespeople, because of the myriad colored wires, and pilots, because of the need to distinguish color-coded lights.

Color Measurement

The fact that we can match any color with a mixture of no more than three primary lights is the basis of *colorimetry*. An understanding of colorimetry is essential for anyone who wishes to specify colors precisely for reproduction.

We can describe a color by the following equation:

$$C \equiv rR + gG + bB \qquad (4.1)$$

where C is the color to be matched, R, G, and B are the primary light sources to be used to create a match, and r, g, and b represent the amounts of each primary light. The $\equiv$ symbol is used to denote a perceptual match—the sample and the mixture of the red, green, and blue (rR, gG, bB) primaries look identical. Figure 4.4 illustrates the concept. Three projectors are set

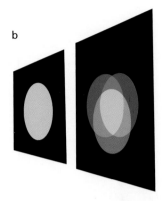

Figure 4.4   A color-matching setup. (a) When the light from three projectors is combined, the results are as shown. Yellow light is a mixture of red and green. Purple light is a mixture of red and blue. Cyan light is a mixture of blue and green. White light is a mixture of red, green, and blue. (b) Any other color can be matched by adjusting the proportions of red, green, and blue light.

up with overlapping beams. In the figure, the beams only partially overlap so that the mixing effect can be illustrated, but in a color-matching experiment they would overlap completely. To match the lilac-colored sample, the projectors are adjusted so that a large amount of light comes from the red and blue projectors and only a small amount of light comes from the green projector.

The *RGB* primaries form the coordinates of a color space, as illustrated in Figure 4.5. If these primaries are physically formed by the phosphor colors of a color monitor, this space defines the gamut of the monitor. In general, a *gamut* is the set of all colors that can be produced by a device or sensed by a receptor system.

It seems obvious that restrictions must be placed on this formulation. So far, we have assumed that the primaries are red, green and blue, but what if we were to choose other primary lights, for example, yellow, blue, and purple? We have stated no rule saying they must be red, green, and blue. How could we possibly reproduce a patch of red light out of combinations of yellow, blue, and purple lights? In fact, we can only reproduce colors that lie within the gamut of the three primaries. Yellow, blue, and purple would simply have a smaller gamut, meaning that if we used them, a smaller range of colors could be reproduced.

The relationship defined in Equation 4.1 is a linear relationship. This has the consequence that if we double the amount of light on the left, we can double the amount of light on each of our primaries and the match will still hold. To make the math simpler, it is also useful to allow the concept of negative light. Thus, we may allow expressions such as

$$C \equiv -rR + gG + bB \tag{4.2}$$

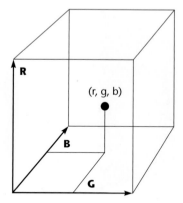

Figure 4.5 The three-dimensional space formed by three primary lights. Any color can be created by varying the amount of light produced by each of the primaries.

Although this concept may seem nonsensical, because negative light does not exist in nature, it is, in fact, practically useful in the following situation. Suppose we have a colored light that cannot be matched because it is outside the gamut of our three primary sources. We can still achieve a match by adding part of one of the primaries to our sample. If the test samples and the *RGB* primaries are all projected as shown in Figure 4.4, this can be achieved by swiveling one of the projectors around and adding its light to the light of the sample.

If the red projector were redirected in this way, we would have

$$C + rR \equiv gG + bB \tag{4.3}$$

which can be rewritten

$$C \equiv -rR + gG + bB \tag{4.4}$$

Once we allow the concept of negative values for the primaries, it becomes possible to state that *any* colored light can be matched by a weighted sum of *any* three distinct primaries.

Change of Primaries

Primaries are arbitrary from the point of view of color mixture—there is no special red, green, or blue light that must be used. Fundamental to colorimetry is the ability to change from one set of primaries to another. This gives us freedom to choose any set of primaries we want. We can choose as primaries the three phosphors of a monitor, three differently colored lasers, or some hypothetical set of lamps. We can even choose to base our primaries on the sensitivities of the human cone receptors. Given a standard way of specifying colors (using a standard set of primaries), we can use a transformation to create that same color on any number of different output devices. This transformation is described in Appendix A.

CIE System of Color Standards

We now have the foundations of a color measurement and specification system. We begin with an easily understood, though impractical, solution based on standardized primary lamps. Red, green, and blue lamps could be manufactured to precise specifications and set up in an instrument so that the amounts of red, green, and blue light falling on a standard white surface could be set by adjusting three calibrated dials, one for each lamp. Identical instruments, each containing sets of colored lamps, would be sent around the world to color experts. They would be very expensive. Then to give a precise color specification to someone with the standard instrument, we would simply need to make a color match by adjusting the dials and sending that person the dial settings. The recipient could then adjust his or her own standard lamps to reproduce the color.

Of course, although this approach is theoretically sound, it is not very practical. Standard primary lamps would be very difficult to maintain and calibrate. But we can apply the principle by creating a set of *abstract* primary lamps defined on the basis of the human receptor characteristics. This assumes that everyone has the same receptor functions. In fact, although humans do not display exactly the same sensitivities to different colors, with the exception of the color deficiencies, they come close. One of the basic concepts in any color standard is that of the *standard observer*. This is a hypothetical person whose color sensitivity functions are held to be typical of all humans. Most serious color specification is done using the Commission Internationale de l'Éclairage (CIE) system of color standards. These are based on standard observer measurements that were made prior to 1931. Color measuring instruments contain glass filters that are derived from the specifications of the human standard observer. One advantage is that glass filters are more stable than lamps.

The CIE system uses a set of abstract primaries called *tristimulus values*; these are labeled *XYZ*. These primaries are chosen for their mathematical properties, not because they match any set of actual lights. One important feature of the system is that the *Y* tristimulus value is the same as luminance. More details of the way the system is derived are given in Appendix B.

Figure 4.6 illustrates the color volume created by the *XYZ* tristimulus primaries of the CIE system. The colors that can actually be perceived are represented as a gray volume entirely contained within the positive space defined by the axes. The colors that can be created by a set of three colored lights, such as the red, green, and blue monitor phosphors, are defined by the pyramid-shaped volume within the *RGB* axes as shown. This is the *monitor gamut*.

The CIE tristimulus system based on the standard observer is by far the most widely used standard for measuring colored light. For this reason, it should always be used when precise color

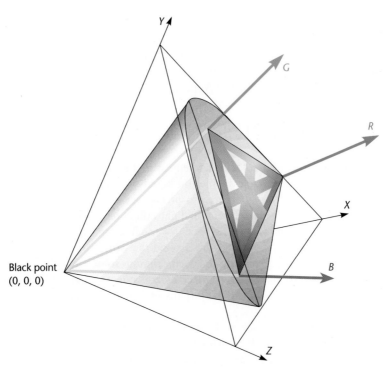

Figure 4.6   The *X*, *Y*, and *Z* axes represent the CIE standard virtual primaries. Within the positive space defined by the axes, the gamut of perceivable colors is represented as a gray solid. The colors that can be created by means of the red, green, and blue monitor primaries are also shown.

specification is required. Because a monitor is a light-emitting device with three primaries, it is relatively straightforward to calibrate a monitor in terms of the CIE coordinates. If a color generated on one monitor is to be reproduced on another, for example, a liquid crystal display, the best procedure is first to convert the colors into the CIE tristimulus values and then to convert them into the primary space of the second monitor.

The specification of surface colors is far more difficult than the specification of lights, because an illuminant must be taken into account and because, unlike lights, pigment colors are not additive. The color that results from mixing paints is difficult to predict. A treatment of surface color measurement is beyond the scope of this book, although later we will deal with perceptual issues related to color reproduction.

Chromaticity Coordinates

The three-dimensional abstract space represented by the *XYZ* coordinates is useful for specifying colors, but it is difficult to understand. As discussed in Chapter 3, there are good reasons for treating lightness, or luminance, information as special. In everyday speech, we often refer to the color of something and its lightness as different and independent properties. Thus, it is useful to have a measure that defines the hue and vividness of a color while ignoring the amount of light. *Chromaticity coordinates* have exactly this property through normalizing with respect to the amount of light.

To transform tristimulus values to chromaticity coordinates, use

$$x = X/(X + Y + Z)$$
$$y = Y/(X + Y + Z)$$
$$z = Z/(X + Y + Z) \tag{4.5}$$

Because $x + y + z = 1$, it is sufficient to use x, y values only. It is common to specify a color by its luminance, Y, and its x, y chromaticity coordinates (x, y, Y). The inverse transformation from x, y, Y to tristimulus values is

$$X = Yx/y$$
$$Y = Y$$
$$Z = (1 - x - y)Y/y \tag{4.6}$$

Figure 4.7 shows a CIE x, y chromaticity diagram and graphically illustrates some of the colorimetric concepts associated with it. Here are some of the useful and interesting properties of the chromaticity diagram:

1. If two colored lights are represented by two points in a chromaticity diagram, the color of a mixture of those two lights will always lie on a straight line between those two points.

2. Any set of three lights specifies a triangle in the chromaticity diagram. Its corners are given by the chromaticity coordinates of the three lights. Any color within that triangle can be created with a suitable mixture of the three lights. Figure 4.7 illustrates this with typical monitor *RGB* primaries.

3. The *spectrum locus* is the set of chromaticity coordinates of pure monochromatic (single-wavelength) lights. All realizable colors fall within the spectrum locus.

4. The *purple boundary* is the straight line connecting the chromaticity coordinates of the longest visible wavelength of red light, about 700 nm, to the chromaticity coordinates of the shortest visible wavelength of blue, about 400 nm.

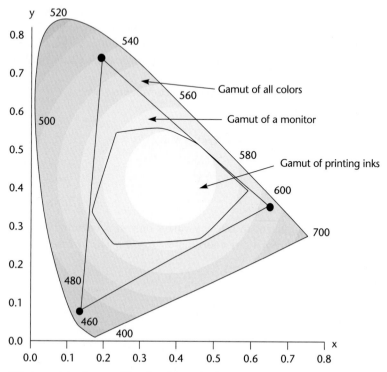

Figure 4.7   CIE chromaticity diagram with various interesting features added. The triangle represents the gamut of a computer monitor with long-persistence phosphors.

5. The chromaticity coordinates of equal-energy white (light having an equal mixture of all wavelengths) are 0.333, 0.333. But when a white light is specified for some application, what is generally required is one of the CIE standard illuminants. The CIE specifies a number that corresponds to different phases of daylight; of these, the most commonly used is D65. D65 was made to be a careful approximation of daylight with an overcast sky. It also happens to be very close to the mix of light that results when both direct sunlight and light from the rest of the sky fall on a horizontal surface. D65 also corresponds to a black-body radiator at 6500 degrees Kelvin. D65 has chromaticity coordinates $x = 0.313$, $y = 0.329$. Another CIE standard illuminant corresponds to the light produced by a typical incandescent tungsten source. This is illuminant A. Illuminant A has chromaticity coordinates $x = 0.448$, $y = 0.407$. This is considerably more yellow than normal daylight.

6. *Excitation purity* is a measure of the distance along a line between a particular pure spectral wavelength and the white point. Specifically, it is the value given by dividing the

distance between the sample and the white point by the distance between the white point and the spectrum line (or purple boundary). This measure defines the vividness of a color. A less technical, but commonly used, term for this quantity is *saturation*. More saturated colors are more vivid.

7. The complementary wavelength of a color is produced by drawing a line between that color and white and extrapolating to the opposite spectrum locus. Adding a color and its complementary color produces white.

The sets of chromaticity coordinates for two sets of typical monitor phosphors follow:

	Short-Persistence Phosphors			Long-Persistence Phosphors		
	Red	*Green*	*Blue*	*Red*	*Green*	*Blue*
x	0.61	0.29	0.15	0.62	0.21	0.15
y	0.35	0.59	0.063	0.33	0.685	0.063

The main difference between the two is that the long-persistence phosphor green (besides the fact that it glows for longer after being bombarded with electrons) is closer to being a pure spectral color than the short-persistence green. This makes the gamut larger. Short-persistence phosphors are useful for frame sequential stereoscopic displays because they reduce the bleeding of the image intended for one eye into the image intended for the other eye.

When a CRT display is used, the CIE tristimulus values of a color formed from some set of red, green, and blue settings can be calculated by the following formula:

$$\begin{bmatrix} X \\ Y \\ Z \end{bmatrix} = \begin{bmatrix} \dfrac{X_R}{Y_R} & \dfrac{X_G}{Y_G} & \dfrac{X_B}{Y_B} \\ 1 & 1 & 1 \\ \dfrac{Z_R}{Y_R} & \dfrac{Z_G}{Y_G} & \dfrac{Z_B}{Y_B} \end{bmatrix} \begin{bmatrix} Y_R \\ Y_G \\ Y_B \end{bmatrix} \tag{4.7}$$

where x_R, y_R, and z_R are the chromaticity coordinates of the particular monitor primaries and Y_R, Y_B, and Y_G are the actual luminance values produced from each phosphor for the particular color being converted. Notice that for a particular monitor the transformation matrix will be constant; only the Y vector will change.

To generate a particular color on a monitor that has been defined by CIE tristimulus values, it is only necessary to invert the matrix and create an appropriate voltage to each of the red, green, and blue electron guns of the monitor. Naturally, to determine the actual value that must be specified, it is necessary to calibrate the monitor's red, green, and blue outputs in terms of luminance and apply gamma correction, as described in Chapter 3. Once this is done, the monitor can be treated as a linear color creation device with a particular set of primaries, depending on its phosphors. For more on monitor calibration, see Cowan (1983). It is also possible to purchase self-calibrating monitors adequate for all but the most demanding applications.

Color Differences and Uniform Color Spaces

Sometimes, it is useful to have a color space in which equal perceptual distances are equal distances in the space. Here are three applications:

Specification of color tolerances: When a manufacturer wishes to order a colored part from a supplier, such as a plastic molding for an automobile, it is necessary to specify the color tolerance within which the part will be accepted. It only makes sense for this tolerance to be based on perception, because ultimately it is the customer who decides whether the door trim matches the upholstery.

Specification of color codes: If we need a set of colors to code data, such as different wires in a cable, we would normally like those colors to be as distinct as possible so that they will not be confused.

Pseudocolor sequences for maps: Many scientific maps use sequences of colors to represent ordered data values. This technique, called *pseudocoloring*, is widely used in astronomy, physics, medical imaging, and geophysics.

The CIE *XYZ* color space is very far from being perceptually uniform. However, in 1978 the CIE produced a set of recommendations on the use of two uniform color spaces that are transformations of the *XYZ* color space. These are called the *CIElab* and the *CIEluv* uniform color spaces. The reason that there are two, rather than one, has to do with the fact that different industries, such as the paint industry, had already adopted one standard or the other. Also, the two standards have somewhat different properties that make them useful for different tasks. Only the *CIEluv* formula is described here. It is generally held to be better for specifying large color differences. However, one measurement made using the *CIElab* color difference formula is worth noting. Using *CIElab*, Hill et al. (1997) estimated that there are between two and six million discriminable colors available within the gamut of a color monitor.

The *CIEluv* equations are:

$$L^* = 116(Y/Y_n)^{1/3} - 16$$
$$u^* = 13L^*(u' - u'_n)$$
$$v^* = 13L^*(v' - v'_n)$$

(4.8)

where

$$u' = \frac{4X}{X + 15Y + 3Z} \quad u'_n = \frac{4X_n}{X_n + 15Y_n + 3Z_n}$$

$$v' = \frac{9Y}{X + 15Y + 3Z} \quad v'_n = \frac{9Y_n}{X_n + 15Y_n + 3Z_n} \tag{4.9}$$

u' and v' are a projective transformation of the x, y chromaticity diagram, designed to produce a perceptually more uniform color space. X_n, Y_n, and Z_n are the tristimulus values of a reference white. To measure the difference between colors ΔE^*_{uv}, the following formula is used:

$$\Delta E^*_{uv} = \sqrt{(\Delta L^*)^2 + (\Delta u^*)^2 + (\Delta v^*)^2} \tag{4.10}$$

The *CIEluv* system retains many of the useful properties of the *XYZ* tristimulus values and the x, y chromaticity coordinates.

The $u'v'$ diagram is shown in Figure 4.8. Its official name is the CIE 1976 uniform chromaticity **Scale** diagram, or UCS diagram. Because u', v' is a projective transformation, it retains the useful property that blends of two colors will lie on a line between the u', v' chromaticity coordinates. (It is worth noting that this is not a property of the *CIElab* uniform color space.)

The u^*, v^* values change the scale of u', v' with respect to the distance from black to white defined by the sample lightness L^* (recall from Chapter 3 that L^* requires Y_n, a reference white in the application environment). The reason for this is straightforward: the darker the colors, the fewer we can see. At the limit, there is only one color: black.

A value of 1 for ΔE^*_{uv} is an approximation to a *just noticeable difference* (JND).

Although they are useful, uniform color spaces provide, at best, only a rough first approximation. Perceived color differences are influenced by many factors. Contrast effects can radically alter the shape of the color space. Small patches of light give different results than large patches. In general, we are much more sensitive to differences between large patches of color. When the patches are small, the perceived differences are smaller, and this is especially true in the yellow–blue direction. Ultimately, with very small samples, small-field tritanopia occurs; this is the inability to distinguish colors that are different in the yellow–blue direction. Figure 4.9 shows two examples of small patches of color on a white background and the same set of colors in larger patches on a black background. Both the white background and the small patches make the colors harder to distinguish.

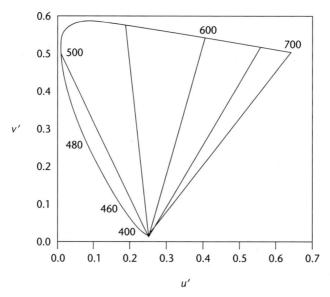

Figure 4.8   CIE *Lu'v'* UCS diagram. The lines radiating from the lower part of the diagram are tritanopic confusion lines. Colors that differ along these lines can still be distinguished by the great majority of color-blind individuals.

Opponent Process Theory

Late in the nineteenth century, German psychologist Ewald Hering proposed the theory that there are six elementary colors and that these colors are arranged perceptually as opponent pairs along three axes: black–white, red–green, and yellow–blue (Hering, 1920). In recent years, this principle has become a cornerstone of modern color theory, supported by a large variety of experimental evidence (see Hurvich, 1981, for a review). Modern opponent process theory has a well established physiological basis: input from the cones is processed into three distinct channels immediately after the receptors. The luminance channel (black–white) is based on input from all the cones. The red–green channel is based on the difference of long- and middle-wavelength cone signals. The yellow–blue channel is based on the difference between the short-wavelength cones and the sum of the other two. These basic connections are illustrated in Figure 4.10.

There are many lines of scientific evidence for the opponent process theory. These are worth examining, because they illuminate a number of applications.

Naming

We often describe colors using combinations of color terms, such as "yellowish green" or "greenish blue." However, certain combinations of terms never appear. People never use "reddish green"

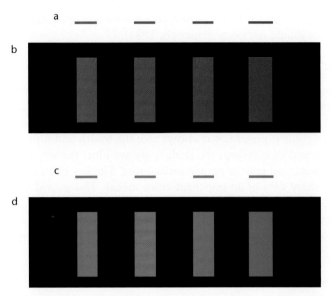

Figure 4.9   (a) Small samples of a yellow-to-blue sequence of colors on a white background. (b) The same yellow-to-blue sequence with larger samples on a black background. (c) Small samples of a green-to-red sequence on a white background. (d) The same green-to-red sequence with larger samples on a black background.

Figure 4.10   In the color opponent process model, cone signals are transformed into black–white (luminance), red–green, and yellow–blue channels.

or "yellowish blue," for example. Because these colors are polar opposites in the opponent color theory, these pairings should not occur (Hurvich, 1981).

Cross-Cultural Naming

In a remarkable study of more than 100 languages from many diverse cultures, anthropologists Berlin and Kay (1969) showed that primary color terms are remarkably consistent across cultures (Figure 4.11). In languages with only two basic color words, these are always black and white; if a third color is present, it is always red; the fourth and fifth are either yellow and then green, or green and then yellow; the sixth is always blue; the seventh is brown, followed by pink, purple, orange, and gray in no particular order. The key point here is that the first six terms define the primary axes of an opponent color model. This provides strong evidence that the neural basis for these names is innate. Otherwise, we might expect to find cultures where lime green or turquoise is a basic color term. The cross-cultural evidence strongly supports the idea that certain colors, specifically, red, green, yellow, and blue, are far more valuable in coding data than others.

Unique Hues

There is something special about yellow. If subjects are given control over a device that changes the spectral hue of a patch of light, and are told to adjust it until the result is a pure yellow, neither reddish nor greenish, they do so with remarkable accuracy. In fact, they are typically accurate within 2 nm (Hurvich, 1981).

Interestingly, there is good evidence for two unique greens. Most people set a pure green at about 514 nm, but about a third of the population sees pure green at about 525 nm (Richards, 1967). This may be why some people argue about the color turquoise; some people consider it to be a variety of green, whereas others consider it to be a kind of blue.

It is also significant that unique hues do not change a great deal when the overall luminance level is changed (Hurvich, 1981). This supports the idea that chromatic perception and luminance perception really are independent.

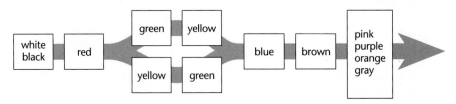

Figure 4.11   This is the order of appearance of color names in languages around the world, according to the research of Berlin and Kay (1969). The order is fixed, with the exception that sometimes yellow is present before green and sometimes the reverse is the case.

Neurophysiology

Neurophysiological studies have isolated classes of cells in the primary visual cortexes of monkeys that have exactly the properties of opponency required by the opponent process theory. Red–green and yellow–blue opponent cells exist, and other configurations do not appear to exist (de Valois and de Valois, 1975).

Categorical Colors

There is evidence that certain colors are canonical in a sense that is analogous to the philosopher Plato's theory of forms. Plato proposed that there are ideal objects, such as an ideal horse or an ideal chair, and that real horses and chairs can be defined in terms of their differences from the ideal. Something similar appears to operate in color naming. If a color is close to an ideal red or an ideal green, it is easier to remember. Colors that are not basic, such as orange or lime green, are not as easy to remember.

There is evidence that confusion between color codes is affected by color categories. Kawai et al. (1995) asked subjects to identify the presence or absence of a chip of a particular color. The subjects took much longer if the chip was surrounded by distracting elements that were of a different color but belonged to the same color category than if the chip was surrounded by distracting elements that were equally distinct according to the sense of a uniform color space but crossed a color category boundary.

Post and Greene (1986) carried out an extensive experiment on the naming of colors produced on a computer monitor and shown in a darkened room. They generated 210 different colors, each in a two-degree (of visual angle) patch with a black surround. Figure 4.12 illustrates the color areas that were given a specific name with at least 75% reliability. A number of points are worth noting:

- The fact that only eight colors plus white were consistently named, even under these highly standardized conditions, strongly suggests that only a very small number of colors can be used effectively as category labels.

- The pure monitor red was actually named orange most of the time. A true color red required the addition of a small amount from the blue monitor primary.

- The specific regions of color space occupied by particular colors should not be given much weight. The data was obtained with a black background. Because of contrast effects, different results are to be expected with white and colored backgrounds.

Properties of Color Channels

From the perspective of data visualization, the different properties of the color channels have profound implications for the use of color. The most significant differences are between the two chromatic channels and the luminance channel, although the two color channels also differ from each other.

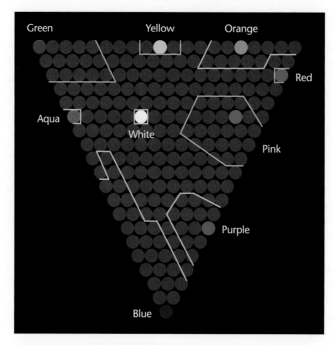

Figure 4.12 The results of an experiment in which subjects were asked to name 210 colors produced on a computer monitor. Outlined regions show the colors that were given the same name with better than 75% probability.

To display data on the luminance channel alone is easy; it is stimulated by patterns that vary only from black to white through shades of gray. But with careful calibration (which must be customized to individual subjects), patterns can be constructed that vary only for the red–green or the yellow–blue channel. A key quality of such a pattern is that its component colors must not differ in luminance. This is called an *isoluminant* or *equiluminous* pattern. In this way, the different properties of the color channels can be explored and compared with the luminance channel capacity.

Spatial Sensitivity

According to a study by Mullen (1985), the red–green and yellow–blue chromatic channels are each only capable of carrying about one-third the amount of detail carried by the black–white channel. Because of this, purely chromatic differences are not suitable for displaying any kind of fine detail. Figure 4.13 illustrates this problem with colored text on an equiluminous background. In the part of the figure where there is only a chromatic difference between the text and the back-

Figure 4.13   Yellow text on a blue gradient. Note how difficult it is to read the text where luminance is equal, despite a large chromatic difference.

ground, the text becomes very difficult to read. Generally, when detailed information of any kind is presented with color coding, it is important that there be considerable luminance contrast in addition to color contrast, especially if the colored patterns are small.

Stereoscopic Depth

It appears to be impossible, or at least very difficult, to see stereoscopic depth in stereo pairs that differ only in terms of the color channels (Lu and Fender, 1972; Gregory, 1977). Thus, stereo space perception is based primarily on information from the luminance channel.

Motion Sensitivity

If a pattern is created that is equiluminous with its background and contains only chromatic differences, and that pattern is set in motion, something strange occurs. The moving pattern appears to move much more slowly than a black-against-white pattern moving at the same speed (Anstis and Cavanaugh, 1983). Thus, motion perception appears to be primarily based on information from the luminance channel.

Form

We are very good at perceiving the shapes of surfaces based on their shading. However, when the shading is transformed from a luminance gradient into a purely chromatic gradient, the impression of surface shape is much reduced. Perception of shape and form appears to be processed mainly through the luminance channel (Gregory, 1977).

To summarize this set of properties, the red–green and yellow–blue channels are inferior to the luminance channel in almost every respect. The general implications for data display are clear. Purely chromatic differences should *never* be used for displaying object shape, object motion, or detailed information such as text. From this perspective, color would seem almost irrelevant and certainly a secondary method for information display. Nevertheless, when it comes to coding information, using color to display data categories is usually the best choice. To see why, we need to look beyond the basic processes that we have been considering thus far.

Color Appearance

The value of color (as opposed to luminance) processing, it would appear, is not in helping us to understand the shape and layout of objects in the environment. Color does not help the hunter aim an arrow accurately. Color does not help us see shape from shading and thereby plan a hike through a valley, although it does help us distinguish vegetation types. Color does not help use stereoscopic depth when we reach out to grasp a tool. But color is useful to the gatherer. Food, in the forest or on the savannah, is often distinct because of its color. This is especially true of fruits and berries. Color creates a kind of visual attribute of objects: this is a red berry. That is a yellow door. Color names are used as adjectives because colors are perceived as attributes of objects. This suggests a most important role for color in visualization—namely, the coding of information. Visual objects can represent complex data entities, and colors can naturally code attributes of those objects.

Color is normally a surface attribute of an object. The *XYZ* tristimulus values of a patch of light physically define a color, but they do not tell us how it will look. Depending on the surrounding colors in the environment and a whole host of spatial and temporal factors, the same physical color can look very different. If it is desirable that color appearance be preserved, it is important to pay close attention to surrounding conditions. In a monitor-based display, a large patch of standardized reference white will help ensure that color appearance is preserved. When colors are reproduced on paper, viewing them under a standard lamp will help preserve their appearance. In the paint and fabric industries, where color appearance is critical, standard viewing booths are used. These booths contain standard illumination systems that can be set to approximate daylight or a standard indoor illuminant, such as a typical tungsten light bulb or halogen lamp.

The mechanisms of surface lightness constancy, discussed at some length in Chapter 3, generalize to trichromatic color perception. Both chromatic adaptation and chromatic contrast occur and play a role in color constancy. Differential adaptation in the cone receptors helps us to discount the color of the illumination in the environment. When there is colored illumination, different classes of cone receptors undergo independent changes in sensitivity. Thus, when the illumination contains a lot of blue light, the short-wavelength cones become relatively less sensitive than the others. The effect of this is to shift the neutral point at which the three receptor types are in equilibrium, such that more blue light must be reflected from a surface for it to seem white. This, of course, is exactly what is necessary for color constancy. That adaptation is effective in maintaining constancy is evident from the fact that not many people are aware how much yellower ordinary tungsten room lighting is than daylight.

Color Contrast

Chromatic contrast also occurs in a way that is similar to the lightness contrast effects discussed and illustrated in Chapter 3. Figure 4.14 shows a color contrast illusion. It has been shown that contrast effects can distort readings from color-coded maps (Cleveland and McGill, 1983; Ware, 1988). Contrast effects can be theoretically accounted for by activity in the color opponent channels (Ware and Cowan, 1982). However, as with lightness contrast, the ultimate purpose of the contrast-causing mechanism is to help us see surface colors accurately by revealing differences between colored patches and background regions.

From the point of view of the monitor engineer and the user of color displays, the fact that colors are perceived relative to their overall context has the happy consequence of making the eye relatively insensitive to poor color balance. A visit to a television store will reveal that when television sets are viewed side by side, the overall color of the pictures can differ strikingly, yet when they are viewed individually, they are all acceptable. Of course, because the state of adaptation is governed by the light of the entire visual field, and a television screen takes up only part of the field, this adaptation will necessarily be incomplete.

Saturation

When describing color appearance in everyday language, people use many terms in rather imprecise ways. Besides using color names such as *lime green, mauve, brown, baby blue,* and so on,

Figure 4.14 A color contrast illusion. The *X* pattern is identical on both sides, but it seems bluer on the red background and pinker on the blue background.

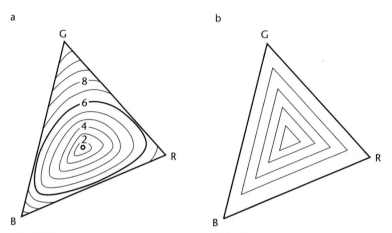

Figure 4.15   (a) The triangle represents the gamut of colors obtained using a computer monitor plotted in CIE chromaticity coordinates. The contours show perceptually determined equal-saturation contours. (b) Equal-saturation contours created using the HSV color space, also plotted in chromaticity coordinates.

people also use adjectives such as *vivid*, *bright*, and *intense* to describe colors that seem especially pure. Because these terms are used so variably, scientists use the technical term *saturation* to denote how pure colors seem to the viewer. A high-saturation color is vivid and a low-saturation color is close to black, white, or gray. In terms of the color opponent channels, high-saturation colors are those that give a strong signal on one or both of the red–green and yellow–blue channels.

Equal saturation contours have been derived from psychophysical experiments (Wyszecki and Stiles, 1982). Figure 4.15(a) shows a plot of equal saturation values in a CIE chromaticity diagram. It is clear that it is possible to obtain much more highly saturated red, green, and blue colors on a monitor than yellow, cyan, or purple values.

Brown

Brown is one of the most mysterious colors. Brown is dark yellow. Whereas people talk about a light green or a dark green, a light blue or a dark blue, yellow is different. When colors in the vicinity of yellow and orange yellow are darkened, they turn to shades of brown and olive green. Unlike red, blue, and green, brown requires that there be a reference white somewhere in the vicinity for it to be perceived. Brown appears qualitatively different to orange yellow. There is no such thing as an isolated brown light in a dark room, but when a yellow or yellowish orange is presented with a bright white surround, brown appears. The relevance to visualization is that if color sets are being devised for the purposes of color coding—for example, a set of blues, a set of reds, and a set of greens—brown may not be recognized as belonging to the set of yellows.

Applications of Color in Visualization

So far, this chapter has been mainly a presentation of the basic theory underlying color vision and color measurement. Now we shift the emphasis to applications of color, for which new theory will be introduced only as needed. We will examine five different application areas: color selection interfaces, color labeling, color sequences for map coding, color reproduction, and color for multidimensional discrete data display. Each of these presents a different set of problems, and each benefits from an analysis in terms of the human perception of color.

Application 1: Color Specification Interfaces and Color Spaces

In data visualization programs, drawing applications, and CAD systems, it is often essential to let users choose their own colors. There are a number of approaches to this user interface problem. The user can be given a set of controls to specify a point in a three-dimensional color space, a set of color names to choose from, or a palette of predefined color samples.

Color Spaces

The simplest color interface to implement on a computer involves giving someone controls to adjust the amounts of red, green, and blue light that combine to make a patch of color on a monitor. The controls can take the form of sliders, or the user can simply type in three numbers. This provides access, in a straightforward way, to any point within the *RGB* color cube shown in Figure 4.5. However, although it is simple, many people find this kind of control confusing. For example, most people do not know that to get yellow you must add red and green. There have been many attempts to make color interfaces easier to use.

One of the most widely used color interfaces in computer graphics is based on the HSV color space (Smith, 1978). This is a simple transformation from hue, saturation, and value (HSV) coordinates to *RGB* monitor coordinates. In Smith's scheme, hue represents an approximation to the visible spectrum by interpolating in sequence from red to yellow to green to blue and back to red. Saturation is the distance from monitor white to the purest hue possible given the limits of monitor phosphors. Figure 4.16 shows how hue and saturation can be laid out in two dimensions, with hue on one axis and saturation on the other, based on the HSV transformation of monitor primaries. As Figure 4.15(b) shows, HSV creates only the crudest approximation to perceptually equal-saturation contours. *Value* is the name given to the black–white axis. Some color specification interfaces based on HSV allow the user to control hue, saturation, and value variables with three sliders.

Color theory suggests that, in a computer interface for selecting colors, there are good reasons for separating a luminance (or lightness) dimension from the chromatic dimensions. A common method is to provide a single slider control for the black–white dimension and to lay out the two opponent color dimensions on a chromatic plane. The idea of laying out colors on a plane has a long history; for example, a color circle is a feature of a color textbook created for artists by

Figure 4.16   This plot shows hue and saturation, based on Smith's transformation (1978) of the monitor primaries.

Rood (1897). With the invention of computer graphics, it has become far simpler to create and control colors, and many ways of laying out colors are now available. Figure 4.17 illustrates a sampling of four different geometric color layouts, each of them embodying the idea of a chromatic plane.

Figure 4.17(a) shows a color circle with red, green, yellow, and blue defining opposing axes. Many such color circles have been devised over the past century. They differ mainly in the spacing of colors around the periphery.

Figure 4.17(b) shows a color triangle with the monitor primaries, red, green, and blue, at the corners. This color layout is convenient because it has the property that mixtures of two colors will lie on a line between them (assuming proper calibration).

Figure 4.17(c) shows a color square with the opponent color primaries, red, yellow, green, and blue, at the corners (Ware and Cowan, 1990).

Figure 4.17(d) shows a color hexagon with the colors red, yellow, green, cyan, blue, and magenta at the corners. This represents a plane through the single-hexcone color model (Smith, 1978). The hexagon representation has the advantage that it gives both the monitor primaries, red, green, and blue, and the print primaries, cyan, magenta, and yellow, prominent positions around the circumference.

To create a color interface using one of these color planes, it is necessary to allow the user to pick a sample from the color plane and adjust its lightness with a luminance slider. In some interfaces, when the luminance slider is moved, the entire plane of colors becomes lighter and darker according to the currently selected level. For those interested in implementing color interfaces, Foley et al. (1990) provide algorithms for a number of color geometries.

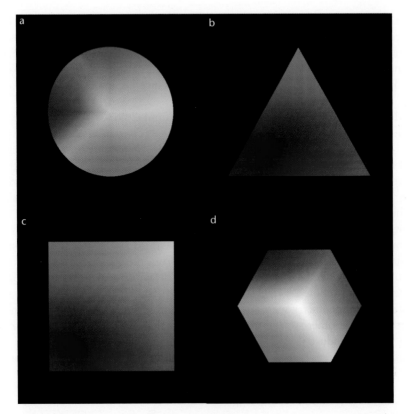

Figure 4.17   There are a number of simple transformations of the *RGB* monitor primaries to provide a color plane with an orthogonal lightness axis. Four of these are illustrated here: (a) Circle. (b) Triangle. (c) Square. (d) Hexagon.

The problem of the best color selection interface is by no means resolved. Experimental studies have failed to show that one way of controlling color is substantially better than another (Schwarz et al., 1987; Douglas and Kirkpatrick, 1996). However, Douglas and Kirkpatrick have provided evidence that good feedback about the location of the color being adjusted in color space can help in the process.

Color Naming

The facts that there are so few widely agreed-upon color names and that color memory is so poor suggest that choosing colors by name will not be useful except for the simplest applications. People agree on red, green, yellow, blue, black, and white as labels, but not much more. Nevertheless, it is possible to remember a rather large number of color names and use them accurately under controlled conditions. Displays in paint stores generally have a standard illuminant and standard background for sample strips containing several hundred samples. Under these circumstances, the specialist can remember and use as many as 1000 color names. But many of the names are idiosyncratic; the colors corresponding to "taupe," "fiesta red," and "primrose" are imprecisely defined for most of us. In addition, as soon as these colors are removed from the standard booth, they will change their appearance because of adaptation and contrast effects.

A standardized color naming system called the Natural Color System (NCS) has been developed based on Hering's opponent color theory (1920). NCS was developed in Sweden and is widely used in England and other European countries. In NCS, colors are characterized by the amounts of redness, greenness, yellowness, blueness, blackness, and whiteness that they contain. As shown in Figure 4.18, red, green, yellow, and blue lie at the ends of two orthogonal axes. Intervening "pure" colors lie on the circle circumference, and these are given numbers by sharing out 100 arbitrary units. Thus, a yellowish orange might be given the value Y70R30, meaning 70 parts yellow and 30 parts red. Colors are also given independent values on a black–white axis by allocating a blackness value between 0 and 100. A third color attribute, intensity (roughly corresponding to saturation), describes the distance from the gray-scale axis. For example, in NCS, the color "spring nymph" becomes 0030-G80Y20, which expands to blackness 00, intensity 30, green 80, and yellow 20 (Jackson et al., 1994). The NCS system combines some of the advantages of a color geometry with a reasonably intuitive and precise naming system.

In North America, other systems are more popular than NCS. The Pantone system is widely used in the printing industry, and the Munsell system is an important reference for surface colors. The Munsell system is useful because it provides a set of standard color chips designed

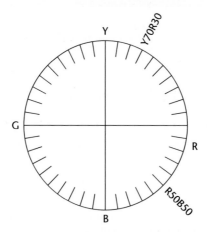

Figure 4.18   The Natural Color System (NCS) circle, defined midway between black and white. Two example color names are shown in addition to the "pure" opponent color primaries. One is an orange yellow and the other is purple.

to represent equal perceptual spacing in a three-dimensional mesh. (Munsell color chips and viewing booths are available commercially, as are Pantone products.) The NCS, Pantone, and Munsell systems were originally designed to be used with carefully printed paper samples providing the reference colors, but computer-based interfaces to these systems have been developed as part of illustration and design packages. Rhodes and Luo (1996) describe a software package that enables transformations between the different systems using the CIE as an intermediate standard.

Color Palette

When the user wishes to use only a small set of standardized colors, providing a color palette is a good solution to the color selection problem. Often, color selection palettes are laid out in a regular order according to one of the color geometries defined previously. It is useful to provide a facility for the user to develop a personal palette. This allows for consistency in color style across a number of visualization displays. Another valuable addition to a color user interface is a method for showing a color sample on differently colored backgrounds. This allows the designer to understand how contrast effects can affect the appearance of particular color samples.

Sometimes a color palette is based on one of the standard color sets used by the fabric industry or the paint industry. If this is the case, the monitor must be calibrated so that colors actually appear as specified. In addition, the lighting surrounding the monitor must be taken into account, as discussed in Chapter 3. Ideally, the monitor should be set up carefully with a standard surround and little or no ambient light falling directly on the screen. This includes having a room light such that the standard white in the set of color samples on the screen closely matches the appearance of a standard white in the room environment.

Application 2: Color for Labeling

The technical name for labeling an object is *nominal information coding*. A nominal code does not have to be orderable; it simply must be remembered and recognized. Color can be extremely effective as a nominal code. When we wish to make it easy for someone to classify visual objects into separate categories, giving the objects distinctive colors is often the best solution. One of the reasons that color is considered effective is that the alternatives are generally worse. For example, if we try to create gray-scale codes that are easily remembered and unlikely to be confused, we find that four is about the limit: white, light gray, dark gray, and black. Given that white will probably be used for the background and black is likely to be used for text, this leaves only two. In addition, using the gray scale as a nominal code may interfere with shape or detail perception. Chromatic coding can often be employed in a way that only minimally interferes with data presented on the luminance channel.

There are many perceptual factors to be considered in choosing a set of color labels.

1. **Distinctness:** A uniform color space, such as *CIEluv*, can be used to determine the degree of perceived difference between two colors that are placed close together. However, when

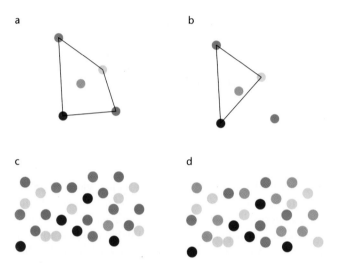

Figure 4.19   The convex hull of a set of colors is defined as the area within a rubber band that is stretched around the colors when they are defined in CIE tristimulus space. Although illustrated in two dimensions here, the concept can easily be extended to three dimensions. (a) Gray is within the convex hull of red, green, yellow, and blue. (b) Red lies outside the convex hull of green, blue, yellow, and gray. (c) The gray dot is difficult to find in a set of red, green, yellow, and blue dots. (d) The red dot is easy to find in a set of green, blue, yellow, and gray dots.

we are concerned with the ability to distinguish a color *rapidly* from a set of other colors, different rules may apply. Bauer et al. (1996) showed that the target color should lie outside the convex hull of the surrounding colors in the CIE color space. This concept is illustrated in Figure 4.19. The issues related to coding for rapid target identification are discussed further in Chapter 5.

2.   **Unique hues:** The unique hues—red, green, yellow, and blue, as well as black and white— are special in terms of the opponent process model. These colors are also special in the color vocabularies of languages worldwide. Clearly, these colors provide natural choices when a small set of color codes is required. In addition, work on color confusion suggests that no two colors should be chosen from the same category, even though they may be relatively far apart in color space. We should avoid using multiple shades of green as codes, for example.

3.   **Contrast with background:** In many displays, color-coded objects can be expected to appear on a variety of backgrounds. Simultaneous contrast with background colors can dramatically alter color appearance, making one color look like another. This is one reason why it is advisable to have only a small set of color codes. A method for reducing contrast effects is to place a thin white or black border around the color-coded object. This device is commonly used with signal lights; for example, train signals are displayed

on large black background discs. In addition, we should never display codes using purely chromatic differences with the background. There should be a significant luminance difference in addition to the color difference.

4. **Color blindness:** Because there is a substantial color-blind population, it may be desirable to use colors that can be distinguished even by people who are color blind. Recall that the majority of color-blind people cannot distinguish colors that differ in a red–green direction. Almost everyone can distinguish colors that vary in a yellow–blue direction, as shown in Figure 4.8. Unfortunately, this drastically reduces the design choices that are available.

5. **Number:** Although color coding is an excellent way to display category information, only a small number of codes can be rapidly perceived. Estimates vary between about five and ten codes (Healey, 1996).

6. **Field size:** Color-coded objects should not be very small; especially if the color differences are in a yellow–blue direction, at least half a degree of visual angle is probably a minimum size. Very small color-coded areas should not be used, to avoid the small-field color blindness illustrated in Figure 4.9. In general, the larger the area that is color-coded, the more easily colors can be distinguished. Small objects that are color-coded should have strong, highly saturated colors for maximum discrimination. When large areas of color coding are used, for example, with map regions, the colors should be of low saturation and differ only slightly from one another. This enables small, vivid color-coded targets to be perceived against background regions. When colors are used to highlight regions of black text, they should be light (minimum luminance contrast with the white paper) and also of low saturation (see Figure 4.20). This will minimize interference with the text.

7. **Conventions:** Color-coding conventions must sometimes be taken into account. Some common conventions are red = hot, red = danger, blue = cold, green = life, green = go. However, it is important to keep in mind that these conventions do not necessarily cross cultural borders. In China, for example, red means life and good fortune, and green means death.

The following is a list of 12 colors recommended for use in coding. They are illustrated in Figure 4.21.

1. Red
2. Green
3. Yellow
4. Blue
5. Black
6. White
7. Pink
8. Cyan
9. Gray
10. Orange
11. Brown
12. Purple

```
import java.applet.Applet;
import java.awt.Graphics;
import java.awt.Color;

public class ColorText extends Applet
{
    public void init ( )
    {
        red = 100;
        green = 255;
        blue = 20;
    }

    public void paint (Graphics g)
    {
        Gr.setColor (new Color (red, green, blue));
        Gr.drawString ("Colored Text". 30,50);
    }

    private int red;
    private int green;
    private int blue;
}
```

Figure 4.20   When large areas are color-coded, low-saturation light colors can be used on a white background. This interferes much less with detailed information in the text.

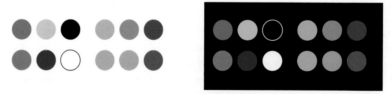

Figure 4.21   A set of 12 colors for use in labeling. The same colors are shown on a white and a black background.

These colors have widely agreed-upon category names and are reasonably far apart in color space. The first four colors, together with black and white, are chosen because they are the unique colors that mark the ends of the opponent color axes. The entire set corresponds to the 11 color names found to be the most common in the cross-cultural study carried out by Berlin and Kay, with the addition of cyan. The colors in the first set of six would normally be used before choosing any from the second set of six.

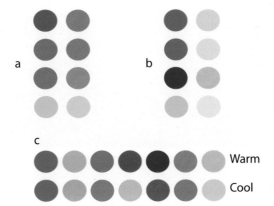

Figure 4.22   Families of colors. (a) Pairs related by hue, family members differ in saturation. (b) Pairs related by hue, family members differ in saturation and lightness. (c) A family of warm hues and a family of cool hues.

Sometimes it is useful to generate codes into families. This can be done by using hue as a primary attribute denoting family membership, with secondary values mapped to a combination of saturation and lightness. Figure 4.22 illustrates. Generally, we cannot expect to get away with more than two different color steps in each family. The canonical red, green, yellow, and blue hues make good categories for defining families. Family members then can be distinguished from one another by saturation, as in Figure 4.22(a), or even better, by saturation and lightness, as in Figure 4.22(b). Interior designers often consider a family of warm colors (nearer to red in color space) to be distinct from a family of cool colors (nearer to blue and green in color space), although the psychological validity of this is questionable.

Application 3: Color Sequences for Data Maps

Pseudocoloring is the technique of representing continuously varying map values using a sequence of colors. Pseudocoloring is used widely for astronomical radiation charts, medical imaging, and many other scientific applications. Geographers use a well-defined color sequence to display height above sea level—lowlands are always colored green, which evokes vegetation, and the scale continues upward, through brown, to white at the peaks of mountains. Figure 4.23 shows a map of gravitational variations over the North Atlantic, displayed with high-gravitation areas coded red and low-gravitation areas coded purple. Intermediate values are coded with a sequence of colors that roughly approximates the visible-light spectrum.

Figure 4.23   Gravitational variation over the North Atlantic is revealed using a spectrum-approximation pseudocolor sequence.

The most common coding scheme used by physicists is a color sequence that approximates the physical spectrum, like that shown in Figure 4.23. Although this sequence is widely used in physics and other disciplines and has some useful properties, it is not a *perceptual* sequence. This can be demonstrated by the following test. Give someone a series of gray paint chips and ask them to place these in order. They will happily comply with either a dark-to-light ordering or a light-to-dark ordering. Give the same person paint chips with the colors red, green, yellow, and blue and ask them to place them in order, and the result will be varied. For most people, the request will not seem particularly meaningful. They may even use an alphabetical ordering. This demonstrates that the whole spectrum is not perceptually ordered, although *short sections* of it are. For example, sections from red to yellow, yellow to green, and green to blue all vary monotonically (they continuously increase or decrease) on both the red–green and yellow–blue channels.

It is useful to consider the problem of selecting a pseudocoloring sequence in terms of Stevens's (1946) taxonomy of measurement scales into nominal, ordinal, interval, and ratio categories.

Nominal Pseudocolor Sequences (Labeling Regions)

A *nominal* pseudocolor sequence is one designed to enable rapid visual classification of regions where the values within the regions have no particular order (i.e., no "greater than" relationship holds for the values). For example, Figure 4.24 gives two examples that classify the physiography of the seabed of the Arctic Ocean. In 4.24(a) only three colors—red, yellow, and green—are used to provide visual segmentation into three distinct regions. In 4.24(b), nine different regions are labeled by color. The considerations in selecting colors for nominal sequences are the same as for color labeling. The colors should be chosen to be visually distinct from one another. In

Figure 4.24 Color sequences designed for classification rather than the display of continuous variables. The physiographic features of the Arctic seafloor are illustrated. *Courtesy of Martin Jakobsson.*

general, a nominal set of colors should be custom designed based on the number of colors required and on the need to display additional symbols on top of the colors. If the overlaid symbols are to be black or dark, then the background color codes should be light, or vice versa, to give luminance contrast. If the overlaid symbols are colored, then the colored areas of the background should have low saturation.

Ordinal Pseudocolor Sequences

An *ordinal* pseudocolor sequence is one in which the monotonic ordering of data values in different parts of the display can be perceived. If value B lies between value A and value C, the color codes should perceptually have the same ordering. For ordinal values to be correctly and rapidly interpreted, it is important that the color sequence increases monotonically with respect to one or more of the color opponent channels. Such a monotonic ordering can be obtained straightforwardly by using a black-white, red-green, or yellow-blue sequence. But it can also be obtained with a saturation sequence or with any relatively straight line through opponent color space. If it is important to show detail in the data, then it is essential to have a sequence that varies according to the luminance (black–white) channel because of the capacity of this channel to convey high spatial frequency information (Ware, 1988; Rogowitz and Treinish, 1996). Figures 4.25(a) and (b) show ozone concentration data presented as a gray-scale sequence and as a color-saturation sequence. The saturation shows far less detail. For comparison, Figure 4.25(c) shows a spectrum approximation. (Images from Rheingans, 1999.) This is not perceptually ordinal but clearly shows different regions of the data map. Sometimes a spectrum approximation sequence can be effective, because the perceptual system tends to segment it into red, green, yellow, and blue regions. As long as the boundaries match significant data classes, the result will be clear.

Sometimes we may wish to overlay pseudocolored information on a shaded surface. In this case, an isoluminant color map should be employed to avoid distorting the perceived surface shape through shape-from-shading information. There will be a loss of ability to show detail through the pseudocoloring, but this cannot be avoided. Although it is often important to have a color key in a visualization that allows values to be read back from the display, it should be noted that the results are likely to be quite inaccurate due to simultaneous contrast between parts of the display (Cleveland and McGill, 1983; Brewer, 1996b). We found that these errors could be substantial: 20% of the scale on average when using gray scales and saturation scales (Ware, 1988). Using a spectrum sequence dramatically reduced contrast errors to less than half a step

Total Ozone

177.   242.   308.   373.   438.

a

Figure 4.25   A map of ozone concentrations in the atmosphere is shown: (a) As a black–white sequence. (b) As a saturation sequence. (c) As a spectrum-approximation sequence. *Images courtesy of Penny Rheingans (Rheingans, 1999).*

b

Total Ozone

177.   242.   308.   373.   438.

c

Figure 4.25 *Continued*

on average. This can be attributed to contrast effects in each opponent channel canceling when a sequence zigzags with respect to the individual color channels.

Some authors have recommended that, for clarity, color sequences should constitute a straight line through a perceptual color space, such as *CIEluv* or *CIElab* (Robertson and O'Callaghan, 1988; Levkowitz and Herman, 1992). This would rule out the spectrum approximation sequence. Further, Spence et al. (1999) found that a color sequence combining variation in brightness, saturation, and hue was the most effective in a task requiring the rapid detection of low and high points in an image. It is possible to construct color sequences that combine the advantages of monotonicity in luminance, so as to show detail, with a variety of colors, to reduce contrast and enable accurate readings from a color key. The result is a kind of spiral in color space that cycles through a variety of hues while continuously increasing in lightness (Ware, 1988). Figure 4.26 gives an example using the same gravity data displayed in Figure 4.23.

Interval Pseudocolor Sequences

An *interval* sequence is one in which each unit step of the sequence represents an equal change in magnitude of the characteristic being displayed across the whole range of the sequence. In terms of color, this suggests using a uniform color space in which equal perceptual steps correspond to equal metric steps (Robertson and O'Callaghan, 1988). Another way to produce clearly discernible intervals is to introduce steps deliberately in the color sequence (a banded color sequence). The example illustrated in Figure 4.27 is not a map but an economic forecast. Increasing uncertainty in the prediction is shown by means of clearly visible color steps, each of which represents a 5% increase in the uncertainty level.

The traditional way to display an interval sequence is through the use of isovalue contours. Contour maps show the pattern of equal heights or other physical attributes with great precision, but using them to understand the overall shape of a terrain or an energy field takes considerable

Figure 4.26   The same data shown in Figure 4.23, pseudocolored with a sequence that provides a kind of upward spiral in color space; each color is lighter than the preceding one.

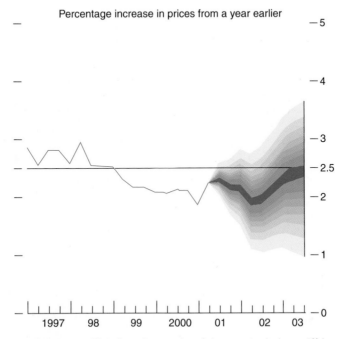

Percentage increase in prices from a year earlier

Figure 4.27   An economic forecast with estimated uncertainty. Color steps each show a 5% increase in uncertainty.

skill and experience. To support unskilled map readers, contours can be usefully combined with pseudocoloring, as shown in Figure 4.28. A well-designed pseudocolor sequence or artificially shaded height map is usually much better for the nonexpert than an unenhanced set of contours. It may also be better for the expert when rapid decision making or data fusion is required.

Ratio Pseudocolors

A *ratio* sequence is an interval sequence that has a true zero and all that this implies: the sign of a value is significant; one value can be twice as large as another. Expressing this in a color sequence is a tall order. No known visualization technique is capable of accurately conveying ratios with any precision. However, a sequence can be designed that effectively expresses a zero point and numbers above and below zero. Brewer (1996a) calls such sequences *diverging* sequences, whereas Spence and Efendov (2001) call them *bipolar* sequences.

Such sequences typically use a neutral value on one or more opponent channels to represent zero, and diverging colors (on one or more channels) to represent positive and negative quantities, respectively. For example, gray may be used to represent zero, increasing redness to represent positive quantities, and increasing blueness to represent negative quantities. In a target-detection study, Spence and Efendof (2001) found that a red–green sequence was most effective,

Figure 4.28   A map containing both contours and a pseudocolor sequence. *Data, courtesy of Dana Yoerger at the Woods Hole Oceanographic Institution, represents a section of the Juan de Fuca Ridgecrest in the northeastern Pacific Ocean.*

confirming the greater information-carrying capacity of this channel than the yellow–blue channel.

The example in Figure 4.29 shows a map of the stock market provided by SmartMoney.com. Market capitalization is represented by area, luminance encodes the magnitude of value change in the past year, and green-red encodes gain-loss. The Web site also gives users the option of a yellow–blue coding, suitable for most color-blind individuals.

Sequences for the Color Blind

Some color sequences will not be perceived by people who suffer from the common forms of color blindness: protanopia and deuteranopia. Both cause an inability to discriminate red from

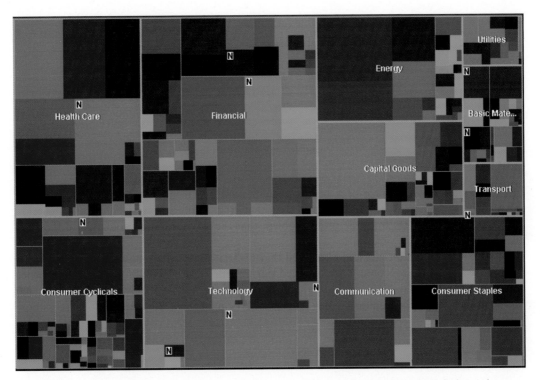

Figure 4.29   A color sequence with black representing zero. Increasing positive values are shown by increasing amounts of red. Increasing negative values are shown by increasing amounts of green. The map itself is a form of treemap (Johnson and Schneiderman, 1991). *Courtesy of SmartMoney.com.*

green. Sequences that vary mainly on a black-to-white scale or on a yellow-to-blue dimension (this includes green to blue and red to blue) will still be clear to color-blind people. Figure 4.30 shows two sequences that will be acceptable to these individuals. Meyer and Greenberg (1988) provide a detailed analysis of color sequences designed for common forms of color blindness.

Bivariate Color Sequences

Because color is three-dimensional, it is possible to display two or even three dimensions using pseudocoloring (Trumbo, 1981). Indeed, this is commonly done in the case of satellite images, in which invisible parts of the spectrum are mapped to the red, green, and blue monitor primaries. Although this mapping is simple to implement and corresponds to capabilities of the display device, (which usually has red, green, and blue phosphors,) such a scheme does not map the data values to perceptual channels. In general, it is better to map data dimensions to perceptual color dimensions. For example

Variable one→hue

Variable two→saturation

or

Variable one→hue

Variable two→lightness

Figure 4.31 gives an example of a bivariate color sequence from Brewer (1996a) that maps one variable to yellow–blue variation and the other to a combination of light–dark variation and saturation. It suffers from the usual problem that the low-saturation colors are difficult to distinguish.

As a word of caution, it should be noted that bivariate color maps are notoriously difficult to read. Wainer and Francolini (1980) carried out an empirical evaluation of a color sequence designed for U.S. census data and found that that it was essentially unintelligible. One approach to a solution is to apply a uniform color space; Robertson and O'Callaghan (1986) discuss how

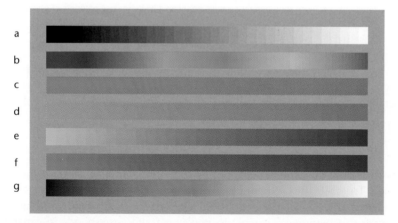

Figure 4.30   Seven different color sequences: (a) Gray scale. (b) Spectrum approximation. (c) Red–green. (d) Saturation. (e) and (f) Two sequences that will be perceived by people suffering from the most common forms of color blindness. (g) A sequence of colors in which each color is lighter than the previous one.

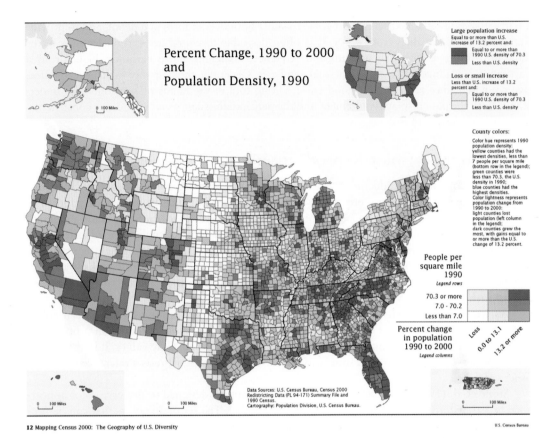

Figure 4.31 A bivariate pseudocoloring scheme using saturation and lightness for one variable and yellow–blue hue for the other. *Courtesy of Cindy Brewer.*

to do this. But distinctness may not lead to something that is interpretable. We do not seem to be able to read different color dimensions in a way that is highly separable. Generally, when the goal is to display two variables on the same map, it may be better to use visual texture, height difference, or another channel for one variable and color for the other, thus mapping data dimensions to more perceptually separable dimensions. Pseudocoloring is only one way to display a 2D scalar field. Often, mapping the scalar field to artificial height and shading the resulting surface with an artificial light source using standard computer graphics techniques is a better alternative. Using shading to reveal map data is discussed in Chapter 7. Using shading in combination with chromatic pseudocoloring is often an effective way to reveal bivariate surfaces. There are many considerations that go into making a color sequence that displays desired quantities without significant distortions, thus making it unlikely that any predefined set of colors will exactly suit a particular data set and visualization goal. To show both overall form and detail, and to provide the ability to read values from a key, it is often desirable to emphasize certain features in the data by using a deliberately nonuniform sequence. Assigning more variation in color to a particular data range will lead to its visual emphasis. Generally, the best way to achieve an effective color sequence is to place a good color editing tool in the hands of someone who understands both the data display requirement and the perceptual issues of color sequence construction (Guitard and Ware, 1990).

Application 4: Color Reproduction

The problem of color reproduction is essentially one of transferring color appearances from one display device, such as a computer monitor, to another device, such as a sheet of paper. The colors that can be reproduced on a sheet of paper depend on such factors as the color and intensity of the illumination. Northern daylight is much bluer than direct sunlight or tungsten light, which are both quite yellow, and is prized by artists for this reason. Halogen light is more balanced. Also, monitor colors can be reproduced only within the range of printing inks; therefore, it is neither possible nor meaningful to reproduce colors directly using a standard measurement system such as the CIE *XYZ* tristimulus values.

As we have discussed, the visual system is built to perceive relationships between colors rather than absolute values. For this reason, the solution to the color reproduction problem lies in preserving the color relationships as much as possible, not the absolute values. It is also important to preserve the white point in some way, because of the role of white as a reference in judging other colors.

Stone et al. (1988) describe a process of gamut mapping designed to preserve color appearance in a transformation between one device and another. The set of all colors that can be produced by a device is called the *gamut* of that device. The gamut of a monitor is larger than that of a color printer, as shown in Figure 4.7. Stone et al. describe the following set of heuristic principles to create good mapping from one device to another:

- The gray axis of the image should be preserved. What is perceived as white on a monitor should become whatever color is perceived as white on paper.

- Maximum luminance contrast (black to white) is desirable.

- Few colors should lie outside the destination gamut.

- Hue and saturation shifts should be minimized.

- An overall increase of color saturation is preferable to a decrease.

Figure 4.32 illustrates, in two dimensions, what is in fact a three-dimensional set of geometric transformations designed to accomplish the principles of gamut mapping. In this example, the process is a transformation from a monitor image to a paper hardcopy, but the same principles and methods apply to transformations between other devices.

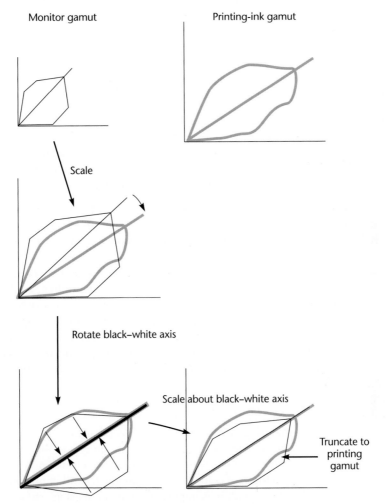

Figure 4.32 Illustration of the basic geometric operations in gamut mapping between devices, as defined by Stone et al. (1988).

1. **Calibration:** The first step is to calibrate the monitor and the printing device in a common reference system. Both can be characterized in terms of CIE tristimulus values. The calibration of the color printer must assume a particular illuminant.

2. **Range scaling:** To equate the luminance range of the source and destination images, the monitor gamut is scaled about the origin until the white of the monitor has the same luminance as the white of the paper on the target printer.

3. **Rotation:** What we perceive as neutral white on the monitor and on the printed paper can be very different, depending on the illumination. In general, in a printed image, the white is defined by the color of the paper. Monitor white is usually defined by the color that results when the red, green, and blue monitor primaries are set to their maximum values. To equate the monitor white with the paper white, the monitor gamut is rotated so as to make the white axes collinear.

4. **Saturation scaling:** Because colors can be achieved on a monitor that cannot be reproduced on paper, the monitor gamut is scaled radially with respect to the black–white axis to bring the monitor gamut within the range of the printing gamut. It may be preferable to leave a few colors outside the range of the target device and simply truncate them to the nearest color on the printing-ink gamut boundary.

For a number of reasons, it may not always be possible to apply these rules automatically. Different images may have different scaling requirements; some may consist of pastel colors that can easily be handled, whereas others may have vivid colors that must be truncated. The approach adopted by Stone et al. is to design a set of tools that support these transformations, making it easy for an educated technician to produce a good result. However, this elaborate process is not feasible with off-the-shelf printers and routine color printing. In these cases, the printer drivers will contain heuristics designed to produce generally satisfactory results. They will contain assumptions about such things as the gamma value of the monitor displaying the original image and methods for dealing with oversaturated colors. Sometimes, the heuristics embedded in devices can lead to problems. In our laboratory, we usually find it necessary to start a visualization process with very muted colors to avoid oversaturated colors on videotape or in paper reproduction.

Another issue that is important in color reproduction is the ability of the output device to display smooth color changes. Neural lateral inhibition within the visual system tends to amplify small artificial boundaries in smooth gradients of color as Mach bands. This sensitivity makes it difficult to display smoothly shaded images without artifacts. Because most output devices cannot reproduce the 16 million colors that can be created with a monitor, considerable effort has gone into techniques for generating a pattern of color dots to create the overall impression of a smooth color change. Making the dots look random is important to avoid aliasing artifacts (discussed in Chapter 2). Unless care is taken, artifacts of color reproduction can produce spurious patterns in scientific images.

Application 5: Color for Exploring Multidimensional Discrete Data

One of the most interesting but difficult challenges for data visualization is to support exploratory data analysis. Visualization can be a powerful tool in data mining, in which the goal is often a kind of general search for relationships and data trends. For example, marketing experts often collect large amounts of data about individuals in potential target populations. The variables that are collected might include age, income, educational level, employment category, tendency to purchase chocolate, and so on. If the marketer can identify a particular cluster of values in this population that are related to the likelihood of purchasing a product, this can result in better targeted, more effective advertising. Each of the measured variables can be thought of as a data dimension. The task of finding particular market segments is one of finding distinct clusters in the multidimensional space that is formed by these many variables.

Sometimes a scientist or a data analyst approaches data with no particular theory to test. The goal is to explore the data for meaningful and useful information in masses of mostly meaningless numbers. Plotting techniques have long been tools of the data explorer. In essence, the process is to plot the data, look for a pattern, and interpret the findings. Thus, the critical step in the discovery process is an act of perception. For example, the four scatter plots in Figure 4.33 illustrate very different kinds of data relationships. In the first, there are two distinct clusters, perhaps suggesting distinct subpopulations of biological organisms. In the second, there is a clear negative linear relationship between two measured variables. In the third, there is a curvilinear, inverted U-shaped relationship. In the fourth, there is an abrupt discontinuity. Each of these patterns will lead to a very different hypothesis about underlying causal relationships between variables. If any of the relationships were previously unknown, the researcher would be rewarded with a discovery.

Problems can arise in exploring data when more than two dimensions of data are to be displayed. It is possible to extend the scatter plot to three dimensions using the techniques for providing strong 3D spatial information, such as stereoscopic displays (see Chapter 8). What do we do, though, about data with more than three dimensions?

One solution for multidimensional data display is the generalized drafter's plot (Chambers et al., 1983) shown in Figure 4.34(a). In this technique, all pairs of variables are used to create two-dimensional scatter plots. Although the generalized drafter's plot can often be useful, it suffers from a disadvantage: it is very difficult to see data patterns that are present only when three or more data dimensions are taken into account.

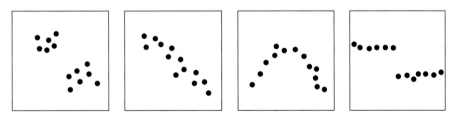

Figure 4.33   Visual exploratory data analysis techniques involve representing data graphically in order to understand relationships between data variables.

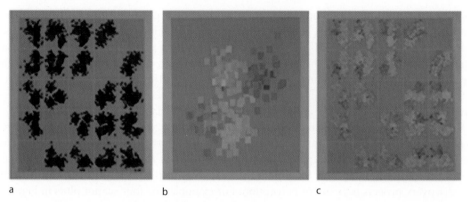

a   b   c

Figure 4.34   Five-dimensional data is presented: (a) In a generalized drafter's plot without color dimension mapping. (b) In a scatter plot with color dimension mapping. (c) In a generalized drafter's plot with color dimension mapping.

Color mapping can be used to extend the number of displayable data dimensions to five or six in a single scatter plot, as shown in Figure 4.34(b). We developed a simple scheme for doing this (Ware and Beatty, 1988). The technique is to create a scatter plot in which each point is a colored patch rather than a black point on a white background. Up to five data variables can be mapped and displayed as follows:

Variable 1 → x-axis position

Variable 2 → y-axis position

Variable 3 → amount of red

Variable 4 → amount of green

Variable 5 → amount of blue

In a careful evaluation of cluster perception in this kind of display, we concluded that color display dimensions could be as effective as spatial dimensions in allowing the visual system to perceive clusters. For this task, at least, the technique produced an effective five-dimensional window into the data space.

There is a negative aspect of the color-mapped scatter plot. Although identifying clusters and other patterns can be easy using this technique, interpreting them can be difficult. A cluster may appear greenish because it is low on the red variable rather than high on the green variable. The use of color can help us to identify the presence of multidimensional clusters and trends, but once the presence of these trends has been ascertained, other methods are needed to analyze them. An obvious solution is to map data variables to the color opponent axes described earlier. However, our experiments with this practice showed that the results were still not easy to interpret and that it was difficult to make efficient use of the color space.

Adding color is by no means the only way to extend a scatter plot to multiple dimensions, although it is one of the best techniques. In Chapter 5, we will consider other methods, which use shape and motion.

Conclusion

There has been more research on the use of color in visualization than any other perceptual issue. Nevertheless, the important lessons are relatively few, and we summarize them here.

*   To show detail in a visualization, *always* have considerable luminance contrast between foreground and background information. Never make the difference only through chromatic variation. This should be obvious in the case of text, although many PowerPoint presentations still violate this rule. It also applies to such problems as the visual display of flow fields, where small color-coded arrows or particle traces are used.

*   Use only a few colors if they are distinct codes. It is easy to select six distinct colors, but if 10 are needed they must be chosen with care. If the background is varied, then attempting to use more than 12 colors as codes is likely to result in failure.

*   Black or white borders around colored symbols can help make them distinct by ensuring a luminance contrast break with surrounding colors.

*   Red, green, yellow, and blue are hard-wired into the brain as primaries. If it is necessary to remember a color coding, these colors are the first that should be considered.

*   When color-coding large areas, use muted colors, especially if colored symbols are to be superimposed.

*   Small color-coded objects should be given high-saturation colors.

*   When a perceptually meaningful ordering is needed, use a sequence that varies monotonically on at least one of the opponent color channels. Examples are red to green, yellow to blue, low saturation to high saturation, and dark to light. Variation on more than one channel is often better, such as pale yellow to dark blue.

*   If it is important to show variations above and below zero, use a neutral value to represent zero and use increases in saturation toward opposite colors to show positive and negative values.

*   Color contrast can cause large errors in the representation of quantity. Contrast errors can be reduced with borders around selected areas, or by using muted, relatively uniform backgrounds.

*   For the reproduction of smooth color sequences, several million colors are needed under optimal viewing conditions. In this case, care must be taken to calibrate the monitor and to take into account monitor gamma values.

- When reproducing complex, continuously shaded images, it is critical to preserve the color relationships and to make sure that, under the particular lighting conditions, neutral values are perceived as neutral.

- Beware of oversaturating colors, especially when a printed image is to be the end product.

It is impossible to keep a discussion of color entirely segregated in one chapter. Color affects every aspect of visualization and is mentioned in many other chapters, especially Chapter 5, which places color in the context of other methods for coding information.

Visual Attention and Information that Pops Out

Consider the eyeball as an information-gathering searchlight, sweeping the visual world under the guidance of the cognitive centers that control our attention. Information is acquired in bursts, a snapshot for each fixation. From an image buffer, the massively parallel machinery of early visual processing finds objects based on salient features of images. Once identified, complex objects are scanned in series, one after another, at about the rate of 25 items per second. This means that we can parse somewhere between four and twelve items before the eye jumps to another fixation. Understanding the steps in this process can help us with many visualization tasks. Here are some examples.

A tactical map display used by a military strategist must simultaneously show many different kinds of information about resources, such as equipment, personnel, and environmental conditions that exist in the field. Ideally, with such a display it should be possible either to attend to a single aspect of the data, such as the deployment of tanks, or, by an act of visual attention, to perceive the whole, complex, interwoven pattern. Understanding early vision is critical in understanding how to make information visually distinct or how to make the integrated patterns stand out.

In a scatter plot, each plotted data point can be made to represent many different kinds of information by using a glyph instead of an undifferentiated circle. A *glyph* is a graphical object designed to convey multiple data values. For information about stocks on the stock exchange, the color of an information glyph might be used to show the price-to-earnings ratio, the size of the glyph to display the growth trend, and the shape of the glyph to represent the type of company—square for technology stocks, round for resources, and so on. But what makes a glyph stand out if it is displayed in this way? This type of graphical tool will be most useful if the interesting stocks can be made to stand out and catch the analyst's eye.

Visual search provides one of the great benefits of visualization. It is possible, in less than a second, to detect a single dark pixel in a 500×500 array of white pixels. This screen can be replaced every second by another, enabling a search of more than 15 million pixels in a minute.

This is an artificial example, because most search tasks are more complex, but it does highlight the incredible parallel search capacity of the visual system.

Attention is both a low-level and a high-level property of vision. This chapter is concerned with the low-level mechanisms that help us understand what is more readily available to attention. A large body of vision research is related to this problem, and in many cases this information can be translated, in a fairly direct way, into design guidelines for data visualization.

Chapter 11 is concerned with the high-level direction of attention for problem solving.

Searching the Visual Field

A problem with most research into attention, according to a recent book by Arien Mack and Irvin Rock, is that almost all perception experiments (except their own) demand attention in the very design (Mack and Rock, 1998). They have a point. Typically, a subject is paid to sit down and pay close attention to a display screen and to respond by pressing a key when some specified event occurs. This is not everyday life. Usually we pay very little attention to what goes on around us.

To understand better how we see when we are not primed for an experiment, Mack and Rock conducted a laborious set of experiments that only required one observation from each experiment. They asked subjects to look at a cross for a fraction of a second and report when one of the arms changed length. So far, this is like most other perception studies. But the real test came when they flashed up something near the cross that the subjects had not been told to expect. Subjects rarely saw this unexpected pattern, even though it was very close to the cross and they were attending to the display. Mack and Rock could only do this experiment once per subject, because as soon as subjects were asked if they had seen the new pattern they would have started looking for "unexpected" patterns, so hundreds of subjects were used. The fact that most subjects did not see a wide range of unexpected targets tells us that humans do not perceive much unless we have at least some expectation and need to see it. In most systems, brief, unexpected events will be missed. Mack and Rock initially claimed from their results that there is no perception without attention. However, because they found that subjects generally noticed larger objects, they were forced to abandon this extreme position.

Useful Field of View

The attention process is concentrated around the fovea, where vision is most detailed. However, we can redirect attention to objects within a single fixation, and the region of visual space we attend to expands and contracts based on task, the information in the display, and the level of stress in the observer. A metaphor for fovea-center attentional field is the searchlight of attention. When we are reading fine print, we can read the words only at the exact point of fixation. But we can take in the overall shape of a larger pattern at a single glance. In the former case, the searchlight beam is as narrow as the fovea, whereas in the latter it is much wider.

A concept called the *useful field of view* (UFOV) has been developed to define the size of the region from which we can rapidly take in information. The UFOV varies greatly, depending on the task and the information being displayed. Experiments using displays densely populated with targets reveal small UFOVs, from 1 to 4 degrees of visual angle (Wickens, 1992). But Drury and Clement (1978) have shown that for low character densities (less than one per degree of visual angle), the useful visual field can be as large as 15 degrees. Roughly, the UFOV varies with target density to maintain a constant number of targets in the attended region. With greater target density, the UFOV becomes smaller and attention is more narrowly focused; with a low target density, a larger area can be attended.

Tunnel Vision and Stress

A phenomenon known as *tunnel vision* has been associated with operators working under extreme stress. In tunnel vision, the UFOV is narrowed so that only the most important information, normally at the center of the field of view, is processed. This phenomenon has been specifically associated with various kinds of nonfunctional behaviors that occur during problem handling in disaster situations. The effect can be demonstrated quite simply. Williams (1985) compared performance on a task that required intense concentration (high foveal load) to one that was simpler. The high-load task involved naming a letter drawn from six alternatives; the low-load task involved naming a letter drawn from two alternatives. They found a dramatic drop in detection rate for objects in the periphery of the visual field (down from 75% correct to 36% correct) as the task load increased. The Williams data shows that we should not think of tunnel vision strictly as a response to disaster. It may generally be the case that as cognitive load goes up, the UFOV shrinks.

The Role of Motion in Attracting Attention

A study by Peterson and Dugas (1972) suggests that the UFOV function can be far larger for detection of moving targets than for detection of static targets. They showed that subjects can respond in less than 1 second to targets 20 degrees from the line of sight, if the targets are moving. If static targets are used, performance falls off rapidly beyond about 4 degrees from fixation. (See Figure 5.1.) This implies a useful field of at least 40 degrees across for the moving-targets task. However, this was merely the largest field that was measured. There is every reason to suppose that the useful visual field for moving targets is even larger; it may well encompass the entire visual field. Thus, motion of icons in user interfaces can be useful for attracting attention to the periphery of the screen (Bartram et al., 2003).

Reading from the Iconic Buffer

Figure 5.2 shows a collection of miscellaneous symbols. If we briefly flash such a collection of symbols on a screen—say, for one-tenth of a second—and then ask people to name as many of

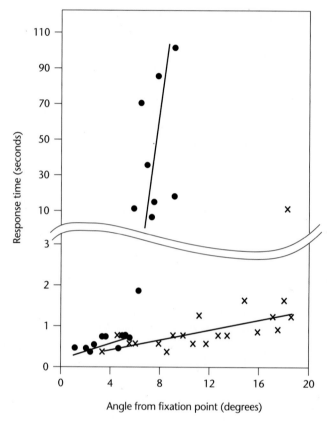

Figure 5.1   Results of a study by Peterson and Dugas (1972). The task was to detect small symbols representing aircraft in a simulation display. The circles show the response times from the appearances of static targets. The crosses show response times from the appearances of moving targets. Note the two different scales.

the symbols as they can, they typically produce a list of three to seven items. Several factors limit the number of items listed. The first is the short-lived visual buffer that allows us to hold the image for about one to two tenths of a second while we read the symbols into our short-term memory. This visual buffer is called *iconic memory*. Its properties were first described in a classic paper by Sperling (1960). See Humphreys and Bruce (1989) for a review. Any information that is retained longer than three-tenths of a second has been read into visual or verbal working memory (discussed in Chapter 11). This is an artificial example, but it has to do with a process that is very general. In each fixation between saccadic eye movements, an image of the world is captured in iconic memory; from this transient store higher-level processes must identify objects,

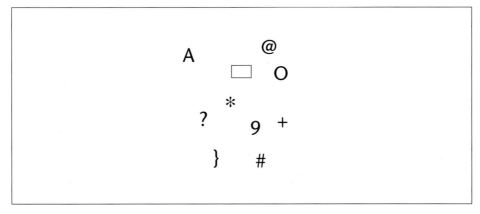

Figure 5.2 How many of these symbols can you remember after a glimpse one-tenth of a second long?

match them with objects previously perceived, and take information into working memory for symbolic analysis.

Preattentive Processing

We can do certain things to symbols to make it much more likely that they will be visually identified even after very brief exposure. Certain simple shapes or colors "pop out" from their surroundings. The theoretical mechanism underlying pop-out is called *preattentive processing* because logically it must occur prior to conscious attention. In essence, preattentive processing determines what visual objects are offered up to our attention. An understanding of what is processed preattentively is probably the most important contribution that vision science can make to data visualization.

Preattentive processing is best introduced with an example. To count the 3s in a table of digits in Figure 5.3(a), it is necessary to scan all the numbers sequentially. To count the 3s in Figure 5.3(b), it is necessary only to scan the red digits. This is because color is preattentively processed.

The typical experiment that is conducted to find out whether something is preattentively processed involves measuring the response time to find a target in a set of distractors; for example, finding the 3s in a set of other numbers. If processing is preattentive, the time taken to find the target should be independent of the number of distractors. Thus, if time to find the target is plotted against number of distractors, the result should be a horizontal line.

Figure 5.4 illustrates a typical pattern of results. The circles illustrate data from a visual target that is preattentively different from the distractors. The time taken to detect whether there is a dark digit in the array of digits shown above is independent of the number of gray digits. The Xs in Figure 5.4 show the results from processing a feature that is not preattentive. The time to respond depends on the number of distractors. The results of this kind of experiment are not

a 85689726984689762689764358922659865986554897689269898
   02462996874026557627986789045679232769285460986772098
   90834579802790759047098279085790847729087590827908754
   98709856749068975786259845690243790472190790709811450
   85689726984689762689764458922659865986554897689269898

b 85689726984689762689764358922659865986554897689269898
   02462996874026557627986789045679232769285460986772098
   90834579802790759047098279085790847729087590827908754
   98709856749068975786259845690243790472190790709811450
   85689726984689762689764458922659865986554897689269898

Figure 5.3   Preattentive processing. (a) To count the 3s in a table of digits, it is necessary to scan all the numbers sequentially. (b) To count the 3s in the next table, it is necessary only to scan the red digits. This is because color is preattentively processed.

Number of distractors

Figure 5.4   Typical results from a study of preattentive processing. The circles show time to perceive an object that is preattentively distinct from its surroundings. Time to process is independent of the number of irrelevant objects (distractors). The Xs show how time to process non-preattentively distinct targets depends on the number of distractors.

always as perfectly clear-cut as Figure 5.4 would suggest. Sometimes there is a small, but still measurable, slope in the case of a feature that is thought to be preattentive. As a rule of thumb, anything that is processed at a rate faster than 10 msec per item is considered to be preattentive. Typical processing rates for non-preattentive targets are 40 msec per item and more (Triesman and Gormican, 1988).

Why is this important? In displaying information, it is often useful to be able to show things "at a glance." If you want people to be able to identify instantaneously some mark on a map as being of type A, it should be differentiated from all other marks in a preattentive way.

There have been literally hundreds of experiments to test whether various kinds of features are processed preattentively. Figure 5.5 illustrates a few of the results. Orientation, size, basic shape, convexity, concavity, and an added box around an object are all preattentively processed. However, the junction of two lines is not preattentively processed; neither is the parallelism of pairs of lines, so it is harder to find the targets in the last two boxes in Figure 5.5.

The reason that preattentive processing has attracted so much attention among researchers is that it is thought to be a way of measuring the primitive features that are extracted in early visual processing (Triesman and Gormican, 1988). However, there is a risk of misinterpreting the findings of such studies. To take a single example, curved lines can be preattentively distinguished from straight lines. Despite this, it may be a mistake to think that there are curved-line detectors in early vision. It may simply be the case that cells responsive to long, straight line segments will not be strongly excited by the curved lines. Of course, it may actually be that early-vision curvature detectors do exist; it is just that the evidence must be carefully weighed. It is not a good idea to propose a new class of detector for everything that exhibits the pop-out effect. The scientific principle of finding the most parsimonious explanation, known as *Occam's razor*, applies here.

The features that are preattentively processed can be organized into a number of categories based on form, color, motion, and spatial position.

Form

- Line orientation

- Line length

- Line width

- Line collinearity

- Size

- Curvature

- Spatial grouping

- Blur

- Added marks

- Numerosity

Color

- Hue

- Intensity

Motion

- Flicker

- Direction of motion

Spatial Position

- 2D position

- Stereoscopic depth

- Convex/concave shape from shading

The results of preattentive processing experiments can be applied directly to the design of symbols for information display. In some cases, it may be desirable that each of many symbols be preattentively distinct from all the others. For example, in the case of a map of the ocean environment, we might wish to be able to scan visually only for scallop beds, only for fish farms, only for cod schools, or only for the fishing boats, assuming that we had all of this data. To make this possible, each type of symbol should be preattentively distinct from the others.

Figure 5.6 shows a set of nine symbols designed so that each is preattentively different from the others. The set could easily be extended—for example, by using blink coding. One thing that is clear from a cursory look at this example is that preattentive symbols become less distinct as the *variety* of distractors increases. It is easy to spot a single hawk in a sky full of pigeons, but if the sky contains a greater variety of birds, the hawk will be more difficult to see. Studies have shown that two factors are important in determining whether something stands out preattentively: the degree of difference of the target from the nontargets, and the degree of difference of the nontargets from each other (Quinlan and Humphreys 1987; Duncan and Humphreys, 1989). For example, yellow highlighting of text works well if yellow is the only color in the display besides black and white, but if there are many colors the highlighting will be less effective. For another example, Chau and Yeh (1995) showed that preattentive segregation by stereoscopic depth decreased as the number of depth layers increased.

It is natural to ask which visual dimensions are preattentively stronger and therefore more salient. Unfortunately, this question cannot be answered, because it always depends on the strength of the particular feature and the context. For example, Callaghan (1989) compared color to orientation as a preattentive cue. The results showed that the preattentiveness of the color depended on the saturation (vividness) and size of the color patch, as well as the degree of difference from surrounding colors. Similarly, the preattentiveness of line orientation depends on the length of the line, the degree to which it differs from surrounding lines, and the contrast of the line pattern with the background.

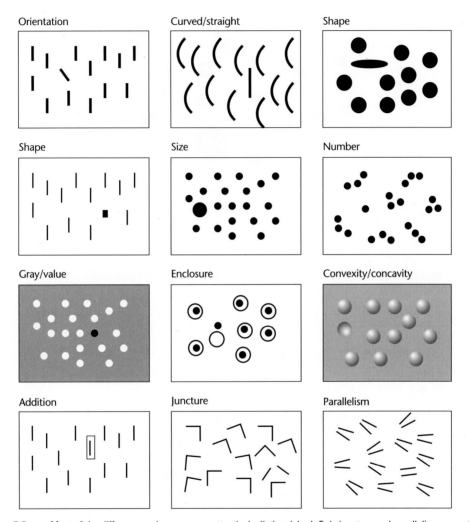

Figure 5.5   Most of the differences shown are preattentively distinguished. Only juncture and parallelism are not.

Numerous studies have addressed the preattentive properties of various combinations of features. It would be impossible to describe all the interactions without writing a complete book on the subject. However, some generalizations are in order. Adding marks to highlight something is generally better than taking them away (Triesman and Gormican, 1988). Thus, it is better to highlight a word by underlining it than to underline all the words in a paragraph except for the target word. It is also the case that simple numerosity is preattentively processed. We can see at

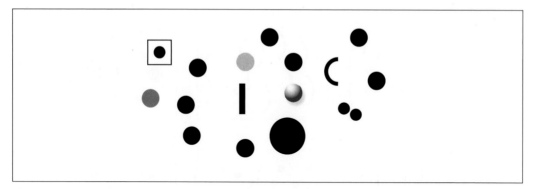

Figure 5.6   A set of symbols in which each of the nine symbol types is preattentively distinct from all the others.

a glance that there are one, two, three, or four objects in a group; this ability appears very early in human development (Dehaene, 1997). Once the number of objects increases beyond four, explicit counting is necessary.

That color is also preattentive has been well established, and the problem of defining a color that will be preattentively distinct from surrounding colors has already been discussed in Chapter 4. To restate a key finding, Bauer et al. (1996) showed that to be preattentively distinct, a color should lie outside the boundary of the region defined by all the other colors in the local part of the display (see Figure 4.19).

Rapid Area Judgments

Most work on preattentive processing has involved the detection of isolated targets. But other tasks can also benefit from rapid processing. In interpreting map data, a common task is to rapidly estimate the area of some region. Healey et al. (1998) showed that fast area estimation can be done on the basis of either the color or the orientation of the graphical elements filling a spatial region. It is a reasonable assumption that all the preattentive cues that have been identified for target identification are also valid for area estimation judgments.

Coding with Combinations of Features

A critical issue for information display is whether more complex patterns can be preattentively processed. For example, what happens if we wish to search for a gray square, not just something that is gray or something that is square? It turns out that this kind of search is slow if the surrounding objects are squares (but not gray ones) and other gray shapes. We are forced to do a serial search of either the gray shapes or the square objects. This is called a *conjunction search*, because it involves searching for the specific conjunction of gray-level and shape attrib-

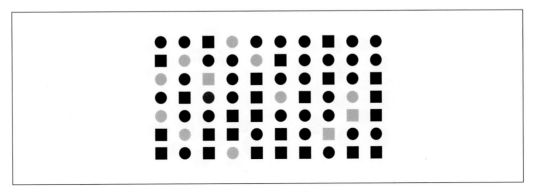

Figure 5.7   Searching for the gray squares is slow because they are identified by conjunction coding.

utes. Figure 5.7 illustrates a conjunction search task in which the targets are represented by three gray squares. Conjunction searches are generally not preattentive, although there are a few very interesting exceptions.

Conjunctions with Spatial Dimensions

Although early research suggested that conjunction searches were never preattentive, it has emerged that there are a number of preattentive dimension pairs that do allow for conjunctive search. Searches can be preattentive when there is a conjunction of spatially coded information and a second attribute, such as color or shape. The spatial information can be position on the *XY* plane, stereoscopic depth, shape from shading, or motion.

Spatial grouping on the *XY* plane: Triesman and Gormican (1988) argue that preattentive search can be restricted by the identification of visual clusters. This is a form of conjunction search: the conjunction of space and color. In Figure 5.8(a), we cannot conjunctively search for green ellipses, but in Figure 5.8(b), we can rapidly search the conjunction of lower grouping and gray target. The fact that the target is also elliptical is irrelevant.

Stereoscopic depth: Nakayama and Silverman (1986) showed that the conjunction of stereoscopic depth and color, or of stereoscopic depth and movement, can be preattentively processed. This may be very useful in producing highlighting techniques allowing for a preattentive search within the set of highlighted items (Bartram and Ware, 2002).

Convexity, concavity, and color: D'Zmura et al. (1997) showed that the conjunction of perceived convexity and color can be preattentively processed. In this case, the convexity is perceived through shape-from-shading information.

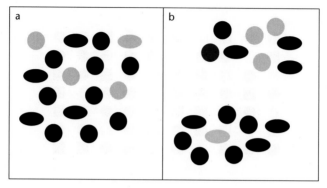

Figure 5.8   Spatial conjunction. The pattern on the left is a classic example of a preattentive conjunction search. To find the gray ellipses, either the gray things or the elliptical things must be searched. However, the example on the right shows that the search can be speeded up by spatial grouping. If attention is directed to the lower cluster, perceiving the gray ellipse is preattentive. This is a preattentive conjunction of spatial location and gray value.

Motion: Driver et al. (1992) determined that motion and target shape can be preattentively scanned conjunctively. Thus, if the whole set of targets is moving, we do not need to look for nonmoving targets. We can preattentively find, for example, the red moving target.

An application in which preattentive spatial conjunction may be useful is found in geographic information systems (GISs). In these systems, data is often characterized as a set of layers: for example, a layer representing the surface topography, a layer representing minerals, and a layer representing ownership patterns. Such layers may be differentiated by means of motion or stereoscopic-depth cues.

Highlighting

The purpose of highlighting is to make some information stand out from other information. This is the most straightforward application of preattentive processing results. The problem of highlighting is easy to solve in homogeneous graphical displays. Yellow background highlighting of text works well for text that is black on white because yellow is a high luminance color that maintains text contrast. When the environment is visually complex, already employing color, texture, and shape, the problem becomes complex. As a rule of thumb, use whatever graphical dimension is least used otherwise in the design. For example, if texture is not used elsewhere, use it. Modern computer graphics permit the use of motion for highlighting. This can be very effective when there is little other motion in the display (Bartram and Ware, 2002). However, making things move may be too strong a cue for many applications.

A new idea for highlighting is the use of blur. Kosara et al. (2002) suggested blurring everything else in the display to make certain information stand out. They call the technique *seman-*

Figure 5.9   Blur can be used to highlight important information by blurring irrelevant information. *Kosara et al. (2002) call this technique semantic depth of field.*

tic depth of field, because it applies the depth of focus effects that can be found in photography to the display of data according to semantic content. As Figure 5.9 illustrates, blur works well, although again there are obvious drawbacks. If the designer is not completely sure what the user should attend to, he or she runs the risk of making important information illegible.

Designing a Symbol Set

One way to think about preattentive processing is to understand that we can easily and rapidly perceive the "odd man out" in visual feature space. If a set of symbols is to be designed to represent different classes of objects on a map display, then these symbols should be as distinct as possible. Military operational maps are an obvious example in which symbols can be used to represent many different classes of targets. (Targets are entities of operational importance that may be friendly or hostile.) A simplified example provides an interesting design exercise.

A tactical map might require the following symbols:

- Aircraft targets
- Tank targets
- Building targets
- Infantry position targets

In addition:

- Each of the target types can be classified as friendly or hostile.

- Targets exist whose presence is suspected but not confirmed.

Finally, there is a need to display features of the terrain itself. Roads, rivers, vegetation types, and topography are all important.

In this example, we encounter many of the characteristic problems of symbol set design. Even though this is a great simplification of the requirements of actual command and control displays, there are still many different types of things to be represented. There is a need for various orthogonal classifications (friendly vs. hostile, static vs. mobile). In some circumstances, conjunction search might be desirable (friendly tanks); in others, it would be useful if whole classes of objects could be rapidly estimated.

A solution to this simplified problem is illustrated in Figure 5.10. The actual symbols for the different target types have all been made preattentively distinct using shape. Color has been used to classify the targets preattentively into friendly and hostile ones. Possible targets are indicated by adding a thin rectangular box. Spatial grouping also helps to distinguish between friendly and hostile targets, but this would not always be the case. In a real application of this type, dozens more different symbols may be required on many different backgrounds, making the design trade-offs much harder.

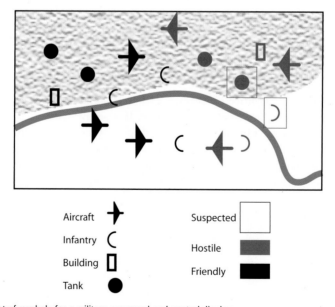

Figure 5.10   A set of symbols for a military command and control display.

Neural Processing, Graphemes, and Tuned Receptors

We now consider the same problem from a neurological perspective. Triesman and others claim that preattentive processing is due to *early* visual processing. What is the neurological evidence for this?

Visual information leaves the retina, passing up the optic nerve, through the neural junction at the lateral geniculate nucleus (LGN), and on to the much richer world of processing in the cortex. The first areas in the cortex to receive visual inputs are called, simply, visual area 1 (V1) and visual area 2 (V2). Most of the output from area 1 goes on to area 2, and together these two regions make up more than 40% of vision processing (Lennie, 1998). There is plenty of neural processing power, as several billion neurons in areas V1 and V2 are devoted to analyzing the signals from only two million nerve fibers coming from the optic nerves of two eyes. This makes possible the massively parallel simultaneous processing of the incoming signals for color, motion, texture, and the elements of form. It is here that the elementary vocabularies of both vision and data display are defined.

Figure 5.11 is derived from Livingston and Hubel's diagram (1988) that summarizes both the neural architecture and the features processed in this area of the brain. A key concept in understanding this diagram is the *tuned receptive field*. In Chapter 3, we saw how single-cell recordings of cells in the retina and the LGN reveal cells with distinctive concentric receptive fields. Such cells are said to be *tuned* to a particular pattern of a white spot surrounded by black or a black spot surrounded by white. In general, a tuned filter is a device that responds strongly to a certain kind of pattern and responds much less, or not at all, to other patterns. In the early visual cortex, some cells respond only to elongated blobs with a particular position and orientation, others respond most strongly to blobs of a particular position moving in a particular direction at a particular velocity, and still others respond selectively to color.

There are cells in V1 and V2 that are differentially tuned to each of the following properties:

- Orientation and size (with luminance) via the Gabor processor described later in this chapter

- Color (two types of signal) via the opponent processing channel mechanisms discussed in Chapter 4

- Elements of local stereoscopic depth

- Elements of motion

Moreover, all these properties are extracted for each point in the visual field. In V1 and V2 and many other regions of the brain, neurons are arranged in the form of a spatial map of the retina. It is a highly distorted map, because the fovea is given more space than the periphery of vision. The receptive fields are smaller for cells that process information coming from the fovea than for cells that process information from peripheral regions of the visual field. Nevertheless, for every

Figure 5.11 Architecture of primary visual areas. *Adapted from Livingston and Hubel (1988).*

point in V1, there is a corresponding area of the visual field in a topographic relationship (adjacency is preserved between areas). It is a massively parallel system in which, for each point in visual space, there are tuned filters for many different orientations, many different kinds of color information, many different directions and velocities of motion, and many different stereoscopic depths.

The Grapheme

It is useful to think of the things that are extracted by the early neural mechanisms as the "phonemes" of perception. *Phonemes* are the smallest elements in speech recognition, the atomic components from which meaningful words are made. In a similar way, we can think of orientation detectors, color detectors, and so on as "visual phonemes," the elements from which meaningful perceptual objects are constructed.

We use the term *grapheme* to describe a graphical element that is primitive in *visual* terms, the visual equivalent of a phoneme. The basis of the grapheme concept is that the pattern that most efficiently excites a neuron in the visual system is exactly the pattern that the neuron is tuned to detect (Ware and Knight, 1995). Thus, the most efficient grapheme is one that matches the receptive field properties of some class of neurons. An orientation detector will be excited most efficiently by a pattern whose light distribution is exactly the same as the sensitivity distribution of the cell. This is simply another way of saying that the detector is tuned to that particular pattern. Once we understand the kinds of patterns the tuned cells of the visual cortex respond to best, we can apply this information to create efficient visual patterns. Patterns based on the receptive field properties of neurons should be rapidly detected and easily distinguished.

A number of assumptions are implicit in this account. They are worth examining critically. One basic assumption is that the rate at which single neurons fire is the key coding variable in terms of human perception. This assumption can certainly be questioned. It may be that what is important is the way in which groups of neurons fire, or perhaps the temporal spacing or synchronization of cell firings. In fact, there is evidence that these alternative information codings may be important, perhaps critical. Nevertheless, few doubt that neurons that are highly sensitive to color differences (in terms of their firing rates) are directly involved in the processing of color and that the same thing is true for motion and shape. Moreover, as we shall see, the behavior of neurons fits well with studies of how people perceive certain kinds of patterns. Thus, there is a convergence of lines of evidence.

We also assume that *early-stage* neurons are particularly important in determining how distinct things seem. We know that at higher levels of processing in the visual cortex, receptive fields are found that are much more complex; they respond to patterns that appear to be composites of the simple receptive field patterns found at earlier stages. The evidence suggests that composite patterns analyzed further up the visual processing chain, are not, in general, processed as rapidly. It seems natural, then, to think of early-stage processing as forming the graphemes, and of later-stage processing as forming the "words," or objects, of perception.

Much of the preattentive processing work already discussed in this chapter can be regarded as providing experimental evidence of the nature of graphemes. The following sections apply the concept to the perception of visual texture and show how knowledge of early mechanisms enables us to create rules for textures that are visually distinct.

The Gabor Model and Texture in Visualization

A number of electrophysiological and psychophysical experiments show that visual areas 1 and 2 contain large arrays of neurons that filter for orientation and size information at each point in the visual field. These neurons have both a preferred orientation and a preferred size (they are said to have *spatial* and *orientation tuning*). These particular neurons are not color-coded; they respond to luminance changes only.

A simple mathematical model used widely to describe the receptive field properties of these neurons is the *Gabor function*. This function is illustrated in Figure 5.12. It consists of the product of a cosine wave grating and a gaussian. Roughly, this can be thought of as a kind of fuzzy bar detector. It has a clear orientation, and it has an excitatory center, flanked by

Figure 5.12   Gabor receptive field, composed of cosine and gaussian components. Multiply the cosine wave grating on the left by the gaussian envelope in the center to get the two-dimensional Gabor function shown on the right. This example has an excitatory center flanked by two inhibitory bars.

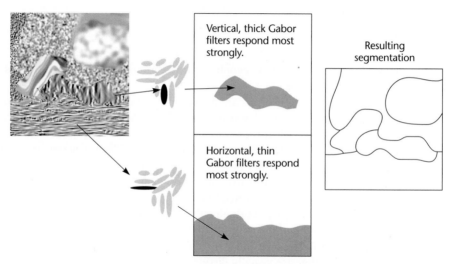

Figure 5.13   The texture segmentation model. Two-dimensional arrays of Gabor detectors filter every part of the image for all possible orientations and sizes. Areas exciting particular classes of detectors form the basis of visually distinct segments of the image.

inhibitory bars. The opposite kind of neuron also exists, with an inhibitory center and an excitatory surround.

Many things about low-level perception can be explained by this model. Gabor-type detectors are used in theories of the detection of contours at the boundaries of objects (form perception), the detection of regions that have different visual textures, stereoscopic vision, and motion perception.

The Gabor function has two components, as illustrated in Figure 5.12: a cosine wave and a gaussian envelope. Multiply them together, and the result is a Gabor function. Mathematically, a Gabor function has the following form (simplified for ease of explanation):

$$\text{Response} = C\cos\left(\frac{Ox}{S}\right)\exp\left(-\frac{(x^2 + y^2)}{S}\right) \qquad\qquad \textbf{(5.1)}$$

The C parameter gives the amplitude or *contrast* value; S gives the overall *size* of the Gabor function by adjusting both the wavelength of the cosine grating and the rate of decay of the gaussian envelope. O is a rotation matrix that *orients* the cosine wave. Other parameters can be added to position the function at a particular location in space and adjust the ratio of the gaussian size to the sine wavelength; however, orientation, size, and contrast are most significant in modeling human visual processing.

Texture Segmentation

One way to apply the Gabor model is in understanding how the visual system *segments* the visual world into regions of distinct visual texture. Suppose we wish to understand how people perceptually differentiate types of vegetation based on the visual textures in a black-and-white satellite image. A model based on Gabor filters provides a good description of the way people perform this kind of texture segmentation task (Bovik et al., 1990; Malik and Perona, 1990).

The segmentation model is illustrated in Figure 5.13. It has three main stages. In the first stage, banks of Gabor filters respond strongly to regions of texture where particular spatial frequencies and orientations predominate. In a later stage, the output from this early stage is low-pass-filtered. (This is a kind of averaging process that creates regions, each having the same general characteristic. At the final stage, the boundaries are identified between regions with strongly dissimilar characteristics.) This model predicts that we will divide visual space into regions according to the predominant spatial frequency and orientation information. A region with large orientation and size differences will be the most differentiated. Also, regions can be differentiated based on the texture contrast. A low-contrast texture will be differentiated from a high-contrast texture with the same orientation and size components.

Tradeoffs in Information Density: An Uncertainty Principle

A famous vision researcher, Horace Barlow, developed a set of principles that have become influential in guiding our understanding of human perception. The second of these, called "the second dogma" (Barlow, 1972), provides an interesting theoretical background to the Gabor model. In the second dogma, Barlow asserted that the visual system is simultaneously optimized in both the spatial–location and spatial–frequency domains. John Daugman (1984) showed mathematically that Gabor detectors satisfy the requirements of the Barlow dogma. They optimally preserve a combination of spatial information (the location of the information in visual space) and oriented-frequency information. A single Gabor detector can be thought of as being tuned to a little packet of orientation and size information that can be positioned anywhere in space.

Daugman (1985) has also shown that a fundamental uncertainty principle is related to the perception of position, orientation, and size. Given a fixed number of detectors, resolution of size can be traded for resolution of orientation or position. We have shown that same principle applies to the synthesis of texture for data display (Ware and Knight, 1995). A gain in the ability to display orientation information precisely inevitably comes at the expense of precision in displaying size information. Given a constant density of data, orientation or size can be specified precisely, but not both.

Figure 5.14 illustrates this tradeoff, expressed by changing the shape and size of the gaussian multiplier function with the same sinusoidal grating. When the gaussian is large, the spatial frequency is specified quite precisely, as shown by the small image in the Fourier transform. When the gaussian is small, position is well specified but spatial frequency is not, as shown by the large image in the Fourier transform. The lower two rows of Figure 5.14 show how the gaussian envelope can be stretched to specify either the spatial frequency or the orientation more precisely. Although a full mathematical treatment of these effects is beyond the scope of this book, the main point is that there are fundamental limits and tradeoffs related to the ways texture can be used for information display. To restate them simply, large display glyphs can only show position imprecisely; precise orientation can be shown at the expense of precise size information, and both trade off against precision in position.

Texture Coding Information

If texture perception can be modeled and understood using the Gabor function as a model of a detector, the same model should be useful in *producing* easily distinguished textures for information display. The ideal grapheme for generating visual textures will be the Gabor function expressed as a luminance profile, as shown in Figure 5.15. A neuron with a Gabor receptive field will respond most strongly to a Gabor pattern with the same size and orientation. Therefore, textures based on Gabor primitives should be easy to distinguish.

Primary Perceptual Dimensions of Texture

A completely general Gabor model has parameters related to orientation, spatial frequency, contrast, and the size and shape of the gaussian envelope. However, in human neural receptive fields, the gaussian and cosine components tend to be coupled so that low-frequency cosine components have large gaussians and high-frequency cosine components have small gaussians (Caelli and Moraglia, 1985). This allows us to propose a simple three-parameter model for the perception and generation of texture.

Orientation O: The orientation of the cosine component

Scale S: The size = 1/(spatial frequency component)

Contrast C: An amplitude or contrast component

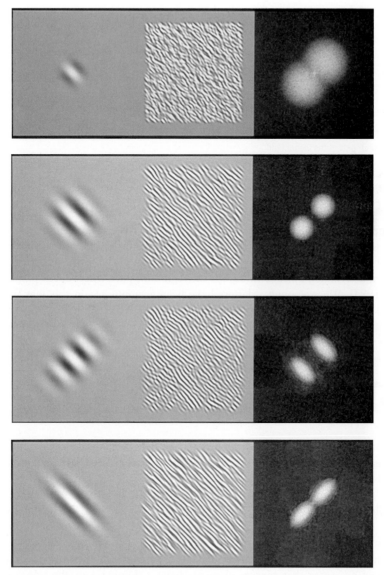

Figure 5.14   In the left-hand column, the same cosine pattern is paired with different gaussian multipliers. In the center column are textures created using each Gabor function by reducing the size by a factor of 5 and spattering it in the field. In the right-hand column are 2D Fourier transforms of the textures.

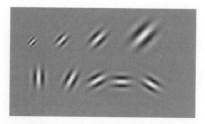

Figure 5.15   Gabor receptive fields shown as gray-scale images. Different sizes and orientations are represented for each part of the visual field.

Generation of Distinct Textures

With this simple model, it is straightforward to generate textures using Gabor functions as primitives. These textures can be varied in orientation, size (1/frequency), or contrast.

One method is to randomly splatter down Gabor functions whose orientation, size, and contrast have been determined by data values for the region in space where each splatter lands (Ware and Knight, 1995). When enough splatters have been accumulated in this way, we will have a continuous map that can represent up to three variables (a trivariate map). We can also map an additional variable to hue, producing a four-variable map.

Data value 1 → Orientation

Data value 2 → Size

Data value 3 → Contrast

Data value 4 → Hue

Figure 5.16 provides an example showing a magnetic field displayed using orientation and size manipulations. Color coding is added to the Gabor textures to illustrate field strength. A word of caution—Figure 5.16 illustrates a direct application of low-level visual theory, but it should not be taken as an optimal display. It is based on a feature-level model; to understand how to better show flow patterns, we need to move up the visual system and consider how patterns are formed from features. A more effective approach to vector field visualization, through pattern perception, is discussed in Chapter 6.

Note that textures need not be made of Gabor patterns for the method or the theory to work. It is only necessary that texture elements have a dominant orientation and spatial frequency. It is also important to note that the fundamental tradeoffs in our ability to represent spatial information using texture are independent of whether or not the Gabor model of texture perception is correct. To take a simple example, if we consider that texture elements, or *textons*, can be made from small graphical shapes representing data, the number of such shapes that can be drawn per unit area is inversely proportional to their size. The location of the packet of

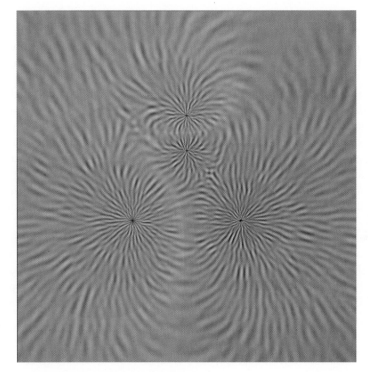

Figure 5.16   Magnetic field shown using Gabor textures.

information can be specified only to a precision determined by the size of the object representing that information.

Spatial-Frequency Channels, Orthogonality, and Maps

Sometimes we may wish to display many different kinds of information in a single map. For example, we might wish to show sea-surface temperature and sea-surface salinity at the same time. Naturally, we would prefer that the different sources of information do not interfere with one another. It would be unfortunate if regions of high salinity appeared to have a greater apparent temperature than they really have, due to visual crosstalk between the way we display temperature and the way we display salinity. Thus, our goal is to create display methods that are *perceptually independent*.

The concept of the *visual processing channel* can be taken directly from vision research and applied to the independence problem. We have already discussed the concept of color channels in Chapter 4. Here, the same idea is applied to spatial information. The idea is that information carried on one channel should not interfere with information displayed on another. It is probably not the case that any of the perceptual channels we shall discuss are fully independent; nevertheless, it is certainly the case that some kinds of information are processed in ways that are more independent than others. A channel that is independent from another is said to be *orthogonal* to it. Here, the concept is applied to the spatial information carried by Gabor detectors.

A given Gabor-type neuron is broadly tuned with respect to orientation and size. The half-width of the spatial tuning curve is approximately a period change (in the sinusoid) of a factor of 3, and the total number of spatial-frequency channels is about four. Wilson and Bergen (1979) determined these values using a masking technique, which essentially determines the extent to which one type of information interferes with another. The resulting estimation of spatial-frequency channels is illustrated in Figure 5.17.

Orientation tuning-in appears to be about ±30 degrees (Blake and Holopigan, 1985). Therefore, textures that differ from one another by more than 30 degrees in orientation will be easily distinguished.

These experimental results can be applied to problems in information display. For textured regions to be visually distinct, the dominant spatial frequencies should differ by at least a factor of 3 or 4, and the dominant orientations should differ by more than 30 degrees, all other factors (such as color) being equal. In general, the more displayed information differs in spatial frequency and in orientation, the more distinct that information will be. In practical applications, this means

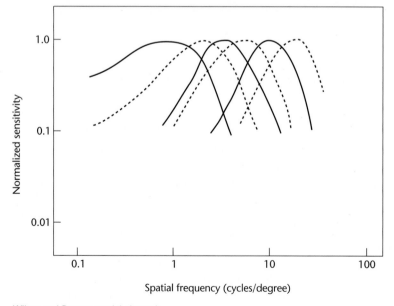

Figure 5.17 Wilson and Bergen spatial channels.

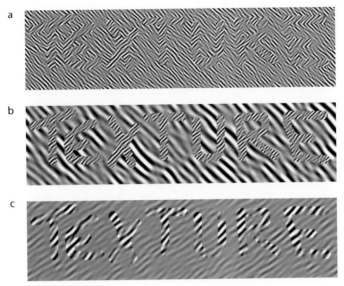

Figure 5.18   The word *TEXTURE* is visible only because of texture differences between the letters and the background; overall luminance is held constant. (a) Only texture orientation is altered. (b) Texture orientation and size are altered. (c) Texture contrast is altered.

that if we want different regions to be distinct because of their texture, the dominant orientations of the patterns should be made as different as possible. In Figure 5.18(a), only orientation is changed between different regions of the display, and although the word *TEXTURE* appears distinct from its background, it is weak. The difference appears much stronger when both the spatial frequency and the orientation differ between the figure and the background, as in Figure 5.18(b). The third way that textures can be made easy to distinguish is by changing the contrast, as illustrated in Figure 5.18(c).

Texture Resolution

The model of texture segmentation described previously predicts performance when people are asked to rapidly classify regions of a display. However, if we ask how small a difference people can *resolve*, we need a different model. When people are allowed to stare at two regions of a display for as long as they like, they can resolve far smaller differences than those perceived in brief presentations.

The *resolvable* size difference for a Gabor pattern is a size change of about 9% (Caelli et al., 1983). The resolvable orientation difference is about 5 degrees (Caelli and Bevan, 1983). These resolutions are much smaller than the channel-tuning functions would predict. This implies that higher-level mechanisms are present to sharpen up the output from individual receptors. The

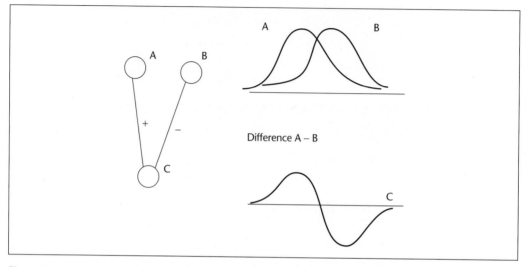

Figure 5.19   Differences between two signals are created by an excitatory and an inhibitory connection.

mechanism is based on inhibition. If a neuron has an excitatory input from one neuron and an inhibitory input from another with a slightly different tuning, the resulting difference signal is much more sensitive to spatial tuning than either of the original signals. This kind of sharpening is common in neural systems; it appears in color systems, edge detection, and heading detection (for navigation). Figure 5.19 illustrates the concept. Neurons A and B both have rather broadly tuned and somewhat overlapping response functions to some input pattern. Neuron C has an excitatory input from A and an inhibitory input from B. The result is that C is highly sensitive to differences between A and B at the crossover point.

Texture Contrast Effects

Textures can appear distorted because of contrast effects, just like the luminance contrast illusions that were described in Chapter 3. Thus, a given texture on a coarsely textured background will appear finer than the same texture on a finely textured background. This phenomenon is illustrated in Figure 5.20. The effect is predicted by higher-order inhibitory connections. It will cause errors in reading data that is mapped to texture element size. Texture orientation can cause contrast illusions in orientation, and this, too, may cause misperception of data. See Figure 5.21.

Other Dimensions of Visual Texture

Although there is considerable evidence to suggest that orientation, size, and contrast are the three dominant dimensions of visual texture, it is clear that the world of texture is much richer

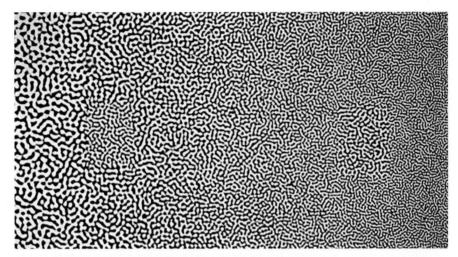

Figure 5.20   Texture contrast effect. The two patches left of center and right of center have the same texture granularity, but texture contrast makes them appear different.

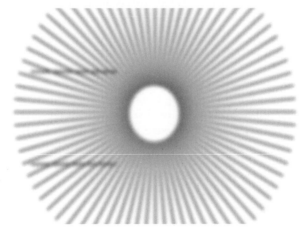

Figure 5.21   The two horizontal lines are parallel, but they appear tilted due to orientation contrast.

than this. The dimensionality of visual texture is very high, as a visual examination of the world around us attests. Think of the textures of wood, brick, stone, fur, leather, and other natural materials. One of the important additional texture dimensions is certainly randomness (Liu and Picard, 1994). Textures that are regular have a very different quality from random ones.

Texture Field Displays

We would do well to learn to use texture more effectively in information displays. The world of visual texture is arguably as rich and expressive as the world of color. Users of GISs commonly require the display of many overlapping variables on the same map, such as geological information, vegetation type, surface topography, and magnetic anomalies. In light of the theory of parallel feature processing, we are now in a position to say something about various solutions that apply visual texture to such problems.

The Exvis tool (Pickett and Grinstein, 1988) mapped data values to various attributes of stick-figure icons such as those shown in Figure 5.22. This package had many display options, including changing the angles of line segments relative to each other, or relative to a reference orientation, and changing the line segment widths. These glyphs could then be displayed in a dense field over a plane producing a visual texture. Although the Exvis developers implemented the capability to map data to icon colors, they worked mostly with angles (Pickett et al., 1995).

What does early visual processing tell us about the Exvis glyph? The theory of visual texture segmentation based on low-level Gabor detectors suggests a problem. With the Exvis glyph, multiple segments of a single glyph can have the same or similar orientations, although each represents a different data dimension. These line segments will be visually confounded when the glyphs are densely displayed, ensuring that unrelated aspects of the underlying data will be visually confounded. Because the orientation tuning of V1 neurons indicates that glyph element orientations should be separated by at least 30 degrees, and because a line-oriented segment will be confused with an identical segment rotated through 180 degrees, fewer than six orientations can be rapidly distinguished.

Weigle et al. (2000) developed a technique called *oriented sliver textures* specifically designed to take advantage of the parallel processing of orientation information. Each variable in a multivariate map was mapped to a 2D array of slivers where all the slivers had the same orientation. Differently oriented 2D sliver arrays were produced for each variable. The values of each scalar map were shown by controlling the amount of contrast between the sliver and the background. Combining all of the sliver fields produced the visualization illustrated in Figure 5.23.

Figure 5.22   The Exvis data glyph used to form visual textures. Different variables are mapped to the angle between line segments and their thickness.

Figure 5.23   The sliver plot of Weigle et al. (2000). Each of the variables shown in the thumbnail patterns in the left part of the above figure is mapped to a differently oriented sliver field. *Courtesy of Chris Weigle.*

The right-hand part of this figure shows the combination of the eight variables illustrated in the thumbnail patterns shown on the left. Weigle et al. conducted a study showing that if slivers were oriented at least 15 degrees from surrounding regions, they stood out clearly. However, the experiment was only carried out with a single sliver at each location (unlike Figure 5.23). To judge the effectiveness of the sliver plot for yourself, try looking for each of the thumbnail patterns in the larger combined plot. The fact that many of the patterns cannot easily be seen suggests that the technique is not effective for so many variables. The tuning of orientation-sensitive cells suggests that slivers should be at least 30 degrees apart to be clearly readable (Blake and Holopigan, 1985), perhaps more, but in Figure 5.23 some differ by only 15 degrees.

   Figure 5.24 shows another sliver plot with only three orientations. This adds a colored background and also uses slivers having both positive and negative contrast with the background. It is easier to see the different patterns in this example.

   Two other examples of high-dimensional data display from Laidlaw and his collaborators (Laidlaw et al. 1998) (Figures 5.25 and 5.26) were created using a very different design strategy.

Figure 5.24 Another example of a sliver plot. Three variables are mapped to three differently oriented slivers. A fourth variable is mapped to the background color. *Courtesy of Chris Weigle.*

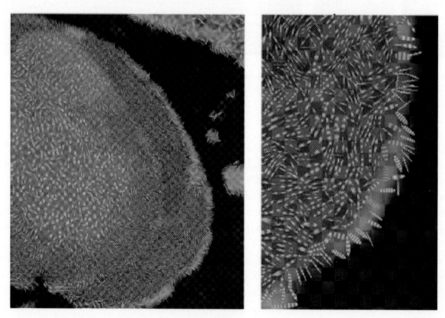

Figure 5.25 A cross section of a mouse spinal column. Seven variables are shown at each location. Part of the image is enlarged on the right. See text for description. *Courtesy of David Laidlaw.*

Figure 5.26   A flow visualization showing six variables relating to fluid flow around a cylinder. *Courtesy of David Laidlaw.*

Rather than attempting to create a simple general technique (like slivers), both figures were hand-crafted in a collaboration between the scientist and the designer. Figure 5.25 shows a cross section of a mouse spinal column. The data has seven values at each location in the image. The image is built up in layers: image intensity, sampling rate determines the grid, elliptical shapes show the in-plane component of principal diffusion and anisotropy, texture on the ellipses shows absolute diffusion rate.

The image in Figure 5.26 is a flow visualization. It displays six variables relating to the flow pattern of a fluid around a cylinder. These values are 2D velocity (two values are mapped to arrow direction and area), vorticity (one value is mapped to color and texture on ellipses), and deformation rate tensor (three values are mapped to shape and orientation of ellipses).

Without specific knowledge of mouse physiology or fluid dynamics, it is impossible to judge the success of these examples. Nevertheless, they provide a vivid commentary on the tradeoffs involved in trying to display high-dimensional multivariate maps. The first point to be made is that none of the preceding three examples (Figures 5.24, 5.25, and 5.26) shows much detail, and there is a good reason for this. We only have one luminance channel, and luminance variation is the only way of displaying detailed information. If we choose to use texture (or any kind of glyph field), we inevitably sacrifice the ability to show detail, because to be clear each glyph element must be displayed using luminance contrast. Larger glyphs mean that less detail can be shown.

There are also tradeoffs when displaying orientation. It may be only possible to display a single orientation clearly at each point in space for the purpose of showing flow patterns. Figure 5.26 suggests that if we need to show differently oriented glyphs in the same region, the glyphs must be widely spaced. This reduces the data density further. Also, Figure 5.26 suggests that the colors of different glyph layers must be very carefully chosen to be dissimilar. This, in turn, severely restricts how color-coding can be used on individual glyphs. In Figure 5.25, each of the elliptical glyphs is textured to display an additional variable. However, the texture striations are at right angles to the ellipse major axes. This camouflages the glyphs, making their orientation more difficult to see. The use of texture will inevitably tend to camouflage glyph shape; if the textures are oriented, the problem will be worse. In general, the more similar the spatial frequencies of the different pattern components, the more likely they are to disrupt one another visually.

The complexity of the design tradeoffs suggests that the problem of creating complex visualizations will be more of a craft than a science for quite some time. The problem is too difficult for automatic assignments of data maps to graphical attributes to be successful. Still, the designer needs to be aware of the perceptual tradeoffs in order to make informed decisions about the best choice of glyph size, shape, and color distribution.

It is also worth pointing out that there are some perceptual dimensions that may be used in addition to color, shape, and texture. In some cases, it is helpful to use stereoscopic depth and motion in displaying multidimensional data. Stereoscopic depth, especially if used with a high-resolution display, can undoubtedly help us perceptually segment data layers. So can motion. Making all of the points in a data layer move coherently, even by a small amount, may make it possible to visually attend to either the static layer or the moving layer (as shown by the possibility of preattentive conjunction search with motion).

Glyphs and Multivariate Discrete Data

In the previous section, we saw how texture could be used to represent continuous map data. In Chapter 4, it was shown that color could be used in a similar way. However, sometimes multivariate *discrete* data is the subject of interest. For example, a marketing specialist may have data for every person in a particular geographical area, including estimates of income, educational level, employment category, and location of residence. The marketer would like to see each person on a map in such a way that the concentrations of individuals with particular sets of attributes can easily be seen. In this way, neighborhoods to be blanketed with flyers might be selected most effectively.

To create a glyph, multiple data attributes are mapped in a systematic way to show the different aspects of the appearance of the graphical object. In the aforementioned marketing example, income might be mapped to the glyph's size, education level to its color, employment category to its shape, and geographic location to the *x,y* location where the glyph is plotted. All the previously discussed results relating to preattentive detection of size, orientation, and color-coding of data apply to the design of glyphs.

Another body of theory that is relevant to glyph design is the theory of integral and separable dimensions, developed by Garner (1974). The kind of multidimensional coding that occurs in the use of glyphs raises questions about the perceptual independence of the display dimensions. Will the color-coding scheme interfere with our perception of glyph size and therefore distort perceived income level? What if we use both color and size to represent a single variable? Will this make the information clearer? The concept of integral vs. separable visual dimensions tells us when one display attribute (e.g., color) will be perceived independently from another (e.g., size). With *integral* display dimensions, two or more attributes of a visual object are perceived holistically and not independently. An example is a rectangular shape, perceived as a holistic combination of the rectangle's width and height. Another is the combination of green light and red light; this is seen holistically as yellow light, and it is difficult to respond independently to the red and green components. With *separable* dimensions, people tend to make separate judgments about each graphical dimension. This is sometimes called *analytic processing*. Thus, if the display dimensions are the diameter of a ball and the color of a ball, they will be processed relatively independently. It is easy to respond independently to ball size and ball color.

Integral and separable dimensions have been determined experimentally in a number of ways. Three experimental paradigms are discussed here. All are related to interactions between pairs of variables. Very little work has been done on interactions among three or more display variables.

Restricted Classification Tasks

In restricted classification tasks, observers are shown sets of three glyphs that are constructed according to the diagram shown in Figure 5.27. Two of the glyphs (A and B) are made the same on one variable. A third glyph (C) is constructed so that it is closer to glyph B in feature space, but this glyph differs from the other two in both of the graphical dimensions. Subjects are asked to group the two glyphs that they think go together best. If the dimensions are integral, A and C are grouped together because they are closest in the feature space. If they are separable, A and B are grouped together because they are identical in one of the dimensions (analytic mode). The clearest example of integral dimensions is color space dimensions. If dimension X is the red—green dimension and dimension Y is the yellow—blue dimension of color space, subjects tend to classify objects (roughly) according to the Euclidean distance between the colors (defined according to one of the uniform color spaces discussed in Chapter 4). Note that even this is not always the case, as the evidence of color categories (also discussed in Chapter 4) shows.

The width and height of an ellipse creates an integral perception of shape. Thus, in Figure 5.28(a), the ellipses B and C appear to be more similar to each other than to the circle A, even though the width of B matches the width of A. If the two dimensions are separable, subjects act in a more analytic manner and react to the fact that two of the objects are actually identical on one of the dimensions. Shape and gray value are separable. Thus, in Figure 5.28(b), either the two gray shapes or the two elliptical shapes will be categorized together. With separable dimensions, it is easy to attend to one dimension or the other.

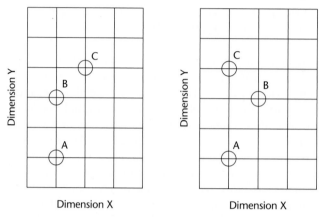

Figure 5.27   When we are considering integral and separable visual dimensions, it is useful to consider a space defined by two display dimensions. One might be size; the other might be color. Or one might be hue and the other might be saturation, both defined in color space.

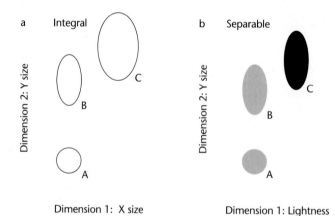

Figure 5.28   (a) The width and height of an ellipse are perceived integrally; therefore, B and C are perceived as more similar. (b) The gray value and the height of an ellipse are perceived as separable; therefore, A and B, which have identical lightness, are perceived as more similar.

Speeded Classification Tasks

Speeded classification tasks tell us how glyphs can visually interfere with each other. In a speeded classification task, subjects are asked to classify visual patterns rapidly according to only one of the visual attributes of a glyph. The other visual attribute can be set up in two different ways: it can be given random values (interference condition), or it can be coded in the same way as the

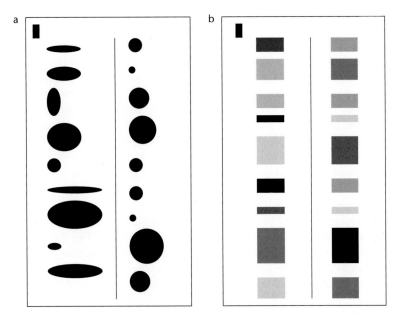

Figure 5.29   Patterns for a speeded classification task. Subjects are required to respond positively only to those glyphs that have the same height as the black bar in the upper-left corner. (a) Integral dimensions. In the first column, a second integral dimension is randomly coded by horizontal size (interference condition). In the second column, width information is redundantly coded with height information. (b) Separable dimension. In the first column, gray information is not correlated with height. In the second column, gray level is a redundant code.

first dimension (redundant coding). If the data dimensions are integral, substantial interference occurs in the first case. With redundant coding, classification is generally speeded for integral dimensions. With separable codes, the results are different. There is little interference from the irrelevant graphical dimension, but there is also little advantage in terms of speeded classification when redundant coding is used. Of course, in some cases, using redundant separable codes may still be desirable. For example, if both color and shape are used for information coding, color-blind individuals will still have access to the information. Figure 5.29 gives examples of the kinds of patterns that are used in experiments.

The lessons to be learned from integral—separable dimension experiments are straightforwardly applied to cases in which each data entity has two attributes. If we want people to respond holistically to a combination of two variables, using integral dimensions will be better. If we want people to respond analytically, making judgments on the basis of one variable or the other, using separable dimensions will be better.

Integral–Separable Dimension Pairs

The preceding analysis has presented integral and separable dimensions as if they were qualitatively distinct. This overstates the case; a continuum of integrality–separability more accurately represents the facts. There is always some interference between different data values presented using different graphical attributes of a single visual object, even between the most separable dimensions. Likewise, the most integral dimensions can be regarded analytically to some extent. We can, for example, perceive the degree of redness and the degree of yellowness of a color, for instance, orange or pink. Indeed, the original experimental evidence for opponent color channels was based on analytic judgments of exactly this type (Hurvich, 1981).

Figure 5.30 provides a list of display dimension pairs arranged on an integral—separable continuum. At the top are the most integral dimensions. At the bottom are the most separable dimensions. Other possible display dimensions are not represented, because of too little evidence for blue and stereoscopic depth. However, it seems likely that stereoscopic depth is quite separable from other dimensions if only two depth layers are involved. The most separable way of coding information, as indicated at the bottom of the list, is to use spatial position to code one of the data dimensions and to use size, shape, or color to code the other. This is exactly what is done in a bar chart in which each bar represents a single value. Figure 5.31 illustrates some of the dimension pairs.

As a theoretical concept, the notion of integral and separable dimensions is undoubtedly simplistic; it lacks mechanism and fails to account for a large number of exceptions and asymmetries that have been discovered experimentally. Eventually, it is to be expected that a more complete body of theory will emerge to account for the ways in which different kinds of visual information are combined. The beauty of the integral—separable distinction lies in its simplicity as a design guideline.

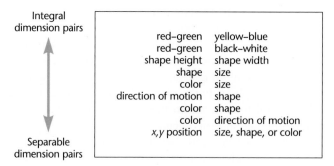

Figure 5.30   This table lists some of the display dimension pairs ranked in order from highly integral to highly separable.

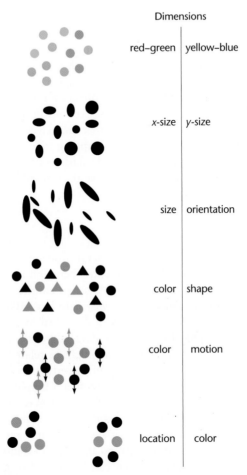

Dimensions

red–green	yellow–blue
x-size	*y*-size
size	orientation
color	shape
color	motion
location	color

Figure 5.31   Examples of glyphs coded according to two display attributes. At the top are more integral coding pairs. At the bottom are more separable coding pairs.

Monotonicity of Visual Attributes

Some visual qualities increase continuously, like size, brightness, or the up direction, and are said to be *monotonic*. Some visual qualities are not monotonic. Orientation is one. It is meaningless to say that one orientation is greater or less than another. The same is true of the phase angle between two oscillating objects. As the phase difference is increased, the objects first appear to move in opposite directions, but as the phase difference continues to increase, they appear to move together again. Phase is cyclic, just as line orientation is cyclic. Hue also lacks a natural order.

Monotonic display variables naturally express relations such as *greater than* or *less than* if they have a direction that we associate with increasing value. For example, in a 3D data space, the up direction is defined by gravity, and using *up* to represent a greater quantity of some variable will be readily interpreted. The axis representing direction *toward* and *away from* the viewpoint is similarly well defined, but the left and right directions do not have as clear a value. In the west, we read left to right but this is learned. Other languages, such as Arabic, have right-to-left ordering. For representing simple quantity, a mapping to any of the following attributes will be effective: size, lightness (on a dark background), darkness (on a light background), vividness (higher saturation) of color, or vertical height above the ground plane. For each of these, an inverse mapping will lead to confusion.

Multidimensional Discrete Data

This is a good place to step back and look at the general problem of multivariate discrete data display in light of the concepts that have been presented here and in the previous chapter. It is worth restating this problem. We are provided with a set of entities, each of which has values on a number of attribute dimensions. For example, we might have 1000 beetles, each measured on 30 anatomical characteristics, or 500 stocks, each described by 20 financial variables. The reason for displaying such data graphically is often for data exploration. We hope to find meaning in the diversity. In the case of the beetles, the meaning might be related to their ecological niche. In the case of the stocks, the meaning is likely to lie in opportunities for profit.

If we decide to use a glyph display, each entity becomes a graphical object and data attributes are mapped to graphical attributes of each glyph. The problem is one of mapping data dimension to the graphical attributes of the glyph. The work on preattentive processing, early visual processing, and integral and separable dimensions suggests that a rather limited set of visual attributes is available to us if we want to understand the values rapidly. Figure 5.32 is a list of the most useful low-level graphical attributes that can be applied to glyph design, with a few summary comments about the number of dimensions available.

Many of these display dimensions are not independent of one another. To display texture, we must use at least one color dimension to make the texture visible. Blink coding will certainly interfere with motion coding. Overall, we will probably be fortunate to display eight dimensional data clearly, using color, shape, spatial position, and motion to create the most differentiated set possible.

There is also the issue of how many resolvable steps are available in each dimension. The number here is also small. When we require rapid preattentive processing, no more than eight colors are available. The number of orientation steps that we can easily distinguish is probably about four. The number of size steps that we can easily distinguish is no more than four, and the values for the other data dimensions are also in the single-digit range. It is reasonable, therefore, to propose that we can represent about 2 bits of information for each of the eight

Visual variable	Dimensionality	Comment
Spatial position of glyph	3 dimensions: *X, Y, Z.*	
Color of glyph	3 dimensions: defined by color opponent theory.	Luminance contrast is needed to specify all other graphical attributes.
Shape	2–3? Dimensions unknown.	The dimensions of shape that can be rapidly processed are unknown. However, evidence suggests that size and degree of elongation are two primary ones.
Orientation	3 dimensions: corresponding to orientation about each of the primary axes.	Orientation is not independent of shape. One object can have rotation symmetry with another.
Surface texture	3 dimensions: orientation, size, and contrast.	Not independent of shape or orientation. Uses up one color dimension.
Motion coding	2–3? Dimensions largely unknown, but phase may be useful.	
Blink coding: The glyph blinks on and off at some rate.	1 dimension.	Motion and blink coding are highly interdependent.

Figure 5.32   Graphical attributes that may be used in glyph design.

graphical dimensions. If the dimensions were truly independent, this would yield 16 displayable bits per glyph (64,000 values). Unfortunately, conjunctions are generally not preattentive. If we allow no conjunction searching, we are left with four alternatives on each of eight dimensions, yielding only 32 rapidly distinguishable alternatives, a far smaller number. Anyone who has tried to design a set of easily distinguishable glyphs will recognize this number to be more plausible.

Stars, Whiskers, and Other Glyphs

There is a family of glyph designs for multidimensional discrete data displays that is interesting to analyze from a perception perspective. In the whisker plot, each data value is represented by a line segment radiating out from a central point, as shown in Figure 5.33(a). The length of the line segment denotes the value of the corresponding data attribute.

A variant of the whisker plot is the star plot (Chambers et al., 1983). This is the same as the whisker plot but with the ends of the lines connected, as in Figure 5.33(b). In general, it is better to use a very small number of orientations, perhaps only three, for really rapid classification of glyphs, as shown in Figure 5.34(b). It may be possible to increase the number of rapidly distinguishable orientations by inverting the luminance polarity of half of the bars, as in Figure 5.34(a). Color and position in space can be used to display other data dimensions. If we map

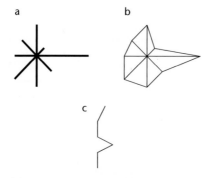

Figure 5.33   Three glyph designs: (a) The whisker or fan plot. (b) A star plot. (c) An Exvis stick icon.

Figure 5.34   (a) It may be possible to increase the number of distinct orientations in a glyph display by changing the luminance polarity of half the line segments. (b) Changing the widths as well as the lengths of segments may also be effective.

three data dimensions to the position of each glyph and two dimensions to the color of the glyph, we can represent eight-dimensional data clearly and effectively. It may also be useful to change the amount of "energy" in glyph segments by altering the line width as well as the length of the line.

When large numbers of glyphs are present in a display, the glyph field becomes a texture field and the theory discussed earlier will apply.

Conclusion

This chapter has provided an introduction to the early stages of vision, in which literally billions of neurons act in parallel to extract elementary aspects of form, color, texture, motion, and stereoscopic depth. The fact that this processing is done for each point of the visual field means that objects differentiated in terms of these simple low-level features pop out and can be noticed easily. Understanding such preattentive processes is the key to designing elements of displays that must be rapidly attended to. Making an icon or a symbol significantly different from its surroundings on one of the preattentive dimensions ensures that it can be detected by a viewer without effort and at high speed.

The lessons from this chapter have to do with fundamental tradeoffs in design choices about whether to use color, shape, texture, or motion to display a particular set of variables. Here is a short summary of the key lessons we have learned from low-level vision:

- Low-level channels tell us about coding dimensions. We can usefully consider color, elements of form (orientation, size), position, simple motion, and stereoscopic depth as separate channels.

- For glyphs to be seen rapidly, they must stand out clearly from all other objects in their near vicinity on at least one coding dimension. In a display of large symbols, a small symbol will stand out. In a display of blue, green and gray symbols or a red symbol will stand out.

- There is more visual interference within channels. The basic rule is that, in terms of low-level properties, like interferes with like. If we have a set of small symbols on a textured background, a texture with a grain size similar to that of the symbols will make them hard to see.

- There is more separability between channels. If we wish to be able to read data values from different data dimensions, each of these values should be mapped to a different data dimension. Mapping one variable to color and another to glyph orientation will make them independently readable. If we map one variable to X-direction size and another to Y-direction size, they will be read more holistically. If we have a set of symbols that are hard to see because they are on a textured background, they can be made to stand out by using another coding channel; having the symbols oscillate will also make them distinct.

Unfortunately, there are no universal rules for mapping multiattribute data to glyphs. The simple techniques, such as star plots, do not allow us to interpret the data rapidly, because we have mapped too much information to line segments having similar orientations that interfere visually with each other. The way to differentiate variables readily is to employ more perceptual channels. Unfortunately, although this solves one problem, it creates another. We have to decide which variable to map to color, to shape, and to texture, and we have to worry about which mappings will be most intuitive for the intended audience. These are difficult design decisions.

In this chapter, we have dealt mainly with how attention is directed within a single fixation of the eye. Attention is also central in controlling eye movements and is a fundamental concept in the processes of visual thinking. We revisit the topic of attention in Chapter 11, which explores how we solve problems through visual thinking.

We have arrived at a transition point in this book. To this point, we have discussed mostly the massively parallel processing of low-level features of early vision and the elementary coding of information. We now turn our attention to the way the brain extracts a few complex objects from elemental information and subjects them to sophisticated analysis. We will also discuss how the brain finds elaborate patterns in data, and eventually we will look at the ways in which information should be integrated and displayed for solving complex problems.

CHAPTER 6

Static and Moving Patterns

Data mining is about finding patterns that were previously unknown or that depart from the norm. The stock-market analyst looks for any pattern of variables that may predict a future change in price or earnings. The marketing analyst is interested in perceiving trends and patterns in a customer database. When we look for patterns, we are making visual queries that are key to visual thinking. Sometimes the queries are vague; we are on the lookout for a variety of structures in the data. Sometimes they are precise, as when we look for a positive trend in a graph. In data exploration, seeing a pattern can often lead to a key insight, and this is the most compelling reason for visualization.

What does it take for us to see a group? How can 2D space be divided into perceptually distinct regions? Under what conditions are two patterns recognized as similar? What constitutes a visual connection between objects? These are some of the perceptual questions addressed in this chapter. The answers are central to visualization, because most data displays are two-dimensional and pattern perception deals with the extraction of structure from 2D space.

Consider again our three-stage model of perception (illustrated in Figure 6.1). At the early stages of feature abstraction, the visual image is analyzed in terms of primitive elements of form, motion, color, and stereoscopic depth. At the next 2D pattern perception stage, the contours are discovered and the visual world is segmented into distinct regions, based on texture, color, motion, and contour. Next, the structures of objects and scenes are discovered, using information about the connections between component parts, shape-from-shading information, and so on. Pattern perception can be thought of as a set of mostly 2D processes occurring between feature analysis and full object perception, although aspects of 3D space perception, such as stereoscopic depth and structure-from-motion, can be considered particular kinds of pattern perception. Finally, objects and significant patterns are pulled out by attentional processes to meet the needs of the task at hand.

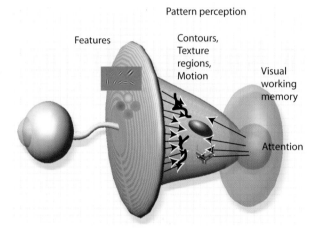

Pattern perception

Features

Contours,
Texture
regions,
Motion

Visual
working
memory

Attention

Figure 6.1   Pattern perception forms a middle ground where the bottom-up processes of feature processing meet the requirements of active attention.

There are radical changes in the kinds of processing that occur at the different stages. In the early stages, massively parallel processing of the entire image occurs. This drives perception from the bottom up. But object and visual search recognition is driven from the top down through active attention, meeting the requirements of visual thinking. At the top level, only three to five objects (or patterns) are held in visual working memory. Pattern perception is the flexible middle ground where objects are extracted from patterns of features. Active processes of attention reach down into the pattern space to keep track of those objects and to analyze them for particular tasks; the essentially bottom-up processing of feature primitives meets the top-down processes of cognitive perception. Rensink (2000) calls the middle ground a "proto-object flux."

Understanding pattern perception provides abstract design rules that can tell us much about how we should organize data so that important structures will be perceived. If we can map information structures to readily perceived patterns, then those structures will be more easily interpreted.

Learning is important in the pattern mechanism. It occurs in the short term through visual priming and in the long term as a kind of skill learning. *Priming* refers to the fact that once we have seen a pattern, it becomes much easier to identify on subsequent appearance. Long-term learning of patterns occurs over hundreds or thousands of trials, but some patterns are much easier to learn than others (Fine and Jacobs, 2002). In this chapter, we consider 2D-pattern perception and what this tells us about information display. In the next two chapters, we consider 3D-space perception, much of which is a form of advanced pattern perception.

Gestalt Laws

The first serious attempt to understand pattern perception was undertaken by a group of German psychologists who, in 1912, founded what is known as the Gestalt school of psychology. The group consisted principally of Max Westheimer, Kurt Koffka, and Wolfgang Kohler (see Koffka, 1935, for an original text). The word *gestalt* simply means *pattern* in German. The work of the Gestalt psychologists is still valued today because they provided a clear description of many basic perceptual phenomena. They produced a set of *Gestalt laws* of pattern perception. These are robust rules that describe the way we see patterns in visual displays, and although the neural mechanisms proposed by these researchers to explain the laws have not withstood the test of time, the laws themselves have proved to be of enduring value. The Gestalt laws easily translate into a set of design principles for information displays. Eight Gestalt laws are discussed here: proximity, similarity, connectedness, continuity, symmetry, closure, relative size, and common fate (the last concerns motion perception and appears later in the chapter).

Proximity

Spatial proximity is a powerful perceptual organizing principle and one of the most useful in design. Things that are close together are perceptually grouped together. Figure 6.2 shows two arrays of dots that illustrate the proximity principle. Only a small change in spacing causes us to change what is perceived from a set of rows, in Figure 6.2(a), to a set of columns, in Figure 6.2(b). In Figure 6.2(c), the existence of two groups is perceptually inescapable. Proximity is not the only factor in predicting perceived groups. In Figure 6.3, the dot labeled *x* is perceived to be part of cluster a rather than cluster b, even though it is as close to the other points in cluster b

Figure 6.2   Spatial proximity is a powerful cue for perceptual organization. A matrix of dots is perceived as rows on the left (a) and columns on the right (b). In (c), because of proximity relationships, we perceive two groupings of dots.

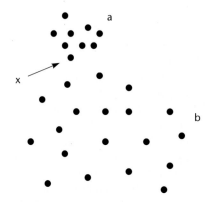

Figure 6.3   The principle of spatial concentration. The dot labeled *x* is perceived as part of group a rather than group b.

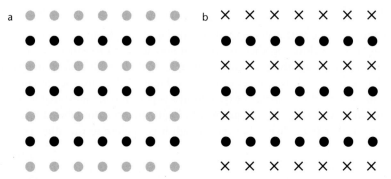

Figure 6.4   According to the Gestalt psychologists, similarity between the elements in alternate rows causes the row percept to dominate.

as they are to each other. Slocum (1983) called this the *spatial concentration principle*. According to this principle, we perceptually group regions of similar element density.

The application of the proximity law in display design is straightforward: the simplest and most powerful way to emphasize the relationships between different data entities is to place them in proximity in a display.

Similarity

The shapes of individual pattern elements can also determine how they are grouped. Similar elements tend to be grouped together. In both Figure 6.4(a) and (b), the similarity of the elements causes us to see the rows most clearly.

a   b

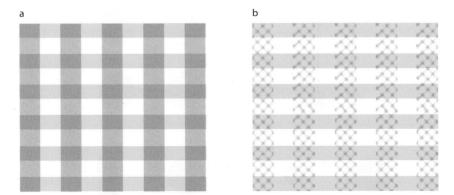

Figure 6.5   (a) Integral dimensions are used to delineate rows and columns. (b) When separable dimensions (color and texture) are used, it is easier to attend separately to either the rows or the columns.

We can also apply lessons from the concept of integral and separable dimensions that was discussed in Chapter 5. Figure 6.5 shows two different ways of visually separating row and column information. In 6.5(a), integral color and gray-scale coding is used. In Figure 6.5(b), green color is used to delineate rows and texture is used to delineate columns. Color and texture are separable dimensions, and the result is a pattern that can be visually segmented either by rows or by columns. This technique can be useful if we are designing so that users can easily attend to either one pattern or the other.

Connectedness

Palmer and Rock (1994) argue that connectedness is a fundamental Gestalt organizing principle that the Gestalt psychologists overlooked. The demonstrations in Figure 6.6 show that connectedness can be a more powerful grouping principle than proximity, color, size, or shape. Connecting different graphical objects by lines is a very powerful way of expressing that there is some relationship between them. Indeed, this is fundamental to the node–link diagram, one of the most common methods of representing relationships between concepts.

Continuity

The Gestalt principle of continuity states that we are more likely to construct visual entities out of visual elements that are smooth and continuous, rather than ones that contain abrupt changes in direction. (See Figure 6.7.)

The principle of good continuity can be applied to the problem of drawing diagrams consisting of networks of nodes and the links between them. It should be easier to identify the sources and destinations of connecting lines if they are smooth and continuous. This point is illustrated in Figure 6.8.

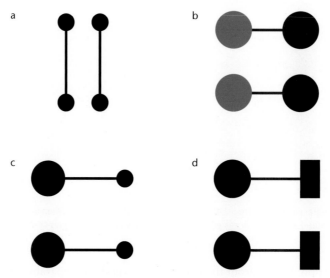

Figure 6.6   Connectedness is a powerful grouping principle that is stronger than (a) proximity, (b) color, (c) size, or (d) shape.

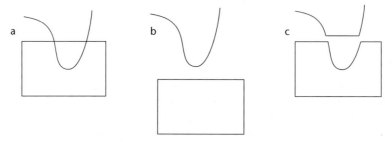

Figure 6.7   The pattern on the left (a) is perceived as a curved line overlapping a rectangle (b) rather than as the more angular components shown in (c).

Symmetry

Symmetry can provide a powerful organizing principle. Figures 6.9 and 6.10 provide two examples. The symmetrically arranged pairs of lines in Figure 6.9 are perceived much more strongly as forming a visual whole than the pair of parallel lines. In Figure 6.10(a), symmetry may be the reason why the cross shape is perceived, as opposed to shapes in 6.10(b), even though the second option is not more complicated. A possible application of symmetry is in tasks in which data analysts are looking for similarities between two different sets of time-series data. It may be easier

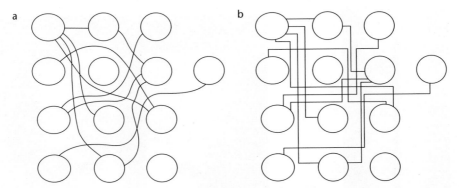

Figure 6.8   In (a), smooth continuous contours are used to connect the elements, whereas in (b), lines with abrupt changes in direction are used. It is much easier to perceive connections when contours connect smoothly.

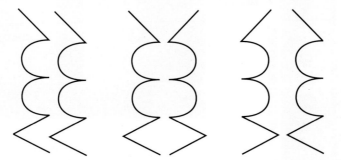

Figure 6.9   The pattern on the left consists of two identical parallel contours. In each of the other two patterns, one of the contours has been reflected about a vertical axis, producing bilateral symmetry. The result is a much stronger sense of a holistic figure.

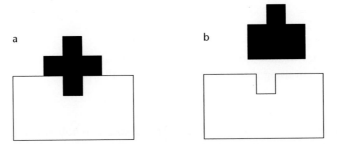

Figure 6.10   We interpret pattern (a) as a cross in front of a rectangle. An alternative, two objects shown in (b) are not perceived, even though the black shape behind the white shape would be an equally simple interpretation. The cross on the rectangle interpretation has greater symmetry (about horizontal axes) for both of the components.

Figure 6.11 An application designed to allow users to recognize similar patterns in different time-series plots. The data represents a sequence of measurements made on deep ocean drilling cores. Two subsets of the extended sequences are shown on the right.

to perceive similarities if these time series are arranged using vertical symmetry, as shown in Figure 6.11, rather than using the more conventional parallel plots.

Closure

A closed contour tends to be seen as an object. The Gestalt psychologists argued that there is a perceptual tendency to close contours that have gaps in them. This can help explain why we see Figure 6.12(a) as a complete circle and a rectangle rather than as a circle with a gap in it as in Figure 6.12(b).

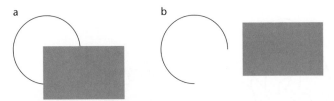

Figure 6.12 The Gestalt principle of closure holds that neural mechanisms operate to find perceptual solutions involving closed contours. Hence in (a), we see a circle behind a rectangle, not a broken ring as in (b).

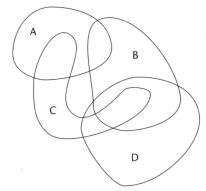

Figure 6.13 An Euler diagram. This diagram tells us (among other things) that entities can simultaneously be members of sets A and C but not of A, B, and C. Also, anything that is a member of both B and C is also a member of D. These rather difficult concepts are clearly expressed and understood by means of closed contours.

Wherever a closed contour is seen, there is a very strong perceptual tendency to divide regions of space into "inside" or "outside" the contour. A region enclosed by a contour becomes a *common region* in the terminology of Palmer (1992). He showed common region to be a much stronger organizing principle than simple proximity. This, presumably, is the reason why Venn-Euler diagrams are such a powerful device for displaying the interrelationships among sets of data. In an Euler diagram, we interpret the region inside a closed contour as defining a set of elements. Multiple closed contours are used to delineate the overlapping relationships among different sets. A Venn diagram is a more restricted form of Euler diagram containing all possible regions of overlap. The two most important perceptual factors in this kind of diagram are closure and continuity.

A fairly complex structure of overlapping sets is illustrated in Figure 6.13, using an Euler diagram. This kind of diagram is almost always used in teaching introductory set theory, and this in itself is evidence for its effectiveness. Students easily understand the diagrams, and they

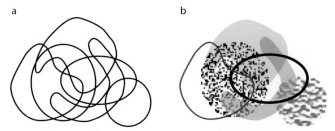

Figure 6.14   An Euler diagram enhanced using texture and color can convey a more complex set of relations than a conventional Euler diagram using only closed contour.

can transfer this understanding to the more difficult formal notation. Stenning and Oberlander (1994) theorize that the ease with which Euler diagrams can be understood results specifically from the fact that they have limited expressive power, unlike fully abstract formal notation.

Although simple contours are generally used in Euler diagrams to show set membership, we can effectively define regions using color and texture as well, as discussed in Chapters 4 and 5. Indeed, by using both we should be able to create Euler diagrams that are considerably more complex and still readily understandable. Figure 6.14 illustrates.

Closed contours are extremely important in segmenting the monitor screen in windows-based interfaces. The rectangular overlapping boxes provide a strong segmentation cue, dividing the display into different regions. In addition, rectangular frames provide frames of reference: the position of every object within the frame tends to be judged relative to the enclosing frame. (See Figure 6.15.)

Relative Size

In general, smaller components of a pattern tend to be perceived as objects. In Figure 6.16, a black propeller is seen on a white background, as opposed to the white areas being perceived as objects.

Figure and Ground

Gestalt psychologists were also interested in what they called *figure–ground* effects. A *figure* is something objectlike that is perceived as being in the foreground. The *ground* is whatever lies behind the figure. The perception of figure as opposed to ground can be thought of as the fundamental perceptual act of identifying objects. All the Gestalt laws contribute to creating a figure, along with other factors that the Gestalt psychologists did not consider, such as texture segmentation (see Chapter 5). Closed contour, symmetry, and the surrounding white area all con-

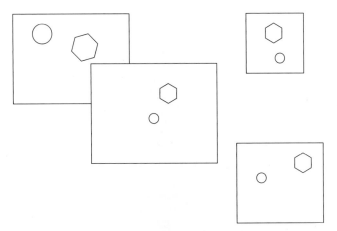

Figure 6.15 Closed rectangular contours strongly segment the visual field. They also provide reference frames. Both the positions and the sizes of enclosed objects are, to some extent, interpreted with respect to the surrounding frame.

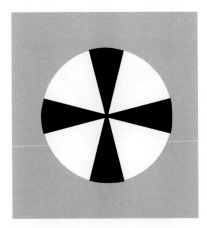

Figure 6.16 The black areas are smaller, and therefore more likely to be perceived as an object. It is also easier to perceive patterns that are oriented horizontally and vertically as objects.

tribute to the perception of the shape in Figure 6.17 as figure, as opposed to a cut-out hole, for example.

Figure 6.18 shows the classic Rubin's Vase figure, in which it is possible to perceive either two faces, nose to nose, or a black vase centered in the display. The fact that the two percepts tend to alternate suggests that competing active processes may be involved in trying to construct figures from the pattern.

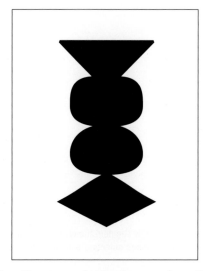

Figure 6.17   Symmetry, surrounding white space, and a closed contour all contribute to the strong sense that this shape is figure, rather than ground.

Figure 6.18   Rubin's Vase. The cues for figure and ground are roughly equally balanced, resulting in a bistable percept of either two faces or a vase.

More on Contours

A contour is a continuous perceived boundary between regions of a visual image. A contour can be defined by a line, by a boundary between regions of different color, by stereoscopic depth, by motion patterns, or by texture. Contours can even be perceived where there are none. Figure 6.19 illustrates an *illusory contour*; a ghostly boundary of a blobby shape is seen even where

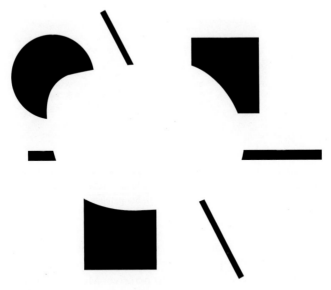

Figure 6.19   Illusory contour.

none is physically present. There is extensive literature on illusory contours (see Kanizsa, 1976, for an early review).

Because the process that leads to the identification of contours is seen as fundamental to object perception, contour detection has received considerable attention from vision researchers. There are a number of detailed neurophysiological models designed to explain how contours can be extracted from the visual image, based on what is known about early visual processing. See Marr (1982), for example.

Higher-order neurophysiological mechanisms of contour perception are not well understood. However, one result is intriguing. Gray et al. (1989) found that cells with collinear receptive fields tend to fire in synchrony. Thus, we do not need to propose higher-order feature detectors, responding to more and more complex curves, to understand the neural encoding of contour information. Instead, it may be that groups of cells firing in synchrony is the way that the brain holds related pattern elements in mind. Theorists have suggested a fast enabling link, a kind of rapid feedback system, to achieve the firing of cells in synchrony. For a review, see Singer and Gray (1995).

Fortunately, because a theoretical understanding is only just emerging, the exact mechanisms involved in contour detection are less relevant to the purpose of designing visualizations than are the circumstances under which we perceive contours. A set of experiments by Field et al. (1993) places the Gestalt notion of *good continuation* on a firmer scientific basis. In these experiments, subjects had to detect the presence of a continuous path in a field of 256 randomly oriented Gabor patches (see Chapter 5 for a discussion of Gabor functions). The setup is illustrated

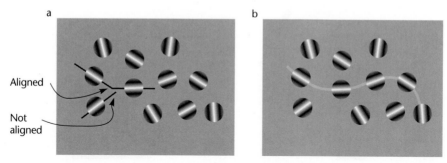

Figure 6.20   A schematic diagram illustrating the experiments conducted by Field et al. (1993). If the elements were aligned as shown in (a) so that a smooth curve could be drawn through some of them, the curve shown in (b) was perceived. In the actual experiments, Gabor patches were used.

schematically in Figure 6.20. The results show that subjects were very good at perceiving a smooth path through a sequence of patches. As one might expect, continuity between Gabor patches oriented in straight lines was the easiest to perceive. More interesting, even quite wiggly paths were readily seen if the Gabor elements were aligned as shown in Figure 6.20(b).

There are direct applications of this result in displaying vector field data. A common technique is to create a regular grid of oriented arrows, such as the one shown in Figure 6.21. When the arrows are displaced so that smooth contours can be drawn between them, the flow pattern is much easier to see.

Perceiving Direction: Representing Vector Fields

The perception of contour leads us naturally to the perceptual problem of representing vector fields. This problem can be broken down into two components: the representation of orientation and the representation of magnitude. Some techniques display one component but not both.

Instead of using little arrows, one obvious and effective way of representing vector fields is through the use of continuous contours; a number of effective algorithms exist for this purpose. Figure 6.22 shows an example from Turk and Banks (1996). This effectively illustrates the direction of the vector field, although it is ambiguous in the sense that for a given contour there can be two directions of flow. Conventional arrowheads can be added, as in Figure 6.21, but the result is visual clutter. In addition, in Figure 6.22 the magnitudes of the vectors are given by line density and inverse line width, and this is not easy to read.

An interesting way to resolve the flow direction ambiguity is provided in a seventeenth-century vector field map of North Atlantic wind patterns by Edmund Halley (discussed in Tufte, 1983). Halley's elegant pen strokes, illustrated in Figure 6.23, are shaped like long, narrow air-foils oriented to the flow, with the wind direction given by the blunt end. Interestingly, Halley also arranges his strokes along streamlines. We verified experimentally that strokes like Halley's are unambiguously interpreted with regard to direction (Fowler and Ware, 1989).

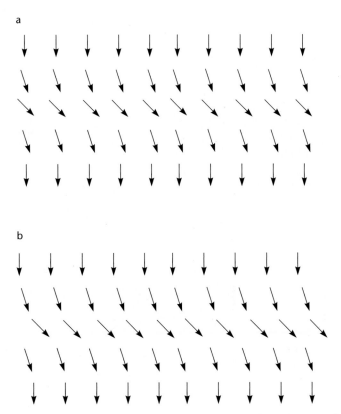

Figure 6.21 The results of Field et al. (1993) suggest that vector fields should be easier to perceive if smooth contours can be drawn through the arrows. (a) A regular grid is used to determine arrow layout. (b) The arrows have been shifted so that smooth contours can be drawn through the arrows. As theory predicts, the latter is more effective.

We also developed a new method for creating an unambiguous sense of vector field direction that involves varying the color along the length of a stroke. This is illustrated in Figure 6.24. There was a strong interaction between the direction of color change and the background color. If one end of the stroke was given the background color, the stroke direction was perceived to be in the direction of color change away from the background color. In our experiments, the impression of direction produced by color change completely dominated that given by shape.

Comparing 2D Flow Visualization Techniques

Laidlaw et al. (2001) carried out an experimental comparison of the six different flow visualization methods illustrated in Figure 6.25 and briefly described as follows.

Figure 6.22   Vector field streamlines are an effective way to represent vector field or flow field data. However, the direction is ambiguous and the magnitude is not clearly expressed (Turk and Banks, 1996).

Figure 6.23   Drawing in a style based on the pen strokes used by Edmund Halley (1696), discussed in Tufte (1983), to represent the trade winds of the North Atlantic. Halley described the wind direction as being given by "the sharp end of each little stroak pointing out that part of the horizon, from whence the wind continually comes."

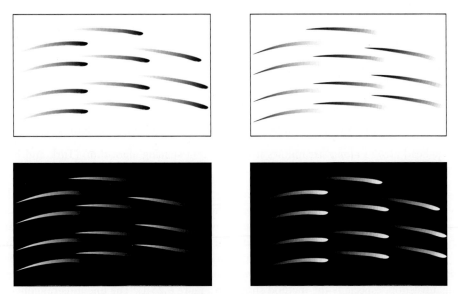

Figure 6.24   Vector direction can be unambiguously given by means of color change relative to the background.

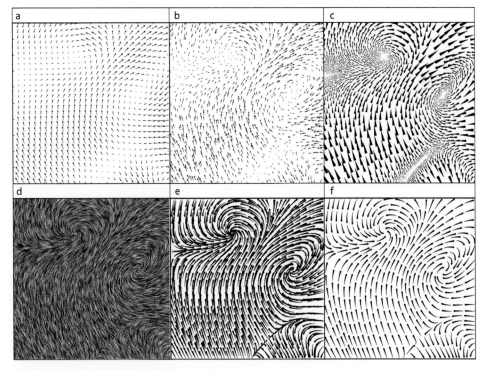

Figure 6.25   Six different flow visualization techniques evaluated by Laidlaw et al., 2001. *Used by permission.*

(a) Arrows on a regular grid. Fixed length.

(b) Arrows on a jittered grid to reduce perceptual aliasing effects. Fixed length.

(c) Triangle icons. Icon size proportional to field strength density inversely related to icon size (Kirby et al., 1999).

(d) Line integral convolution (Cabral and Leedom, 1993).

(e) Large-head arrows along a streamline using a regular grid (Turk and Banks, 1996).

(f) Large-head arrows along streamlines using constant spacing algorithm. (Turk and Banks, 1996).

In order to evaluate any visualization, it is necessary to specify a set of tasks. Laidlaw et al. (2001) had subjects identify critical points as one task. These are points in a vector or flow field where the vectors have zero magnitude. The results showed the arrow-based methods illustrated in Figure 6.25(a) and (b) to be the least effective for identifying the locations of these points. A second task involved perceiving advection trajectories. An *advection trajectory* is the path taken by a particle dropped in a flow. The streamline methods of Turk and Banks proved best for showing advection, especially the method shown in Figure 6.25(f). The line integral convolution method, shown in Figure 6.25(d), was by far the worst for advection, probably because it does not unambiguously identify direction.

Although the study done by Laidlaw et al. (2001) is the first serious comparative evaluation of the effectiveness of vector field visualization methods, it is by no means exhaustive. There are alternative visualizations, and those shown have many possible variations: longer and shorter line segments, color variations, and so on. In addition, the tasks studied by Laidlaw et al. do not include all of the important visualization tasks that are likely to be carried out with flow visualizations. Here is a more complete list:

- Identifying the location and nature of critical points

- Judging an advection trajectory

- Perceiving patterns of high and low velocity

- Perceiving patterns of high and low vorticity (sometimes called *curl*)

- Perceiving patterns of high and low turbulence

Both the kinds and the scale of patterns that are important will vary from one application to another; small-scale detailed patterns, such as eddies, will be important to one researcher, whereas large-scale patterns will interest another.

The problem of optimizing flow display may not be quite so complex and multifaceted as it would first seem. If we ignore the diverse algorithms and think of the problem in purely visual terms, then the various display methods illustrated in Figures 6.22 through 6.25 have many characteristics in common. They all consist principally of contours oriented in the flow direction, although these contours have different characteristics in terms of length, width, and shape. The line integral convolution method illustrated in Figure 6.25(d) produces a very different-looking, blurry result; however, something similar could be computed using blurred contours. Contours that vary in shape and gray value along their lengths could be expressed with two or three parameters. The different degrees of randomness in the placement of contours could be parameterized. Thus, we might consider the various 2D flow visualization methods as part of a family of related methods—different kinds of flow oriented contours. Considered in this way, the display problem becomes one of optimizing the various parameters to reveal important aspects of the data for a particular set of tasks and not so much a problem of developing new algorithms.

Perception of Transparency: Overlapping Data

In many visualization problems, it is desirable to present data in a layered form. This is especially common in geographic information systems (GISs). Sometimes, a useful technique is to present one layer of data as if it were a transparent layer over another. However, there are many perceptual pitfalls in doing this. The contents of the different layers will always interfere with each other to some extent, and sometimes the two layers will fuse perceptually so that it is not possible to determine to which layer a given object belongs.

In simple displays, as in Figure 6.26(a), the two main determinants of perceived transparency are good continuity (Beck and Ivry, 1988) and the ratio of colors or gray values in the different pattern elements. A reasonably robust rule for transparency to be perceived is $x < y < z$ or $x > y > z$ or $y < z < w$ or $y > z > w$, where x, y, z, and w refer to gray values arranged in the pattern shown in Figure 6.26(b) (Masin, 1997). Readers who are interested in perceptual rules of transparency should consult Metelli (1974).

Another way to represent layers of data is to show each layer as a see-through texture or screen pattern (Figure 6.27). Watanabe and Cavanaugh (1996) explored the conditions under which people perceive two distinct overlapping layers, as opposed to a single fused composite texture. They called the effect *laciness*. In Figure 6.27(a) and (b), two different overlapping rectangles are clearly seen, but in (c), only a single textured patch is perceived. In (d), the percept is bistable. Sometimes it looks like two overlapping squares containing patterns of "–" elements; sometimes a central square containing a pattern of "+" elements seems to stand out as a distinct region.

In general, when we present layered data, we can expect the basic rules of perceptual interference, discussed in Chapter 5, to apply. Similar patterns interfere with one another. Graphical patterns that are similar in terms of color, spatial frequency, motion, and so on, tend to interfere more with one another than do those with dissimilar components.

One possible application of transparency in user interfaces is to make pop-up menus transparent so that they do not interfere with information located behind them. Harrison and Vincente (1996) investigated the interference between background patterns and foreground trans-

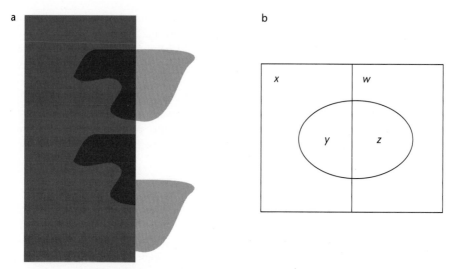

Figure 6.26   In (a), transparency is perceived only when good continuity is present and when the correct relationship of the colors is present. See text for an explanation of (b).

parent menus. They found that it took longer to read from the menu with text or wireframe drawings in the background than with continuously shaded images in the background. This is exactly what would be expected from an interference model. Because a continuously shaded image lacks the high-frequency detail of a wireframe image or text, there will be less interference between the two. The advantages of transparent layered displays must be weighed against the perceptual interference between the layers. For the designer to minimize visual interference, layers must be maximally separated in the different visual channels. Color, texture, motion, and stereoscopic depth channels can all be used in any combination, depending on the design requirements. The more channels used, the better the separation will be.

Pattern Learning

If pattern perception is, as claimed, fundamental to extraction of meaning from visualizations, then an important question arises. Can we learn to see patterns better? Artists talk about seeing things that the rest of us cannot see, and ace detectives presumably spot visual clues that are invisible to the beat officer.

What is the scientific evidence that people can learn to see patterns better? The results are mixed. There have been some studies of pattern learning where almost no learning occurred. An often-cited example is the visual search for the simple conjunction of features such as color and shape (Treisman and Gelade, 1980). But other studies have found learning for certain patterns (Logan, 1994). A plausible explanation is that pattern learning occurs least for simple, basic

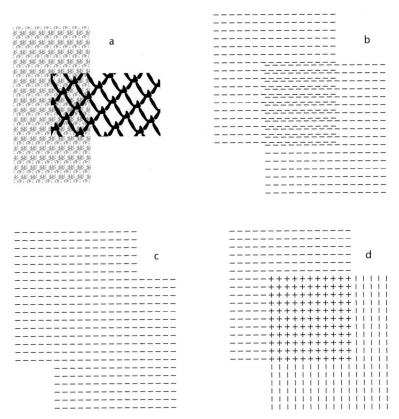

Figure 6.27   Watanabe and Cavanaugh (1996) called the texture equivalent of transparency *laciness*. This figure is based on their work.

patterns processed early in the visual system, and most for complex, unfamiliar patterns processed late in the visual system.

Fine and Jacobs (2002) reviewed 16 different pattern-learning experiments and found very different amounts of learning. The studies they looked at all contained large numbers of trials (in which a subject would attempt to see a particular pattern in a display) distributed over several days. They found that for simple pattern perception tasks, such as the ability to resolve a grating pattern like that shown in Figure 6.28(a), almost no learning occurred. This task depends on early-stage visual processing, for which the neural machinery is consolidated in the first few months of life. In tasks involving patterns of intermediate complexity, some learning does occur. For example, seeing spatial frequency differences within a pattern such as that shown in Figure 6.28(b) can be learned (Fine and Jacobs, 2000). This is a "plaid" pattern constructed by summing a variety of the sinusoidal gratings. Processing of such patterns is thought to occur

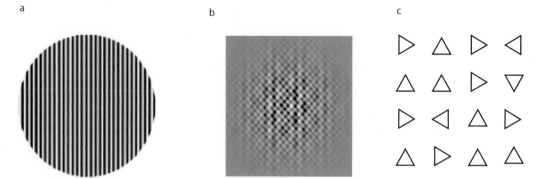

Figure 6.28   Three patterns used in perceptual learning studies.

mostly at an intermediate stage of the visual system. The most learning was found in higher-level pattern tasks, such as detecting the downward pointing triangles in Figure 6.28(c) (Sigman and Gilbert, 2000).

Another factor that affects learning is the degree to which a particular pattern is already familiar. We would not expect much change in a subject's ability to identify letters of the alphabet in a short experiment, because most people have already been exposed to millions of alphabetic characters. Rapid learning can only be expected for patterns that are unfamiliar. The change in rate of learning over time is captured by the *power law of practice*, which has the following form:

$$\log(T_n) = C - \alpha \log(n) \tag{6.1}$$

This law states that log of the time T_n to respond on the nth trial is inversely proportional to the log of the number of trials. The constant C is the time taken on the first trial (or block of trials).

The power law of practice is usually applied to manual skill learning, but it has also been shown to apply to the perception of complex patterns. Kolers (1975) found that a power law applied to the task of learning to read inverted text. His results are illustrated in Figure 6.29. Initially, it took subjects about 15 minutes to read a single inverted page, but when over 100 pages had been read, the time was reduced to 2 minutes. Although Figure 6.29 shows a straight-line relationship between practice and learning, this is only because of the logarithmic transformation of the data. The relationship is actually very nonlinear. Consider a hypothetical task where people improve by 30% from the first day's practice to the second day. Doubling the amount of practice has resulted in a 30% gain. According to the power law, someone with 10 years of experience at the same task will take a further 10 years to improve by 30%. In other words, practice yields decreasing gains over time.

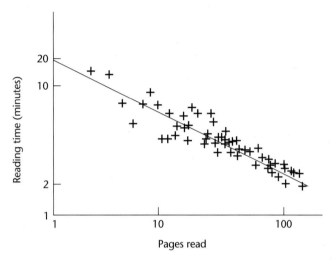

Figure 6.29   The time to read a page of inverted text is plotted against the number of pages read. Both axes have logarithmic spacing. Data replotted from Newell and Rosenbloom (1981).

In addition to long-term pattern-learning skills, there are also priming effects that are much more transient. Whether these constitute learning is still the subject of debate. *Priming* refers to the phenomenon that once a particular pattern has been recognized, it will be much easier to identify in the next few minutes or even hours. This is usually thought of as a kind of heightened receptivity within the visual system, but some theorists consider it to be visual learning. In either case, once a neural pathway has been activated, its future activation becomes facilitated. For a modern theory of perceptual priming based on neural mechanisms, see Huber and O'Reilly (2003).

What are the implications of these findings for visualization? One is that people can learn pattern-detection skills, although the ease of gaining these skills will depend on the specific nature of the patterns involved. Experts do indeed have special expertise. The radiologist interpreting an X-ray, the meteorologist interpreting radar, and the statistician interpreting a scatter plot will each bring a differently tuned visual system to bear on his or her particular problem. People who work with visualizations must learn the skill of seeing patterns in data. In terms of making visualizations that contain easily identified patterns, one strategy is to rely on pattern-finding skills that are common to everyone. These can be based on low-level perceptual capabilities, such as seeing the connections between objects linked by lines. We can also rely on skill transfer. If we know that our users are cartographers, already good at reading terrain contour maps, we can display other information, such as energy fields, in the form of contour maps. The evidence from priming studies suggests that when we want people to see particular patterns, even familiar ones, it is a good idea to show them a few examples ahead of time.

The Perceptual Syntax of Diagrams

Diagrams are always hybrids of the conventional and the perceptual. Diagrams contain conventional elements, such as abstract labeling codes, that are difficult to learn but formally powerful. They also contain information that is coded according to perceptual rules, such as Gestalt principles. Arbitrary mappings may be useful, as in the case of mathematical notation, but a good diagram takes advantage of basic perceptual mechanisms that have evolved to perceive structure in the environment. By presenting examples, the following sections describe the visual grammar of two different kinds of diagrams: node–link diagrams and the layered maps used in GISs.

The Grammar of Node–Link Diagrams

For a mathematician, a graph is a structure consisting of nodes and edges (links between the nodes). See Figure 6.30 for examples. There is a specialized academic field called *graph drawing* whose goal is to make graphs that are pleasantly laid out and easy to read. In graph drawing, layout algorithms are optimized according to aesthetic rules, such as the minimization of link crossings, displaying symmetry of structure and minimizing bends in links (Di Battista et al., 1999). Path bendiness and the number of link crossings have both been shown empirically to degrade performance on the task of finding the shortest path between two nodes (Ware et al., 2002). However, for the most part, there has been little attempt either to systematically apply our knowledge of pattern perception to problems in graph drawing or to use empirical

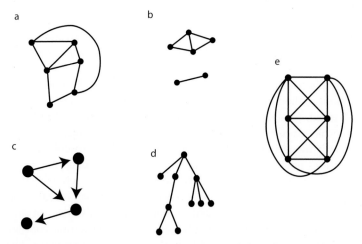

Figure 6.30   Node–link diagrams, technically called graphs: (a) A graph. (b) A graph with two connected components. (c) A directed graph. (d) A tree structure graph. (e) A nonplanar graph. It cannot be laid out on a plane without links crossing.

methods to determine that graphs laid out according to aesthetic principles are, in fact, easier to understand.

In the following paragraphs, we broaden the concept of a graph to consider a very large class of diagrams that we will call, generically, node–link diagrams. The essential characteristic of these diagrams is that they consist of *nodes*, representing various kinds of entities, and *links*, representing relationships between the entities. Dozens of different diagrams have this basic form, including software structure diagrams, data-flow diagrams, organization charts, and software modeling diagrams. Figure 6.31 provides four examples commonly used in software engineering. The set of abstractions common to node–link diagrams is so close to ubiquitous that it can be called a visual grammar. The nodes are almost always outline boxes or circles, usually representing the entities in a system. The connecting lines generally represent different kinds of relationships, transitions, or communication paths between nodes. Experimental work shows that visualizing *interdependencies* between program elements helps program understanding (Linos et al., 1994).

The various reasons why we may be justified in calling these graphical codes perceptual are distributed throughout this book, but are addressed mostly in this chapter and Chapter 5. The

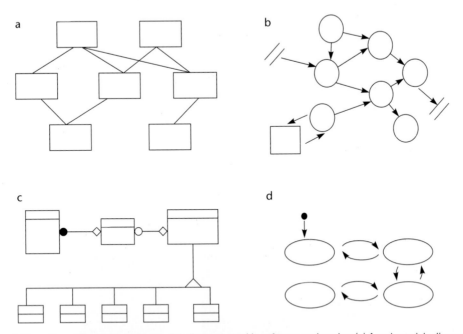

Figure 6.31   Four different kinds of node–link diagrams used in software engineering: (a) A code module diagram. (b) A data flow diagram. (c) An object modeling diagram. (d) A state transition diagram. Each of these diagrams would normally contain text labels on the nodes and the arcs.

fundamental argument is that closed contours are basic in defining visual objects. Thus, although a circular line may be only a mark drawn on paper, at some level in the visual system it is object-like. Similarly, two objects can be connected by a line, and this visual connection has the ability to represent any of a number of relationships.

Although lines get their expressive power from neural mechanisms designed to interpret objects, they are fundamentally ambiguous. Kennedy (1974) has elucidated many ways in which contours (lines) can represent aspects of the environment. Some of them are illustrated in Figure 6.32. A circle can represent a ring, a flat disk, a ball, a hole, or the boundary between two objects (a disk in a hole). This nicely illustrates the mixture of perception and convention that is common to diagrams. Our visual systems are capable of interpreting a line contour in any of these ways. In real-world scenes, additional information is available to clarify ambiguous contours. In a diagram, the contour may remain perceptually ambiguous and some convention may be necessary to remove the ambiguity. In one kind of diagram, a circle may represent an object; in another, it may represent a hole; in a third, it may represent the boundary of a geographic region. The diagram convention tells us which interpretation is correct.

A general data model that uses a form of node–link diagram is the entity-relationship model. It is widely used in computer science and business modeling (Chen, 1976). In entity relationships, *modeling entities* can be objects and parts of objects, or more abstract things such as parts of organizations. *Relationships* are the various kinds of connections that can exist between entities. For example, an entity representing a wheel will have a part-of relationship to an entity representing an automobile. A person may have a customer relationship to a store. Both entities and relationships can have *attributes*. Thus, a particular customer might be a preferred customer. An attribute of an organization might be the number of its employees. There are standard diagrams for use in entity-relationship modeling, but we are not concerned with these here. We are more

Figure 6.32   The line circle shown at the top left can represent many kinds of objects: a wire ring, a disk, a ball, a cut-out hole, or the boundary between a disk and the hole in which it resides.

interested in the different ways diagrams can be constructed to represent entities, relationships, and attributes in an easily perceived manner.

The following list is a description of the general ways in which entities and relationships can be expressed using node–link diagrams. This can be regarded loosely as a visual syntax. These are conjectured to be good display mappings, although none has been proved through scientific study to be the best. Each of the elements in the list has a perceptual, rather than conventional, basis for the way it conveys meaning. Most of these elements are discussed more extensively elsewhere in this book. Figure 6.33 provides a set of matching illustrations.

1. A closed contour in a node–link diagram generally represents an entity of some kind. It might be part of a body of software, or a person in an organization.

2. The shape of the closed contour is frequently used to represent an entity type (an attribute of the entity).

3. The color of an enclosed region represents an entity type (an attribute).

4. The size of an enclosed region can be used to represent the magnitude of an entity (a scalar attribute).

5. Lines that partition a region within a closed contour can delineate subparts of an entity. This may correspond to a real-world multipart object.

6. Closed-contour regions may be aggregated. The result is readily seen as a composite entity.

7. A number of closed-contour regions within a larger closed contour can represent conceptual containment.

8. Placing closed contours spatially in an ordered sequence can represent conceptual ordering of some kind.

9. A line linking entities represents some kind of relationship between them.

10. A line linking closed contours can have different colors, or other graphical qualities such as waviness. This effectively represents an attribute or type of a relationship.

11. The thickness of a connecting line can be used to represent the magnitude of a relationship (a scalar attribute).

12. A contour can be shaped with tabs and sockets to indicate which components have particular relationships.

13. Proximity of components can represent groups.

The vast majority of node–link diagrams currently in use are very simple. For the most part, these diagrams use identical rectangular or circular nodes and constant-width lines, like those shown in Figure 6.31. Although such generic diagrams are very effective in conveying patterns of structural relationships among entities, they are often poor at showing the types of entities

Graphical Code	Visual Instantiation	Semantics
1. Closed contour.		Entity, object, node.
2. Shape of closed region.		Entity type.
3. Color of enclosed region.		Entity type.
4. Size of enclosed region.		Entity value. Larger = more.
5. Partitioning lines within enclosed region.		Entity partitions are created, e.g., TreeMaps.
6. Attached shapes.		Attached entities. Part-of relations.
7. Shapes enclosed by contour.		Contained entities.
8. Spatially ordered shapes.		A sequence.
9. Linking line.		Relationship between entities.
10. Linking-line quality.		Type of relationship between entities.
11. Linking-line thickness.		Strength of relationship between entities.
12. Tab connector.		A fit between components.
13. Proximity.		Groups of components.

Figure 6.33   The visual grammar of diagram elements (node–link diagrams).

and the types of relationships. Attributes, when they are shown, are often provided in the form of text labels attached to the boxes and lines, although occasionally dashed lines and other variations are used to denote types.

Clearly, there are ways to extend this vocabulary that are perceptually sound. Chapter 7 introduces the concept of a *geon diagram* as a graphical device that uses 3D objects, with surface texture and color, to represent entities and relationships. There is a range of possibilities between the rectangular-box-and-line diagram and fully rendered, colored, and textured 3D objects. We can make diagram boxes that are more objectlike, with shape and texture denoting various attributes, and we can depict relationships using thin tubes. Most of the different ways of representing attributes shown in Figure 6.33 are rarely used, although they are relatively easy to implement with modern computer graphics.

The Grammar of Maps

A second visual grammar can be found in the way maps are designed and interpreted. Only three basic kinds of graphical marks are common to most maps: areas, line features, and point features (Mark and Franck, 1996). Figure 6.34 illustrates this basic grammar of maps and shows how these three elements can work in isolation and in combination.

1, 2, 3. Geographical areas are usually denoted by closed contours, tinted areas, or textured areas. Often, in a map, all three methods can be used; for example, lines to represent county boundaries, color-coding to represent climate, and texture to represent vegetation.

4. Geographical linear features represent either boundaries or elongated geographical regions. The difference between geographical areas and linear features is sometimes related to scale. At a small scale, a river will be represented by a thin line of constant width; at a larger scale, it can become an extended geographical area.

5. Dots or other small symbols are used to represent *point features*, although whether or not something is a point feature depends on the scale. At a large scale, an entire city may be represented by a single dot; at a small scale, a dot might be used to show the locations of churches, schools, or tourist attractions.

6. A dot on a line means that the entity denoted by the point feature is on, or attached to, the entity denoted by the linear feature. For example, a city is "on" a river.

7. A dot within a closed contour means that the entity denoted by the point feature lies within the boundaries of the area feature. For example, a town is within a province.

8. A line crossing a closed-contour region means that a linear feature traverses an area feature. For example, a road passes through a county.

9. A line that ends in a closed-contour region means that a linear feature ends or starts within an area feature. For example, a river flows out of a park.

10. Overlapping contour regions denoted by contour, color, or texture denote overlapping spatial entities. For example, a forested region may overlap a county boundary.

Graphical Code	Visual Instantiation	Semantics
1. Closed contour.		Geographic region.
2. Colored region.		Geographic region.
3. Textured region.		Geographic region.
4. Line.		Linear map features such as rivers, roads, etc. Depends on scale.
5. Dot.	•	Point features such as town, building. Depends on scale.
6. Dot on line.		Point feature such as town on linear feature such as road.
7. Dot in closed contour.		Point feature such as town located within a geographic region.
8. Line crosses closed-contour region.		Linear feature such as river crossing geographic region.
9. Line exits closed-contour region.		A linear feature such as a river terminates in a geographic region.
10. Overlapping contour, colored regions, textured regions.		Overlapping geographically defined areas.

Figure 6.34   The visual grammar of map elements.

Maps need not be used only for geographical information. Johnson and Shneiderman (1991) developed a visualization technique they call a *treemap*, for displaying information about the tree data structures commonly used in computer science. Figure 6.35 shows an example of a tree data structure presented in treemap form and in a conventional node–link diagram.

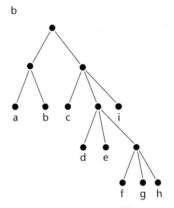

Figure 6.35   (a) A treemap representation of hierarchical data. Areas represent the amount of data stored in parts of the tree data structure. (b) The same tree structure, represented using a node–link diagram.

The original treemap was based on the following algorithm. First the rectangle is divided with a vertical partition according to the number of branches from the root of the tree. Next, each subrectangle is similarly divided, but with horizontal partitions. This process is repeated to the "leaves" of the tree. The area of each leaf on the tree corresponds to the amount of information that is stored there.

The great advantage of the treemap over conventional tree views is that the amount of information on each branch of the tree can be easily visualized. Because the method is space-filling, it can show quite large trees containing thousands of branches. The disadvantage is that the hierarchical structure is not as clear as it is in a more conventional tree drawing, which is a specialized form of node–link diagram.

Patterns in Motion

To this point, we have mainly discussed the use of static patterns to represent data, even though the data is sometimes dynamic—as in the case of a vector field representing a pattern of moving liquid or moving gas. We can also use motion as a display technique to represent data that is either static or dynamic. The perception of dynamic patterns is not understood as well as the perception of static patterns. But we are very sensitive to patterns in motion and, if we can learn to use motion effectively, it may be a good way to display certain aspects of data.

We start by considering the problem of how to represent data communications with computer animation. One way of doing this is to use a graphical object to represent each packet of information and then to animate that package from the information source to its destination.

First we consider the simplest case—data represented by a series of identical and equally spaced graphical elements, as shown in Figure 6.36. In this case, there is a fundamental limitation on the throughput that can be represented. In a computer animation sequence, the basic process is a loop that involves drawing the animated object, displaying it, moving it, and then redrawing it. When this cycle is repeated fast enough, a sequence of static pictures is seen as a smoothly moving image. The limitation on perceived data throughput arises from the amount that a given object can be moved before it becomes confused with another object in the next frame—this is called the *correspondence problem*.

If we define the distance between pattern elements as λ, we are limited to a maximum displacement of $\lambda/2$ on each frame of animation before the pattern is more likely to be seen as moving in the reverse direction from that desired. The problem is illustrated in Figure 6.36(a).

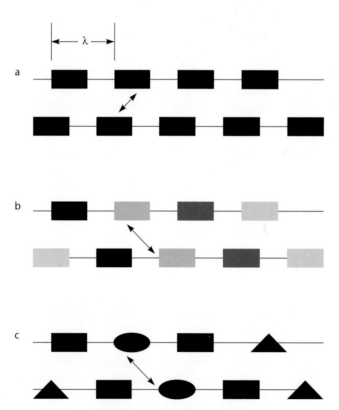

Figure 6.36   If motion is represented using a regular sequence of identical and equally spaced elements, there is a strict limit on the throughput that can be perceived. This limit can be extended by varying the sizes and shapes of the graphical elements.

When all the elements are identical, the brain constructs correspondences based on object proximity in successive frames. This is sometimes called the *wagon-wheel effect,* because of the tendency of wagon wheels in Western movies to appear to be rotating in the wrong direction. Experiments by Fleet (1998) suggest that the maximum change per frame of animation for motion to reliably be seen in a particular direction is about $\lambda/3$ for the basic representation shown in Figure 6.36(a). Given an animation frame rate of 60 frames per second, this establishes an upper bound of 20 messages per second that can be represented.

There are many ways in which the correspondence limitation can be overcome by giving the graphical elements a different shape, orientation, or color. Two possibilities are illustrated in Figure 6.36(b) and (c). In one, the gray values of the elements are varied from message to message; in the other, the shapes of the elements are varied. Research with element shapes suggests that correspondence of shape is more important than correspondence of color in determining perceived motion (Caelli et al., 1993). In a series of experiments that examined a variety of enhanced representations like those illustrated in Figure 6.36(b) and (c), Fleet (1998) found that the average phase shift per animation frame could be increased to 3λ before correspondence was lost. Given an animation frame rate of 60 frames per second, this translates to an upper bound of 180 messages per second that can be represented using animation.

Of course, when the goal is to visualize high traffic rates, there is no point in representing individual messages in detail. Most digital communications systems transfer millions of data packets per second. What is important at high data rates is an impression of data volumes, the direction of traffic flow, and large-scale patterns of activity.

Form and Contour in Motion

A number of studies have shown that people can see relative motion with great sensitivity. For example, contours and region boundaries can be perceived with precision in fields of random dots if defined by differential motion alone (Regan, 1989; Regan and Hamstra, 1991). Human sensitivity to such motion patterns rivals our sensitivity to static patterns; this suggests that motion is an underutilized method for displaying patterns in data.

For purposes of data display, we can treat motion as an attribute of a visual object, much as we consider size, color, and position to be object attributes. We evaluated the use of simple sinusoidal motion in enabling people to perceive correlations between variables (Limoges et al., 1989). We enhanced a conventional scatter plot representation by allowing the points to oscillate sinusoidally, either horizontally or vertically (or both) about a center point. An experiment was conducted to discover whether the frequency, phase, or amplitude of point motion was the most easily "read." The task was to distinguish a high correlation between variables from a low one. A comparison was made with more conventional graphical techniques, including using point size, gray value, and *x,y* position in a conventional scatter plot. The results showed that data mapped to phase was perceived best; in fact, it was as effective as most of the more conventional techniques, such as the use of point size or gray value. In informal studies, we also showed that motion appears to be effective in revealing clusters of distinct data points in a multidimensional data space (see Figure 6.37). Related data shows up as clouds of points moving together in elliptical paths, and these can be easily differentiated from other clouds of points.

Moving Frames

Perceived motion is highly dependent on its context. Johansson (1975) has demonstrated a number of grouping phenomena that show that the brain has a strong tendency to group moving objects in a hierarchical fashion. One of the effects he investigated is illustrated in Figure 6.38. In this example, three dots are set in motion. The two outer dots move in synchrony in a horizontal direction. The third dot, located between the other two, also moves in synchrony but in an oblique direction. However, the central dot is not perceived as moving along an oblique path. Instead, what is perceived is illustrated in 6.38(b). An overall horizontal motion of the entire group of dots is seen; within this group, the central dot also appears to move vertically.

A rectangular frame provides a very strong contextual cue for motion perception. It is so strong that if a bright frame is made to move around a bright static dot in an otherwise

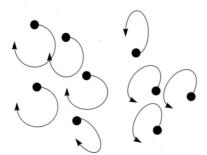

Figure 6.37   An illustration of the elliptical motion paths that result when variables are mapped to the relative phase angles of oscillating dots. The result is similar elliptical motion paths for points that are similar. In this example, two distinct groups of oscillating dots are clearly perceived.

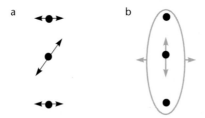

Figure 6.38   When dots are set in synchronized motion, as shown in (a), what is actually perceived is shown in (b). The entire group of dots is seen to move horizontally, and the central dot moves vertically within the group.

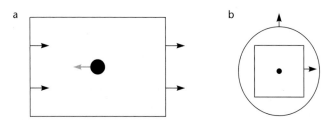

Figure 6.39   (a) When a stationary dot is placed within a moving frame in a dark room, it is the dot that is perceived to move in the absence of other cues. (b) The effect is hierarchical.

completely dark environment, it is often the static dot that appears to move (Wallach, 1959). Wallach also showed that the effect works in a hierarchical fashion. Thus, the perceived motion of the static dot in Figure 6.39(b) is strongly influenced by the motion of a surrounding square frame, but it is much less influenced by the motion of the circle outside the square.

Computer animation is often used in a straightforward way to display dynamic phenomena, such as a particle flow through a vector field. In these applications, the main goal from a perceptual point of view is to bring the motion into the range of human sensitivities. The issue is the same for viewing high-speed or single-frame movie photography. The motions of flowers blooming or bullets passing through objects are speeded up and slowed down, respectively, so that we can perceive the dynamics of the phenomena. Humans are reasonably sensitive to motion ranging from a few millimeters per second to a few hundred millimeters per second for objects viewed at normal screen distances. Generally, the data animator should aim for motion in the midrange of a few centimeters per second. (See Chapter 2 for some of the basic issues related to motion sensitivity.)

The use of motion to help us distinguish patterns in abstract data is at present only a research topic, albeit a very promising one. One application of the research results is the use of frames to examine dynamic flow field animations. Frames can be used as an effective device for highlighting local relative motion. If we wish to highlight the local relative motion of a group of particles moving through a fluid, a rectangular frame that moves along with the group will create a reference area within which local motion patterns can emerge.

Another way in which motion patterns are important is in helping us to perceive visual space and rigid 3D shapes. This topic is covered in Chapter 8 in the context of the other mechanisms of space perception.

Expressive Motion

Using moving patterns to represent motion on communication channels, or in vector fields, is a rather obvious use of motion for information display, but there are other, more subtle uses. There appears to be a vocabulary of expressive motion comparable in richness and variety to the vocabulary of static patterns explored by the Gestalt psychologists. In the following sections, some of the more provocative results are discussed, together with their implications for data visualization.

Perception of Causality

When we see a billiard ball strike another and set the second ball in motion, we perceive that the motion of the first ball *causes* the motion of the second, according to the work of Michotte (translated 1963). Michotte's book *The Perception of Causality* is a compendium of dozens of experiments, each showing how variations in the basic parameters of velocity and event timing can radically alter what is perceived. He conducted detailed studies of the perception of interactions between two patches of light and came to the conclusion that the perception of causality can be as direct and immediate as the perception of simple form. In a typical experiment, illustrated in Figure 6.40, one rectangular patch of light moved from left to right until it just touched a second patch of light, then stopped. At this point, the second patch of light would start to move. This was before the advent of computer graphics, and Michotte conducted his experiments with an apparatus that used little mirrors and beams of light. Depending on the temporal relationships between the moving-light events and their relative velocities, observers reported different kinds of causal relationships, variously described as "launching," "entraining," or "triggering."

Precise timing is required to achieve perceived causality. For example, Michotte found that for the effect he called *launching* to be perceived, the second object had to move within 70 milliseconds of contact; after this interval, subjects still perceived the first object as setting the second object in motion, but the phenomenon was qualitatively different. He called it *delayed launching*. Beyond about 160 milliseconds, there was no longer an impression that one event caused the other; instead, unconnected movements of the two objects were perceived. Figure 6.41 provides a reproduction of some of his results. For causality to be perceived, visual events must be synchronized within at least one-sixth of a second. Given that virtual-reality animation often occurs at only about 10 frames per second, events should be frame-accurate for clear causality to be perceived.

If an object makes contact with another and the second object moves off at a much greater velocity, a phenomenon that Michotte called *triggering* is perceived. The first object does not seem to cause the second object to move by imparting its own energy; rather, it appears that contact triggers propelled motion in the second object.

Figure 6.40   Michotte (1963) studied the perception of causal relationships between two patches of light that always moved along the same line but with a variety of velocity patterns.

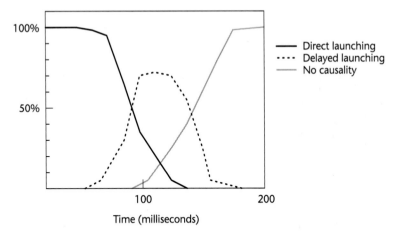

Figure 6.41   From Michotte (1963). When one object comes into contact with another and the second moves off, the first motion may be seen to cause the second if the right temporal relationships exist. The graph shows how different kinds of phenomena are perceived, depending on the delay between the arrival of one object and the departure of the other.

More recent developmental work by Leslie and Keeble (1987) has shown that infants at only 27 weeks of age can perceive causal relations such as launching. This would appear to support the contention that such percepts are in some sense basic to perception.

The significance of Michotte's work for data visualization is that it provides a way to increase the expressive range beyond what is possible with static diagrams. In a static visualization, the visual vocabulary for representing relationships is quite limited. To show that one visual object is related to another, we can draw lines between them, we can color or texture groups of objects, or we can use some kind of simple shape coding. The only way to show a causal link between two objects is by using some kind of conventional code, such as a labeled arrow. However, such codes owe their meaning more to our ability to understand conventional coded language symbols than to anything essentially perceptual. This point about the differences between language-based and perceptual codes is elaborated in Chapter 9. What Michotte's work gives us is the ability to significantly enrich the vocabulary of things that can be immediately and directly represented in a diagram.

Perception of Animate Motion

In addition to the fact that we can perceive causality using simple animation, there is evidence that we are highly sensitive to motion that has a biological origin. In a series of now-classic studies, Gunnar Johansson attached lights to the limb joints of actors (Johansson, 1973). He then produced moving pictures of the actors carrying out certain activities, such as walking and

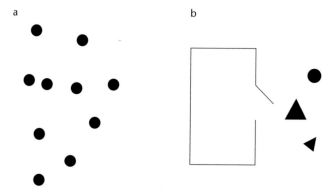

Figure 6.42   (a) In Johansson's (1973) experiments, a pattern of moving dots was produced by making a movie of actors with lights attached to parts of their bodies. (b) Heider and Semmel (1944) made a movie of simple geometric shapes moving through complex paths. Viewers of both kinds of displays attribute anthropomorphic characteristics to what they see.

dancing. These pictures were made so that only the points of light were visible, and, in any given still frame, all that was perceived was a rather random-looking collection of dots, as shown in Figure 6.42(a). A remarkable result from Johansson's studies was that viewers of the animated movies were immediately conscious of the fact that they were watching human motion. In addition, they could identify the genders of the actors and the tasks they were performing. Some of these identifications could be made after exposures lasting only a small fraction of a second.

Another experiment pointing to our ability to recognize form from motion was a study by Heider and Semmel (1944). In this study, an animated movie was produced incorporating the motion of two triangles and a circle, as shown in Figure 6.42(b). People viewing this movie readily attributed human characteristics to the shapes; they would say, for example, that a particular shape was angry, or that the shapes were chasing one another. Moreover, these interpretations were consistent across observers. Because the figures were simple shapes, the implication is that patterns of motion were conveying the meaning. Other studies support this interpretation. Rimé et al. (1985) did a cross-cultural evaluation of simple animations using European, American, and African subjects, and found that motion could express such concepts as kindness, fear, or aggression, and there was considerable similarity in these interpretations across cultures, suggesting some measure of universality.

Enriching Diagrams with Simple Animation

The research findings of Michotte, Johansson, Rimé, and others suggest that the use of simple motion can powerfully express certain kinds of relationships in data. Animation of abstract shapes can significantly extend the vocabulary of things that can be conveyed naturally beyond what is possible with a static diagram. The key result, that motion does not require the support of complex depictive representations (of animals or people) to be perceived as animate, means that simplified motion techniques may be useful in multimedia presentations. The kinds of animated critters that are starting to crawl and hop over Web pages are often unnecessary and distracting. Just as elegance is a virtue in static diagrams, so is it a virtue in diagrams that use animation. A vocabulary of simple expressive animation requires development, but research results strongly suggest that this will be a productive and worthwhile endeavor. The issue is pressing, because animation tools are becoming more widely available for information display systems. More design work and more research are needed.

Conclusion

The brain is a powerful pattern-finding engine; indeed, this is the fundamental reason why visualization techniques are becoming important. There is no other way of presenting information so that structures, groups, and trends can be discovered among hundreds of data values. If we can transform data into the appropriate visual representation, its structure may be revealed. However, not all patterns are equally easy to perceive. The brain appears to be especially good at discovering linear features and distinct objects, so much so that the discovery of spurious patterns should always be a concern. Because the brain is a pattern-finding engine, patterns may be perceived even where there is only visual noise.

Much of the material presented in this chapter, especially the Gestalt laws of pattern perception, leads to rules that seem obvious to any visual designer. Nevertheless, it is surprising how often these design rules are violated. A common mistake is that related data glyphs are placed far apart in displays. Another is that closed contours are used in ways that visually segment a display into regions that make it difficult, rather than easy, to comprehend related information. The use of windows is often to blame, because they result in strong framing effects, which can cause confusion if used inconsistently.

For information to be clearly related, the visual structure should reflect relationships between data entities. Placing data glyphs in spatial proximity, linking them with lines, or enclosing them within a contour will provide the necessary visual structure to make them seem related. In terms of seeing patterns in rather abstract data displays, perception of contours is likely to be especially important. The visual system contains a number of mechanisms for finding contours. These contours can be simple lines, dots, or other features in a linear pattern; boundaries between regions of different textures, different colors, different motion; or even illusory contours.

For the researcher and for those interested in finding novel display techniques, the effective use of motion is suggested as a fertile area for investigation. Patterns in moving data points can be perceived easily and rapidly. Given the computing power of modern personal computers, the opportunity exists to make far greater use of animation in visualizing information.

In considering pattern perception, we should always bear in mind that the perception of abstract patterns is probably not a primary purpose of visual perception. Rather, pattern-finding mechanisms are part of the neural machinery that divides the world into visual objects. For example, the reason that closed contours are so compelling in segmenting space is that they normally define objects in our environment; they do not have any special significance in and of themselves. In the next chapter, we consider ways in which 3D objects are perceived and ways in which object displays can be used to organize information.

CHAPTER 7

Visual Objects and Data Objects

The object metaphor is pervasive in the way we think about abstract data. Object-oriented programming is one example; the body politic is another. Object-related concepts are also basic in modern systems design. A modular system is one that has easily understood and easily replaced components. Good modules are *plug-compatible* with one another; they are discrete and separate parts of a system. In short, the concept of a module has a lot in common with the perceptual and cognitive structures that define visual objects. This suggests that visual objects may be an excellent way to represent modular system components. A visual object provides a useful metaphor for encapsulation and cohesiveness, both important concepts in defining modular systems.

For our present purposes, an *object* can be thought of as any identifiable, separate, and distinct part of the visual world. Information about visual objects is cognitively stored in a way that ties together critical features, such as oriented edges and patches of color and texture, so that they can be identified, visually tracked, and remembered. Because visual objects cognitively group visual attributes, if we can represent data values as visual features and group these features into visual objects, we will have a very powerful tool for organizing related data.

Two radically different theories have been proposed to explain object recognition. The first is image-based. It proposes that we recognize an object by matching the visual image with something roughly like a snapshot stored in memory. The second type of theory is structure-based. It proposes that is analyzed in terms of primitive 3D forms and the structural interrelationships between them. Both of these models have much to recommend them, and it is entirely plausible that each is correct in some form. It is certainly clear that the brain has multiple ways of analyzing visual input. Certainly, both models provide interesting insights into how to display data effectively.

Image-Based Object Recognition

We begin with some evidence related to picture and image perception. People have a truly remarkable ability to recall pictorial images. In an arduous experiment, Standing et al. (1970) presented subjects with a list of 2560 pictures at a rate of one every 10 seconds. This was like the family slide show from hell, it took them more than seven hours spread over a four-day period. Amazingly, when subsequently tested, subjects were able to distinguish pictures from others not previously seen, with better than 90% accuracy.

People can also recognize objects in images that are presented very rapidly. Suppose you asked someone, "Is there a dog in one of the following pictures?" and then showed them a set of images, rapidly, all in the same place, at a rate of 10 per second. Remarkably, they will be able to detect the presence, or absence, of a dog in one of the images most of the time. This experimental technique is called *rapid serial visual presentation* (RSVP). Experiments have shown that the maximum rate for the ability to detect common objects in images is about 10 images per second (Potter and Levy, 1969; Potter, 1976).

A related phenomenon is *attentional blink*. If, in a series of images, a second dog were to appear in an image within 350 ms of the first, people do not notice it (or anything else). This moment of blindness is the attentional blink (Coltheart, 1999). It is conjectured that the brain is still processing the first dog, even though the image is gone, and this prohibits the identification of other objects in the sequence.

It is useful to make a distinction between recognition and recall. We have a great ability to recognize information that we have encountered before, as the picture memory experiment of Standing et al. shows. However, if we are asked to reconstruct visual scenes—for example, to recall what happened at a crime scene—our performance is much worse. Recognition is much better than recall. This suggests that a major use of visual images can be as an aid to memory. An image that we recognize can help us remember events or other information related to that image. This is why icons are so effective in user interfaces; they help us to recall the functionality of computer programs.

More support for image-based theories comes from studies showing that three-dimensional objects are recognized most readily if they are encountered from the same view direction as when they were initially seen. Johnson (2001) studied subjects' abilities to recognize bent pipe structures. Subjects performed well if the same viewing direction was used in the initial viewing and in the test phase; they performed poorly if a different view direction was used in the test phase. But subjects were also quite good at identification from exactly the opposite view direction. Johnson attributed this unexpected finding to the importance of silhouette information. Silhouettes would have been similar, although flipped left-to-right from the initial view.

Although most objects can easily be recognized independent of the size of the image on the retina, image size does have some effect. Figure 7.1 illustrates this. When the picture is seen from a distance, the image of the Mona Lisa face dominates; when it is viewed up close, smaller objects become dominant: a gremlin, a bird, and a claw emerge. Experimental work by Biederman and

Figure 7.1   When the image of the Mona Lisa is viewed from a distance, the face dominates. But look at it from 30 cm, and the gremlin hiding in the shadows of the mouth and nose emerges. When component objects have a size of about 4 degrees of visual angle, they become maximally visible. *Adapted from the work of the Tel Aviv artist Victor Molev.*

Cooper (1992) suggests that the optimal size for recognizing a visual object is about 4 to 6 degrees of visual angle. This gives a useful rule of thumb for the optimal size for rapid presentation of visual images so that we can best see the visual patterns contained in them.

Another source of evidence for image-based object recognition comes from priming effects. The term *priming* refers to the fact that people can identify objects more easily if they are given prior exposure to some relevant information. Most priming studies have been carried out using verbal information, but Kroll and Potter (1984) showed that *pictures* of related objects, such as a cow and a horse, have a mutually priming effect. This is similar to the priming effect between the words *cow* and *horse*. However, they found little cross-modality priming; the word *cow* provided only weak priming for a picture of a horse. It is also possible to prime using purely visual information, that is, information with no semantic relationship. Lawson et al. (1994) devised a series of experiments in which subjects were required to identify a specified object in a series of briefly presented pictures. Recognition was much easier if subjects had been primed by visually similar images. They argued that this should not be the case if objects are recognized on the basis of a high-level, 3D structural model of the kind that we will discuss later in this chapter; only image-based storage can account for their results.

Priming effects can occur even if information is not consciously perceived. Bar and Biederman (1998) showed pictorial images to subjects, so briefly that it was impossible for them to identify the objects. They used what is called a *masking technique*, a random pattern shown immediately after the target stimulus to remove the target from the iconic store, and they rigorously tested to show that subjects performed at chance levels when reporting what they had seen. Nevertheless, 15 minutes later, this unperceived exposure substantially increased the chance of recognition on subsequent presentation. Although the information was not consciously perceived, exposure to the particular combination of image features apparently primed the visual system to make subsequent recognition easier. They found that the priming effect decreased substantially if the imagery was displaced sideways. They concluded that the mechanism of priming is highly image-dependent and not based on high-level semantic information.

Palmer et al. (1981) showed that not all views of an object are equally easy to recognize. They found that many different objects have something like a *canonical view* from which they are most easily identified. From this and other evidence, a theory of object recognition has been developed, proposing that we recognize objects by matching the visual information with internally stored viewpoint-specific exemplars, or "prototypes" (Edelman and Buelthoff, 1992; Edelman, 1995). According to this theory, the brain stores a number of key views of objects. These views are not simple snapshots; they allow recognition despite simple geometric distortions of the image that occur in perspective transformation. This explains why object perception survives the kinds of geometric distortions that occur when a picture is viewed and tilted with respect to the observer. However, there are strict limits on the extent to which we can change an image before recognition problems occur. For example, numerous studies show that face recognition is considerably impaired if the faces are shown upside down (Rhodes, 1995).

Adding support to the multiple-view, image-based theory of object recognition is neurophysiological data from recordings of single cells in the inferotemporal cortexes of monkeys. Perrett et al. (1991) discovered cells that respond preferentially to particular views of faces. Figure 7.2 shows some of their results. One cell (or cell assembly) responds best to a three-quarter view of a face; another, to profiles, either left or right; still another responds to a view of a head from any angle. We can imagine a kind of hierarchical structure, with the cell assemblies that respond to particular views feeding into higher-level cell assemblies that respond to any view of the object.

Applications of Images in User Interfaces

The fact that visual images are easily recognized after so little exposure suggests that icons in user interfaces should make excellent memory aids, helping us recall the functionality of parts of complex systems. Icons that are readily recognized may trigger activation of related concepts

Figure 7.2 The responses of three cells in the temporal cortex of a monkey to faces in different orientations. At the top is a cell most sensitive to a right profile. The middle cell responds well to either profile. The cell at the bottom responds well to a face irrespective of orientation. *Adapted from Perrett et al. (1991).*

in the semantic network of long-term memory. Icons are also helpful because to some extent they can represent pictorially the things they are used to reference.

Priming may be useful in helping people search for particular patterns in data. The obvious way of doing this is to provide sample images of the kind of pattern being sought and repeating the samples at frequent intervals during the search process. An example would be the use of images of sample viruses in a medical screening laboratory.

Searching an Image Database

Presenting images rapidly in sequence may be a useful way to allow users to scan picture databases (Wittenburg et al., 1998; de Bruijn et al., 2000). The fact that people can search rapidly for an image in a sequence of up to 10 pictures per second suggests that presenting images using RSVP may be efficient. Contrast this with the usual method of presenting image collections in a regular grid of small thumbnail images. If it is necessary to make an eye movement to fixate each thumbnail image, it will not be possible to scan more than three to four images per second.

Even though RSVP is promising, there are a number of design problems that must be solved in building a practical interface. Once a likely candidate image is identified as being present in an RSVP sequence, it must still be found. By the time a user responds with a mouse click several images will have passed, more if the user is not poised to press the stop button. Thus, either controls must be added for backing up through the sequence, or part of the sequence must be fanned out in a conventional thumbnail array to confirm that candidate's presence and study it further (Spence, 2002; Wittenburg et al., 1998).

Personal Image Memory Banks

Based on straightforward predictions about the declining cost and increasing capacity of computer memory, it will soon be possible to have a personal memory data bank containing video and sound data collected during every waking moment of a person's lifetime. This could be achieved with an unobtrusive miniature camera, perhaps embedded in a pair of eyeglasses, and assuming continuing progress in solid-state storage, the data could be stored in a device weighing a few ounces and costing a few hundred dollars. Storing speech information will be even more straightforward. The implications of such devices are staggering. Among other things, it would be the ultimate memory aid—the user would never have to forget anything. However, a personal visual memory device of this kind would need a good user interface. One way of searching the visual content might be by viewing a rapidly presented sequence of selected frames from the video sequence. Perhaps 100 per day would be sufficient to jog the user's memory about basic events. Video data compressed in this way might make it possible to review a day in a few seconds, and a month in a few minutes.

Structure-Based Object Recognition

Image-based theories of object recognition imply a rather superficial level of analysis of visual objects. However, there is evidence that a much deeper kind of structural analysis must also occur. Figure 7.3 shows two novel objects, probably never seen by the reader before. Yet despite the fact that the *images* of these two objects are very different from one another, they can be rapidly recognized as representations of the same object. No image-based theory can account for this result.

Geon Theory

Figure 7.4 provides a somewhat simplified overview of a neural-network model of structural object perception, developed by Hummel and Biederman (1992). This theory proposes a hierarchical set of processing stages leading to object recognition. Visual information is decomposed first into edges, then into component axes, oriented blobs, and vertices. At the next layer, three-dimensional primitives such as cones, cylinders, and boxes, called *geons*, are identified. A selection of geons is illustrated in Figure 7.5. Next, the structure is extracted that specifies how the geon components interconnect; for example, in a human figure, the arm cylinder is attached near the top of the torso box. Finally, object recognition is achieved.

Silhouettes

Silhouettes appear to be especially important in determining how we perceive the structure of objects. The fact that simplified line drawings are often silhouettes may, in part, account for our ability to interpret them. At some level of perceptual processing, the silhouette boundaries of objects and the simplified line drawings of those objects excite the same neural contour-extraction mechanisms. Halverston (1992) noted that modern children tend to draw objects on the basis of the most salient silhouettes, as did early cave artists. Many objects have particular

Figure 7.3   These two objects are rapidly recognized as identical, or at least very similar, despite the very different visual images they present.

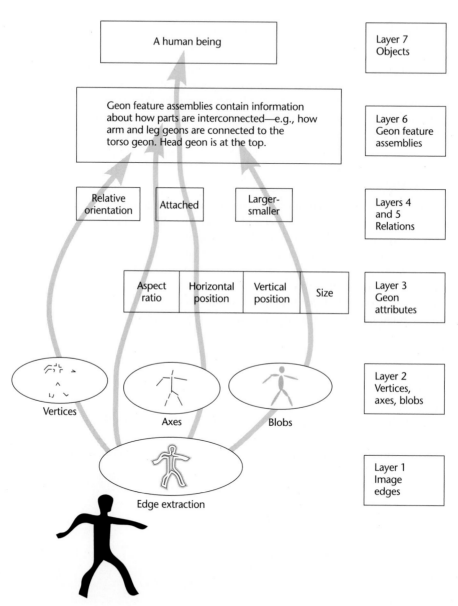

Figure 7.4   A simplified view of Hummel and Biederman's (1992) neural-network model of form perception.

Figure 7.5   According to Biederman's geon theory, the visual system interprets 3D objects by identifying 3D component parts called geons.

silhouettes that are easily recognizable; think of a teapot, a shoe, a church, a person, or a violin. These *canonical* silhouettes are based on a particular view of an object, often from a point at right angles to a major plane of symmetry. Figure 7.6 illustrates canonical views of a teapot and a person.

David Marr suggested ways in which the brain might use silhouette information to extract the structures of objects (Marr, 1982). He argued that "buried deep in our perceptual machinery" are mechanisms that contain constraints determining how silhouette information is interpreted. Three rules are embedded in this perceptual machinery:

1. Each line of sight making up a silhouette grazes the surface exactly once. The set of such points is the *contour generator*. The idea of the contour generator is illustrated in Figure 7.7.

2. Nearby points on the contour of an image arise from nearby points on the contour generator of the viewed object.

3. All the points on the contour generator lie on a single plane.

Under Marr's default assumptions, contour information is used in segmenting an image into its component solids. Marr and Nishihara (1978) suggested that concave sections of the silhouette contour are critical in defining the ways different solid parts are perceptually defined. Figure 7.8 illustrates a crudely drawn animal that we nevertheless readily segment into head, body, neck,

Figure 7.6   Many objects have canonical silhouettes, defined by the viewpoints from which they are most easily recognized. In the case of the man, the overall posture is unnatural, but the component parts—hands, feet, head, and so on—are all given in canonical views.

Contour generator

Figure 7.7   According to Marr, the perceptual system makes assumptions that occluding contours are smoothly connected and lie in the same plane. *Adapted from Marr (1982).*

Figure 7.8   Concave sections of the silhouette define subparts of the object and are used in the construction of a structural skeleton. *Adapted from Marr and Nishihara (1978).*

Figure 7.9   A photograph of a hand and a simplified line drawing of the hand. Ryan and Schwartz (1956) showed that a cartoon image was recognized more rapidly than a photograph.

legs, and so on. Marr and Nishihara also suggested a mechanism whereby the axes of the parts become cognitively connected to form a structural skeleton.

One of the consequences of structural theories of perception is that certain simplified views should be easier to read. There are practical advantages to this. For example, a clear diagram may sometimes be more effective than a photograph. This is exactly what Ryan and Schwartz (1956) showed when they found that a hand could be perceived more rapidly in the form of a simplified line drawing than in the form of a photograph (see Figure 7.9).

But this result should not be overgeneralized. Other studies have shown that time is required for detailed information to be perceived (Price and Humphreys, 1989; Venturino and Gagnon, 1992). Simplified line drawings may be most appropriate only when rapid responses are required.

Although image-based theories and structure-based theories of object recognition are usually presented as alternatives, it may be that both kinds of processes occur. If geons are extracted based on concavities in the silhouette, certain views of a complex object will be much easier to recognize. Further, it may well be that viewpoint-dependent aspects of the visual image are stored in addition to the 3D structure of the object. Indeed, it seems likely that the brain is capable of storing many kinds of information about an object or scene if they have some usefulness. The implication is that even though 3D objects in a diagram may be more effective in some cases, care should be taken to provide a good 2D layout.

Faces

Faces are special objects in human perception. Infants learn about faces faster than other objects. It is as if we are born with visual systems primed to learn to recognize important humans, such as our own mothers (Morton and Johnson, 1991; Bruce and Young, 1998; Bushnell et al., 1989). A specific area of our brains, the right middle fusiform gyrus, is especially important in face perception (Puce et al., 1995; Kanwisher et al., 1999; Kanwisher et al., 1997). This area is

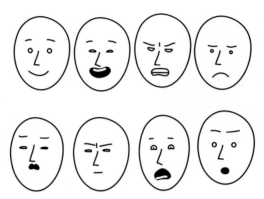

Figure 7.10 Happiness, elation, anger, sadness, disgust, determination, fear, surprise.

also useful for recognizing other complex objects, such as automobiles; although it is not essential as a Volkswagen detector, we cannot recognize faces without it.

Faces have an obvious importance in communication, because we use facial expression to communicate our emotion and degree of interest. Cross-cultural studies by Paul Ekman and coworkers strongly suggests that certain human expressions are universal communication signals, correctly interpreted across cultures and social groups (Ekman and Friesen, 1975; Ekman, 2003). Ekman identified six universal expressions: anger, disgust, fear, happiness, sadness and surprise. These are illustrated in Figure 7.10, along with determination and elation (a variation on happiness). The motion of facial features is also important in conveying emotion. Animated images are necessary to convey a full range of nuanced emotion; it is especially important to show motion of the eyebrows (Basilli, 1978; Sadr et al., 2003).

Facial expressions are produced by the contractions of facial muscles. The *facial action coding system* (FACS) is a widely applied method of measuring and defining groups of facial muscles and their effect on facial expression (Ekman et al., 1988). The eyebrows and mouth are particularly significant in emotion signaling, but the shape of the eyes is also important. There is evidence that false smiles can be distinguished from true smiles from the particular expression around the eyes that occurs with contraction of a muscle that orbits the eye (Ekman et al., 1988; Ekman, 2003). This muscle contracts with true smiles but not with false ones. According to Ekman (2003) it is difficult, if not impossible, to control this voluntarily and thus fake a "true" smile.

The main application of FACS theory in computer displays has been in the creation of computer avatars that convey human emotion (Kalra et al., 1993; Ruttkay et al., 2003). Appropriate emotional expression may help make a virtual salesperson more convincing. In computer-aided instruction, the expression on a human face could reward or discourage.

The Object Display and Object-Based Diagrams

Wickens (1992) is primarily responsible for the concept of an *object display* as a graphical device employing "a single contoured object" to integrate a large number of separate variables. Wickens theorized that mapping many data variables onto a single object will guarantee that these variables are processed together, in parallel. This approach, he claimed, has two distinct advantages. The first is that the display can reduce visual clutter by integrating the variables into a single visual object. The second is that the object display makes it easier for an operator to integrate multiple sources of information.

Among the earlier examples of object displays are Chernoff faces, named after their inventor, Herman Chernoff (1973). In this technique, a simplified image of a human face is used as a display. Examples are shown in Figure 7.11. To turn a face into a display, data variables are mapped to different facial features, such as the length of the nose, the curvature of the mouth, the size of the eye, the shape of the head, etc. There are good psychological reasons for choosing what might seem to be a rather whimsical display object. Faces are probably the most important class of objects in the human environment. Even newborn babies can rapidly distinguish

Figure 7.11 Chernoff faces. Different data variables are mapped to the sizes and shapes of different facial features.

faces from nonfaces with scrambled features, suggesting that we may have special neural hardware for dealing with faces. Jacob et al. (1976) carried out a classification task using a series of displays that were progressively more objectlike. The displays included Chernoff faces, tables, star plots, and the whisker plots described in Chapter 5. They found that the more objectlike displays, including Chernoff face plots, enabled faster, more accurate classification.

Chernoff faces have not generally been adopted in practical visualization applications. The main reason for this may be the idiosyncratic nature of faces. When data is mapped to faces, many kinds of perceptual interactions can occur. Sometimes the combination of variables will result in a particular stereotypical face, perhaps a happy face or a sad face, and this will be identified more readily. In addition, there are undoubtedly great differences in our sensitivity to the different features. We may be more sensitive to the curvature of the mouth than to the height of the eyebrows, for example. This means that the perceptual space of Chernoff faces is likely to be extremely nonlinear. In addition, there are almost certainly many uncharted interactions between facial features, and these are likely to vary from one viewer to another.

Often, object displays will be most effective when the components of the objects have a natural or metaphorical relationship to the data being represented. For example, Figure 7.12 illustrates how a storage vessel in a chemical plant might be represented using both a conventional bar chart and a customized object display. The variables in the object diagram are represented as follows:

- Size of cylinder represents tank capacity.
- Height of liquid represents volume of material stored.
- Texture of liquid represents the chemical composition.
- Color of liquid represents liquid temperature.
- Diameter of pipe represents outflow capacity.
- Status of the valve and thickness of the outgoing fluid stream represent rate at which liquid is being drawn from the tank.

In this example, the object display has a number of clear advantages. It can reduce accidental misreadings of data values. Mistakes are less likely because components act as their own descriptive icons. In addition, the structural architecture of the system and the connections between system components are always visible, and this may help in diagnosing the causes and effects of problems. Conversely, the disadvantage of object displays is that they lack generality. Each display must be custom-designed for the particular application and, ideally, should be validated with a user population to ensure that the data representation is clear and properly interpreted. This requires far more effort than displaying data as a table of numbers or a simple bar chart.

Figure 7.12 Two representations of the same data. The object diagram on the right combines six variables in an easily interpreted, cohesive representation.

The Geon Diagram

Biederman's geon theory, outlined earlier, can be applied directly to object display design. If cylinders and cones are indeed perceptual primitives, it will make sense to construct diagrams using these geon elements. This should make the diagrams easy to interpret if a good mapping can be found from the data to a geon structure. The geon diagram concept is illustrated in Figure 7.13(a). Geons are used to represent the major components of a compound data object, whereas the architecture of the data object is represented by the structural skeleton linking the geons. The size of a geon becomes a natural metaphor for the relative importance of a data entity, or its complexity or relative value. The strength of the connections between the components is given by the necklike linking structures. Additional attributes of entities and relationships can be coded by coloring and texturing them.

We evaluated the geon diagram concept in a comparison with Unified Modeling Language (UML) diagrams (Irani et al., 2001). UML is a widely used, standardized diagramming notation for representing complex systems. Equivalent diagrams were constructed by matching geon elements to UML elements (see Figure 7.13). We found that when the task involved rapid identification of substructures in a larger diagram, participants performed both faster and with only half the errors using the geon diagrams. Another experiment showed that geon diagrams were easier to remember.

In Biederman's theory, surface properties of geons, such as their colors and textures, are secondary characteristics. This makes it natural to use the surface color and texture of the geon to represent data attributes of a data object. The important mappings between data and a geon diagram are as follows:

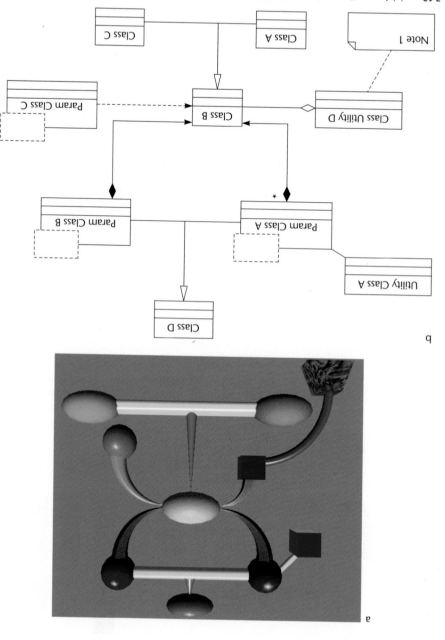

Figure 7.13 (a) A geon diagram constructed using a subset of Biederman's geon primitives. The primitive elements can also be color-coded and textured. (b) A Unified Modeling Language (UML) equivalent.

Major components of a complex data object	→	Geons
Architectural links between data object components	→	Limbs consisting of elongated geons—connections between limbs reflect architectural structure of data
Minor subcomponents	→	Geon appendices—small geon components attached to larger geons
Component attributes	→	Geon color, texture, and symbology mapped onto geons

Although the geon diagram is a 3D representation, there are reasons to pay special attention to the way it is laid out in 2D in the *x,y* plane. As discussed earlier, some silhouettes are especially effective in allowing the visual system to extract object structure. Thus, a common-sense design rule is to lay out structural components principally on a single plane. A diagramming method resembling the bas-relief stone carvings common in classical Rome and Greece may be optimal. Such carvings contain careful 3D modeling of the component objects, combined with only limited depth and a mainly planar layout.

Abstract semantics may be expressible, in a natural way, through the way geons are interconnected. In the everyday environment, there is meaning to the relative positioning of objects that is understood at a deep, possibly innate level. Because of gravity, *above* is different from *below*. If one object is inside another, it is perceived as either contained by that other object or a part of it. Irani et al. (2001) suggested that the semantics inherent in the different kinds of relationships of real-world objects might be applied to diagramming abstract concepts. Based on this idea, the researchers developed a set of graphical representations of abstract concepts. Some of the more successful of these mappings are illustrated in Figure 7.14 and listed as follows:

- Sometimes we wish to show different *instances* of the same generic object. Geon theory predicts that having the same shape should be the best way of doing this. Geon shape is dominant over color, which is a secondary attribute. Thus the elbow shapes in Figure 7.14(a) are seen as two instances of the same object, whereas the two green objects are not.

- Having an object inside another transparent object is a natural representation of a *part-of* relationship. The inside objects seem part of the outside objects, as in Figure 7.14(b).

- One object above and touching another, as shown in Figure 7.14(c), is easily understood as representing a *dependency* relationship.

- A thick bar between two objects is a natural representation of a *strong* relationship between two objects; a thinner, transparent bar represents a *weak* relationship. See Figure 7.14(d).

Perceiving the Surface Shapes of Objects

Not all things in the world are made up of closed, discrete components like geons. For example, there are undulating terrains that have no clearly separable components. Although to some extent we can decompose such a landscape into features such as hills and valleys, these are not essential to perceiving the shape of any given area of the surface. Examples of continuous surfaces that are important in visualization include digital elevation maps representing the topography of the land or the ocean floor, maps of physical properties of the environment, such as pressure and temperature, and maps representing mathematical functions that are only distantly related to the raw data. The general terms for this class of data object are *two-dimensional scalar field* and *univariate map*. The two traditional methods for displaying scalar field information are the contour map, which originated in cartography, and the pseudocolor map, discussed in Chapter 4.

Spatial Cues for Representing Scalar Fields

From a Gibsonian point of view, the obvious way to represent a univariate map is to make it into a physical surface in the environment. Some researchers occasionally do just this; they construct plaster or foam models of data surfaces. But the next best thing may be to use computer graphics techniques to shade the data surface with a simulated light source and give it a simulated color and texture to make it look like a real physical surface. Such a simulated surface can be viewed using a stereoscopic viewing apparatus, by creating different perspective images, one for each eye. These techniques have become so successful that the auto industry is using them to design car bodies in place of the full-sized clay models that were once constructed by hand to show the curves of a design. The results have been huge cost savings and a considerably accelerated design process.

Figure 7.14 Certain spatial relationships between objects can readily represent abstract concepts. (a) That objects belong to the same class is better shown by shape than by color. (b) A part-of relationship. (c) A dependency relationship. (d) Strong and weak relationships.

An important issue in the creation of univariate maps is determining how to represent surface shape most effectively. Four principal sets of visual cues for surface shape perception have been studied: shading models, surface texture, stereoscopic depth, and motion parallax.

Shading Models

The basic shading model used in computer graphics to represent the interaction of light with surfaces has already been discussed in Chapter 2. It has four basic components, as follows:

Lambertian shading: Light reflected from a surface equally in all directions

Specular shading: The highlights reflected from a glossy surface

Ambient shading: Light coming from the surrounding environment

Cast shadows: Shadows cast by an object, either on itself or on other objects

Figure 7.15 illustrates the shading model, complete with cast shadows, applied to a digital elevation map of San Francisco Bay. As can be seen, even this simple lighting model is capable of producing a dramatic image of a surface topography. A key question in choosing a shading model for data visualization is not its degree of realism, but how well it reveals the surface shape. There is some evidence that more sophisticated lighting may be harmful in representing surfaces.

Figure 7.15   A shaded representation of San Francisco Bay, shown as if the water had been drained out of it. Data courtesy of Jim Gardner, U.S. Geological Survey. Image constructed using IVS Fledermaus software.

Experiments by Ramachandran (1988) suggest that the brain assumes a *single* light source from *above* in determining whether a particular shaded area is a bump or a hollow. (See Figure 7.16.) The kinds of complex shadows that result from multiple light sources and radiosity modeling may be visually confusing rather than helpful. Chapter 8 presents evidence that cast shadows provide spatial information relevant to the layout of objects in space rather than their surface shapes.

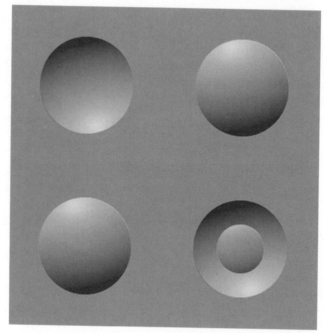

Figure 7.16　The brain generally assumes that lighting comes from above. The bumps in this image become hollows when the picture is turned upside down.

Surface Texture

Surfaces in nature are generally textured. Gibson (1986) took the position that surface texture is an essential property of a surface. A nontextured surface, he said, is merely a patch of light. The way in which textures wrap around surfaces can provide valuable information about surface shape.

Texturing surfaces is especially important when they are viewed stereoscopically. This becomes obvious if we consider that a uniform nontextured polygon contains no *internal* stereo-scopic information about the surface it represents. Under uniform lighting conditions, such a surface also contains no orientation information. When a polygon is textured, every texture element provides stereoscopic depth information relative to neighboring points. Figure 7.17 shows a stereoscopic pair of images representing a textured surface.

Without texture, it is usually impossible to distinguish one transparent curved surface from another transparent curved surface lying beneath it. Figure 7.18 shows an illustration from Interrante et al. (1997) containing experimental see-through textures designed to reveal one curved surface lying above another. The concept of *laciness*, discussed in Chapter 6, is relevant here, because it tells us something about how to make layers visually distinct. Stereoscopic viewing considerably enhances our ability to see one surface through another, semitransparent one.

Integration of Cues for Surface Shape

Given the many factors that may be involved in surface shape perception, the question arises as to which of them are most helpful. To study this problem, Norman et al. (1995) used computer graphics to render smoothly shaded rounded objects like the one shown in Figure 7.19. They manipulated the entire list of variables given above—specular shading, Lambertian shading, texture, stereo, and motion parallax—in a multifactor experiment. Stereo and motion were studied only in combination with the other cues because without shading or texture, neither stereo nor motion cues can be effective. The subjects' task was to indicate surface orientation at a number of selected points by manipulating the 3D glyph shown in Figure 7.20.

Norman et al. found *all* of the cues they studied to be useful in perceiving surface orientation, but the relative importance of the cues differed from one subject to another. For some subjects, motion appeared to be the stronger cue; for others, stereo was stronger. A summary of their results with motion and stereo data combined is given in Figure 7.21. Motion and stereo both reduced errors dramatically when used in combination with *any* of the surface representations. Overall, the combination of shading (either specular or Lambertian) with either stereo or motion was either the best or nearly the best combination for all the subjects.

There have been other studies of the relative importance of different cues to the perception of surface shape. Todd and Mingolla (1983) found surface texture to be more effective in determining surface shape than either Lambertian shading or specular shading. However, because of the lack of a convincing general theory for the combination of spatial cues, it is difficult to generalize from experiments such as this. Many of the results may be valid only for specific textures

Figure 7.17   A stereo pair showing a textured surface.

used, for example. The fact that there are large individual differences is another barrier to reaching general conclusions. Random textures, such as those used by Norman et al. (1995), may not be as effective in revealing shape as texture that follows the surface in some way (Interrante et al., 1997; Kim et al., 1993). For these reasons, it is not meaningful to make general statements such as "Lambertian shading is more useful than texture." The values of the different cues will also depend on the specific task. For example, specular highlights can be extremely useful in revealing fine surface details, as when a light is used to show scratches on glass. At other times, highlights will obscure patterns of surface color.

Interaction of Shading and Contour

The boundary contours of objects can interact with surface shading to change dramatically the perception of surface shape. Figure 7.22 is adapted from Ramachandran (1988). It shows two

Figure 7.18   Texture designed to reveal surface shape. *From Interrante et al. (1997).*

Figure 7.19   Textured, shaded, irregular objects were used by Norman et al. (1995) in experiments to determine which visual information contributes most to the perception of surface shape.

Figure 7.20   Interactive glyph used by Norman et al. (1995) to measure perception of surface orientation.

shapes that have exactly the same shading but different silhouette contours. The combination of silhouette contour information with shading information is convincing in both cases, but the surface shapes that are perceived are very different. This tells us that shape-from-shading information is inherently ambiguous; it can be interpreted in different ways, depending on the contours.

Contours that are drawn on a shaded surface can also drastically alter the perceived shape of that surface. Figure 7.23 has added shaded bands that provide internal contour information. As in Figure 7.22, the actual pattern of shading within each of the two images, and within the bands, is the same. It is the contour information that makes one surface shape appear so different from the other. This technique can be used directly in displaying shaded surfaces to make a shape easier to perceive.

One of the most common ways to represent surfaces is to use a contour map. A contour map is a plan view representation of a surface with isoheight contours, usually spaced at regular

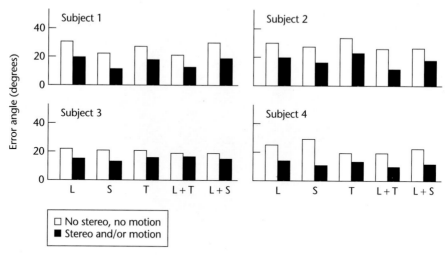

Figure 7.21   Results of the study of shape perception by Norman et al. (1995). The average errors in adjusted orientation are shown for five different surface representations. The different representations are labeled as follows: (L) Lambertian shading, (S) specular highlight shading, (T) texture with no shading, (L + T) Lambertian shading with texture, and (L + S) Lambertian shading with specular highlights. The four sets of histograms represent results from four different subjects.

Figure 7.22   When scanned from left to right, the sequences of gray values in these two patterns are identical. The external contour interacts with the shading information to produce the perception of two very differently shaped surfaces.

intervals. Conceptually, each contour can be thought of as the line of intersection of a horizontal plane with a particular value in a scalar height field, as illustrated in Figure 7.24. Although reading contour maps is a skill that requires practice and experience, contour maps should not necessarily be regarded as entirely arbitrary graphical conventions. Contours are visually ambiguous with respect to such things as degree of slope and direction of slope; this information is given only in the printed labels that are attached to them. However, it is likely that the contours in contour maps get at least some of their expressive power because they provide a limited perceptual code. As we have seen, both occluding (silhouette) contours and surface contours are effective in providing shape information. Although contour-map contours are not silhouettes, they obey one of the cognitive restrictions that Marr (1982) proposed for occluding contours,

Figure 7.24 A contour is created by the intersection of a plane with a scalar field.

Figure 7.23 The left-to-right gray sequence in these patterns is identical. The internal contours interact with the shading information to produce the perception of two very differently shaped surfaces.

namely, that contours are assumed to be planar. They also provide texture gradient information. Thus, contour maps are a good example of a hybrid code; they make use of a perceptual mechanism, and they are also partly conventional.

There are many ways to make oriented textures conform to a surface. Texture lines can be constructed to follow the fall-line (down slope), to be horizontal contours, to be at right angles to maximum curvature direction, or to be orthogonal to the line of site of a viewer, to present a few examples. Kim et al. (1993) investigated combinations of first and second principal directions of curvature contours, as illustrated in Figure 7.25. All of the textured surfaces were artificially lit using standard computer graphics shading algorithms. Subjects made smaller errors in surface orientation judgments when two contour directions were used to form a mesh, as in Figure 7.25(a). Nevertheless, this study and Norman et al. (1995) found that errors averaged 20 degrees. This is surprisingly large and suggests that further gains are possible.

Guidelines for Displaying Surfaces

Taken together, the evidence suggests that to represent a surface clearly it may be possible to do better than simply create a photorealistic rendering of a scene using the most sophisticated techniques of computer graphics. A simplified lighting model—for example, a single light source located at infinity—may be more effective than complex rendering using multiple light sources. The importance of contours and the easy recognizability of cartoon representation suggest that an image may be enhanced for display purposes by using techniques that are nonrealistic.

Taking all these caveats into consideration, some guidelines may be useful for the typical case:

1. A simple lighting model, based on a single light source, should normally be used. The light source should be from above and to one side and infinitely distant.

2. Both Lambertian and moderate specular surface reflection should be modeled. More sophisticated lighting modeling, such as the interreflection of light between surfaces, should be avoided for reasons of clarity.

3. Specular reflection is especially useful in revealing fine surface detail. Because specular reflection depends on both the viewpoint and the position of the light source, the user should be given interactive control of the lighting direction, and the amount of specular reflection to specify where the highlights will appear.

4. Cast shadows should be used if possible, but only if the shadows do not interfere with other displayed information. The shadows should be computed to have blurred edges to make a clear distinction between shadow and surface pigment changes.

5. Surfaces should be textured, especially if they are to be viewed in stereo. However, the texturing should ideally be low-contrast so as not to interfere with shading information. Textures that have linear components are more likely to reveal surface shape than textures with randomly stippled patterns.

Figure 7.25 Surface-revealing texture patterns (Kim et al., 2003). (a) Two-directional texture pattern following first and second principal directions. (b) One-directional texture pattern following first principal curvature direction. (c) One-directional line-integral convolutions texture following first principal curvature direction. (d) No texture. Reproduced with permission.

6. Where appropriate hardware is available, both structure-from-motion (by rotating the surface) and stereoscopic viewing will enhance the user's understanding of 3D shape. These may be especially useful when one textured transparent surface overlays another.

Bivariate Maps: Lighting and Surface Color

In many cases, it is desirable to represent more than one continuous variable over a plane. This representation is called a *bivariate* or *multivariate map*. From the ecological optics perspective discussed in Chapter 1, the obvious bivariate map solution is to represent one of the variables as a shaded surface and the other as color coding on that surface. A third variable might use variations in the surface texture. These are the patterns we have evolved to perceive. An example is given in Figure 7.26, where one variable is a height map of the ocean floor and the surface color represents sonar backscatter strength. In this case, the thing being visualized is actually a physical 3D surface. However, the technique also works when both variables are abstract. For example, a radiation field can be expressed as a shaded height map and a temperature field can be represented by the surface color.

If this colored and shaded surface technique is used, some obvious tradeoffs must be observed. Since luminance is used to represent shape-from-shading by artificially illuminating the surface, we should not use luminance (at least not much) in coloring the surface. Therefore, the surface coloring must be done mainly using the chromatic opponent channels discussed in Chapter 4. But because of the inability of color to carry high–spatial frequency information, only rather gradual changes in color can be perceived. Therefore, in designing a multivariate surface display, rapidly changing information should always be mapped to luminance. For a more

Figure 7.26   A bivariate map showing part of the Stellwagen Bank National Marine Sanctuary (Mayer et al., 1997). One variable shows angular response of sonar backscatter, color-coded and draped on the depth information given through shape-from-shading. *Courtesy of Larry Mayer.*

detailed discussion of these spatial tradeoffs, see Robertson and O'Callaghan (1988), Rogowitz and Treinish (1996), and Chapter 4 of this book.

A similar set of constraints applies to the use of visual texture. Normally it is advisable to use luminance contrast in displaying texture, but this will also tend to interfere with shape-from-shading information. Thus, if we use texture to convey information, we have less available visual bandwidth to express surface shape and surface color. We can gain a relatively clear and easily interpreted trivariate map, but only so long as we do not need to express a great deal of detail. Using color, texture, and shape-from-shading to display different continuous variables does not increase the total amount of information that can be displayed per unit area, but it does allow multiple map variables to be independently perceived.

Cushion Maps

The treemap visualization technique was introduced in Chapter 6 and illustrated in Figure 6.36 (Johnson and Shneiderman, 1991). As discussed, a problem with treemaps is that they do not convey tree structure well, although they are extremely good at showing the sizes and groupings of the leaf nodes. An interesting solution devised by van Wijk and van de Wetering (1999) makes use of shading. They applied a hierarchical shading model to the treemap so that areas representing large branches are given an overall shading. Regions representing smaller branches are given their own shading within the overall shading. This is repeated down to the leaf nodes, which have the smallest scale shading. The illustration shown in Figure 7.27 shows a computer file system. As can be seen, the hierarchical structure of the system is quite clear.

Integration

In this chapter, we have seen a number of ways in which different spatial variables interact to help us recognize objects, their structures, and their surfaces. However, there has been no discussion of how the brain organizes these different kinds of information. What is the method by which the shape, color, size, texture, and other attributes of an object are stored and indexed? Unfortunately, this is still a largely open question. Only some highly speculative theories exist.

One suggestion is the theoretical concept of the *object file*, introduced by Kahneman and Henik (1981) to account for human perceptual organization. An object file is a temporary cognitive structure that stores or indexes all aspects of an object: its color, size, orientation, texture, and even its name and other semantic links (Kahneman et al., 1992). An object file can be thought of as a cognitive data structure that maintains links to all the perceived attributes of an object. An object file allows us to keep track of objects in the visual field, and from one fixation to the

Figure 7.27   The cushion map is a variation on a treemap that uses shape-from-shading information to reveal hierarchical structure. *Courtesy of Jack van Wijke.*

next when they temporarily disappear behind other objects. Work by Pylyshyn and Storm (1988) and Yantis (1992) suggests that only a small number of visual objects, somewhere between two and four, can be maintained simultaneously in this way. Because of this, the display designer should drastically restrict the number of complex objects that are required simultaneously for any complex decision-making task.

Because both linguistic and visual information is included in the object file, it explains a number of well known psychological effects. One effect is that almost any information about an object, either visual or verbal, can be used to prime for that object. If there were a strong separation between visual and verbal information, we would not expect a verbal priming cue, for example, the word *bark*, to make it easier to identify a picture of a dog. But in fact, verbal priming does improve object recognition, at least under certain circumstances.

However, as discussed earlier in this chapter, there are also many priming effects that are strongest within a sensory modality; this is part of the evidence for separate verbal and visual processing centers. The concept of the object data structure also accounts for interference effects.

In the Stroop effect, subjects read a list of color words such as *red*, *yellow*, *green* and *blue* (Stroop, 1935). If the words themselves are printed with colored inks and the colors do not match the word meanings—for example, the word *blue* is colored red—people read more slowly. This shows that visual and verbal information must be integrated at some level, perhaps in something like Kahneman and Henik's object file.

Speculating further, the cognitive object file also provides an explanation of why object displays can be so effective. Essentially, the object display is the graphical analog of a cognitive object file. However, the strong grouping afforded by an object display can be a double-edged sword. A particular object display may suit one purpose but be counterproductive for another. Object-based displays are likely to be most useful when the goal is to give an unequivocal message about the relationship of certain data variables. For example, when the goal is to represent a number of pieces of information related to a part of a chemical plant, the object display can be clear and unambiguous. Conversely, when the goal is information discovery, the object display may not be useful because it will be strongly biased toward a particular structure. Other, more abstract representations will be better because they more readily afford multiple interpretations. Chapter 9 offers more discussion of the relationship between verbal and visual information and presents a number of rules for integrating the two kinds of information.

Conclusion

The notion of a visual object is central to our understanding of the higher levels of visual processing. In a sense, the object can be thought of as the point at which the image becomes thought. Objects are units of cognition as well as things that are recognized in the environment.

There is strong evidence to support both viewpoint-dependent recognition of objects and the theory that the brain creates 3D structural models of objects. Therefore, in representing information as objects, both kinds of perceptually stored information should be taken into account. Even though data may be represented as a 3D structure, it is critical that this structure be laid out in such a way that it presents a clear 2D image. Special attention should be paid to silhouette information, and if objects are to be rapidly recognized, they should be presented in a familiar orientation.

Visual processing of objects is very different from the massive processing of low-level features described in Chapter 5. Only a very small number of complex visual objects, perhaps only one or two, can be held in mind at any given time. This makes it difficult to find novel patterns that are distributed over multiple objects. However, there is a kind of parallelism in object perception. Although only one visual object may be processed at a time, all the features of that object are processed together. This makes the object display the most powerful way of grouping disparate data elements together. Such a strong grouping effect may not always be desirable; it may inhibit the perception of patterns that are distributed across multiple objects. However, when strong visual integration is a requirement, the object display is likely to be the best solution.

Once we choose to represent visual objects in a data display, we encounter the problem of what degree of abstraction or realism should be employed. There is a tradeoff between literal realism, which leads to unequivocal object identification, and abstraction, which leads to more general-purpose displays. Most interesting is the possibility that we can create a kind of hyper-realism through our understanding of the mechanisms of perception. By using simplified lighting models and enhanced contours, together with carefully designed colors and textures, the important information in our data may be brought out with optimal clarity.

processes depth-cue information to provide an accurate perception of space. Following is a list of the more important depth cues. They are divided into categories according to whether they can be reproduced in a static picture (*monocular static*) or a moving picture (*monocular dynamic*) or require two eyes (*binocular*).

Monocular Static (Pictorial):

- Linear perspective

- Texture gradient

- Size gradient

- Occlusion

- Depth of focus

- Cast shadows

- Shape-from-shading

- Depth-from-eye accommodation (this is nonpictorial)

Monocular Dynamic (Moving Picture):

- Structure-from-motion (kinetic depth, motion parallax)

Binocular:

- Eye convergence

- Stereoscopic depth

Shape-from-shading information has already been discussed in Chapter 7. The other cues are discussed in this chapter. More attention is devoted to stereoscopic depth perception than to the other depth cues, not because it is the most important, but because it is relatively complex and because it is difficult to use stereoscopic depth effectively.

Perspective Cues

Figure 8.1 shows how perspective geometry can be described for a particular viewpoint and a picture plane. The position of each feature on the picture plane is determined by extending a ray from the viewpoint to that feature in the environment. If the resulting picture is subsequently scaled up or down, the correct viewpoint is specified by similar triangles, as shown. If the eye is placed at the specified point with respect to the picture, the result is a correct perspective view of the scene. A number of the depth cues are direct results of the geometry of perspective. These are illustrated in Figures 8.2 and 8.3.

Space Perception and the Display of Data in Space

We live in a three-dimensional world (actually, four dimensions if time is included). In the short history of visualization research, most graphical display methods have required that data be plotted on sheets of paper, but computers have evolved to the point that this is no longer necessary. Now we can create the illusion of 3D space behind the monitor screen, changing over time if we desire. The big question is why we should do this. There are clear advantages to conventional 2D techniques, such as the bar chart and the scatter plot. Designers already know how to draw diagrams and represent data effectively in two dimensions, and the results can easily be included in books and reports. Of course, one compelling reason for an interest in 3D space perception is the explosive advance in 3D computer graphics. Because it is so inexpensive to display data in an interactive 3D virtual space, people are doing it—often for the wrong reasons. It is inevitable that there is now an abundance of ill conceived 3D design, just as the advent of desktop publishing brought poor use of typography and the advent of cheap color brought ineffective and often garish use of color. Through an understanding of space perception, we hope to reduce the amount of poor 3D design and clarify those instances in which 3D representation is really useful.

The first half of this chapter presents an overview of the different factors involved in the perception of 3D space. The second half gives a task-based analysis of the ways in which different kinds of spatial information are used in performing seven different tasks, ranging from tracing paths in 3D networks to judging the morphology of surfaces to appreciating an aesthetic impression of spaciousness. The way we use spatial information differs greatly, depending on the task at hand. Docking one object with another and trying to trace a path in a tangled web of virtual wires require different ways of seeing.

Depth Cue Theory

The visual world provides many different sources of information about 3D space. These sources are usually called *depth cues,* and a large body of research is related to the way the visual system

Figure 8.1   The geometry of linear perspective is obtained by sending a ray from each point in the environment through a picture plane to a single fixed point. Each point on the picture plane is colored according to the light that emanates from the corresponding region of the environment. The result is that objects vary in size on the picture plane in inverse proportion to their distance from the fixed point. If an image is created according to this principle, the correct viewpoint is determined by similar triangles, as shown in the upper right.

Figure 8.2   Perspective cues arising from perspective geometry include the convergence of lines and the fact that more distant objects become smaller on the picture plane.

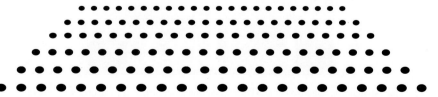

Figure 8.3   A texture gradient is produced when a uniformly textured surface is projected onto the picture plane.

- Parallel lines converge to a single point.

- Objects at a distance appear smaller on the picture plane than do nearby objects. Objects of known size may have a very powerful role in determining the perceived size of adjacent unknown objects. Thus, an image of a person placed in a picture of otherwise abstract objects gives a scale to the entire scene.

- Uniformly textured surfaces result in texture gradients in which the texture elements become smaller with distance.

In the real world, we generally perceive the actual size of an object rather than the size at which it appears on a picture plane (or on the retina). This phenomenon is called *size constancy*. The degree to which size constancy is obtained is a useful measure of the relative effectiveness of depth cues. However, when we perceive pictures of objects, we enter a kind of dual perception mode. To some extent, we have a choice between accurately perceiving the size of the depicted object as though it were in a 3D space and accurately perceiving the size of the object at the picture plane (Hagen, 1974). The amount and effectiveness of the depth cues used will, to some extent, make it easy to see in one mode or the other. The picture-plane sizes of objects in a very sketchy schematic picture are easy to perceive. Conversely, the real 3D sizes of objects will be more readily perceived with a highly realistic moving picture, although large errors will be made in estimating picture-plane sizes.

In terms of the total amount of information available from an information display, there is little evidence that a perspective picture lets us see more than a nonperspective image. A study by Cockburn and McKenzie showed that perspective cues added no advantage to a version of the Data Mountain display of Robertson et al. (1998). The version shown in Figure 8.4(b) was just as effective as the one in Figure 8.4(a). However, both of these versions make extensive use of other depth cues (occlusion and height on the picture plane).

a

Figure 8.4   (a) Variations on Robertson et al.'s (1998) Data Mountain Display. *Courtesy of Andy Cockburn.*

b

Figure 8.4   *Continued* (b) Same as part (a) but without perspective.

Pictures Seen from the Wrong Viewpoint

It is obvious that most pictures are not viewed from their correct centers of perspective. In a movie theater, only one person can occupy this optimal viewpoint (determined by the focal length of the original camera and the scale of the final picture). When a picture is viewed from an incorrect viewpoint, the laws of geometry suggest that significant distortions should occur. Figure 8.5 illustrates this. If the mesh shown in Figure 8.5 is projected on a screen with a geometry based on viewpoint (a), but it is actually viewed from position (b), it should be perceived to stretch along the line of sight as shown (if the visual system were a simple geometry processor). However, although people report seeing some distortion initially when looking at moving pictures from the wrong viewpoint, they become unaware of the distortion after a few minutes. Kubovy (1986) calls this the *robustness of linear perspective*. Apparently, the human visual system overrides some aspects of perspective in constructing the 3D world that we perceive.

One of the mechanisms that can account for this lack of perceived distortion may be based on a built-in perceptual assumption that objects in the world are rigid. Suppose that the mesh in Figure 8.5 is smoothly rotated about a vertical axis, projected assuming viewpoint (a) but viewed from point (b). It should appear as a nonrigid, elastic body. But perceptual processing is constrained by a rigidity assumption, and this causes us to see a stable, nonelastic three-dimensional object.

Under extreme conditions, some distortion is still seen with off-axis viewing of moving pictures. Hagen and Elliott (1976) showed that this residual distortion is reduced if the projective geometry is made more parallel. This can be done by simulating long–focal length lenses, which may be a useful technique if displays are intended for off-axis viewing.

Various technologies exist that can track a user's head position with respect to a computer screen and thereby estimate the position of the eye(s). With this information, a 3D scene can be

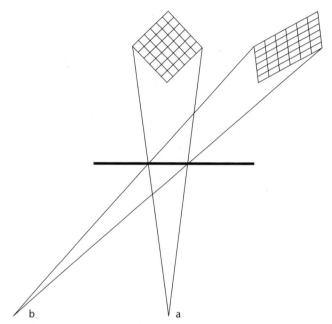

b.   a

Figure 8.5   When a perspective picture is seen from the wrong viewpoint (point b), simple geometry predicts that large distortions should be seen. However, they are generally not seen or, when seen, are minimal.

computed and viewed so that the perspective is "correct" at all times by adjusting the viewpoint parameters in the computer graphics software (Deering, 1992; Ware et al., 1993). There are two reasons why this might be desirable, despite the fact that incorrect perspective viewing of a picture seems generally unimportant. The first reason is that as an observer changes position, the perspective image will change accordingly, resulting in motion parallax. Motion parallax is itself a depth cue, as discussed later in the structure-from-motion section. The second reason is that in some virtual-reality systems, it is possible to place the subject's hand in the same space as the virtual computer graphics imagery. When we make visually guided hand movements toward some object in the world, we are constantly correcting our movements based on visual feedback. If this were done using computer graphics imagery to represent a virtual object and a virtual image of the subject's hand, head-coupled perspective could be necessary to keep the subject's body sense (kinesthetic feedback) of hand position aligned with his or her visual feedback. An example of an experimental setup is shown in Figure 8.6. However, research has shown that as long as continuous visual feedback is provided, *without excessive lag*, people can adjust rapidly to simple changes in the eye–hand relationship (Held et al., 1966). The effects of lag on performance are discussed further in Chapter 10.

Figure 8.6   A user is attempting to trace 3D blood vessels in an interface that puts his hand in the same space as the virtual computer graphics imagery. *From Serra et al., 1997.*

When virtual-reality head-mounted displays are used, it is essential that the perspective be coupled to a user's head movement, because the whole point is to allow users to change viewpoint in a natural way. Experimental evidence supports the idea that head-coupled perspective enhances the sense of presence in virtual spaces more than stereoscopic viewing (Arthur et al., 1993; Pausch et al., 1996).

Occlusion

If one object overlaps or occludes another, it appears closer to the observer. See Figure 8.7. This is probably the strongest depth cue, but it provides only binary information. An object is either behind or in front of another; no information is given about the distance between them. A kind of partial occlusion occurs when one object is transparent or translucent. In this case, there is a color difference between the parts of an object that lie behind the transparent plane and the parts that are in front of it. This can be useful in positioning one object inside another (Zhai et al., 1994).

Figure 8.7   An object that occludes another appears closer to the viewer.

Occlusion can be useful in design; for example, the tabbed cards illustrated in Figure 8.8(a) use occlusion to provide rank-order information, in addition to rapid access to individual cards. Although modern graphical user interfaces (GUIs) are usually described as being 2D, they are actually 3D in a nontrivial way. Overlapping windows rely on our understanding of occlusion to be effective. See Figure 8.8(b).

Depth of Focus

When we look around, our eyes change focus to bring the images of fixated objects into sharp focus on the fovea. As a result, the images of both nearby and more distant objects become blurred. The equations that determine depth of focus are presented in Chapter 2. Focus effects are important in separating foreground objects from background objects, as shown in Figure 8.9. Perhaps because of its role as a depth cue, simulating depth of focus is an excellent way to highlight information by blurring everything except that which is critical. Unfortunately, the technique is computationally expensive and thus currently limited in utility.

Focus can be considered a pictorial depth cue only if the object of fixation can be predicted. In normal vision, our attention shifts and our eyes refocus dynamically depending on the distance of the object fixated. Chapter 2 describes a system designed to change focus information based on measured point of fixation in a virtual environment.

Cast Shadows

Cast shadows are a very potent cue to the height of an object above a plane, as illustrated in Figure 8.10(a). They can function as a kind of indirect depth cue—the shadow locates the object with respect to some surface in the environment. In the case of Figure 8.10, this surface is not present in the illustration but is assumed by the brain. In a multifactor experiment, Wanger et al. (1992) found that shadows provided the strongest "depth" cue when compared to texture, projection type, frames of reference, and motion. But it should be noted that they used a checkerboard as a base plane to provide the actual distance information. Cast shadows function

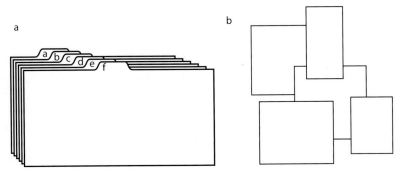

Figure 8.8   (a) Careful use of occlusion enables small tabs to provide access to larger objects. (b) Window interfaces use occlusion.

Figure 8.9   The eye adjusts to bring objects of interest into sharp focus. As a result, objects at different distances become blurred.

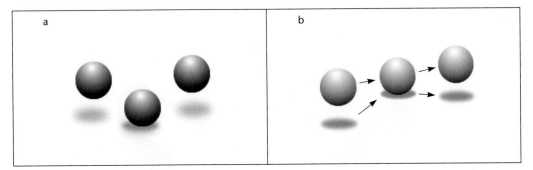

Figure 8.10   (a) Shadows can provide a strong cue for the relative height of objects above a plane. (b) The effect becomes even stronger with motion. The ball actually appears to bounce when the ball and shadow are animated to follow the trajectories shown.

best as a height-above-surface cue when there is a relatively small distance between the object and the surface, and they can be especially effective in showing when an object is very close to the point of contact (Madison et al., 2001).

Cast shadows are useful in distinguishing information that is layered a small distance above a planar surface, as illustrated in Figure 8.11. This technique can be applied to layered map displays of the type used in geographical information systems (GISs). In complex environments, where objects are arranged throughout 3D space, cast shadows can be confusing rather than helpful, because it may not be possible to determine perceptually which object cast a particular shadow.

Kersten et al. (1997) showed that cast shadows are especially powerful when objects are in motion. One of their demonstrations is illustrated in Figure 8.10(b). In this case, the *apparent* trajectory of a ball moving in 3D space is caused to change dramatically depending on the path of the object's *shadow*. The image of the ball actually travels in a straight line, but the ball appears to bounce because of the way the shadow moves. In this study, shadow motion was shown to be a stronger depth cue than change in size with perspective.

It seems likely that shadows can be correctly interpreted without being realistic. Kersten et al. (1996) found no effect of shadow quality in their results. However, one of the principal cues in distinguishing shadows from nonshadows in the environment is the lack of sharpness in shadow edges. Fuzzy shadows are likely to lead to less confusing images.

Shape-from-Shading

See Chapter 7 for a discussion of the perception of surface shape-from-shading information. We can add one more point here. Shading information can be useful in emphasizing the affordances of display widgets such as buttons and sliders, even in displays that are very flat. Figure 8.12 illustrates a slider enhanced with shading. This technique is widely used in today's GUIs.

Figure 8.11   Cast shadows can be useful in making data appear to stand out above an opaque plane.

Figure 8.12   Even with mostly 2D interfaces, subtle shading can make sliders and other widgets look like objects that can be manipulated.

Eye Accommodation

The eye changes focus to bring attended objects into sharp focus on the retina. However, because we are only capable of focusing to one-half of a diopter, this means that accommodation can provide limited information about the distance to nearby objects (Hochberg, 1971). Accommodation does not appear to be used to judge distance directly, but it is used in computing the size of nearby objects (Wallach and Floor, 1971).

Structure-from-Motion

When an object is in motion or when we ourselves move through the environment, the result is a dynamically changing pattern of light on the retina. Structure-from-motion information is generally divided into two different classes: motion parallax and the kinetic depth effect.

An example of *motion parallax* occurs when we look sideways out of a car or train window. Things nearby appear to be moving very rapidly, whereas objects close to the horizon only appear to move gradually. Overall, there is a velocity gradient, as illustrated in Figure 8.13(a). When we move forward through a cluttered environment, the result is a very different expanding pattern of motion, like that shown in Figure 8.13(b). Wann et al. (1995) showed that subjects were able to control their headings with an accuracy of 1 to 2 degrees when they were given feedback from a wide-screen field of dots through which they had to steer. There is also evidence for specialized neural mechanisms sensitive to the time to contact with visual moving targets. These may enable animals to become aware of objects on a collision course (Wang and Frost, 1992).

The *kinetic depth effect* can be demonstrated with a wire bent into a complex 3D shape and projected onto a screen, as shown in Figure 8.13(c). Casting the shadow of the wire will suffice for the projection. The result is a two-dimensional line, but if the wire is rotated, the three-dimensional shape of the wire immediately becomes apparent (Wallach and O'Connell, 1953). The kinetic depth effect dramatically illustrates a key concept in understanding space perception. The brain generally assumes that objects are rigid in 3D space, and the mechanisms of object perception incorporate this constraint. The moving shadow of the rotating bent wire is perceived as a rigid 3D object, not as a wiggling 2D line. It is easy to simulate this in a computer graphics system by creating an irregular line, rotating it about a vertical axis, and displaying it using standard graphics techniques.

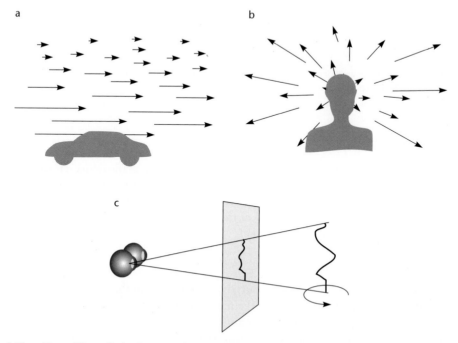

Figure 8.13   Three different kinds of structure-from-motion information. (a) The velocity gradient that results when the viewer is looking sideways out of a moving vehicle. (b) The velocity field that results when the viewer is moving forward through the environment. (c) The kinetic depth information that results when a rotating rigid object is projected onto a screen.

For many tasks, structure-from-motion information is at least as important as stereoscopic depth in providing us with information about the spatial layout of objects in space (Rogers and Graham, 1979). It helps us determine both the 3D shapes of objects and the large-scale layout of objects in space. Structure-from-motion is the reason for the effectiveness of fly-through animated movies that take an observer through a data space.

Eye Convergence

When we fixate an object with both eyes, they must converge to a degree dictated by the distance of the object. This *vergence* angle is illustrated in Figure 8.14. Given the two line-of-sight vectors, it is a matter of simple trigonometry to determine the distance to the fixated object. However, the evidence suggests that the human brain is not good at this geometric computation except for objects within arm's length (Viguier et al., 2001). The vergence sensing system appears capable of quite rapid recalibration in the presence of other spatial information (Fisher and Cuiffreda, 1990).

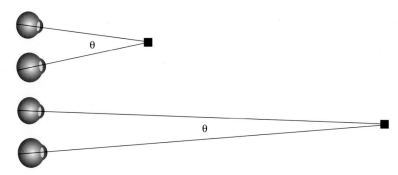

Figure 8.14   The vergence angle θ varies as the eyes fixate on near and far objects.

Stereoscopic Depth

There is an often-expressed opinion that stereoscopic displays allow "truly" three-dimensional images. In advertising literature, potential buyers are urged to buy stereoscopic display equipment and "see it in 3D." As should be plain from this chapter, stereoscopic disparity is only one of many depth cues that the brain uses to analyze 3D space, and it is by no means the most useful one. If fact, as much as 20% of the population may be stereo-blind, yet they function perfectly well and in fact are often unaware that they have a disability. Nevertheless, stereoscopic displays can provide a particularly compelling sense of a three-dimensional virtual space, and for certain tasks they can be extremely useful.

The basis of stereoscopic depth perception is forward-facing eyes with overlapping visual fields. On average, human eyes are separated by about 6.4 centimeters; this means that the brain receives slightly different images, which can be used to compute relative distances of pairs of objects. Stereoscopic depth is a technical subject, and we therefore begin by defining some of the terms.

Figure 8.15 illustrates a simple stereo display. Both eyes are fixated on the vertical line (a for the right eye, c for the left eye). A second line d in the left eye's image is fused with b in the right eye's image. The brain resolves the discrepancy in line spacing by perceiving the lines as being at different depths, as shown.

Angular disparity is the difference between the angular separation of a pair of points imaged by the two eyes (disparity = $\alpha - \beta$). *Screen disparity* is the distance between parts of an image on the screen (screen disparity = $(c - d) - (a - b)$).

If the disparity between the two images becomes too great, double vision, called *diplopia,* occurs. Diplopia is the appearance of the doubling of part of a stereo image when the visual system fails to fuse the images. The 3D area within which objects can be fused and seen without double images is called *Panum's fusional area.* In the worst case, Panum's fusional area has remarkably little depth. At the fovea, the maximum disparity before fusion breaks down is only

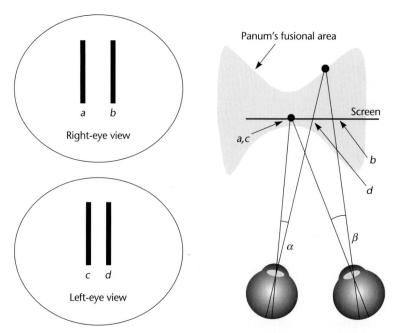

Figure 8.15 A simple stereo display. Different images for the two eyes are shown on the left. On the right, a top-down view shows how the brain interprets this display. The vertical lines *a* and *b* in the right-eye image are perceptually fused with *c* and *d*, respectively, in the left-eye image.

1/10 degree, whereas at 6 degrees eccentricity (of the retinal image from the fovea), the limit is 1/3 degree (Patterson and Martin, 1992).

It is worthwhile to consider what these numbers imply for monitor-based stereo displays. A screen with 30 pixels/cm, viewed at 57 cm, will have 30 pixels per degree of visual angle. The 1/10-degree limit on the visual angle before diplopia occurs translates into about three pixels of screen disparity. This means that we can only display three whole-pixel-depth steps before diplopia occurs, either in front of or behind the screen. It also means that in the worst case, it will only be possible to view a virtual image that extends in depth a fraction of a centimeter from the screen (assuming an object on the screen is fixated). However, it is important to emphasize that this is a worst-case scenario. It is likely that antialiased images will allow better-than-pixel resolution, for exactly the same reason that vernier acuities can be achieved to better-than-pixel resolution (discussed in Chapter 2). In addition, the size of Panum's fusional area is highly dependent on a number of visual display parameters, such as the exposure duration of the images and the size of the targets. Both moving targets and blurred images can be fused at greater disparities, and the fusional area becomes larger, with lateral separation of the image components (Patterson and Martin, 1992). Depth judgments can also be made outside the fusional area, although these are less accurate.

Stereopsis is a superacuity. We can resolve disparities of only 10 seconds of arc at better than chance. This means that we should be able to see a depth difference between an object at 1 kilometer and an object at infinity, under optimal viewing conditions.

Problems with Stereoscopic Displays

It is common for users of 3D visualization systems with stereoscopic display capabilities to disable stereo viewing once the novelty has worn off, and view the data using a monocular perspective. There are a number of reasons that stereoscopic displays are disliked. Double-imaging problems tend to be much worse in stereoscopic computer displays than in normal viewing of the 3D environment. One of the principal reasons for this is that in the real world, objects farther away than the one fixated are out of focus on the retina. Because we can fuse blurred images more easily than sharply focused images, this reduces diplopia problems in the real world. In addition, focus is linked to attention and foveal fixation. In the real world, double images of nonattended peripheral objects generally will not be noticed. Unfortunately, in present-day computer graphics systems, particularly those that allow for real-time interaction, depth of focus is never simulated. All parts of the computer graphics image are therefore equally in focus, even though some parts of the image may have large disparities. Thus, the double images that occur in stereoscopic computer graphics displays are very obtrusive.

Frame Cancellation

Valyus (1966) coined the phrase *frame cancellation* to describe a common problem with stereoscopic displays. If the stereoscopic depth cues are such that a virtual image should appear in front of the screen, the edge of the screen appears to occlude the virtual object, as shown in Figure 8.16. Occlusion overrides the stereo depth information, and the depth effect collapses. This is typically accompanied by a double image of the object that should appear in front.

The Vergence–Focus Problem

When we change our fixation between objects placed at different distances, two things happen: the convergence of the eyes changes (vergence), and the focal lengths of the lenses in the eyes accommodate to bring the new object into focus. The vergence and the focus mechanisms are coupled in the human visual system. If one eye is covered, the vergence and the focus of the *covered* eye change as the uncovered eye accommodates objects at different distances. This illustrates vergence being driven by focus. The converse also occurs: a change in vergence can drive a change in focus.

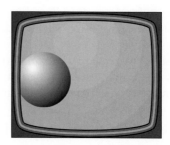

Usable working volume

Figure 8.16   Frame cancellation occurs when stereoscopic disparity cues indicate that an object is in front of the monitor screen. Because the edge of the screen clips the object, this acts as an occlusion depth cue and the object appears to be behind the window, canceling the stereo depth effect. Because of this, the usable working volume of a stereoscopic display is restricted as shown.

In a stereoscopic display, all objects lie in the same focal plane, regardless of their apparent depth. However, accurate disparity and vergence information may fool the brain into perceiving them at different depths. Screen-based stereo displays provide disparity and vergence information, but no focus information. The failure to present focus information correctly, coupled with vergence, may cause a form of eyestrain (Wann et al., 1995; Mon-Williams and Wann, 1998). This problem is present in both stereoscopic head-mounted systems and monitor-based stereo displays. Wann et al. concluded that vergence and focus cross-coupling "prevents large depth intervals of three-dimensional visual space being rendered with integrity through dual two-dimensional displays." This may account for the common reports of eyestrain occurring with dynamic stereoscopic displays.

Distant Objects

The problems with stereoscopic viewing are not always related to disparities that are too large. Sometimes disparities may be too small. The stereoscopic depth cue is most useful for 30 meters or less from the viewer. Beyond this, disparities are too small to be resolved. For practical purposes, most useful stereoscopic depth is obtained within distances of less than 10 meters from the viewer and may be optimal for objects held roughly at arm's length.

Making Effective Stereoscopic Displays

Because stereoscopic depth perception is a superacuity, the ideal stereoscopic display should have very high resolution, much higher than the typical desktop monitor. On current monitors, the fine detail is produced by pixels, and in a stereoscopic display the pixelation of features such as fine lines will generate false binocular correspondences. High-resolution displays enable the presentation of fine texture gradients and hence disparity gradients that are the basis for stereoscopic surface shape perception.

There are also ways of mitigating the diplopia, frame cancellation, and vergence–focus problems described previously, although they will not be fully solved until true 3D displays become commercially viable. All the solutions involve reducing screen disparities by artificially bringing the computer graphics imagery into the fusional area. Valyus (1966) found experimentally that the diplopia problems were acceptable if no more than 1.6 degrees of disparity existed in the display. Based on this, he proposed that the screen disparity should be less than 0.03 times the distance to the screen. However, this provides only about ±1.5 cm of useful depth at normal viewing distances. Using a more relaxed criterion, Williams and Parrish (1990) concluded that a practical viewing volume falls between –25% and +60% of the viewer-to-screen distance. This provides a more usable working space.

One obvious solution to the problem of creating useful stereoscopic displays is simply to create small virtual scenes that do not extend much in front of or behind the screen. However, in many situations this is not practical—for example, if we wish to make a stereoscopic view of extensive terrain. A more general solution is to compress the range of stereoscopic disparities so that they lie within a judiciously enlarged fusional area, such as that proposed by Williams and Parrish. A method for doing this is described in the next two sections.

But before going on, we must consider a potential problem. We should be aware that tampering with stereoscopic depth may cause us to misjudge distance. There is conflicting evidence as to whether this is likely. Some studies have shown stereoscopic disparity to be relatively unimportant in making absolute depth judgments. For example, Wallach and Karsh (1963) found that when they rotated a wireframe cube viewed in stereo, only half the subjects they were trying to recruit were even aware of a doubling in their eye separation. Because increasing eye separation increases stereo disparities, this should have resulted in a grossly distorted cube. The fact that distortion was not perceived indicates that kinetic depth-effect information and rigidity assumptions are much stronger than stereo information. Ogle (1962) argued that stereopsis gives us information about the *relative* depths of objects that have small disparities; when it comes to judging the overall layout of objects in space, other depth cues dominate. Yet, under certain circumstances, accurate depth may be made on the basis of stereoscopic disparities (Durgin et al., 1995). More research will be needed before we have a really clear picture of the way stereoscopic depth is combined with other depth information in the brain. Also, many experiments show large individual differences in how we use the different kinds of depth information, so we will never have a simple "one-size-fits-all" account.

Overall, we can conclude that the brain is very flexible in weighing evidence from the different depth cues and that disparity information can be scaled by the brain depending on other available information. Thus, it should be possible to manipulate artificially the overall pattern of stereo disparities and enhance local 3D space perception without distorting the overall sense of space if other strong cues to depth, such as linear perspective, are provided. We (Ware et al., 1998) investigated dynamically changed disparities by smoothly varying the stereoscopic eye separation parameter. We found that a subject's disparity range could be changed by about 30% over two seconds, without them even noticing, as long as the change was smooth.

Cyclopean Scale

One simple method that we have developed to deal with diplopia problems is called a *cyclopean scale* (Ware et al., 1998). As illustrated in Figure 8.17, this manipulation involves scaling the virtual environment about the midpoint between the observer's estimated eye positions. The scaling variable is chosen so that the nearest part of the scene comes to a point just behind the monitor screen. To understand the effects of this operation, it is worthwhile to consider first that scaling a virtual world about a single viewpoint does not result in any change in computer graphics imagery (assuming depth of focus is not taken into account). Thus, the cyclopean scale does not change the overall sizes of objects as they are represented on a computer screen. The cyclopean scale has a number of benefits for stereo viewing:

- More distant objects, which would normally not benefit from stereo viewing because they are beyond the range where significant disparities exist, are brought into a position where usable disparities are present.

- The vergence–focus discrepancy is reduced. At least for the part of the virtual object that lies close to the screen, there is no vergence—focus conflict.

- Virtual objects that are closer to the observer than to the screen are also scaled so that they lie behind the screen. This removes the possibility of frame cancellation.

Virtual Eye Separation

The cyclopean scale, although useful, does not remove the possibility of disparities that result in diplopia. In order to do so, it is necessary to compress or expand the disparity range. To understand how this can be accomplished, it is useful to consider a device called a *telestereoscope*. This

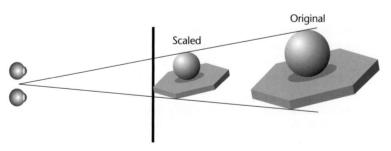

Figure 8.17   Cyclopean scale: A virtual environment is resized about a center point midway between the left and right viewpoints.

uses a system of mirrors to increase the effective separation of the eyes, as shown in Figure 8.18. A telestereoscope is generally used to increase disparities when distant objects are viewed. However, the same principle can also be used to decrease the range of disparities by optically moving the eyes closer together.

Figure 8.19 illustrates the concept of virtual eye separation and demonstrates how the apparent depth of an object decreases if the virtual viewpoints have a wider eye separation than the actual viewpoint. We consider only a single point in the virtual space. If E_v is the virtual eye separation and E_a is the actual eye separation of an observer, the relationship between depth in the virtual image (z_v) and in the viewed stereo image (z_s) is a ratio:

$$\frac{E_v}{E_a} = \frac{z_S(z_v + z_e)}{z_v(z_S + z_e)} \tag{8.1}$$

where z_e represents the distance to the screen. By rearranging terms, we can get the stereo depth expressed as a function of the virtual depth and the virtual eye separation.

$$z_S = \frac{z_e z_v E_v}{E_a Z_v + E_a z_e - E_v z_v} \tag{8.2}$$

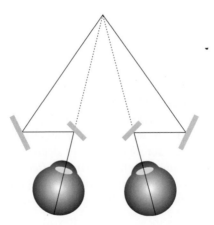

Figure 8.18   A telestereoscope is a device that increases the effective eye separation, thereby increasing stereoscopic depth information (disparities).

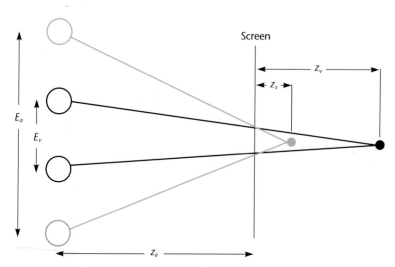

Figure 8.19   The geometry of virtual eye separation. In this example, the stereoscopic depth is decreased by computing an image with a virtual eye separation that is smaller than the actual eye separation. Stereoscopic depth can just as easily be increased.

If the virtual eye separation is smaller than the actual eye separation, stereo depth is decreased. If the virtual eye separation is larger than the actual eye separation, stereo depth is increased. $E_v = E_a$ for "correct" stereoscopic viewing of a virtual scene, although for the reasons stated, this may not be useful in practice. When $E_v = 0.0$, both eyes get the same image, as in single-viewpoint graphics. Note that stereo depth and perceived depth are not always equal. The brain is an imperfect processor of stereo information, and other depth cues may be much more important in determining the perceived depth.

Experimental evidence shows that subjects given control of their eye-separation parameters have no idea of what the "correct" setting should be (Ware et al., 1998). When asked to adjust the virtual eye-separation parameter, subjects tended to decrease the eye separation for scenes in which there was a lot of depth, but actually increased eye separation beyond the normal (enhancing the sensation of stereoscopic depth) when the scene was flat. This behavior can be mimicked by an algorithm designed to test automatically the depth range in a virtual environment and adjust the eye-separation parameters appropriately (after cyclopean scale). We have found the following function to work well for a large variety of digital terrain models. It uses the ratio of the nearest point to the farthest point in the scene to calculate the virtual eye separation in centimeters.

$$\text{EyeSeparation} = 2.5 + 5.0*(\text{NearPoint/FarPoint})^2 \qquad \textbf{(8.3)}$$

This function increases the eye separation to 7.5 cm for shallow scenes (as compared to a normal value of 6.4 cm) and reduces it to 2.5 cm for very deep scenes.

Artificial Spatial Cues

There are effective ways to provide information about space that are not based directly on the way information is provided in the normal environment, although the best are probably effective because they make use of existing perceptual mechanisms.One common technique that is used to enhance 3D scatter plots is illustrated in Figure 8.20. A line is dropped from each data point to the ground plane. Without these lines, only a 2D judgment of spatial layout is possible. With the lines, it is possible to estimate 3D position. Kim et al. (1991) showed that this artificial spatial cue can be at least as effective as stereopsis in providing 3D position information.

It should be understood that although the vertical line segments in Figure 8.20 can be considered artificial additions to the plot, there is nothing artificial about the way they operate as depth cues. Gibson (1986) pointed out that one of the most effective ways to estimate the sizes of objects is with reference to the ground plane. Adding the vertical lines creates a link to the ground plane and the rich texture size and linear perspective cues embedded in it. They function in the same way as cast shadows, only they are generally easier to interpret, given that cast shadows can be confusing with certain lighting directions.

Computer graphics systems sometimes provide a facility for what vision researchers call *proximity luminance covariance* (Dosher et al., 1986), which is simply (but rather confusingly) called *depth cueing* by computer graphics texts. Depth cueing in computer graphics is the ability to vary the color of an object depending on its distance from the viewpoint, as illustrated in Figure 8.21. Normally, this is done so that more distant objects are faded toward

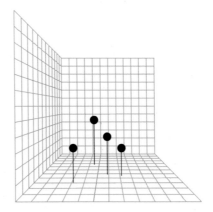

Figure 8.20   Dropping lines to a ground plane is an effective artificial spatial cue.

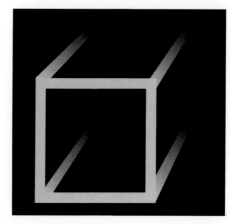

Figure 8.21   Proximity luminance covariance as a depth cue. Object color is altered with distance in the direction of the background color. This simulates extreme atmospheric effects.

the background color, becoming darker if the background is dark and lighter if the background is light.

Proximity luminance covariance mirrors an environmental depth cue sometimes called *atmospheric depth*. This refers to the reduction in contrast of distant objects in the environment, especially under hazy viewing conditions. However the depth cueing is used in computer graphics, it is generally much more extreme than any atmospheric effects that occur in nature, and for this reason it can be considered an "artificial" cue. Dosher et al. (1986) showed that proximity luminance covariance could function as an effective depth cue but was weaker than stereo for static displays. With moving displays, however, proximity luminance covariance became a relatively stronger cue in making an ambiguous 3D scene unambiguous.

Depth Cues in Combination

In computer graphics–based data displays, the designer has considerable freedom about which depth cues to include in a data visualization and which to leave out. One approach would be to simply include all of them. However, this is not always the best solution. There can be considerable costs associated with creating a stereoscopic display or with using real-time animation to take advantage of structure-from-motion cues. Other cues, such as depth-of-focus information, are difficult or impossible to compute in the general case, because without knowing what object the observer is looking at, it is impossible to determine what should be shown in focus and what should be shown out of focus. A general theory of space perception should make it possible to determine which depth cues are likely to be most valuable. Such a theory would provide information about the relative values of different depth cues when they are used in combination.

Unfortunately, there is no single, widely accepted unifying theory of space perception, although the issue of how depth cues interact has been addressed by a number of studies. For example, the weighted-average model assumes that depth perception is a weighted linear sum of the depth cues available in a display (Bruno and Cutting, 1988). Alternatively, depth cues may combine in a geometric sum (Dosher et al., 1986). Young et al. (1993) proposed that depth cues are combined additively, but are weighted according to their apparent reliability in the context of other cues and relevant information. However, there is also evidence that some depth cues— in particular, occlusion—work in a logical binary fashion rather than contributing to an arithmetic or geometric sum. For example, if one object overlaps another in the visual image, it is perceived as closer to the observer.

Most of the work on the combination of spatial information implicitly contains the notions that spatial information is combined into a single cognitive model of space and that this model is used as a resource in performing all spatial tasks. This theoretical position is illustrated in Figure 8.22. However, evidence is accumulating that this unified model of cognitive space is fundamentally flawed.

The alternative model is that depth cues are combined expeditiously, depending on task requirements (Bradshaw et al., 2000; Fine and Jacobs, 1999). For example, Wanger et al. (1992)

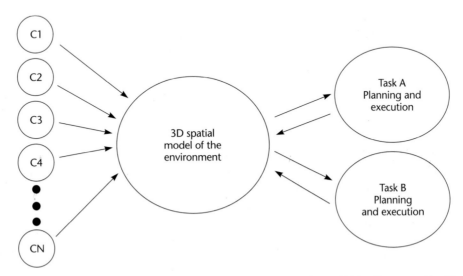

Figure 8.22　Most models of 3D space perception assume that depth cues (C1 . . . CN) feed into a cognitive 3D model of the environment. This, in turn, is used as a resource for task planning and execution.

showed that cast shadows and motion parallax cues both helped in the task of orienting one virtual object to match another. Correct linear perspective (as opposed to parallel orthographic perspective) actually increased errors; thus, it acted as a kind of negative depth cue for this particular task. However, when the task was one of translating an object, linear perspective was the most useful of the cues, and motion parallax did not help at all. Bradshaw et al. (2000) showed that stereopsis is critical in setting objects at the same distance from the observer, but motion parallax is more important for a different layout task involving the creation of a triangle laid out in depth. This alternative model is illustrated in Figure 8.23. Depending on whether the task is threading a needle or running through a forest, different depth cues are most informative, and judgments are made depending on the best available evidence.

An application designer's choice is not whether to design a 3D or 2D interface, but rather how much 3D to use, because depth cues can be applied somewhat independently. For example, in a static picture we use all the monocular pictorial depth cues, but not motion parallax or stereoscopic disparity. If we add structure-from-motion information, we get what we see at the movie theater. If we add stereo to a static picture, the result is the kind of stereoscopic viewer

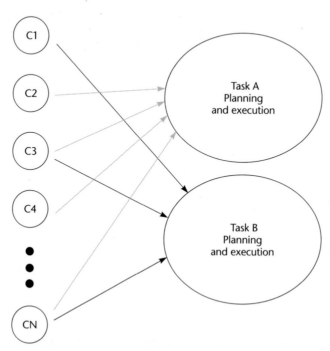

Figure 8.23   Experimental evidence shows that depth cues (C1 ... CN) are weighted very differently for different tasks, suggesting that there is no unified cognitive spatial model.

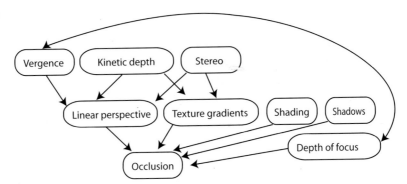

Figure 8.24   A dependency graph for depth cues. Arrows indicate how depth cues depend on each other for undistorted appearance.

popular in Victorian times. We can also use far fewer depth cues. Modern desktop GUIs only use occlusion for windows, some minor shading information to make the menus and buttons stand out, and a cast shadow for the cursor.

However, there are some restrictions on our freedom to arbitrarily choose combinations of depth cues. Figure 8.24 shows a dependency graph for depth cues. An arrow means that a particular cue depends on another cue to appear correctly. This graph does not show absolute rules that cannot be broken, but it does imply that breaking the rules will have undesirable consequences. For example, the graph shows that kinetic depth depends on correct perspective. It is possible break this rule and show kinetic depth with a parallel (orthographic) perspective. The undesirable consequence is that a rotating object will appear to distort as it rotates. This graph is transitive; all of the depth cues depend on occlusion being shown properly, because they all depend on something that in turn depends on occlusion. Thus, occlusion is, in a sense, the most basic depth cue; it is difficult to break the occlusion dependency rule and have a perceptually coherent scene.

Task-Based Space Perception

The obvious advantage of a theory of space perception that takes the task into account is that it can be directly applied to the design of interactive 3D information displays. The difficulty is that the number of tasks is potentially large, and many tasks that appear at first sight to be simple and unified are found, upon more detailed examination, to be multifaceted. Nevertheless, taking the task into account is unavoidable; perception and action are intertwined. If we are to understand space perception, we must understand the purpose of perceiving. The best hope for progress lies in identifying a small number of elementary tasks that are as common as possible. Once this is done, informed design decisions can be made. The remainder of this chapter is devoted to analyzing the following tasks:

- Tracing data paths in 3D graphs
- Judging the morphology of surfaces and surface target detection
- Finding patterns of points in 3D space
- Judging the relative positions of objects in space
- Judging the relative movement of self within the environment
- Reaching for objects
- Judging the "up" direction
- Feeling a sense of presence

This list of eight tasks is at best only a beginning; each has many variations. One additional task, navigation (or *wayfinding*), is discussed in Chapter 10.

Tracing Data Paths in 3D Graphs

Many kinds of information structures can be represented as networks of nodes and arcs, technically called *graphs*. Figure 8.25 shows an example of object-oriented computer software represented using a 3D graph. Nodes in the graph stand for various kinds of entities, such as modules, classes, variables, and methods. The 3D spars that connect the entities represent various kinds of relationships characteristic of object-oriented software, such as inheritance, function calls, and variable usage.

Information structures are becoming so complex that there has been considerable interest in the question of whether a 3D visualization will reveal more information than a 2D visualization.

One special kind of graph is a tree, illustrated in Figure 8.26. Trees are a standard technique for representing hierarchical information, such as organizational charts or the structure of information in a computer directory. The *cone tree* is a graphical technique for representing tree graph information in 3D (Robertson et al., 1993). It shows the tree branches arranged around a series of circles, as illustrated in Figure 8.27. The inventors of the cone tree claim that as many as 1000 nodes may be displayable without visual clutter using cone trees—clearly more than could be contained in a 2D layout. However, 3D cone trees require more complex user interactions to access some of the information than are necessary for 2D layouts.

Empirical evidence also exists that shows that the number of errors in detecting paths in 3D tree structures is substantially reduced if a 3D display method is used. Sollenberger and Milgram (1993) investigated a task involving two 3D trees with intermeshed branches. The task was to discover to which of two tree roots a highlighted leaf was attached. Subjects carried out the task both with and without stereo depth, and with and without rotation to provide kinetic depth. Their results showed that both stereo and kinetic depth viewing reduced errors, but that kinetic depth was the more potent cue.

Figure 8.25   The structure of object-oriented software code is represented as a graph in 3D.

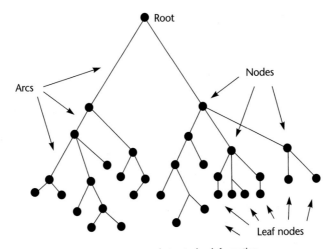

Figure 8.26   A tree is one of the most common ways of structuring information.

Figure 8.27   The cone tree developed by Robertson et al. (1993).

However, an abstract tree structure is not necessarily a good candidate for 3D visualization, for the reason that a tree data structure can always be laid out on a 2D plane in such a way that none of the paths cross (path crossings are the main reason for errors in path-tracing tasks). Conversely, more general graph structures, such as that illustrated in Figure 8.28, usually cannot be laid on a plane without some paths crossing and therefore would benefit more from 3D viewing techniques.

To study the effects of stereo and kinetic depth cues on 3D visualization of graphs, we systematically varied the size of a graph laid out in 3D and measured path-tracing ability with both stereoscopic and motion depth cues (Ware and Franck, 1996). Our results, illustrated in Figure 8.28, showed a factor-of-1.6 increase in the complexity that could be viewed when stereo was added to a static display, but a factor-of-2.2 improvement when kinetic depth cues were added. A factor-of-3.0 improvement occurred with both stereo and kinetic depth cues. These results held for a wide range of graph sizes. A subsequent experiment showed that the advantage of kinetic depth cues applied whether the motion was coupled to movements of the head or movements of the hand, or consisted of automatic oscillatory rotation of the graph.

Occlusion is one additional depth cue that should make it easier to differentiate arcs if they are colored differently, because occlusion makes it easier to see which arcs lie above and beneath. It seems unlikely that other depth cues will contribute much to a path-tracing task. There is no

Figure 8.28   The plot shows how the errors increase as the number of nodes increases in a 3D graph representing stereo and motion depth cues.

obvious reason that we should expect perspective viewing to aid the comprehension of connections between nodes in a 3D graph, and this was confirmed empirically by our study (Ware and Franck, 1996). There is also no reason to suppose that shading and cast shadows would provide any significant advantage in a task involving connectivity, although shading might help in revealing the orientation of the arcs.

Judging the Morphology of Surfaces and Surface Target Detection

Shape-from-shading and texture cues are extremely important in revealing surface shape, as discussed in Chapter 7. Here is some additional information on the value of stereoscopic and motion parallax information.

Experimental evidence suggests that the relative contribution of structure-from-motion and stereoscopic depth depends on very specific task-related factors. Surface shape detection is not a simple problem. A study of the judged *heights* of cones showed that stereo depth was much more effective than structure-from-motion (Durgin et al., 1995). Conversely, Tittle et al. (1995) showed that structure-from-motion information was more important than stereo information in judging the *gradient* of a textured surface. Disparity curvature information may be considerably more important than absolute disparities in judging the shapes of surfaces, because this information is relatively invariant with viewing distance. Rogers and Cagnello (1989) showed that the kind of curvature matters. In a stereoscopic display, we are approximately twice as sensitive to the curvature of a horizontally oriented cylinder as we are to that of a vertically oriented cylinder.

There are also temporal factors to be taken into consideration. When we are viewing stereoscopic displays, it can take several seconds for the impression of depth to build up. However, stereoscopic depth and structure-from-motion information interact strongly. With moving stereoscopic displays, the time to fusion can be considerably shortened (Patterson and Martin, 1992). In determining shape from surfaces made from random dot patterns, using both stereoscopic and motion depth cues, Uomori and Nishida (1994) found that kinetic depth information dominated the initial perception of surface shape, but after an interval of four to six seconds, stereoscopic depth came to dominate.

Overall, it is clear that the way different depth cues combine in judgments of surface shape is highly complex. The relative values of stereo and structure-from-motion depend on the viewing distance, the texture of the surface, the kind of surface shape, and the viewing time. Because of this, when arbitrary surface shapes are being viewed, stereoscopic depth, kinetic depth, shape-from-shading, and surface textures can all add to our understanding of surface shape. The most important cues for any particular surface will vary, but including them all will ensure that good shape information is always presented.

Stereoscopic depth can also be used to enhance real-world imagery. Kalaugher (1985) developed an intriguing technique that enabled a fusion of real-world imagery and photographic imagery. His method is simply to take a slide viewer out into the field, to the same place where a photographic slide image of the scene was previously taken. One eye is then used to view the photographic image while the other eye views the actual scene. Using this technique, it is possible to either enhance or reduce stereoscopic depth simply by moving laterally. Kalaugher reported that with this viewing technique, otherwise invisible features in the real world, such as ledges on distant cliffs, could be seen. A variation of the technique can also be used to view changes in a landscape, such as landslides. When the eyes are alternately covered, these appear as anomalous depth or as movement effects.

Patterns of Points in 3D Space

The scatter plot is probably the most effective method for finding unknown patterns in 2D discrete data. In a 3D scatter plot, three data variables are used to position a point with respect to the *XYZ* axes. The resulting 3D scatter plot is usually rotated around a vertical axis, exploiting structure-from-motion to reveal its structure (Donoho et al., 1988). This technique can be added to the color- and shape-enhanced scatter plots discussed in Chapters 4 and 5.

There has been little or no empirical work on the role of depth cues in perceiving structures such as clusters and correlations in 3D. Nevertheless, a number of conclusions can be deduced from our understanding of the way depth cues function.

Perspective cues will not help us perceive depth in a 3D scatter plot, because a cloud of small, discrete points has no perspective information. If the points all have a constant and relatively large size, weak depth information will be produced by the size gradient. Similarly, with small points, occlusion will not provide useful depth information, but if the points are larger, some ordinal depth information will be perceivable. If there are a large number of points, cast shadows will not provide information, because it will be impossible to determine the association between a given point and its shadow. Shape-from-shading information will be missing, because a point has no orientation information. Each point will reflect light equally, no matter where it is placed and no matter where the light source is placed.

Hence, it is likely that the only important depth cues that will be useful in a 3D scatter plot are stereoscopic depth and structure-from-motion. There seems to be little doubt that using both will be advantageous. As with the perception of surfaces, discussed above, the relative advantages of the different cues will depend on a number of factors. Stereo depth will be optimal for fine depth discriminations between points that lie near one another in depth. Structure-from-motion will be more important for points that lie farther apart in depth.

One of the problems with visualizing clouds of data points is that the overall shape of the cloud cannot easily be seen, even when stereo and motion cues are provided. One way to add extra shape information to a cloud of discrete points is to add shape-from-shading information artificially. It is possible to treat a cloud of data points as though each point were actually a small, flat oriented object. These flat particles can be artificially oriented, if they lie near the boundary of the point cloud, to reveal the shape of the cloud when shading is applied. In this way, perception of the cloud's shape can be considerably enhanced, and shape information can be perceived without additional stereo and motion cues. At the same time, the positions of individual points can be perceived. Figure 8.29 illustrates this.

Judging Relative Positions of Objects in Space

Judging the relative positions of objects is a complex task, performed very differently depending on the overall scale and the context. When very fine depth judgments are made in the near vicinity, as in the task of threading a needle, stereopsis is the strongest single cue. Stereoscopic depth perception is a superacuity and is optimally useful for objects held at about arm's length. For these fine tasks, motion parallax is not very important, as evidenced by the fact that people hold their heads still when threading needles.

In larger environments, stereoscopic depth can play no role at all at distances beyond 30 m. Conversely, when we are judging the overall layout of objects in a larger environment, motion

Figure 8.29   A cloud of discrete points is represented by oriented particles. The orientation is determined by using an inverse-square law of attraction between the particles. When the cloud is artificially shaded, its shape is revealed (Li, 1997).

parallax, linear perspective, cast shadows, and texture gradients all contribute, depending on the exact spatial arrangement.

Gibson (1986) noted that much of size constancy can be explained by a referencing operation with respect to a textured ground plane. The sizes of objects that rest on a uniformly textured ground plane can be obtained by reference to the texture element size. Objects slightly above the ground plane can be related to the ground plane through the shadows they cast. In artificial environments, a very strong artificial reference can be provided by dropping a vertical line to the ground plane. A practical aid to visualizing spatial layout is a regular grid or checkerboard on the floor and walls, as illustrated in Figure 8.20. A grid provides a strong linear perspective cue, as well as a reference texture that may be optimal for many applications.

Judging the Relative Movement of Self within the Environment

When we are navigating through a virtual environment representing an information space, there are a number of frames of reference that may be adopted. For example, an observer may feel she is moving through the environment or that she is stationary and the world is moving past. In virtual-environment systems that are either helmet-mounted or monitor-based, the user rarely actually moves physically any great distance, because real-world obstacles lie in the way. If self-movement is perceived, it is generally an illusion. Note that this applies only to linear motion, not to rotations; users with helmet-mounted displays can usually turn their heads quite freely.

A sensation of self-movement can be strongly induced even when the subject is not moving. This phenomenon, called *vection*, has been studied extensively. When observers are placed inside a large moving visual field—created either by a physical drum or by means of computer graphics within a virtual-reality helmet—they invariably feel that they are moving, even though they are not. A number of visual parameters influence the amount of vection that is perceived:

Field size: In general, the larger the area of the visual field that is moving, the stronger the experience of self-motion (Howard and Heckman, 1989).

Foreground/background: Much stronger vection is perceived if the moving part of the visual field is perceived as background more distant from the observer than foreground objects (Howard and Heckman, 1989). In fact, vection can be perceived even with quite a small moving field, if that field is perceived to be relatively distant. The classic example occurs when someone is sitting in a train at a station and the movement of an adjacent vehicle (seen through a window) causes that person to feel he or she is moving even though this is not the case.

Frame: Vection effects are considerably increased if there is a static foreground frame between the observer and the moving background (Howard and Childerson, 1994).

Stereo: Stereoscopic depth can determine whether a moving pattern is perceived as background or foreground, and thereby increase or decrease vection (Lowther and Ware, 1996).

In aircraft simulators and other vehicle simulators, it is highly desirable that the user experiences a sense of motion, even though the simulator's actual physical motion is relatively small or non-existent. One of the unfortunate side effects of this perceived motion is simulator sickness. The symptoms of simulator sickness can appear within minutes of acute exposure to perceived extreme motion. Kennedy et al. (1989) report that between 10 and 60% of users of immersive displays report some symptoms of simulator sickness. This high incidence may ultimately be a major barrier to the adoption of fully immersive display systems.

Simulator sickness is thought to be caused by conflicting cues from the visual system and the vestibular system of the inner ear. When most of the visual field moves, the brain usually interprets this as a result of self-motion. But if the observer is in a simulator, no corresponding information comes from the vestibular system. According to this theory, the contradictory information results in nausea.

There are ways to ensure that simulator sickness does occur, and ways of reducing its effects. Turning the head repeatedly while moving in a simulated virtual vehicle is almost certain to induce nausea (DiZio and Lackner, 1992). This means that a virtual ride should never be designed in which the participant is expected to look from side to side while wearing a helmet-mounted display. Simulator sickness in immersive virtual environments can be mitigated by initially restricting the participant's experience to short periods of exposure, lasting only a few minutes each day. This allows the user to build up a tolerance to the environment, and the periods of exposure can gradually be lengthened (McCauley and Sharkey, 1992).

Reaching for Objects

A number of researchers have investigated how eye–hand coordination changes when there is a mismatch between feedback from the visual sense and the proprioceptive sense of body position.

A typical experiment involves subjects pointing at targets while wearing prisms that displace the visual image relative to the proprioceptive information from their muscles and joints. Subjects adapt rapidly to the prism displacement and point accurately. Work by Rossetti et al. (1993) suggests that there may be two mechanisms at work, a long-term, slow-acting mechanism that is capable of spatially remapping misaligned systems, and a short-term mechanism that is designed to realign the visual and proprioceptive systems within a fraction of a second. These results have been confirmed in studies with fish-tank VR systems, showing that a large translational offset between the hand position and the object being manipulated with the hand has only a small effect on performance (Ware and Rose, 1999).

Rotational mismatches between what is seen and what is held may have a much greater negative impact on eye–hand coordination than translational mismatches. Experiments with prisms that invert the visual field have shown that it can take months to reach behavior approaching normal performance under this condition, and adaptation may never be complete (Harris, 1965).

Designers of 3D display systems must make choices about which depth cues to include. In a full-blown virtual reality system, the goal is to include all of the depth cues at the highest fidelity possible, but in practical systems for molecular modeling or 3D computer-aided design, various tradeoffs must be made. Two of the options are whether to use a stereoscopic display and whether to provide motion parallax through perspective coupled to head position. Both require an investment in technology not normally provided with computer workstations. The evidence suggests that having a stereoscopic display is more important than the motion parallax that occurs through the motion of the user's head with respect to the objects of attention (Boritz and Booth, 1998; Arsenault and Ware, in press). It appears that users can adapt rapidly to a stereoscopic view from an incorrect viewpoint.

Actually providing a sense of physical contact with nearby objects is also important in calibrating the proprioceptive system, especially for grasping (Mackenzie and Iberall, 1994). Unfortunately, this component of natural object interaction is proving very difficult to simulate. Although VR displays can produce excellent 3D sound and reasonable simulation of visual space, the simulation of touch is still very poor. There is no technology that can produce a physically touchable virtual object at any desirable location within a reasonably large volume of space, although such simulations can be made for small volumes of space by devices such as the PHANTOM (Massie and Salisbury, 1994). This means that it is possible to create small-scale virtual environments that allow for touch and high-resolution stereo display, but not to create large-scale data spaces with the same haptic affordances.

Judging the "Up" Direction

In abstract 3D data spaces (for example, molecular models), there is often no sense of an "up" direction, and this can be confusing. The "up" direction is defined both by gravity, sensed by the vestibular system in the inner ear, and by the presence of the ground on which we walk. Much of the research that has been done on perceived "up" and "down" directions has been done as part of space research, to help us understand how people can best orient themselves in a gravity-free environment.

Nemire et al. (1994) showed that linear perspective provides a strong cue in defining objects perceived at the same horizontal level. They showed that a linear grid pattern on the virtual floor and walls of a display strongly influenced what the participants perceived as horizontal; to some extent, this overrode the perception of gravity. Other studies have shown that placing recognizable objects in the scene very strongly influences a person's sense of self-orientation. The presence of recognizable objects with a known normal orientation with respect to gravity, such as a chair or a standing person, can strongly influence which direction is perceived as up (Howard and Childerson, 1994). Both of these results can easily be adapted to virtual environments. Providing a clear reference ground plane and placing recognizable objects on it can define, to some extent, a vertical polarity for a data space.

The Aesthetic Impression of 3D Space (Presence)

One of the most nebulous and ill-defined tasks related to 3D space perception is achieving a sense of *presence*. What is it that makes a virtual object or a whole environment seem vividly three-dimensional? What is it that makes us feel that we are actually present in an environment?

Much of presence has to do with a sense of engagement, and not necessarily with visual information. A reader of a powerfully descriptive novel may *visualize* (to use the word in its original cognitive sense) himself or herself in a world of the author's imagination—for example, watching Ahab on the back of the great white whale, Moby-Dick.

Presence is somewhat anomalous in a task-based classification of spatial information, because presence as such does not have a clear task associated with it. It is simply the sense of being there. Nevertheless, a number of practical applications require a sense of presence. For an architect designing a virtual building to present to a client, the feeling of spaciousness and the aesthetic quality of that space may be all-important. In virtual tourism, where the purpose is to give a potential traveler a sensation of what the Brazilian rain forest is really like, presence is also crucial.

A number of studies have used virtual-reality techniques for phobia desensitization. In one study by North et al. (1996), patients who had a fear of open spaces (agoraphobia) were exposed to progressively more challenging virtual open spaces. The technique of progressive desensitization involves taking people closer and closer to the situations that cause them fear. As they overcome their fears at one level of exposure, they can be taken to a slightly more stressful situation. In this way, they can overcome their phobias, one step at a time. The reason for using VR simulations in phobia desensitization is to provide control over the degree of presence and to reduce the stress level by enabling the patient to exit the stressful environment instantaneously. After treatment in a number of virtual environments, the experimental subjects of North et al. scored lower on a standardized Subjective Units of Discomfort test.

In developing a virtual-reality theme park attraction for Disneyland, Pausch et al. (1996) observed that high frame rate and high level of detail were especially important in creating a sense of presence for users "flying on a magic carpet." Presenting a stereoscopic display did not enhance the experience. Empirical studies have also shown that high-quality structure-from-motion information contributes more to a sense of presence than does stereoscopic display (Arthur et al., 1993). However, the sense of presence may also be divided into subtasks. Hendrix and Barfield (1996) found stereoscopic viewing to be very important when subjects were asked to rate the extent to which they felt they could reach for and grasp virtual objects, but it did not contribute at all to the sense of the overall realism of the virtual condition. Hendrix and Barfield also found that having a large field of view was important to creating a sense of presence.

Conclusion

High-quality, interactive 3D displays are now becoming cheap, although even mediocre-quality VR systems are still expensive. But creating a 3D visualization environment is considerably more difficult than creating a 2D system with similar capabilities. We still lack design rules for 3D environments, and many interaction techniques are competing for adoption.

The strongest argument for the ultimate ascendancy of 3D visualization systems, and 3D user interfaces in general, must be that we live in a 3D world and our brains have evolved to recognize and interact with 3D. The 3D design space is self-evidently richer than the 2D design space, because a 2D space is a part of 3D space. It is always possible to flatten out part of a 3D display and represent it in 2D.

Nevertheless, it also should be cautioned that going from 2D to 3D adds far less visual information than might be supposed. Consider the following simple argument. On a line of a computer display, we can perceive 1000 distinct pixels. On a plane of the same display, we can display $1000 \times 1000 = 1,000,000$ pixels. But going to a stereoscopic display only increases the number of pixels by a factor of 2. Even this is an overestimate, because it assumes that the images presented to the two eyes are completely independent, whereas in fact they must be highly correlated for us to perceive stereoscopic depth. We may only be able to fuse stereoscopically images that differ by 10% or so. Of course, as we have shown in this chapter, motion parallax can enable us to see more information, and in the case of 3D networks, a network about three times as large can be perceived with stereo and motion parallax. The other depth cues, such as occlusion and linear perspective, certainly help us perceive a coherent 3D space, but as the study of Cockburn and McKenzie (2001) suggests, we should not automatically assume that 3D provides more readily accessible information.

This chapter has been about the use of 3D spaces to display information. It should not be assumed; however, that a 3D display is automatically superior to a 2D solution. Deciding whether or not to use a 3D display must involve deciding whether there are sufficient important subtasks for which 3D is clearly beneficial. The complexity and the consistency of the user interface for the whole application must be weighed in the decision. Even if 3D is better for one or two sub-tasks, the extra cost involved and the need for nonstandard interfaces for the 3D components may suggest that a 2D solution would be better overall. In terms of overall assessment, the cost of navigation is an essential component, and many 3D navigation methods are considerably slower than 2D alternatives. Even if we can show somewhat more information in 3D, the rate of information access may be slower. Issues relating to overall system costs are dealt with in Chapters 10 and 11.

CHAPTER 9

Images, Words, and Gestures

This chapter addresses the relationship between visual information and verbal or textual information. Most visualizations are not purely graphical; they are composites, combining images with text or spoken language. But why do we need words? And when will images and words each be most effective? How should labels be used in diagrams? How should visual and verbal material be integrated in multimedia presentations? A particularly thorny but interesting problem is whether or not we should be using visual languages to program computers. Although computers are rapidly becoming common in every household, very few householders are programmers. It has been suggested that visual programming languages may make it easier for "nonprogrammers" to program computers.

We begin by considering the differences between visual and verbal means of communication, then move on to the application areas.

Coding Words and Images

Bertin, in his seminal work, *Semiology of Graphics* (1983), distinguishes two distinct sign systems. One cluster of sign systems is associated with auditory information processing and includes mathematical symbols, natural language, and music. The second cluster is based on visual information processing and includes graphics, together with abstract and figurative imagery. More recently, the dual coding of Paivio (1987) proposes that there are fundamentally different types of information stored in working memory; he calls them *imagens* and *logogens*. Roughly speaking, imagens denote the mental representation of visual information, whereas logogens denote the mental representation of language information.

Visual imagens consist of objects, natural groupings of objects, and whole parts of objects (for example, an arm), together with spatial information about the way they are laid out in a particular environment, such as a room. Logogens store basic information pertaining to language, although not the sounds of the words. Logogens are processed by a set of functional subsystems that provide support for reading and writing, understanding and producing speech, and logical thought. Logogens need not necessarily be tied to speech. Even in the profoundly deaf, the same language subsystems exist and are used in the reading and production of Braille and sign language.

The architecture of dual coding theory is sketched in Figure 9.1. Visual–spatial information enters through the visual system and is fed into association structures in the nonverbal imagen system. Visual text is processed, but is then fed into the association structures of logogens. Acoustic verbal stimuli are processed primarily through the auditory system and then fed into the logogen system. Logogens and imagens, although based on separate subsystems, can be strongly interlinked. For example, the word *cat* and language-based concepts related to cats will be linked to visual information related to the appearance of cats and their environment.

Much of this theory is uncontroversial. It has been known for decades that there are different neural processing centers for verbal information (speech areas of the temporal cortex) and visual information (the visual cortex). But the idea that we can "think" visually is relatively recent. One line of evidence comes from mental imaging. When people are asked to compare the size of a light bulb with the size of a tennis ball, or the green of a pea with the green of a Christmas tree, most claim that they use mental images of these objects to carry out the task (Kosslyn, 1994). Other studies by Kosslyn and his coworkers show that people treat objects in mental images as if they have real sizes and locations in space. Recently, positron emission tomography (PET) has been used to reveal which parts of the brain are active during specific tasks. This shows that when people are asked to perform tasks involving mental imaging, the visual processing

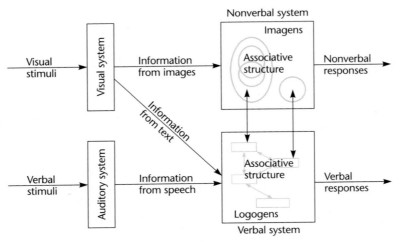

Figure 9.1   According to dual-coding theory, visual and verbal information is stored in different systems with different characteristics. *Adapted from Paivio (1987).*

centers in the brain are activated. Also, when they mentally change the size and position of an imagined object, different visual areas of the brain are activated (Kosslyn et al., 1993). In addition, if visual processing centers in the brain are damaged, mental imaging ability is disrupted (Farah et al., 1992). It would seem that when we see a cow and when we mentally visualize a cow, the same neural pathways are excited, at least in part.

Indeed, modern visual memory theory takes the position that visual object processing and visual object recognition are part of the same process. To some extent, the visual memory traces of objects and scenes are stored as part of the processing mechanism; thus it is not necessary for an object to be fully processed for recognition to take place (Beardsley, 1997). This can account for the great superiority of recognition over recall. We can easily recognize that we have seen something before, but reproducing it in a drawing or with a verbal description is much harder.

The Nature of Language

Noam Chomsky revolutionized the study of natural language because he showed that there are aspects of the syntactic structure of language that generalize across cultures (Chomsky, 1965). A central theme of his work is the concept that there are "deep structures" of language, representing innate cognitive abilities based on inherited neural structures. In many ways, this work forms the basis of modern linguistics. The fact that Chomsky's analysis of language is also a cornerstone of the theory of computer languages lends support to the idea that natural languages and computer languages have the same cognitive basis.

There is a critical period for normal language development that extends to about age 10. However, language is most easily acquired in the interval from birth to age three or four. If we do not obtain fluency in *some* language in our early years, we will never become fluent in any language.

Sign Language

Being *verbal* is not a defining characteristic of natural language. Sign languages are interesting because they are exemplars of true visual languages. If we do not acquire sign languages early in life, we will never become very adept at using them. Groups of deaf children spontaneously develop rich sign languages that have the same deep structures and grammatical patterns as spoken language. These languages are as syntactically rich and expressive as spoken language (Goldin-Meadow and Mylander, 1998). There are many sign languages; British sign language is a radically different language from American sign language, and the sign language of France is similarly different from the sign language of francophone Québec (Armstrong et al., 1994). Sign languages grew out of the communities of deaf children and adults that were established in the 19th century, arising spontaneously from the interactions of deaf children with one another. Sign languages are so robust that they thrived despite efforts of well-meaning teachers to suppress them in favor of lip reading—a far more limiting channel of communication.

Although in spoken languages words do not resemble the things they reference (with a few rare exceptions), signs are based partly on similarity. For example, see the signs for a tree

Figure 9.2   Three different sign-language representations of a tree. Note that they are all very different and all incorporate motion *From Bellugi and Klima (1976).*

illustrated in Figure 9.2. Sign languages have evolved rapidly. The pattern appears to be that a sign is originally created on the basis of a form of similarity in the shape and motion of the gesture, but over time, the sign becomes more abstract and similarity becomes less and less important (Deuchar, 1990). It is also the case that even signs apparently based on similarity are only recognized correctly about 10% of the time without instruction, and many signs are fully abstract.

Language Is Dynamic and Distributed over Time

We take in spoken, written, and sign language serially; it can take a few seconds to hear or read a short sentence. Armstrong et al. (1994) argue that in important ways, spoken language is essentially dynamic. Verbal expression does not consist of a set of fixed, discrete sounds; it is more accurately described as a set of vocal gestures producing dynamically changing sound patterns. The hand gestures of sign language are also dynamic, even when denoting static objects, as Figure 9.2 illustrates. There is a dynamic and inherently temporal phrasing at the syntactic level in the sequential structure of nouns and verbs. Even written language becomes a sequence of mentally recreated dynamic utterances when it is read.

In contrast with the dynamic, temporally ordered nature of language, relatively large sections of static pictures and diagrams can be understood in parallel. We can comprehend a complex visual structure in a fraction of a second, based on a single glance.

Visual and Spoken Language

The difficulty of writing and understanding computer programs has led to the development of a number of so-called *visual languages* in the hope that these can make the task easier. But we must be very careful in discussing these as languages. Visual programming languages are mostly static diagramming systems, so different from spoken languages that using the word *language* for both can be more misleading than helpful. Linguists and anthropologists commonly use the term *natural language* to refer to the spoken and written communications that make up our everyday human communication. Many of the cognitive operations required for computer programming have more in common with natural language than with visual processing.

Consider the following instructions that might be given to a mailroom clerk:

Take a letter from the top of the In tray.

Put a stamp on it.

Put the letter in the Out tray.

Continue until all the letters have stamps on them.

This is very like the following short program, which beginning programmers are often asked to write:

```
Repeat
   get a line of text from the input file
   change all the lowercase letters to uppercase
   write the line to the output file
Until (there is no more input)
```

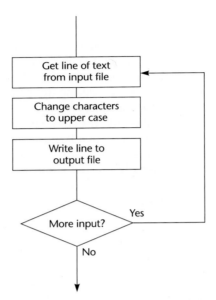

Figure 9.3 A flowchart is often a poor way to represent information that can be readily expressed in natural language–like pseudocode.

This example program can also be expressed in the form of a graphical language called a *flowchart* (see Figure 9.3).

Flowcharts provide a salutary lesson to those who design visual programming languages. Flowcharts were once part of every introductory programming text, and it was often a contractual requirement that large bodies of software be documented with flowcharts describing the code structure. Once almost universally applied, flowcharts are now almost defunct. Why did flowcharts fail? It seems reasonable to attribute this to a lack of commonality with natural language. We have already learned to make *while* statements and *if–then* structured expressions in everyday communications. Using natural language–like pseudocode transfers this skill. But a graphical flowchart representing the same program must be translated before it can be interpreted in the natural-language processing centers.

Nevertheless, some information is much better described in the form of a diagram. A second example illustrates this. Suppose that we wish to express a set of propositions about the management hierarchy of a small company.

Jane is Jim's boss.

Jim is Joe's boss.

Anne works for Jane.

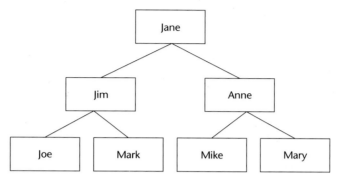

Figure 9.4   A structure diagram shows a hypothetical management hierarchy.

Mark works for Jim.

Anne is Mary's boss.

Anne is Mike's boss.

This pattern of relationships is far more clearly expressed in a diagram, as shown in Figure 9.4.

These two examples suggest that visual language, in the form of static diagrams, has certain expressive capabilities that are very different from, and perhaps complementary to, natural language. Diagrams should be used to express structural relationships among program elements, whereas words should be used to express detailed procedural logic.

However, the existence of the sign languages of the deaf suggests that there can be visual analogs to natural language and hence that effective visual programming languages are potentially possible. If they are to be developed, however, they must be dynamically phrased, rely heavily on animation, and ideally be learned early in life. We will return to this concept later in this chapter.

Images vs. Words

The greatest advantage of words over graphical communication, either static or dynamic, is that spoken and written natural language is ubiquitous. It is by far the most elaborate, complete, and widely shared system of symbols that we have available. For this reason alone, it is only when there is a clear advantage that visual techniques are preferred. In general, words should provide the general framework for the narrative of an extended communication. They can also be used for the detailed structure.

Having said that, often the visualization designer has the task of deciding whether to represent information visually, using words, or both. Other, related choices involve the selection of static or moving images and spoken or written text. If both words and images are used, methods for linking them must be selected. Useful reviews of cognitive studies that bear on these issues have been summarized and applied to multimedia design by a number of authors, including Strothotte and Strothotte (1997), Najjar (1998), and Faraday (1998). What follows is a summary of some of the key findings, beginning with the issue of when to use images vs. words. We start with static images, then consider animated images before moving to discuss the problem of combining images and words.

Static Images vs. Words

As a general comment, images are better for spatial structures, location, and detail, whereas words are better for representing procedural information, logical conditions, and abstract verbal concepts. Here are some more detailed points:

- Images are best for showing structural relationships, such as links between entities and groups of entities. Bartram (1980) showed that planning trips on bus routes was better achieved with a graphical representation than with tables.

- Tasks involving localization information are better conveyed using images. Haring and Fry (1979) showed improved recall of compositional information for pictorial, as opposed to verbal, information.

- Visual information is generally remembered better than verbal information, but not for abstract images. A study by Bower et al. (1975) suggested that it is important that visual information be meaningful and capable of incorporation into a cognitive framework for the visual advantage to be realized. This means that an image memory advantage cannot be relied on if the information is new and is represented abstractly and out of context.

- Images are best for providing detail and appearance. A study by Dwyer (1967) suggests that the amount of information shown in a picture should be related to the amount of time available to study it. A number of studies support the idea that first we comprehend the shape and overall structure of an object, then we comprehend the details (Price and Humphreys, 1989; Venturino and Gagnon, 1992). Because of this, simple line drawings may be most effective for quick exposures.

- Text is better than graphics for conveying abstract concepts, such as freedom or efficiency (Najjar, 1998).

- Procedural information is best provided using text or spoken language, or sometimes text integrated with images (Chandler and Sweller, 1991). Static images by themselves are not effective in providing complex, nonspatial instructions.

- Text is better than graphics for conveying program logic.

- Information that specifies conditions under which something should or should not be done is better provided using text or spoken language (Faraday, 1998).

Animated Images vs. Words

Computer animation opens up a whole range of new possibilities for conveying information. The work of researchers such as Michotte (1963), Heider and Simmel (1944), and Rimé et al. (1985), discussed in Chapter 6, shows that people can perceive events such as hitting, pushing, and aggression when geometric shapes are moved in simple ways. None of these things can be expressed with any directness using a static representation, although many of them can be well expressed using words. Thus, animation brings graphics closer to words in expressive capacity.

- Possibly the single greatest enhancement of a diagram that can be provided by animation is the ability to express causality (Michotte, 1963). With a static diagram, it is possible to use some device, such as an arrow, to denote a causal relationship between two entities. But the arrowhead is a conventional device that perceptually shows that there is *some* relationship, not that it has to do with causality. The work of Michotte shows that with appropriate animation and timing of events, a causal relationship will be directly and unequivocally perceived.

- An act of communication can be expressed by means of a symbol representing a message moving from the message source object to the message destination object (Stasko, 1990). For example, Figure 9.5 shows a part of a message-passing sequence between parts of a

Figure 9.5   The "snakes" concept (Parker et al., 1998). *Image courtesy of NVision Software Systems.*

distributed program using a graphical technique called *snakes* (Parker et al., 1998). Animation moves the head of the snake from one software component to the next as the locus of computation moves; the tail of the snake provides a sense of recent history. Although a verbal or text description of this is possible, it would be difficult to describe adequately the behavior of *multiple* process threads, whereas multiple snakes readily can express this.

- A structure can be transformed gradually using animation. In this way, processes of restructuring or rearrangement can be made explicit. However, only quite simple mechanisms can be readily interpreted. Based on studies that required the inference of hidden motion, Kaiser et al. (1992) theorized that a kind of "naïve physics" is involved in perceiving action. This suggests that certain kinds of mechanical logic will be readily interpreted—for example, a simple hinge motion—but that complex interactions will not be interpreted correctly.

- A sequence of data movements can be captured with animation. The pioneering movie *Sorting Out Sorting* used animation to explain a number of different computer sorting algorithms by clearly showing the sequence in which elements were moved (Baecker, 1981). The smooth animated movement of elements enabled the direct comprehension of data movements in a way that could not be achieved using a static diagram.

- Some complex spatial actions can be conveyed using animation (Spangenberg, 1973). An animation illustrating the task of disassembling a machine gun was compared to a sequence of still shots. The animation was found to be superior for complex motions, but verbal instructions were just as effective for simple actions, such as grasping some component part. Based on a study of mechanical troubleshooting, Booher (1975) concluded that an animated description is the best way to convey perceptual-motor tasks, but that verbal instruction is useful to qualify the information. Teaching someone a golf swing would be better achieved with animation than with still images.

Links between Images and Words

The central claim of multimedia is that providing information in more than one medium of communication will lead to better understanding (Mousavi et al., 1995). Mayer et al. (1999) and others have translated this into a theory based on *dual coding*. They suggest that if active processing or related material takes place in both visual and verbal cognitive subsystems, learning will be better. It is claimed that dual coding of information will be more effective than single-modality coding. According to this theory, it is not sufficient for material to be simply presented and passively absorbed; it is critical that both visual and verbal representation be actively constructed, together with the connections between them.

Supporting multimedia theory, studies have shown that images and words in combination are often more effective than either in isolation (Faraday and Sutcliffe, 1997; Wadill and McDaniel, 1992). Faraday and Sutcliffe (1999) showed that multimedia documents with frequent and explicit links between text and images can lead to better comprehension. Fach and Strothotte (1994) theorized that using graphical connecting devices between text and imagery can explicitly form cross-links between visual and verbal associative memory structures. Care should be taken in linking words and images. For obvious reasons, it is important that words be associated with the appropriate images. These links between the two kinds of information can be static, as in the case of text and diagrams, or dynamic, as in the case of animations and spoken words.

Static Links

When text is integrated into a static diagram, the Gestalt principles discussed in Chapter 6 apply, as Figure 9.6 shows. Simple proximity is commonly used in labeling maps. A line drawn around the object and the text creates a common region; this can also be used to associate groups of objects with a particular label. Arrows and speech balloons linking text and graphics also apply the principle of connectedness.

Beyond merely attaching text labels to parts of diagrams, there is the possibility of integrating more complex procedural information. Chandler and Sweller (1991) showed that a set of instructional procedures for testing an electrical system were understood better if blocks of text were integrated with the diagram, as shown in Figure 9.7. In this way, process steps could be read immediately adjacent to the relevant visual information. Sweller et al. (1990) used the concept of *limited-capacity working memory* to explain these and similar results. They argue that when the information is integrated, there is a reduced need to store information temporarily while switching back and forth between locations.

There can be a two-way synergy between text and images. Faraday and Sutcliffe (1997) found that propositions given with a combination of imagery and speech were recalled better than propositions given only through images. Pictures can also enhance memory of text. Wadill and McDaniel (1992) provided images that were added redundantly to a text narrative; even though no new information was presented, the images enhanced recall.

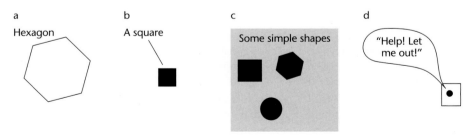

Figure 9.6   Various Gestalt principles are used to guide the linking of text and graphics: (a) Proximity. (b) Continuity/connectedness. (c) Common region. (d) Common region combined with connectedness.

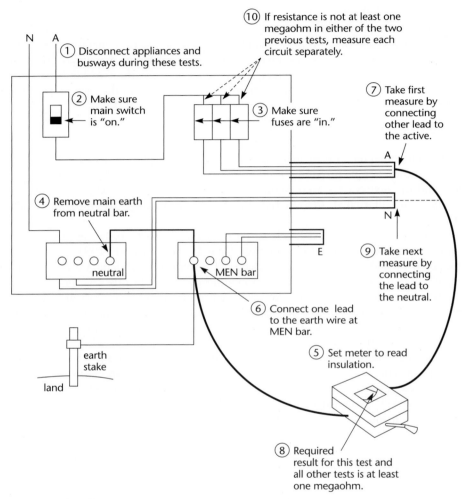

Figure 9.7   An illustration used in a study by Chandler and Sweller (1991). A sequence of short paragraphs is integrated with the diagram to show how to conduct an electrical testing procedure.

The nature of text labels can strongly influence the way visual information is encoded. Jorg and Horman (1978) showed that when images were labeled, the choice of a general label (such as *fish*) or a specific label (such as *flounder*) influenced what would later be identified as previously seen. The broader-category label caused a greater variety of images to be identified (mostly erroneously). In some cases, it is desirable that people generalize specific instances into broader, more abstract categories, so this effect may sometimes be used to advantage.

Gestures as Linking Devices

When possible, spoken information—rather than text information—should accompany images, because the text necessarily takes visual attention away from the imagery. If the same information is given in spoken form, the auditory channel can be devoted to it, whereas the visual channel can be devoted to the imagery (Mousavi et al., 1995). The most natural way of linking spoken material with visual imagery is through hand gestures.

Deixis

In human communication theory, a gesture that links the subject of a spoken sentence with a visual reference is known as a *deictic gesture*, or simply *deixis*. When people engage in conversation, they sometimes indicate the subject or object in a sentence by pointing with a finger, glancing, or nodding in a particular direction. For example, a shopper might say "Give me that one," while pointing at a particular wedge of cheese at a delicatessen counter. The deictic gesture is considered to be the most elementary of linguistic acts. A child can point to something desirable, usually long before she can ask for it verbally, and even adults frequently point to things they wish to be given without uttering a word. Deixis has its own rich vocabulary. For example, an encircling gesture can indicate an entire group of objects or a region of space (Levelt et al., 1985; Oviatt et al., 1997).

To give a name to a visual object, we point and speak its name. Teachers will often talk through a diagram, making a series of linking deictic gestures. To explain a diagram of the respiratory system, a teacher might say, "*This tube* connecting the *larynx* to the *bronchial pathways* in the lungs is called the *trachea*," with a gesture toward each of the important parts.

Deictic techniques can be used to bridge the gap between visual imagery and spoken language. Some shared computer environments are designed to allow people at remote locations to work together while developing documents and drawings. Gutwin et al. (1996) observed that in these systems, voice communication and shared cursors are the critical components in maintaining dialog. It is generally thought to be much less important to transmit an image of the person speaking. Another major advantage of combining gesture with visual media is that this *multimodal* communication results in fewer misunderstandings (Oviatt, 1999; Oviatt et al., 1997), especially when English is not the speaker's native language.

Oviatt et al. (1997) showed that, given the opportunity, people like to point and talk at the same time when discussing maps. They studied the ordering of events in a multimodal interface to a mapping system, in which a user could both point deictically and speak while instructing another person in a planning task using a shared map. The instructor might say something like "Add a park here," or "Erase this line," while pointing to regions of the map. One of their findings was that pointing generally preceded speech; the instructor would point to something and then talk about it.

Interestingly, the reverse order of events may be appropriate when we are integrating text (as opposed to spoken language) with a diagram. In a study of eye movements, Faraday and Sutcliffe (1999) found that people would read a sentence, then look for the reference in an accompanying diagram. Based on this finding, they created a method for making it easy for users to make the appropriate connections. A button at the end of each sentence caused the relevant part of the image to be highlighted or animated in some way, thus enabling readers to switch attention rapidly to the correct part of the diagram. They showed that this did indeed result in greater understanding.

This research suggests two rules of thumb:

- If spoken words are to be integrated with visual information, the relevant part of the visualization should be highlighted just before the start of the relevant speech segment.

- If written text is to be integrated with visual information, links should be made at the end of each relevant sentence or phrase.

Deictic gestures can be more varied than simple pointing. For example, circular encompassing gestures can be used to indicate a whole group of objects, and different degrees of emphasis can be added by making a gesture more or less forceful.

Symbolic Gestures

In everyday life, we use a variety of gestures that have symbolic meaning. A raised hand signals that someone should stop moving. A wave of the hand signals farewell. Some symbolic gestures can be descriptive of actions. For example, we might rotate a hand to communicate to someone that they should turn an object. McNeill (1992) called these gestures *kinetographics*.

With input devices such as the Data Glove that capture the shape of a user's hand, it is possible to program a computer to interpret a user's hand gestures. This idea has been incorporated into a number of experimental computer interfaces. In a notable study carried out at MIT, researchers explored the powerful combination of hand gestures and speech commands (Thorisson et al., 1992). A person facing the computer screen first asked the system to

"Make a table"

This caused a table to appear on the floor in the computer visualization. The next command,

"On the table, place a vase,"

was combined with a gesture placing the fist of one hand on the palm of the other hand to show the relative location of the vase on the table. This caused a vase to appear on top of the table. Next, the command,

"Rotate it like this,"

was combined with a twisting motion of the hand causing the vase to rotate as described by the hand movement.

Although such systems are still experimental, there is evidence that combining words with gestures in this way will ultimately result in communication that is more effective and less error-prone (Mayer and Sims, 1994).

Expressive Gestures

Gestures can have an expressive dimension in addition to being deictic. Just as a line can be given a variety of qualities by being made thick, thin, jagged, or smooth, so can a gesture be made expressive (McNeill, 1992; Amaya et al., 1996). A particular kind of hand gesture, called a *beat*, sometimes accompanies speech, emphasizing critical elements in a narrative. Bull (1990) studied the way political orators use gestures to add emphasis. Vigorous gestures usually occurred at the same time as vocal stress. Also, the presence of both vigorous gestures and vocal stress often resulted in applause from the audience. In the domain of multimedia, animated pointers sometimes accompany a spoken narrative, but often quite mechanical movements are used to animate the pointer. Perhaps by making pointers more expressive, critical points might be brought out more effectively.

Visual Momentum in Animated Sequences

Moving the viewpoint in a visualization can function as a form of narrative control. Often a virtual camera is moved from one part of a data space to another, drawing attention to different features. In some complex 3D visualizations, a sequence of *shots* is spliced together to explain a complex process. Hochberg and Brooks (1978) developed the concept of *visual momentum* in trying to understand how cinematographers link different camera shots together. As a starting point, they argued that in normal perception, people do not take more than a few glances at a simple static scene; following this, the scene "goes dead" visually. In cinematography, the device of the cut enables the director to create a kind of heightened visual awareness, because a new perspective can be provided every second or so. The problem faced by the director is that of maintaining perceptual continuity. If a car travels out of one side of the frame in one scene, it should arrive in the next scene traveling in the same direction, otherwise the audience may lose track of it and pay attention to something else. Wickens (1992) has extended the visual momentum concept to create a set of four principles for user interface design:

1. Use consistent representations. This is like the continuity problem in movies, which involves making sure that clothing, makeup, and props are consistent from one cut to another. In visualization, this means that the same visual mappings of data must be preserved. This includes presenting similar views of a 3D object.

2. Use graceful transitions. Smooth animations between one scale view and another allow context to be maintained. Also, the technique of smoothly morphing a large object into a small object when it is "iconified" helps to maintain the object's identity.

3. Highlight anchors. Certain visual objects may act as visual reference points, or *anchors*, tying one view of a data space to the next. An anchor is a constant, invariant feature of a displayed world. Anchors become reference landmarks in subsequent views. When cuts are made from one view to another, ideally, several anchors should be visible from the previous frame. The concept of landmarks is discussed further in Chapter 10.

4. Display continuous overview maps. Common to many adventure video games and navigation systems used in aircraft or ground vehicles is the use of an *overview map* that places the user in a larger spatial context. This is usually supplemented by a more detailed local map. The same kind of technique can be used with large information spaces. The general problem of providing focus and context is also discussed further in Chapter 10.

Another technique used in cinematography is the *establishing shot*. Hochberg (1986) showed that identification of image detail was better when an establishing shot preceded a detail shot than when the reverse ordering was used. This suggests that an overview map should be provided first when an extended spatial environment is being presented.

Animated Visual Languages

When people discuss computer programs, they frequently anthropomorphize, describing software objects as if they were people sending messages to each other and reacting to those messages by performing certain tasks. This is especially true for programs written using object-oriented programming techniques. Some computer languages explicitly incorporate anthropomorphism. ToonTalk is one such language (Kahn, 1996). ToonTalk uses animated cartoon characters in a cartoon city as the programming model. Houses stand for the subroutines and procedures used in conventional programming. Birds are used as message carriers, taking information from one house to another. Active methods are instantiated by robots, and comparison tests are symbolized by weight scales. The developers of ToonTalk derived their motivation from the observation that even quite young children can learn to control the behavior of virtual robots in games such as Nintendo's Mario Brothers.

A ToonTalk example given by Kahn is programming the swapping of values stored in two locations. This is achieved by having an animated character take one object, put it to the side, take the second object and place it in the location of the first, and then take the first object and move it to the second location. Figure 9.8 illustrates this procedure.

KidSim is another interactive language, also intended to enable young children to acquire programming concepts using direct manipulation of graphical interfaces (Cypher and Smyth, 1995). Here is the authors' own description:

KidSim is an environment that allows children to create their own simulations. They create their own characters, and they create rules that specify how the characters are to

Figure 5. Sequence of snapshots showing the creation of a ToonTalk program to swap two items

```
temp = x;
x = y;
y = temp;
```

Figure 6. Swapping two items in C

Figure 9.8   A swap operation carried out in ToonTalk. In this language, animated characters can be instructed to move around and carry objects from place to place, just as they are in video games (Kahn, 1996b).

behave and interact. KidSim is programmed by demonstration, so that users do not need to learn a conventional programming language.

In KidSim, as in ToonTalk, an important component is programming by example using direct manipulation techniques. In order to program a certain action, such as a movement of an object, the programmer moves the object using the mouse and the computer infers that this is a

Figure 9.9   Creating a "Move Right" rule in KidSim. The user shapes a spotlight to outline the square to the right of the character, then drags the character into the adjacent square. At the bottom, the initial and final states for the rule are displayed (Cypher and Smyth, 1995).

programming event that should occur when a certain set of conditions is met. For example, when an actor gets close to a rock, the actor should jump over the rock.

Programming by example always requires that the programmer make a number of assumptions about how the system should behave. In KidSim, programs are based on graphical rewrite rules—a picture is replaced by another picture specified by demonstration. Figure 9.9 illustrates how the rule "If there is an empty space to the right of me, move me into it" is created. The programmer must first specify the area to which the rule applies and then drag the object from its old position to the new position. There are implicit assumptions that the user must make: the rule will apply wherever the picture object occurs on the screen, and the rule is repeated in an animation cycle.

The use of animated characters as program components can often lead to false assumptions about the programs that use them. Humans and animals get tired and bored, and can be expected to give up repetitive activities quite soon unless they are strongly motivated. Therefore, a child programming a computer with animated characters will expect them to stop and do something else after a while. But this is a poor metaphor for computers, which do not get tired or bored and can continue doing the same repetitive operation millions of times. Ultimately, both the strengths and the weaknesses of programming with animated characters will derive from the rich variety of visual metaphors that become available. Like all metaphors, they will be helpful if they are apt and harmful if they are not.

Rader et al. (1997) carried out an extensive independent evaluation of KidSim in two class-rooms over the course of a year. The system was deliberately introduced without explicit teach-ing of the underlying programming concepts. They found that children rapidly learned the interactions needed to draw animated pictures but failed to gain a deep understanding of the programs. The children often tried to generalize the behavior they saw in ways that the machine did not understand. Students sometimes found it frustrating when they set up conditions they thought should cause some action, and then nothing happened.

A study by Palmiter et al. (1991) provided two kinds of instructions for a procedural task; one was an animated demonstration, the other was a written text. They found that immediately following instruction, the animated demonstration produced better performance. However, a week later, the results reversed; those who received written instructions did better. They explained these results by suggesting that in the short term, subjects could simply mimic what they had recently seen if they were given animated instructions. In the longer term, the effort of inter-preting the written instructions produced a deeper symbolic coding of the information that was better retained over time.

Conclusion

Some of the advantages of visual representation, such as better comprehension of patterns and spatial relationships in general, seem clear and well documented. It is when we try to pin down the advantages of words that we run into difficulty. Indeed, some of the statements made, and supported by experimental results, appear to be contradictory. For example, some authors have suggested that procedural information is better described using words than images. But there appear to be counterexamples. The Gantt chart is a widely used graphical tool for project plan-ning, and this is surely visual procedural information. Also, the study cited earlier by Bartram (1980), showing that visual representation of bus routes is better for planning a bus trip can be described as procedural planning.

It is possible that there is ultimately no kind of information for which words are demon-strably superior—all things being equal. But of course, they are not equal. Natural language pro-vides us with the most developed and widely used symbol system available. We are all experts at it, having been trained intensively from an early age. We are not similarly experts at visual communication. The sign languages of the deaf show that a rich and complete visual equivalent is possible, but these alternative natural languages are inaccessible to most of us. Given the dominance of words as a medium of communication, visualizations will necessarily be hybrids, claiming ground only where a clear advantage can be obtained.

We should use images and words together whenever possible. Concepts presented using both kinds of coding are understood and remembered better. We evidently have cognitive subsystems dealing with both visual and verbal information (as discussed in Chapter 10), and it is possible that using both together may allow us to do more cognitive work. But to obtain a positive benefit from multimedia presentations, cross-references must be made so that the words and images can be integrated conceptually. Both time and space can be used to create these cross-links. The deictic gesture, wherein someone points at an object while speaking about it, is probably the most elementary of visual–verbal linking device. It is deeply embedded in human discourse and probably provides the cognitive foundation for other linking devices.

The material presented in this chapter suggests a number of conclusions about how we should design easy-to-learn computer programming languages. They should be hybrids of visual and natural language codes. Structure should be presented visually, and perhaps also created visually using direct manipulation techniques. Modules can be represented as visual objects, easily connected by drawing lines between them or by snapping them together. Detailed logical procedures should be programmed using words, not graphics. Ultimately, the use of speech recognition software may help beginning programmers with the difficulty of using a keyboard. They may use pointing gestures to bind the spoken words to the relevant parts of the diagrams.

CHAPTER 10

Interacting with Visualizations

A good visualization is not just a static picture or a 3D virtual environment that we can walk through and inspect like a museum full of statues. A good visualization is something that allows us to drill down and find more data about anything that seems important. Ben Shneiderman has coined what he calls a "mantra" to guide visual information-seeking behavior and the interfaces that support it: "Overview first, zoom and filter, then details on demand," (Shneiderman, 1998). But in reality we are just as likely to see an interesting detail, zoom out to get an overview, find some related information in a lateral segue, and then zoom in again to get the details of the original object of interest. The important point is that a good computer-based visualization is an interface that can support all of these activities. Ideally, every data object on a screen will be active and not just a blob of color on the screen. It will be capable of displaying more information as needed, disappearing when not needed, and accepting user commands to help with the thinking processes.

Interactive visualization is a process made up of a number of interlocking feedback loops that fall into three broad classes. At the lowest level is the *data manipulation loop,* through which objects are selected and moved using the basic skills of eye–hand coordination. Delays of even a fraction of a second in this interaction cycle can seriously disrupt the performance of higher-level tasks. At an intermediate level is an *exploration and navigation loop,* through which an analyst finds his or her way in a large visual data space. As people explore a new town, they build a cognitive spatial model using key landmarks and paths between them; something similar occurs when they explore data spaces.

But exploration can be generalized to more abstract searching operations. Kirsh and Maglio (1994) define a class of epistemic actions as activities whereby someone hopes to better understand or perceive a problem. At the highest level is a *problem-solving loop* through which the analyst forms hypotheses about the data and refines them through an augmented visualization process. The process may be repeated through multiple visualization cycles as new data is added, the problem is reformulated, possible solutions are identified, and the visualization is revised or replaced. Sometimes the visualization may act as a critical externalization of the problem, forming a crucial extension of the cognitive process.

This chapter deals with two of the three loops: low-level interaction and exploration. General problem solving is discussed in Chapter 11.

Data Selection and Manipulation Loop

There are a number of well established "laws" that describe the simple, low-level control loops needed in tasks such as the visual control of hand position or the selection of an object on the screen.

Choice Reaction Time

Given an optimal state of readiness, with a finger poised over a button, a person can react to a simple visual signal in about 130 msec (Kohlberg, 1971). If the signals are very infrequent, the time can be considerably longer. Warrick et al. (1964) found reaction times as long as 700 msec under conditions such that there could be as much as two days between signals. The participants were engaged in routine typing, so they were at least positioned appropriately to respond. If people are not positioned at workstations, their responses will naturally take longer.

Sometimes, before someone can react to a signal, he or she must make a choice. A simple choice reaction-time task might involve pressing one button if a red light goes on and another if a green light goes on. This kind of task has been studied extensively. It has been discovered that reaction times can be modeled by a simple rule called the *Hick–Hyman law* for choice reaction time (Hyman, 1953).

According to this law,

$$\text{Reaction time} = a + b \log_2(C) \qquad \textbf{(10.1)}$$

where C is the number of choices and a and b are empirically determined constants. The expression $\log_2(C)$ represents the amount of information processed by the human operator, expressed in bits of information.

Many factors have been found to affect choice reaction time—the distinctness of the signal, the amount of visual noise, stimulus–response compatibility, and so on—but under optimal conditions, the response time per bit of information processed is about 160 msec plus the time to set up the response. Thus, if there are eight choices (3 bits of information), the response time will typically be on the order of the simple reaction time plus approximately 480 msec. Another important factor is the degree of accuracy required—people respond faster if they are allowed to make mistakes occasionally, and this effect is called a *speed–accuracy tradeoff*. For a useful overview of factors involved in determining reaction time, see Card et al. (1983).

2D Positioning and Selection

In highly interactive visualization applications, it is useful to have graphical objects function not only as program output—a way of representing data—but also as program input, a way of finding out more about data.

Selection using a mouse or some similar input device (such as a joystick or trackball) is one of the most common interactive operations in the modern graphical user interface, and it has been extensively studied. A simple mathematical model provides a useful estimation of the time taken to select a target that has a particular position and size:

$$\text{Selection time} = a + b \log_2(D/W + 1.0) \qquad \textbf{(10.2)}$$

where D is the distance to the center of the target, W is the width of the target, and a and b are constants determined empirically. These are different for different devices.

This formula is known as Fitts' law, after Paul Fitts (1954). The term $\log_2 (D/W + 1.0)$ is known as the *index of difficulty* (ID). The value $1/b$ is called the *index of performance* (IP) and is given in units of bits per second. There are a number of variations in the index-of-difficulty expression, but the one given here is the most robust (MacKenzie, 1992). Typical IP values for measured performance made with the fingertip, the wrist, and the forearm are all in the vicinity of 4 bits per second (Balakrishnan and MacKenzie, 1997). To put this into perspective, consider moving a cursor 16 cm across a screen to a small (0.5 cm) target. The index of difficulty will be about 5 bits. The selection will take more than a second longer than selecting a target that is already under the cursor.

Fitts' law can be thought of as describing an iterative process of eye–hand coordination, as illustrated in Figure 10.1. The human starts by judging the distance to the target and initiates the hand movement. On successive iterations, a corrective adjustment is made to the hand movement based on visual feedback showing the cursor position. The number of iterations around the control loop increases both as the distance to the target gets larger and as the size of the target gets smaller. The logarithmic nature of the relationship derives from the fact that on each iteration, the task difficulty is reduced in proportion to the remaining distance.

In many of the more complex data visualization systems, as well as in experimental data visualization systems using 3D virtual-reality (VR) technologies, there is a significant lag between a hand movement and the visual feedback provided on the display (Liang et al., 1991; Ware and Balakrishnan, 1994).

Fitts' law, modified to include lag, looks like this:

$$\text{Mean time} = a + b \, (\text{Human Time} + \text{MachineLag}) \log_2 (D/W + 1.0) \qquad \textbf{(10.3)}$$

According to this equation, the effects of lag increase as the target gets smaller. Because of this, a fraction-of-a-second lag can result in a subject's taking several seconds longer to perform a simple selection task. This may not seem like much, but in a VR environment intended to make everything seem easy and natural, lag can make the simplest task difficult.

Fitts' law is part of ISO standard 9214-9, which sets out protocols for evaluating user performance and comfort when using pointing devices with visual display terminals. It is invaluable as a tool for evaluating potential new input devices.

Hover Queries

The most common kind of selection action with a computer is done by dragging a cursor over an object and clicking the mouse button. The *hover query* dispenses with the mouse click. Extra information is revealed about an object when the mouse cursor passes over it. Usually it is implemented with a delay; for example, the function of an icon is shown by a brief text message after

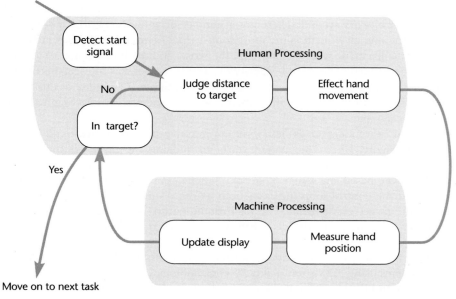

Figure 10.1   The visually guided reaching control loop. The human processor makes adjustments based on visual feedback provided by the computer.

hovering for a second or two. However, a hover query can function without a delay, making it very fast. The enables the mouse cursor to be dragged over a set of data objects, rapidly revealing the data contents and perhaps allowing an interactive query rate of several per second in special circumstances.

Path Tracing

Fitts' law deals with single, discrete actions, such as reaching for an object. Other tasks, such as tracing a curve or steering a car, involve continuous ongoing control. In such tasks, we are continually making a series of corrections based on visual feedback about the results of our recent actions. Accot and Zhai (1997) used Fitts' law to derive a prediction about continuous steering tasks. Their derivation revealed that the speed at which tracing could be done should be a simple function of the width of the path:

$$v = W/\tau \qquad \qquad \textbf{(10.4)}$$

where v is the velocity, W is the path width, and τ is a constant that depends on the motor control system of the person doing the tracing. In a series of experiments, the researchers found an almost perfect linear relationship between speed of path-following and the path width, confirming their theory. The actual values of τ lay between .05 and .11 sec, depending on the specific task. To make this more concrete, consider the problem of tracing a pencil along a 2 mm–wide path. Their results suggest that this will be done at a rate of between 1.8 and 4 cm/sec.

Two-Handed Interaction

In most computer interfaces, users select and move graphical objects around the screen with a mouse held in one hand, leaving the other unoccupied. But in interacting with the everyday world, we frequently use both our hands. This leads us to the question of how we might make the computer interface better by taking advantage of both hands (Buxton and Myers, 1986).

The most important principle that has been discovered relating to the way tasks should be allocated to the two hands is Guiard's *kinematic chain theory* (Guiard, 1987). According to this theory, the left hand and the right hand form a kinematic chain, with the left hand providing a frame of reference for movements with the right, in right-handed individuals. For example, if we sculpt a small object out of modeling clay, we are likely to hold it in the left hand and do the detailed shaping with the right. The left hand reorients the piece and provides the best view, whereas the right pokes and prods within that frame of reference.

A number of interface designers have incorporated this principle into demonstrably superior interfaces for various tasks (Bier et al., 1993, Kabbash et al., 1994). For example, in an innovative computer-based drawing package, Kurtenbach et al. (1997) showed how templates, such as the French curve, could be moved rapidly over a drawing with the left hand while an artist used his or her right hand to paint around the shape.

Another way that using the left hand can be beneficial is in positioning tools for easy access. In interactive drawing packages, users spend a lot of time moving between the drawing and various menus, positioned off to the side of the screen. The *toolglass* and *magic lens* approach, developed by Bier et al. (1993), got around this problem by allowing users to use the left hand to position tool palettes and the right hand to do normal drawing operations. This allowed for very quick changes in color or brush characteristics. As an additional design refinement, they also made some of the tools transparent (hence toolglasses).

In an application more relevant to information visualization, Stone et al. (1994) developed the magic lens idea as a set of interactive information filters implemented as transparent windows that the user can move over an information visualization with the left hand. The magic lens could be programmed to be a kind of data X-ray, revealing normally invisible aspects of the data. For example, a magic lens view of a map might show some or all of the regions with high rainfall, or alternatively, the geology underneath. In the magic lens design, the right hand can be used in a conventional way, to control a cursor that can then be used to click within the magic lens, to make selections or position objects.

Learning

Over time, people become more skilled at any task, barring fatigue, sickness, or injury. A simple expression known as the *power law of practice* describes the way task performance speeds up over time.

$$\log(T_n) = C - \alpha \log(n) \tag{10.5}$$

where $C = \log(T_1)$ is based on the time to perform the task on the first trial and, T_n is the time required to perform the nth trial, and α is a constant that represents the steepness of the learning curve.

One of the ways in which skilled performance is obtained is through the *chunking* of small subtasks into programmed motor procedures. The beginning typist must make a conscious effort to hit the letters *t, h,* and *e* when typing the word *the,* but the brains of experienced typists can execute preprogrammed bursts of motor commands so that the entire word can be typed with a single mental command to the motor cortex. Skill learning is characterized by more and more of the task becoming automated and encapsulated. To encourage skill automation, the computer system should provide rapid and clear feedback of the consequences of user actions (Hammond, 1987).

Control Compatibility

Some control movements are easier to learn than others, and this depends heavily on prior experience. If you move a computer mouse to the right, causing an object on the screen to move to the right, this positioning method will be easy to learn. A skill is being applied that was gained very early in life and has been refined ever since. But if the system interface has been created such that a mouse movement to the right causes a graphical object to move to the left, this will be incompatible with everyday experience and positioning the object will be difficult. In the behaviorist tradition of psychology, this factor is generally called *stimulus–response (S–R) compatibility*. In modern cognitive psychology, the effects of S–R compatibility are readily understood in terms of skill learning and skill transfer.

In general, it will be easier to execute tasks in computer interfaces if the interfaces are designed in such a way that they take advantage of previously learned ways of doing things. Nevertheless, some inconsistencies are easily tolerated, whereas others are not. For example, many user interfaces amplify the effect of a mouse movement so that a small hand movement results in a large cursor movement. Psychologists have conducted extensive experiments that involve changing the relationship between eye and hand. If a prism is used to laterally displace what is seen relative to what is felt, people can adapt in minutes or even seconds (Welch and Cohen, 1991). This is like using a mouse that is laterally displaced from the screen cursor being controlled.

On the other hand, if people are asked to view the world inverted with a mirror, it can take weeks of adaptation for them to learn to operate in an upside-down world (Harris, 1965). Snyder and Pronko (1952) had subjects wear inverting prisms continuously for a month. At the end of this period, reaching behaviors seemed error-free, but the world still seemed upside-down. This suggests that if we want to achieve good eye–hand coordination in an interface, we do not need to worry too much about matching hand translation with virtual object translation, but we should worry about matching the axis or rotation.

Some imaginative interfaces designed for virtual reality involve extreme mismatches between the position of the virtual hand and the proprioceptive feedback from the user's body. In the Go-Go Gadget technique (named after the cartoon character, Inspector Gadget), the user's virtual hand is stretched out far beyond his or her actual hand position to allow for manipulation of objects at a distance (Poupyrev et al., 1996).

Studies by Ramachandran (1999) provide interesting evidence that even under extreme distortions people may come to act as if a virtual hand is their own, particularly if touch is stimulated. In one of Ramachandran's experiments, he hid a subject's hand behind a barrier and showed the subject a grotesque rubber Halloween hand. Next, he stroked and patted the subject's actual hand and the Halloween hand in exact synchrony. Remarkably, in a very short time, the subject came to perceive that the Halloween hand was his or her own. The strength of this identification was demonstrated when the researcher hit the Halloween hand with a hammer. The subjects showed a strong spike in galvanic skin response (GSR), indicating a physical sense of shock. No shock was registered without the stroking. The important point from the perspective of virtual reality interfaces is that even though the fake hand and the subjects' real hand were in quite different places, a strong sense of identification occurred.

Consistency with real-world actions is only one factor in skill learning. There are also the simple physical affordances of the task itself. It is easier for us to make certain body movements than others. Very often we can make computer-mediated tasks easier to perform than their real-world counterparts. When designing a house, we do not need to construct it virtually with bricks and concrete. The magic of computers is that a single button click can often accomplish as much as a prolonged series of actions in the real world. For this reason, it would be naïve to conclude that computer interfaces should evolve toward VR simulations of real-world tasks or even enhanced Go-Go Gadget–style interactions.

Vigilance

A basic element of many interaction cycles is the detection of a target. Although several aspects of this have already been discussed in Chapter 5, a common and important problem remains to be covered—the detection of infrequently appearing targets.

The invention of radar during World War II created a need for radar operators to monitor radar screens for long hours, searching for visual signals representing incoming enemy aircraft. Out of this came a need to understand how people can maintain *vigilance* while performing monotonous tasks. This kind of task is common to airport baggage X-ray operators, industrial quality-control inspectors, and the operators of large power grids. Vigilance tasks commonly involve visual targets, although they can be auditory. There is extensive literature concerning vigilance (see Davies and Parasuraman, 1980, for a detailed review). Here is an overview of some of the more general findings, adapted from Wickens (1992):

1. Vigilance performance falls substantially over the first hour.

2. Fatigue has a large negative influence on vigilance.

3. To perform a difficult vigilance task effectively requires a high level of sustained attention, using significant cognitive resources. This means that dual tasking is not an option during an important vigilance task. It is not possible for operators to perform some useful task in their "spare time" while simultaneously monitoring for some difficult-to-perceive signal.

4. Irrelevant signals reduce performance. The more irrelevant visual information is presented to a person performing a vigilance task, the harder it becomes.

Overall, people perform poorly on vigilance tasks, but there are a number of techniques that can improve performance. One method is to provide reminders at frequent intervals about what the targets will look like. This is especially important if there are many different kinds of targets. Another is to take advantage of the visual system's sensitivity to motion. A difficult target for a radar operator might be a slowly moving ship embedded in a great many irrelevant noise signals. Scanlan (1975) showed that if a number of radar images are stored up and rapidly replayed, the image of the moving ship can easily be differentiated from the visual noise. Generally, anything that can transfer the visual signal into the optimal spatial or temporal range of the visual system should help detection. If the signal can be made perceptually different or distinct from irrelevant information, this will also help. The various factors that make color, motion, and texture distinct can all be applied. These are discussed in Chapters 4 and 5.

Exploration and Navigation Loop

View navigation is important in visualization when the data is mapped into an extended and detailed visual space. The problem is complex, encompassing theories of pathfinding and map use, cognitive spatial metaphors, and issues related to direct manipulation and visual feedback.

Figure 10.2 sketches the basic navigation control loop. On the human side is a cognitive logical and spatial model whereby the user understands the data space and his or her progress through it. If the data space is maintained for an extended period, parts of its spatial model may become encoded in long-term memory. On the computer side, the visualization may be updated and refined from data mapped into the spatial model.

Here, we start with the problem of 3D locomotion; next, we consider the problem of pathfinding, and finally move on to the more abstract problem of maintaining focus and context in abstract data spaces.

Locomotion and Viewpoint Control

Some data visualization environments show information in such a way that it looks like a 3D landscape, not just a flat map. This is done with remote sensing data from other planets, or with maps of the ocean floor or other data related to the terrestrial environment. The data landscape idea has also been applied to abstract data spaces such as the World Wide Web (see Figure 10.3 for an example). The idea is that we should find it easy to navigate through data presented in this way because we can harness our real-world spatial interpretation and navigation skills.

James Gibson (1986) offers an environmental perspective on the problem of perceiving for navigation:

A path affords pedestrian locomotion from one place to another, between the terrain features that prevent locomotion. The preventers of locomotion consist of obstacles, barriers, water margins, and brinks (the edges of cliffs). A path must afford footing; it must be relatively free of rigid foot-sized obstacles.

Gibson goes on to describe the characteristics of obstacles, margins, brinks, steps, and slopes. According to Gibson, locomotion is largely about perceiving and using the affordances offered for navigation by the environment. (See Chapter 1 for a discussion of affordances). His perspective can be used in a quite straightforward way in designing virtual environments, much as we might design a public museum or a theme park. The designer creates barriers and paths in order to encourage visits to certain locations and discourage others.

We can also understand navigation in terms of the depth cues presented in Chapter 8. All the perspective cues are important in providing a sense of scale and distance, although the stereoscopic cue is important only for close-up navigation in situations such as walking through a crowd. When we are navigating at higher speed, in an automobile or a plane, stereoscopic depth is irrelevant, because the important parts of the landscape are beyond the range of stereoscopic

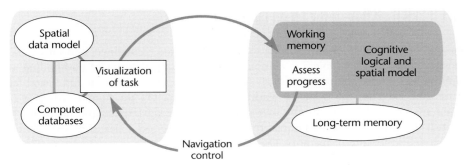

Figure 10.2   The navigation control loop.

Figure 10.3   Web sites arranged as a data landscape (T. Bray, 1996).

discrimination. Under these conditions, structure-from-motion cues and information based on perceived objects of known size are critical.

It is usually assumed that smooth-motion flow of images across the retina is necessary for judgment of the direction of self-motion within the environment. But Vishton and Cutting (1995) investigated this problem using VR technology, with subjects moving through a forestlike virtual environment, and concluded that relative displacement of identifiable objects over time was the key, not smooth motion. Their subjects could do almost as well with a low frame rate, with images presented only 1.67 times per second, but performance declined markedly when updates were less than 1 per second. The lesson for the design of virtual navigation aids is that these environments should be sparsely populated with discrete but separately identifiable objects—there must be enough landmarks that several are always visible at any instant, and frame rates ideally should be at least 2 per second. However, it should also be recognized that although judgments of heading are not impaired by low frame rates, other problems will result. Low frame rates cause lag in visual feedback and, as discussed previously, this can introduce serious performance problems.

Spatial Navigation Metaphors

Interaction metaphors are cognitive models for interaction that can profoundly influence the design of interfaces to data spaces. Here are two sets of instructions for different viewpoint control interfaces:

1. "Imagine that the model environment shown on the screen is like a real model mounted on a special turntable that you can grasp, rotate with your hand, move sideways, or pull towards you."

2. "Imagine that you are flying a helicopter and its controls enable you to move up and down, forward and back, left and right."

With the first interface metaphor, if the user wishes to look at the right-hand side of some part of the scene, she must rotate the scene to the left to get the correct view. With the second interface metaphor, the user must fly her vehicle forward, around to the right, while turning in toward the target. Although the underlying geometry is the same, the user interface and the user's conception of the task are very different in the two cases.

Navigation metaphors have two fundamentally different kinds of constraints on their usefulness. The first of these constraints is essentially cognitive. The metaphor provides the user with a model that enables the prediction of system behavior given different kinds of input actions. A good metaphor is one that is apt, matches the system well, and is also easy to understand. The second constraint is more of a physical limitation. A particular metaphor will naturally make some actions physically easy to carry out, and others difficult to carry out, because of its implementation. For example, a walking metaphor limits the viewpoint to a few feet above ground level and the speed to a few meters per second. Both kinds of constraints are related to Gibson's concept of affordances—a particular interface affords certain kinds of movement and not others, but it must also be *perceived* to embody those affordances.

Note that, as discussed in Chapter 1, we are going beyond Gibson's view of affordances here. Gibsonian affordances are properties of the *physical* environment. In computer interfaces, the physical environment constitutes only a small part of the problem, because most interaction is mediated through the computer and Gibson's concept as he framed it does not strictly apply. We must extend the notion of affordances to apply to both the physical characteristics of the user interface and the representation of the data. A more useful definition of an interface with the right affordances is one that makes the possibility for action plain to the user and gives feedback that is easy to interpret.

Four main classes of metaphors have been employed in the problem of controlling the viewpoint in virtual 3D spaces. Figure 10.4 provides an illustration and summary. Each metaphor has a different set of affordances.

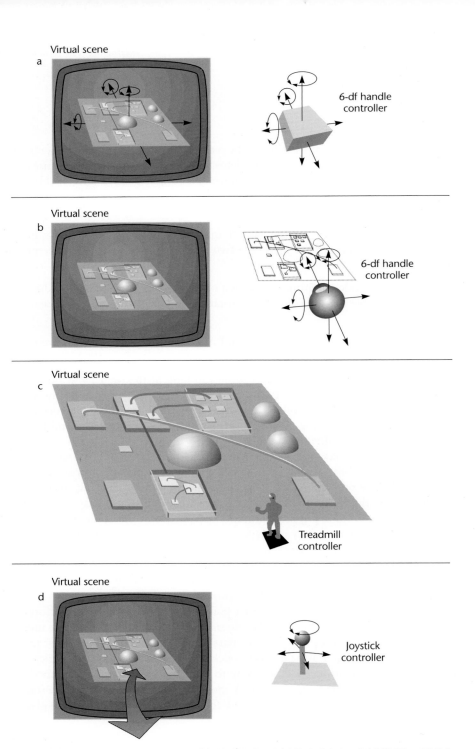

Figure 10.4 Four different navigation metaphors: (a) World-in-hand. (b) Eyeball-in-hand. (c) Walking. (d) Flying.

1. World-in-hand. The user metaphorically grabs some part of the 3D environment and moves it (Houde, 1992; Ware and Osborne, 1990). Moving the viewpoint closer to some point in the environment actually involves pulling the environment closer to the user. Rotating the environment similarly involves twisting the world about some point as if it were held in the user's hand. A variation on this metaphor has the object mounted on a virtual turntable or gimbal. The world-in-hand model would seem to be optimal for viewing discrete, relatively compact data objects, such as virtual vases or telephones. It does not provide affordances for navigating long distances over extended terrains.

2. Eyeball-in-hand. In the eyeball-in-hand metaphor, the user imagines that she is directly manipulating her viewpoint, much as she might control a camera by pointing it and positioning it with respect to an imaginary landscape. The resulting view is represented on the computer screen. This is one of the least effective methods for controlling the viewpoint. Badler et al. (1986) observed that "consciously calculated activity" was involved in setting a viewpoint. Ware and Osborne (1990) found that although some viewpoints were easy to achieve, others led to considerable confusion. They also noted that with this technique, physical affordances are limited by the positions in which the user can physically place her hand. Certain views from far above or below cannot be achieved or are blocked by the physical objects in the room.

3. Walking. One way of allowing inhabitants of a virtual environment to navigate is simply to let them walk. Unfortunately, even though a large extended virtual environment can be created, the user will soon run into the real walls of the room in which the equipment is housed. Most VR systems require a handler to prevent the inhabitant of the virtual world from tripping over the real furniture. A number of researchers have experimented with devices like exercise treadmills so that people can walk without actually moving. Typically, something like a pair of handlebars is used to steer. In an alternative approach, Slater et al. (1995) created a system that captures the characteristic up-and-down head motion that occurs when people walk in place. When this is detected, the system moves the virtual viewpoint forward in the direction of head orientation. This gets around the problem of bumping into walls, and may be useful for navigating in environments such as virtual museums. However, the affordances are still restrictive.

4. Flying. Modern digital terrain visualization packages commonly have fly-through interfaces that enable users to smoothly create an animated sequence of views of the environment. Some of these are more literal, having aircraftlike controls. Others use the flight metaphor only as a starting point. No attempt is made to model actual flight dynamics; rather, the goal is to make it easy for the user to get around in 3D space in a relatively unconstrained way. For example, we (Ware and Osborne 1990) developed a flying interface that used simple hand motions to control velocity. Unlike real aircraft, this interface makes it as easy to move up, down, or backward as it is to move forward. They reported that subjects with actual flying experience had the most difficulty; because of

their expectations about flight dynamics, pilots did unnecessary things such as banking on turns and were uncomfortable with stopping or moving backward. Subjects without flying experience were able to pick up the interface more rapidly. Despite its lack of realism, this was rated as the most flexible and useful interface when compared to others based on the world-in-hand and eyeball-in-hand metaphors.

The optimal navigation method depends on the exact nature of the task. A virtual walking interface may be the best way to give a visitor a sense of presence in an architectural space; something loosely based on the flying metaphor may be a more useful way of navigating through spatially extended data landscapes. The affordances of the virtual data space, the real physical space, and the input device all interact with the mental model of the task that the user has constructed.

Wayfinding, Cognitive, and Real Maps

In addition to the problem of moving through an environment in real time, there is the metalevel problem of how people build up an understanding of larger environments over time. This problem is usually called *wayfinding*. It encompasses both the way in which people build mental models of extended spatial environments and the way they use physical maps as aids to navigation.

Unfortunately, this area of research is plagued with a diversity of terminology. Throughout the following discussion, bear in mind that there are two clusters of concepts, and the differences between these clusters relate to the dual coding theory discussed in Chapter 9.

One cluster includes the related concepts of declarative knowledge, procedural knowledge, topological knowledge, and categorical representations. These concepts are fundamentally logical and nonspatial.

The other cluster includes the related concepts of spatial cognitive maps and coordinate representations. These are fundamentally spatial.

Seigel and White (1975) proposed that there are three stages in the formation of wayfinding knowledge. First, information about key landmarks is learned; initially there is no spatial understanding of the relationships between them. This is sometimes called *declarative knowledge*. We might learn to identify a post office, a church, and the hospital in a small town.

Second, *procedural knowledge* about routes from one location to another is developed. Landmarks function as decision points. Verbal instructions often consist of procedural statements related to landmarks, such as "Turn left at the church, go three blocks, and turn right by the gas station." This kind of information also contains *topological knowledge,* because it includes connecting links between locations. Topological knowledge has no explicit representation of the spatial position of one landmark relative to another.

Third, a *cognitive spatial map* is formed. This is a representation of space that is two-dimensional and includes quantitative information about the distances between the different locations of interest. With a cognitive spatial map, it is possible to estimate the distance between any two points, even though we have not traveled directly between them, and to make statements such as "The university is about one kilometer northwest of the train station."

In Seigel and White's initial theory and in much of the subsequent work, there has been a presumption that spatial knowledge developed strictly in the order of these three stages: declarative knowledge, procedural knowledge, and cognitive spatial maps. Recent evidence from a study by Colle and Reid (1998) contradicts this. They conducted an experimental study using a virtual building consisting of a number of rooms connected by corridors. The rooms contained various objects. In a memory task following the exploration of the building, subjects were found to be very poor at indicating the relative positions of objects located in different rooms, but they were good at indicating the relative positions of objects within the same room. This suggests that cognitive spatial maps form easily and rapidly in environments where the viewer can see everything at once is the case for objects within a single room. It is more likely that the paths from room to room were captured as procedural knowledge. The practical application of this is that overviews should be provided wherever possible in extended spatial information spaces.

The results of Colle and Reid's study fit well with a somewhat different theory of spatial knowledge proposed by Kosslyn (1987). He suggested that there are only two kinds of knowledge, not necessarily acquired in a particular order. He called them *categorical* and *coordinate* representations. For Kosslyn, categorical information is a combination of both declarative knowledge and topological knowledge, such as the identities of the landmarks and the paths between them. Coordinate representation is like the cognitive spatial map proposed by Seigel. A spatial coordinate representation would be expected to arise from the visual imagery obtained with an overview. Conversely, if knowledge were constructed from a sequence of turns along corridors when the subject was moving from room to room, the natural format would be categorical.

Landmarks provide the links between categorical and spatial coordinate representations. They are important both for cognitive spatial maps and for topological knowledge about routes. Vinson (1999) created a generalized classification of landmarks based on Lynch's classification (1960) of the "elements" of cognitive spatial maps. Figure 10.5 summarizes Vinson's design guidelines for the different classes of landmarks. This broad concept includes paths between locations, edges of geographical regions, districts, nodes such as public squares, and the conventional ideal of a point landmark such as a statue.

Vinson also created a set of design guidelines for landmarks in virtual environments. The following rules are derived from them:

- There should be enough landmarks that a small number are visible at all times.

- Each landmark should be visually distinct from the others.

- Landmarks should be visible and recognizable at all navigable scales.

- Landmarks should be placed on major paths and at intersections of paths.

Creating recognizable landmarks in 3D environments can be difficult because of multiple viewpoints. Darken et al. (1998) reported that Navy pilots typically fail to recognize landmark terrain features on a return path, even if these were identified correctly on the outgoing leg of a low-flying exercise. This suggests that terrain features are not encoded in memory as fully three-

Lynch's Types	Examples	Functions
Paths	Street, canal, transit line	Channel for navigator movement
Edges	Fence, riverbank	Indicates district limits
Districts	Neighborhood	Reference region
Nodes	Town square, public building	Focal point for travel
Landmarks	Statue	Reference point into which we cannot enter

Figure 10.5   The functions of different kinds of landmarks in a virtual environment. *Adapted from Vinson (1999).*

dimensional structures, but rather are remembered in some viewpoint-dependent fashion. (See Chapter 7 for a discussion of viewpoint-dependent object memory.)

An interesting way to assist users in the encoding of landmarks for navigation in 3D environments was developed by Elvins et al. (1997). They presented subjects with small 3D subparts of a virtual cityscape that they called *worldlets,* as illustrated in Figure 10.6. The worldlets provided 3D views of key landmarks, presented in such a way that observers could rotate them to obtain a variety of views. Subsequently, when they were tested in a navigation task, subjects who had been shown the worldlets performed significantly better than subjects who had been given pictures of the landmarks, or subjects who had simply been given verbal instructions.

Cognitive maps can also be acquired directly from an actual map much more rapidly than by traversing the terrain. Thorndyke and Hayes-Roth (1982) compared people's ability to judge distances between locations in a large building. Half of them had studied a map for half an hour or so, whereas the other half never saw a map but had worked in the building for many months. The results showed that for estimating the straight-line Euclidean distance between two points, a brief experience with a map was equivalent to working in the building for about a year. However, for estimating the distance along the hallways, the people with experience in the building did the best.

To understand map-reading skills, Darken and Banker (1998) turned to orienteering, a sport that requires athletes to run from point to point over rugged and often difficult terrain with the aid of a map. Experienced orienteers are skilled map readers. One cognitive phenomenon the researchers observed was related to an initial scaling error rapidly remedied; they observed that "initial confusion caused by a scaling error is followed by a 'snapping' phenomenon where the

Figure 10.6   Elvins et al. (1998) conceived the idea of worldlets as navigation aids. Each worldlet is a 3D representation of a landmark in a spatial landscape. (a) A straight-on view of the landmark. (b) The region extracted to create the worldlet. (c) The worldlet from above. (d) The worldlet from street level. Worldlets can be rotated to facilitate later recognition from an arbitrary viewpoint.

world that is seen is instantaneously snapped into congruence with the mental representation" (Darken et al., 1998). This suggests that wherever possible, aids should be given to identify matching points on both an overview map and a focus map.

Frames of Reference

The ability to generate and use something cognitively analogous to a map can be thought of as applying another perspective or *frame of reference* to the world. A map is like a view from above. Cognitive frames of reference are often classified into *egocentric* and *exocentric*. According to this classification, a map is just one of many exocentric views—views that originate outside of the user.

The egocentric frame of reference is, roughly speaking, our subjective view of the world. It is anchored to the head or torso, not the direction of gaze (Bremmer et al., 2001). Our sense of what is ahead, left, and right does not change as we rapidly move our eyes around the scene, but it does change with body and head orientation.

As we explore the world, we change our egocentric viewpoint primarily around two axes of rotation. We turn our bodies mostly around a vertical axis (pan) to change heading, and swivel our heads on the neck (also pan) about a similar vertical axis for more rapid adjustments in view direction. We also tilt our heads forward and back, but generally not to the side (roll). Thus, human angle of view control normally has only two degrees of freedom. These heading (pan) and tilt rotational degrees of freedom are illustrated in Figure 10.7.

A consequence of the fact that we are most familiar with only two of the three degrees of freedom of viewpoint rotation is that when displaying maps, either real or in a virtual environment, we are most comfortable with only two degrees of freedom of rotation. Figure 10.8 illus-

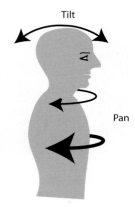

Figure 10.7   Primary rotation axes of egocentric coordinates.

Figure 10.8   View-control widgets for examining geographic data. Note that the rotational degrees of freedom match the rotational degrees of freedom of egocentric coordinates. The three views show different amounts of tilt. The handle on the top widgets can be dragged left and right around the ring to change the view heading.

trates an interface for rotating geographical information spaces constructed to have the same two degrees of freedom (Ware et al., 2001). The widgets allow rotation around the center point (equivalent to turning the body) and tilt from horizontal up into the plane of the screen (equivalent to forward-and-back head tilt), but they do not allow rotation about the line of site through the center of the screen (equivalent to the rarely used sideways head tilt).

Because we tend to move our bodies forward, and only rarely sideways, a simple interface to simulate human navigation can be constructed with only three degrees of freedom, two for rotations (heading and tilt) and one to control forward motion in the direction of heading. If a fourth degree of freedom is added, it may be most useful to allow for something analogous to head turning. This allows for sideways glances while traveling forward.

The term *exocentric* simply means external. In 3D computer graphics, exocentric frames of reference are used for applications such as monitoring avatars in video games, controlling virtual cameras in cinematography, and monitoring the activities of remote or autonomous vehicles. Obviously, there is an infinity of exocentric views. The following is a list of some of the more important and useful ones.

Another person's view For some tasks, it can be useful to take the egocentric view of someone else who is already present in our field of view. Depending on the angular disparity in the relative directions of gaze, this can be confusing, especially when the other person is facing us. In the ClearBoard system (Ishii and Kobayashi, 1992), a remote collaborator appeared to be writing on the other side of a pane of glass. By digitally reversing the image, a common left–right frame of reference was maintained.

Over-the-shoulder view A view from just behind and to the side of the head of an individual. This view is commonly used in cinematography.

God's-eye view Following a vehicle or avatar from above and behind. Figure 10.9(a) illustrates. This view is very common in video games. Because it provides a wider field of

Figure 10.9   (a) God's-eye view of a moving vehicle shown by the tube object in the foreground. (b) Wingman's view of the same vehicle.

view, it can be better for steering a remote vehicle than the more obvious choice, an egocentric view from the vehicle itself (Wang and Milgram, 2001).

Wingman's view Following a vehicle or avatar while looking at it from the side. Figure 10.9(b) illustrates. Exocentric views that follow a moving object, such as the God's-eye or wingman's views, are sometimes called *tethered* (Wang and Milgram, 2001).

Map view A top-down view.

Whether an egocentric or an exocentric frame of reference is likely to be most useful depends on the task (McCormick et al., 1998). Some tasks, such as steering a virtual vehicle, are better done with an egocentric view or an exocentric God's-eye tethered view. Other tasks involving global spatial awareness, such as estimating the distance between a set of objects, can be performed better with an exocentric map view.

If we have multiple views simultaneously, then the links between views can be made visually explicit (Ware and Lewis, 1995; Plumlee and Ware, 2003). Figure 10.10 illustrates

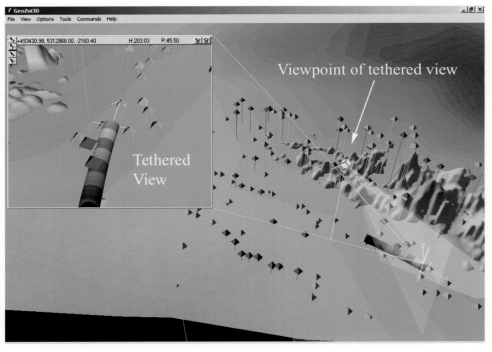

Figure 10.10   The subwindow in the upper left corner provides a tethered view. The overview contains a number of graphical devices to make the tethering explicit (Plumlee and Ware, 2003).

graphical methods for showing where the tethered view is with respect to a larger overview. These include a viewpoint proxy, a transparent pyramid showing the direction and angle of the tethered view, and lines that visually link the secondary window with its source.

None of the exocentric views has been studied as much as the map view.

Map Orientation

How should a map be displayed? Two alternatives have been extensively studied: the track-up display, shown in Figure 10.11(b), and the north-up display, shown in Figure 10.11(a). A *track-up map* is oriented so that the straight-ahead direction, from the point of view of the navigator, is the up direction on the map. The second alternative is to display the map so that north is always up, at the top of the map.

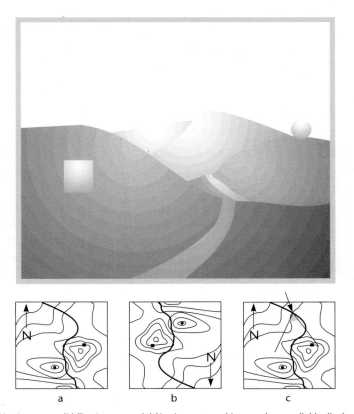

a   b   c

Figure 10.11   (a) North-up map. (b) Track-up map. (c) North-up map with user view explicitly displayed.

One way of considering the map orientation problem is in terms of control compatibility. Imagine yourself in a car, driving south from Berlin, Germany, to Rome, Italy. With a north-up map, a right turn becomes a left direction on the map. Many people find this confusing and reorient the map, even though this means that the place names are upside-down. Experimental studies of map use confirm this, showing that fewer errors are made when subjects use a track-up map (Eley, 1988). However, the north-up map does have advantages. Expert navigators often prefer this orientation because it provides a common frame of reference for communicating with someone else.

It is possible to enhance a north-up map and make it almost as effective as a track-up map, even for novices. Aretz (1991) provided a north-up map for helicopter navigators, but with the addition of a clear indicator of the forward field of view of the navigator. This significantly enhanced the ability of the user to orient himself or herself. Figure 10.11(c) illustrates this kind of enhanced map.

Supporting Visualizations with Maps

The research suggests a number of ways that visualizations can be enhanced with maps:

- Overview maps should be provided when an information space is large. Given how hard it is to build up a mental map by exploring an environment, an overview can substantially reduce the cognitive load.

- User location and direction of view within the map should be indicated. A common way of doing this is with a *You are here* arrow.

- Imagery of key landmarks should be provided. A landmark image on a map should be constructed from a viewpoint that will occur when the wayfinder encounters the actual landmark.

It should be borne in mind that procedural instructions can be more useful than a map when the task itself requires navigating from landmark to landmark. In this case, the cognitive representation of the task is likely to be topological. If the problem is to guide a user from node to node through a virtual information space, providing a sequence of instructions may be more appropriate than providing a map. A verbal or written set of procedural instructions can also be enhanced with landmark imagery.

Focus, Context, and Scale

We have been dealing with the problem of how people navigate through 3D data spaces, under the assumption that the methods used should reflect the way we navigate in the real world. The various navigation metaphors are all based on this assumption. However, there are a number of successful spatial navigation techniques that do not use an explicit interaction metaphor, but do involve visual spatial maps. These techniques make it easy to move rapidly between views at different scales; because of this, they are said to solve the *focus–context* problem. If we think of the problem of wayfinding as one of discovering specific objects or locations in a larger landscape, the focus–context problem is simply a generalization of this, the problem of finding detail in a larger context. The focus–context problem is not always spatial; there are also structural and temporal variations.

Spatial scale Spatial-scale problems are common to all mapping applications. For example, a marine biologist might wish to understand the spatial behavior of individual codfish within a particular school off the Grand Banks of Newfoundland. This information is understood in the context of the shape of the continental shelf and the boundary between cold Arctic water and the warm waters of the Gulf Stream.

Structural scale Complex systems can have structural components at many levels. A prime example is computer software. This has structure within a single line of code, structure within a subroutine or procedure (perhaps 50 lines of code), structure at the object level for object-oriented code (perhaps 1000 lines of code), structure at the packet level, and structure at the system level. Suppose that we wish to visualize the structure of a large program, such as a digital telephone switch (comprising as many as 20 million lines of code); we may wish to understand its structure through as many as six levels of detail.

Temporal scale Many data visualization problems involve understanding the timing of events at very different scales. For example, in understanding data communications, it can be useful to know the overall traffic patterns in a network as they vary over the course of a day. It can also be useful to follow the path of an individual packet of information through a switch over the course of a few microseconds.

It is worth noting that the focus–context problem has already been solved by the human visual system. The brain continuously integrates detailed information from successive fixations of the fovea with the less detailed information that is available at the periphery. This is combined with data coming from the prior sequence of fixations. For each new fixation, the brain must somehow match key objects in the previous view with those same objects moved to new locations. Differing levels of detail are supported in normal perception because objects are seen at much lower resolution at the periphery of vision than in the fovea. Because we have no difficulty in recognizing objects at different distances, this also means that scale-invariance operations are supported in normal perception. The best solutions to the problem of providing focus and context in a display are likely to take advantage of these perceptual capabilities.

Although the spatial scale of a map, the structural levels of detail of a computer program, and the temporal scale in communications monitoring are very different application domains, they can all be represented by means of spatial layouts of data and they belong to a class of related visualization problems. The same interactive techniques can usually be applied. In the following sections, we consider the perceptual properties of four different visualization techniques to solve the focus–context problem: distortion, rapid zooming, elision, and multiple windows.

Distortion Techniques

A number of techniques have been developed that spatially distort a data representation, giving more room to designated points of interest and decreasing the space given to regions away from those points. What is of specific interest is spatially expanded at the expense of what is not, thus providing both focus and context. Figure 10.12 illustrates one such method, called *intelligent zooming* (Bartram et al., 1994). Parts of the graph are dynamically repositioned and resized based on selected points of interest, and selected nodes are expanded to show their contents. Some techniques have been designed to work with a single focus, such as the hyperbolic tree browser (Lamping et al., 1995), shown in Figure 10.13. Others allow multiple foci to be simultaneously expanded, for example, the table lens (Rao and Card, 1994) illustrated in Figure 10.14. Many

Figure 10.12   A view of the intelligent zoom system developed by Bartram et al. (1998).

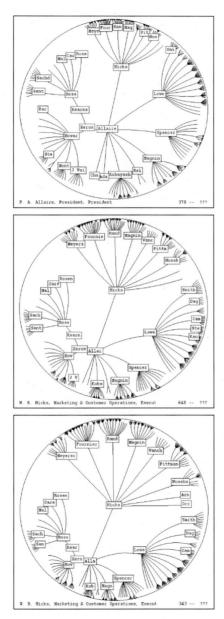

Figure 10.13   Hyperbolic tree browser from Lamping et al. (1995). The focus can be changed by dragging a node from the periphery into the center.

Figure 10.14　Table lens from Rao and Card (1994). Multiple row- and column-wise centers of focus can be created.

of these methods use simple algebraic functions to distort space based on the distance from each focus.

An obvious perceptual issue related to the use of distorting focus–context methods is whether the distortion makes it difficult to identify important parts of the structure. This problem can be especially acute when actual geographical maps are expanded. For example, Figure 10.15 from Sarkar and Brown (1994) shows a distorted view of a map of major cities in North America, together with communications paths between them. The focus is on St. Louis, with the graph expanded at that point, whereas all other regions are reduced in size. The result achieves the goal of making the information about St. Louis and neighboring cities clearer, at the expense of an extreme distortion of the shape of the continent. Compromises are possible; Bartram et al. (1994) do not distort the focal information locally presented in the graph nodes, but they do distort the overall graph layout (see Figure 10.12).

Rapid Zooming Techniques

In rapid zooming techniques, a large information landscape is provided, although only a part of it is visible in the viewing window at any instant. The user is given the ability to zoom rapidly into and out of points of interest, which means that although focus and context are not simultaneously available, the user can move rapidly and smoothly from focus to context and back. If

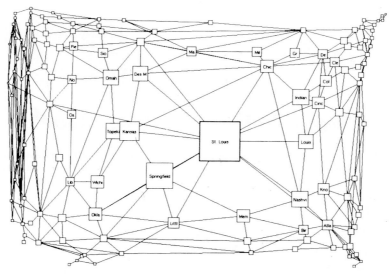

Figure 10.15 Fish-eye view of links between major American cities. The focus is on St. Louis (Sarkar and Brown 1994).

rapid smooth scaling is used, the viewer can perceptually integrate the information over time. The Pad and Pad++ syastems (Bederson and Hollan, 1994) are based on this principle. They provide a large planar data landscape, with an interface using a simple point-and-click technique to move rapidly in and out. Care has been taken to make the animation smooth and continuous.

Mackinlay et al. (1990) invented a rapid-navigation technique for 3D scenes that they called *point of interest navigation*. This method moves the user's viewpoint rapidly, but smoothly, to a point of interest that has been selected on the surface of some object. At the same time, the view direction is smoothly adjusted to be perpendicular to the surface. A variant of this is to base the navigation on an object. Parker et al. (1998) developed a similar technique that is object- rather than surface-based; clicking on an object scales the entire 3D "world" about the center of that object while simultaneously bringing it to the center of the workspace. This is illustrated in Figure 10.16.

In all these systems, the key perceptual issues are the rapidity and ease with which the view can be changed from a focal one to an overview and back. Less than a second of transition time is probably a good rule of thumb, but the animation must be smooth to maintain the identity of objects in their contexts. To maintain a sense of location, landmark features should be designed to be recognized consistently, despite large changes in scale.

Figure 10.16   In the NV3D systems (Parker et al., 1998), clicking and holding down the mouse causes the environment to be smoothly scaled as the selected point is moved to the center of the 3D workspace.

Elision Techniques

In visual *elision,* parts of a structure are hidden until they are needed. Typically, this is achieved by collapsing a large graphical structure into a single graphical object. This is an essential component of the Bartram et al. (1994) system, illustrated in Figure 10.12, and of the NV3D system (Parker et al., 1998; see Figure 8.25). In these systems, when a node is opened, it expands to reveal its contents.

The elision idea can be applied to text as well as to graphics. In the *generalized fish-eye* technique for viewing text data (Furnas, 1986), less and less detail is shown as the distance from the focus of interest increases. For example, in viewing code, the full text is shown at the focus; farther away, only the subroutine headers are made visible, and the code internal to the subroutine is elided.

Elision in visualization is analogous to the cognitive process of chunking, discussed earlier, whereby small concepts, facts, and procedures are cognitively grouped into larger "chunks." Replacing a cluster of objects that represents a cluster of related concepts with a single object is very like chunking. This similarity may be the reason that visual elision is so effective.

Multiple Windows

It is common, especially in mapping systems, to have one window that shows an overview and several others that show expanded details. The major perceptual problem with the multiple-window technique is that detailed information in one window is disconnected from the overview (context information) shown in another. A solution is to use lines to connect the boundaries of the zoom window to the source image in the larger view. Figure 10.17 illustrates a zooming window interface for an experimental calendar application. Multiple windows show day, month, and year views in separate windows (Card et al., 1994). The different windows are connected by lines that integrate the focus information in one table within the context provided by another. Figure 10.18 shows the same technique used in a 3D zooming user interface. The great advan-

Figure 10.17   The spiral calendar (Card et al., 1994). The problem with multiple-window interfaces is that information becomes visually fragmented. In this application, information in one window is linked to its context within another by a connecting transparent overlay.

tage of the multiple-window technique over the others listed previously is that it is both nondistorting and able to show focus and context simultaneously.

Rapid Interaction with Data

In a data exploration interface, it is important that the mapping between the data and its visual representation be fluid and dynamic. Certain kinds of interactive techniques promote an experience of being in direct contact with the data. Rutkowski (1982) calls it the principle of *transparency;* when transparency is achieved, "the user is able to apply intellect directly to the task; the tool itself seems to disappear." There is nothing physically direct about using a mouse to drag a slider on the screen, but if the temporal feedback is rapid and compatible, the user can obtain the illusion of direct control. A key psychological variable in achieving this sense of control is the responsiveness of the computer system. If, for example, a mouse is used to select an object or to rotate a cloud of data points in 3D space, as a rule of thumb visual feedback should be provided within 1/10 second for people to feel that they are in direct control of the data (Shneiderman, 1987).

Interactive Data Display

Often data is transformed before being displayed. Interactive data mapping is the process of adjusting the function that maps the data variables to the display variables. A nonlinear mapping

Figure 10.18   The GeoZui3D system allows for subwindows to be linked in a variety of ways (Plumlee and Ware, 2003). In this illustration the focus of one subwindow is linked to an undersea vehicle docking. A second subwindow provides an overview of a group of undersea vehicles. The faint translucent triangles in the overview show the position and direction of the subwindow views.

between the data and its visual representation can bring the data into a range where patterns are most easily made visible. Figure 10.19 illustrates this concept. Often the interaction consists of imposing some transforming function on the data. Logarithmic, square root, and other functions are commonly applied (Chambers et al., 1983). When the display variable is color, techniques such as histogram equalization and interactive color mapping can be chosen (see Chapter 4). For large and complex data sets, it is sometimes useful to limit the range of data values that are visible and mapped to the display variable; this can be done with sliders.

Ahlberg et al. (1992) call this kind of interface *dynamic queries* and have incorporated it into a number of interactive multivariate scatter-plot applications. By adjusting data range sliders, subsets of the data can be isolated and visualized. An example is given in Figure 10.20, showing a dynamic query interface to the Film Finder application (Ahlberg et al., 1992). Dragging the

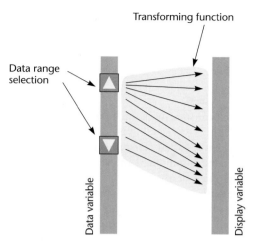

Figure 10.19 In a visualization system, it is often useful to change interactively the function that maps data values to a display variable.

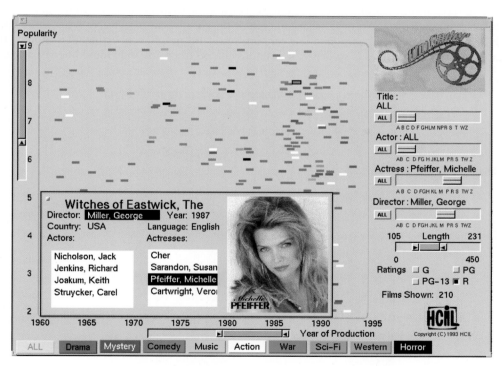

Figure 10.20 The Film Finder application of Ahlberg and Shneiderman (1987) used dynamic query sliders to allow rapid interactive updating of the set of data points mapped from a database to the scatter-plot display in the main window. *Courtesy of Matthew Ward.*

Year of Production slider at the bottom causes the display to update rapidly the set of films shown as points in the main window.

Another interactive technique is called *brushing* (Becker and Cleveland, 1987). This enables subsets of the data elements to be highlighted interactively in a complex representation. Often data objects, or different attributes of them, simultaneously appear in more than one display window, or different attributes can be distributed spatially within a single window. In brushing, a group of elements selected through one visual representation becomes highlighted in all the displays in which it appears. This enables visual linking of components of heterogeneous complex objects. For example, data elements represented in a scatter plot, a sorted list, and a 3D map can all be visually linked when simultaneously highlighted.

Brushing works particularly well with a graphical display technique called *parallel coordinates* (Inselberg and Dimsdale, 1990). Figure 10.21 shows an example in which a set of automobile statistics are displayed: miles per gallon, number of cylinders, horsepower, weight, and so on. A vertical line (parallel coordinate axis) is used for each of these variables. Each automobile is represented by a vertical height on each of the parallel coordinates, and the entire automobile is represented by a compound line running across the graph, connecting all its points. But because the pattern of lines is so dense, it is impossible to trace any individual line visually and

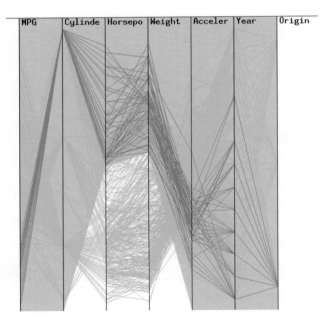

Figure 10.21   In a parallel-coordinates plot, each data dimension is represented by a vertical line. This example illustrates brushing. The user can interactively select a set of objects by dragging the cursor across them. *From: XmdvTool (http://davis.wpi.edu/~xmdv). Courtesy of Matthew Ward (1990).*

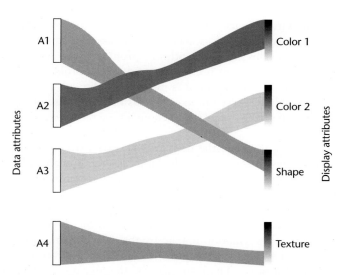

Figure 10.22   In some interactive visualization systems, it is possible to change the mapping between data attributes and the visual representation.

thereby understand the characteristics of a particular automobile. With brushing, a user can select a single point on one of the variables, which has the result of highlighting the line connecting all the values for that automobile. This produces a kind of visual profile. Alternatively, it is possible to select a range on one of the variables, as illustrated in Figure 10.21, and all the lines associated with that range become highlighted. Once this is done, it is easy to understand the characteristics of a set of automobiles (those with low mileage, in this case) across all the variables.

As discussed in Chapter 5, it is possible to map different data attributes to a wide variety of visual variables: position, color, texture, motion, and so on. Each different mapping makes some relationships more distinct and others less distinct. Therefore, allowing a knowledgeable user to change the mapping interactively can be an advantage. (See Figure 10.22.) Of course, such mapping changes are in direct conflict with the important principle of consistency in user interface design. In most cases, only the sophisticated visualization designer should change display mappings.

Conclusion

This chapter has been about the how to make the graphic interface as fluid and transparent as possible. Doing so involves supporting eye–hand coordination, using well-chosen interaction metaphors, and providing rapid and consistent feedback. Of course, transparency comes from practice. A violin has an extraordinarily difficult user interface, and to reach virtuosity may take thousands of hours, but once virtuosity is achieved, the instrument will have become a transparent medium of expression. This highlights a thorny problem in the development of novel interfaces. It is very easy for the designer to become focused on the problem of making an interface that can be used rapidly by the novice, but it is much more difficult to research designs for the expert. It is almost impossible to carry out experiments on expert use of radical new interfaces for the simple reason that no one will ever spend enough time on a research prototype to become truly skilled.

Having said that, efforts to refine the user interface are extremely important. One of the goals of cognitive systems design is to tighten the loop between human and computer, making it easier for the human to obtain important information from the computer via the display. Simply shortening the amount of time it takes to select some piece of information may seem like a small thing, but information in human visual and verbal working memories is very limited; even a few seconds of delay or an increase in the cognitive load, due to the difficulty of the interface, can drastically reduce the rate of information uptake by the user. When a user must stop thinking about the task at hand and switch attention to the computer interface itself, the effect can be devastating to the thought process. The result can be the loss of all or most of the cognitive context that has been set up to solve the real task. After such an interruption, the train of thought must be reconstructed, and research on the effect of interruptions tells us that this can drastically reduce cognitive productivity (Field and Spence, 1994; Cutrell et al., 2000).

CHAPTER 11

Thinking with Visualizations

One way to approach the design of an information system is to consider the *cost of knowledge*. Pirolli and Card (1995) drew an analogy with the way animals seek food to gain insights about how people seek information. Animals minimize energy expenditure to get the required gain in sustenance; humans minimize effort to get the necessary gain in information. Foraging for food has much in common with the seeking of information because, like edible plants in the wild, morsels of information are often grouped, but separated by long distances in an information wasteland. Pirolli and Card elaborated the idea to include information "scent"—like the scent of food, this is the information in the current environment that will assist us in finding more succulent information clusters.

The result of this approach is a kind of cognitive information economics. Activities are analyzed according to the value of what is gained and the cost incurred. There are two kinds of costs: resource costs and opportunity costs (Pirolli, 2003). *Resource costs* are the expenditures of time and cognitive effort incurred. *Opportunity costs* are the benefits that could be gained by engaging in other activities. For example, if we were not seeking information about information visualization, we might profitably be working on software design.

In some ways, an interactive visualization can be considered an *internal* interface between human and computer components in a problem-solving system. We are all becoming cognitive cyborgs in the sense that a person with a computer-aided design program, access to the Internet, and other software tools is capable of problem-solving strategies that would be impossible for that person acting unaided. A businessman plotting projections based on a spreadsheet business model can combine business knowledge with the computational power of the spreadsheet to plot scenarios rapidly, interpret trends visually, and make better decisions.

In this chapter, our concern is with the economics of cognition and the cognitive cost of knowledge. Human attention is a very limited resource. If it is taken up with irrelevant visual noise, or if the rate at which visual information is presented on the screen poorly matches the rate at which people can process visual patterns, then the system will not function well.

There are two fundamental ways in which visualizations support thinking: first, by supporting *visual queries* on information graphics, and second, by extending memory. For visual queries to be useful, the problem must first be cast in the form of a query pattern that, if seen, helps solve part of the problem. For example, finding a number of big red circles in a GIS display may indicate a problem with water pollution. Finding a long, red, fairly straight line on a map can show the best way to drive between two cities. Once the visual query is constructed, a visual search strategy, through eye movements and attention to relevant patterns, provides answers.

Memory extension comes from the way a display symbol, image, or pattern can rapidly evoke nonvisual information and cause it to be loaded from long-term memory into verbal-propositional processing centers.

This chapter presents the theory of how we think with visualizations. First, the memory and attention subsystems are described. Next, visual thinking is described as a set of embedded processes. Throughout, guidelines are provided for designing visual decision support systems.

Memory Systems

Memory provides the framework that underlies active cognition, whereas attention is the motor. As a first approximation, there are three types of memory: iconic, working, and long-term. There may also be a fourth, intermediate store that determines what from working memory finds its way into long-term memory. *Iconic memory* is a very brief image store, holding what is on the retina until it is replaced by something else or until several hundred milliseconds have passed (Sperling, 1960). *Long-term memory* is the information that we retain from everyday experience, perhaps for a lifetime. Consolidation of information into long-term memory only occurs, however, when active processing is done to integrate the new information with existing knowledge (Craik and Lockhart, 1972). *Visual working memory* holds the visual objects of immediate attention. These can be either external or mental images. In computer science terms, this is a register that holds information for the operations of visual cognition.

Visual Working Memory

The most critical cognitive resource for visual thinking is called *visual working memory*. Theorists disagree on details of exactly how visual working memory operates, but there is broad agreement on basic functionality and capacity—enough to provide a solid foundation for a theory of visual thinking. Closely related alternative concepts are the visuospatial sketchpad (Marr, 1982), visual short-term memory (Irwin, 1992), and visual attention (Rensink, 2002). Here is a list of some key properties of visual working memory:

- Visual working memory is separate from verbal working memory.

- Capacity is limited to a small number of simple visual objects and patterns, perhaps three to five simple objects.

- Positions of objects are stored in an egocentric map. Perhaps nine locations are stored, but only three to five are linked to specific objects.

- Attention controls what visual information is held and stored.

- The time to change attention is about 100 msec.

- The semantic meaning or gist of an object or scene (related more to verbal working memory) can be activated in about 100 msec.

- For items to be processed into long-term memory, deeper semantic coding is needed.

Working memory is not a single system; rather, it has a number of interlinked but separate components. There are separate systems for processing auditory and visual information, as well as subsystems for body movements and verbal output (Thomas et al., 1999). There may be additional stores for sequences of cognitive instructions and for motor control of the body. Kieras and Meyer (1997), for example, proposed an *amodal control memory*, containing the operations needed to accomplish current goals, and a general-purpose working memory, containing other miscellaneous information. A similar control structure is called the *central executive* in Baddeley and Hitch's model (1974), illustrated in Figure 11.1.

A detailed discussion of nonvisual working memory processes is beyond the scope of this book. Complete overview models of cognitive processes, containing both visual and nonvisual subsystems can be found in the Anderson ACT-R model (Anderson et al., 1997) and the executive process interactive control (EPIC) developed by Kieras and his coworkers (Kieras and Meyer, 1997). The EPIC architecture is illustrated in Figure 11.2. Summaries of the various working memory theories can be found in Miyake and Shah (1999).

That visual thinking results from the interplay of visual and nonvisual memory systems cannot be ignored. However, rather than getting bogged down in various theoretical debates about particular nonvisual processes, which are irrelevant to the perceptual issues, we will hereafter refer to nonvisual processes generically as *verbal-propositional* processing.

It is functionally quite easy to separate visual and verbal-propositional processing. Verbal-propositional subsystems are occupied when we speak, whereas visual subsystems are not. This allows for simple experiments to separate the two processes. Postma and De Haan (1996) provide a good example. They asked subjects to remember the locations of a set of easily recognizable objects—small pictures of cats, horses, cups, chairs, tables, etc.—laid out in two dimensions on a screen. Then the objects were placed in a line at the top of the display and the subjects were

Figure 11.1   The multicomponent model of working memory of Baddeley and Hitch (1974).

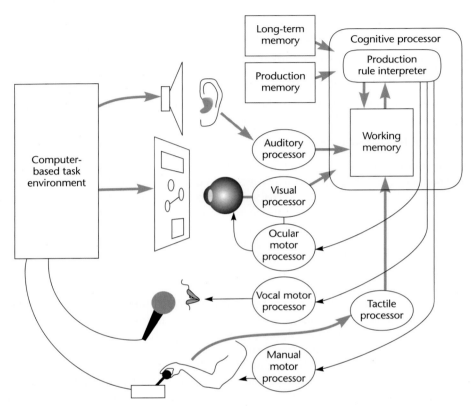

Figure 11.2   A unified extended cognitive model containing both human and machine processing systems. *Adapted from Kieras and Meyer, (1997).*

asked to reposition them—a task the subjects did quite well. In another condition, subjects were asked to repeat a nonsense syllable, such as *blah*, while in the learning phase; in this case they did much worse. However, saying *blah* did not disrupt memory for the *locations* themselves; it only disrupted memory for what was at the locations. This was demonstrated by having subjects place a set of disks at the positions of the original objects, which they could do with relative accuracy. In other words, when *blah* was said in the learning phase, subjects learned a set of locations but not the objects at those locations. This technique is called *articulatory suppression* (Postma and DeHaan, 1996; Postma et al., 1998).

Presumably, the reason why saying *blah* disrupted memory for the objects is that this information was translated into a verbal-propositional coding when the objects were attended.

Visual Working Memory Capacity

Position is not the only information stored in visual working memory; some abstract shape, color, and texture information is also retained. Visual working memory can be roughly defined as the visual information retained from one fixation to the next. This appears to be limited to about three to five simple objects (Irwin, 1992; Xu, 2002; Luck and Vogel 1997; Melcher, 2001). The exact number depends on the task and the kind of pattern. Figure 11.3(a) illustrates the kinds of patterns used in a series of experiments by Vogel et al. (2001). In these experiments, one set of objects was shown for a fraction of a second (e.g., 400 msec), followed by a blank of more than 0.5 sec. After the blank, the same pattern was shown, but with one attribute of an object altered—for example, its color or shape. The results from this and a large number of similar studies have shown that about three objects can be retained without error, but these objects can have color, shape, and texture. If the same amount of color, shape, and texture information is distributed across more objects, memory declines for each of the attributes.

Only quite simple shapes can be stored in this way. For example, each of the mushroom shapes shown in Figure 11.3(b) uses up two visual memory slots (Xu, 2002). Subjects do no better if the stem and the cap are combined than if they are separated. Intriguingly, Vogel et al. (2001) found that if colors were combined with concentric squares, as shown in Figure 11.3(c), then six colors could be held in visual working memory, but if they were put in side-by-side squares, only three colors could be retained. Melcher (2001) found that more information could be retained if longer viewing was permitted: up to five objects after a four-second presentation.

What are the implications for data glyph design? (A *glyph*, as discussed in Chapter 5, is a visual object that displays one or more data variables.) If it is important that a data glyph be held in visual working memory, then it is important that its shape allows it to be encoded according to visual working memory capacity. For example, Figure 11.4 shows two ways of representing the same data. One consists of an integrated glyph containing a colored arrow showing orientation, by arrow direction; temperature, by arrow color; and pressure, by arrow width. A second representation distributes the three quantities among three separate visual objects: orientation by

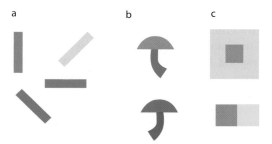

Figure 11.3   Patterns used in studies of the capacity of visual working memory. *(a) From Vogel et al. (2001). (b) From Xu (2002). (c) From Vogel et al. (2001).*

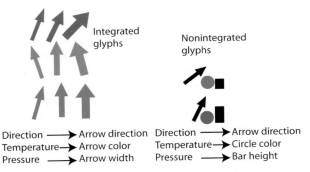

Figure 11.4   If multiple data attributes are integrated into a single glyph, more information can be held in visual working memory.

an arrow, temperature by the color of a circle, and air pressure by the height of a rectangle. The theory of visual working memory and the results of Vogel et al. (2001) suggest that three of the former glyphs could be held in visual working memory, but only one of the latter.

Object Files, Coherence Fields, and Gist

What exactly is held in working memory? Kahneman et al. (1992) coined the term *object file* to describe the temporary grouping of a collection of visual features together with other links to verbal-propositional information. They hypothesized that an object file would consist of a neural activation pattern having the equivalent of pointers reaching into the part of the brain where visual features are processed, as well as pointers to verbal working memory structures and to stored motor memories concerned with the appropriate body movements to make in response.

What we perceive is mostly determined by the task at hand, whether it is finding a path over rocks or finding the lettuce in a grocery store. Perception is tuned by the task requirements to give us what is most likely to be useful. In the first example we see the rocks immediately in front of us. In the second we see green things on the shelves. We can think of perception as occurring through a sequence of active *visual queries* operating through a focusing of attention to give us what we need. The neural mechanism underlying the query may be a rapid tuning of the pattern perception networks to respond best to patterns of interest (Dickinson et al. 1997). Rensink (2002, 2000) coined the term *nexus* to describe this instantaneous grouping of information by attentional processing.

Another term sometimes used to describe a kind of summary of the properties of an object or a scene is *gist*. Gist is used mainly to refer to the properties that are pulled from long-term memory as the image is recognized. Visual images can activate verbal-propositional information in as little as 100 msec (Potter, 1976). Gist consists of both visual information about the typical structure of an object and links to relevant verbal-propositional information. We may also store the gist of a whole environment, so that when we see a familiar scene, the interior of a car, for example, a whole visual framework of the typical locations of things will be activated. We can think of an object file as the temporary structure in working memory, whereas gist is a longer-term counterpart.

Change Blindness

One of the consequences of the very small amount of information held in visual working memory is a phenomenon known as *change blindness* (Rensink, 2000). Because we remember so little, it is possible to make large changes in a display between one view and the next and people generally will not notice, unless the change is to something they have recently attended. If a change is made while the display is being fixated, the inevitable blink will draw attention to it. But if changes are made mid–eye movement, midblink, or after a short blanking of the screen (Rensink, 2002), the change generally will not be seen. Iconic memory information in retinal coordinates decays within about 200 msec (Phillips, 1974). By the time 400 msec have elapsed, what little remains is in visual working memory.

 An extraordinary example of change blindness is a failure to detect a change from one person to another in midconversation. Simons and Levin (1998) carried out a study in which an unsuspecting person was approached by a stranger holding a map and asking for directions. The conversation that ensued was interrupted by two workers carrying a door and during this interval another actor, wearing different clothes, was substituted to carry on the conversation. Remarkably, most people did not notice the substitution.

 To many people, the extreme limitation on the capacity of visual working memory seems quite incredible. How can we experience a rich and detailed world, given such a shallow internal representation? The answer to this dilemma is that the world "is its own memory" (O'Regan, 1992). We perceive the world to be rich and detailed, not because we have an internal detailed model, but simply because whenever we wish to see detail we can get it, either by focusing attention on some aspect of the visual image at the current fixation or by moving our eyes to see the detail in some other part of the visual field. We are unaware of the jerky eye movements by which we explore the world; we are only aware of the complexity of the environment detail being brought into working memory on a need-to-know, just-in-time fashion (O'Regan, 1992; Rensink, 2002; Rensink et al., 1997). This is in agreement with the idea of visual queries being basic to perception.

Spatial Information

For objects acquired in one fixation to be reidentified in the next requires some kind of buffer that holds locations in egocentric coordinates as opposed to retina-centric coordinates (Hochberg, 1968). This also allows for the synthesis of information obtained from successive fixations. Figure 11.5 illustrates the concept. Neurophysiological evidence from animal studies suggests that the lateral interparietal area near the top of the brain (Colby, 1998) appears to play a crucial role in linking eye-centered coordinate maps in the brain with egocentric coordinate maps.

Figure 11.5   A spatial map of objects that have recently been held by attention is a necessary part of visual working memory.

Egocentric-spatial location memory also holds remarkably little information, although probably a bit more than the three objects that Vogel et al. (2001) suggest. It may be possible to remember some information about approximately nine locations (Postma et al., 1998). Three of these may contain links to object files, whereas the remaining ones specify only that there is something at a particular region in space, but very little more. Some evidence suggests that fixation of a particular object may be essential for that object and its location to be held from one fixation to the next (Hollingworth and Henderson, 2002).

Some visual information is retained over several seconds and several fixations. Potter (2002) provided evidence for this. Subjects viewed a rapid serial presentation of 10 pictures at the rate of six per second and afterwards were able to identify whether a particular picture was in the set about 60% of the time. This suggests that some residual gist is retained over many visual changes in scene. A recent and very intriguing study by Melcher (2001) suggests that we can build up information about several scenes that are interspersed. When the background of a scene was shown, subjects could recall some of the original objects, even though several other scenes had intervened. This implies that a distinctive screen design could help with visual working memory when we switch between different views of a data space. We may be able to cognitively swap in and swap out different data "scenes," albeit each with a low level of detail.

An interesting question is how many moving targets can be held from one fixation to the next. The answer seems to be about four or five. Pylyshyn and Storm (1988) carried out experiments in which visual objects moved around on a display in a pseudo-random fashion. A subset of the objects was visually marked by changing color, but then the marking was turned off. If there were five or fewer marked objects, subjects could continue to keep track of them, even though they were now all black. Pylyshyn coined the term *FINST*, for *fingers of instantiation*, to describe the set of pointers in a cognitive spatial map that would be necessary to support this task. The number of individual objects that can be tracked is somewhat larger than the three found by Vogel et al. (2001), although it is possible that the moving objects may be grouped perceptually into fewer chunks (Yantis, 1992).

Attention

The studies showing that we can hold three or four objects in visual working memory required intense concentration on the part of the participants. Most of the time, when we interact with displays or just go about our business in the everyday world, we will not be attending that closely. In a remarkable series of studies, Mack and Rock (1998) tricked subjects into not paying attention to the subject of the experiment, although they wanted to make sure that subjects were at least looking in the right direction. They told subjects to attend to a cross pattern for changes in the length of one of the arms; perfect scores on this task indicated they had to be attending. Then the researchers presented a pattern that the subject *had not been asked to look for*. They found that even though the unexpected pattern was close to, or even on, the point of fixation, most of the time it was not seen. The problem with this kind of study is that the ruse can only be used once. As soon as you ask subjects if they saw the unexpected pattern, they will start looking for unexpected patterns. Mack and Rock therefore used each subject for only one trial; they used literally hundreds of subjects in a series of studies.

Mack and Rock called the phenomenon *inattentional blindness*. It should not be considered as a peculiar effect only found in the laboratory. Instead this kind of result probably reflects everyday reality much more accurately than the typical psychological experiment in which subjects are paid to closely attend. Most of the time we simply do not register what is going on in our environment unless we are looking for it. The conclusion must be that attention is central to all perception.

Although we are blind to many changes in our environment, some visual events are more likely to cause us to change attention than others are. Mack and Rock found that although subjects were blind to small patterns that appeared and disappeared, they still noticed larger visual events, such as patterns larger than one degree of visual angle appearing near the point of fixation.

Jonides (1981) studied ways of moving a subject's attention from one part of a display to another. He looked at two different ways, which are sometimes called pull cues and push cues. In a *pull cue*, a new object appearing in the scene pulls attention toward it. In a *push cue*, a symbol in the display, such as an arrow, tells someone where a new pattern is to appear. It appears to take only about 100 msec to shift attention based on a pull cue but can take between 200 and 400 msec to shift attention based on a push cue.

Visual attention is not strictly tied to eye movements. Although attending to some particular part of a display often does involve an eye movement, there are also attention processes operating within each fixation. The studies of Triesman and Gormican (1988) and others (discussed in Chapter 5) showed that we process simple visual objects serially at a rate of about one every 40–50 msec. Because each fixation typically will last for 100–300 msec, this means that our visual systems process two to six objects within each fixation, before we move our eyes to attend visually to some other region.

Attention is also not limited to specific locations of a screen. We can, for example, choose to attend to a particular pattern that is a component of another pattern, even though the patterns overlap spatially (Rock and Gutman, 1981). Thus, we can choose to attend to the curved pattern or to the rectangular shape in Figure 11.6. We can also choose to attend to a particular attribute if it is preattentively distinct (Treisman 1985). For example, on a field of black text with parts highlighted in red, we can choose to attend only to the red items. Having whole groups of objects that move is especially useful in helping us to attend selectively (Bartram and Ware, 2002). We can attend to the moving group or the static group, with relatively little interference between them.

The selectivity of attention is by no means perfect. Even though we may wish to focus on one aspect of a display, other information is also processed, apparently to quite a high level. The well known Stroop effect illustrates this (Stroop, 1935). In a set of words printed in different colors, as illustrated in Figure 11.7, if the words themselves are color names that do not match the ink colors, subjects name the colors more slowly than if the colors match the words. This means that the words are processed automatically; we cannot entirely ignore them even when we want to. More generally, it is an indication that all highly learned symbols will automatically invoke verbal-propositional information that has become associated with them.

The Role of Motion in Attracting Attention

As we conduct more of our work in front of computer screens, there is an increasing need for signals that can attract a user's attention. Often someone is busy with a primary task, perhaps filling out forms or composing email, while at the same time events may occur on other parts of the display, requiring attention. These *user interrupts* can alert us to an incoming message from

Figure 11.6   We can attend to either the curved orange shape or the black rectangle, even though they overlap in space.

RED GREEN YELLOW BLUE BLACK GREEN PURPLE BLUE BLACK
ORANGE GREEN RED GREEN YELLOW BLUE BLACK GREEN PURPLE
BLUE BLACK ORANGE BLACK GREEN RED

GREEN RED BLUE YELLOW PURPLE RED BLACK BLUE BLACK GREEN
ORANGE BLUE RED PURPLE YELLOW RED BLACK YELLOW GREEN
ORANGE BLACK GREEN RED GREEN

Figure 11.7   As quickly as you can, try to name the colors of the words in the set at the top. Then try to name the colors in the set below. Even though both tasks involve ignoring the words themselves, people are slowed down by the mismatch. This is called the Stroop effect.

a valued customer or a signal from a computer agent that has been out searching the Internet for information on the latest flu virus. There are four basic visual requirements for a user interrupt:

- A signal should be easily perceived, even if it is outside of the area of immediate focal attention.

- If the user wishes to ignore the signal and attend to another task, the signal should continue to act as a reminder.

- The signal should not be so irritating that it makes the computer unpleasant to use.

- It should be possible to endow the signal with various levels of urgency.

Essentially, the problem is how to attract the user's attention to information outside the central parafoveal region of vision (approximately the central six degrees). For a number of reasons, the options are limited. We have a low ability to detect small targets in the periphery of the visual field. Peripheral vision is color blind, which rules out color signals (Wyszecki and Stiles, 1982). Saccadic suppression during eye movements means that some transitory event occurring in the periphery will generally be missed if it occurs during an eye movement (Burr and Ross, 1982). Taken together, these facts suggest that a single, abrupt change in the appearance of an icon is unlikely to be an effective signal.

The set of requirements suggests two possible solutions. One is to use auditory cues. In certain cases, these are a good solution, but they are outside the scope of this book. Another solution is to use blinking or moving icons. In a study involving shipboard alarm systems, Goldstein and Lamb (1967) showed that subjects were capable of distinguishing five flash patterns with approximately 98% reliability and that they responded with an average delay of approximately 2.0 seconds. But anecdotal evidence indicates that a possible disadvantage of flashing lights or blinking cursors is that users find them irritating. Unfortunately, many Web page designers generate a kind of animated chart junk: small, blinking animations with no functional purpose are often used to jazz up a page. Moving icons may be a better solution. Moving targets are detected more easily in the periphery than static targets (Peterson and Dugas, 1972). In a series of dual task experiments, Bartram et al. (2003) had subjects carry out a primary task, either text editing or playing Tetris or Solitaire, while simultaneously monitoring for a change in an icon at the side of the display in the periphery of the visual field. The results showed that having an icon move was far more effective in attracting a user's attention than having it change color or shape. The advantage increased as the signal was farther from the focus of attention in the primary task.

Another advantage of moving or blinking signals is that they can persistently attract attention, unlike a change in an icon, such as the raising of a mailbox flag, which fades rapidly from attention. Also, although rapid motions are annoying, slower motions need not be and they can still support a low-level of awareness (Ware et al., 1992).

Interestingly, more recent work has suggested that it may not be motion per se that attracts attention, but the appearance of a new object in the visual field (Hillstrom and Yantis, 1994;

Enns et al., 2001). This seems right; after all, we are not constantly distracted in an environment of swaying trees or people moving about on a dance floor. It also makes ecological sense; when early man was outside a cave, intently chipping a lump of flint into a hand axe, or when early woman was gathering roots out on the grassland, awareness of emerging objects in the periphery of vision would have had clear survival value. Such a movement might have signaled an imminent attack. Of course, the evolutionary advantage goes back much further than this. Monitoring the periphery of vision for moving predators or prey would provide a survival advantage for most animals. Thus, the most effective reminder might be an object that moves into view, disappears, and then reappears every so often. In a study that measured the eye movements made while viewing multimedia presentations, Faraday and Sutcliffe (1997) found that the onset of motion of an object generally produced a shift of attention to that object.

Rensink's Model

Rensink (2002) has recently developed a model that ties together many of the components we have been discussing. Figure 11.8 illustrates. At the lowest level are the elementary visual features that are processed in parallel and automatically. These correspond to elements of color, edges, motion, and stereoscopic depth. From these elements, prior to focused attention, low-level precursors of objects, called *proto-objects*, exist in a continual state of flux. At the top level, the mechanism of attention forms different visual objects from the proto-object flux. Note that Rensink's proto-objects are located at the top of his "low-level vision system." He is not very specific on the nature of proto-objects, but it seems reasonable to suppose that they have char-

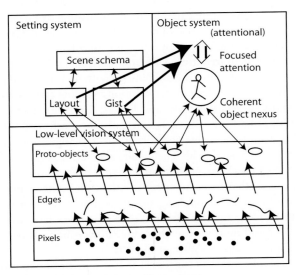

Figure 11.8 A model of visual attention. *Adapted from Rensink (2002).*

acteristics similar to the mid-level pattern perception processes in the three-stage model laid out in this book.

Rensink uses the metaphor of a hand to represent attention, with the fingers reaching down into the proto-object field to instantiate a short-lived object. After the grasp of attention is released, the object loses its coherence and the components fall back into the constituent proto-objects. There is little or no residue from this attentional process. Other components of the model are a layout map containing location information and the rapid activation of object gist.

The central role of attention in Rensink's model suggests a way that visual queries can be used to modify the grasp of attention and pull out the particular patterns we need to support problem solving. For example, we might need to know how one module connects to another in a software system. To obtain this information, a visual query is constructed to find out if lines connect certain boxes in the diagram. This query is executed by focusing visual attention on those graphical features.

The notion of proto-objects in a continuous state of flux suggests, also, how visual displays can provide a basis for creative thinking, because they allow multiple visual interpretations drawn from the same visualization. Another way to think about this is that different patterns in the display become cognitively highlighted, as we consider different aspects of a problem.

Eye Movements

We constantly make eye movements to seek information. Moving our eyes causes different parts of the visual environment to be imaged on the high-resolution fovea, where we can see detail. These movements are frequent. For example, as you read this page, your eye is making between two and five jerky movements, called *saccades*, per second.

Here are the basic statistics describing three important types of eye movement:

1. Saccadic movements: In a visual search task, the eye moves rapidly from fixation to fixation. The dwell period is generally between 200 and 600 msec, and the saccade takes between 20 and 100 msec. The peak velocity of a saccade can be as much as 900 deg/sec (Hallett, 1986; Barfield et al., 1995).

2. Smooth-pursuit movements: When an object is moving smoothly in the visual field, the eye has the ability to lock onto it and track it. This is called a *smooth-pursuit* eye movement. This ability also enables us to make head and body movements while maintaining fixation on an object of interest.

3. Convergent movements (also called *vergence* movements): When an object moves toward us, our eyes converge. When it moves away, they diverge. Convergent movements can be either saccadic or smooth.

Saccadic eye movements are said to be *ballistic*. This means that once the brain decides to switch attention and make an eye movement, the muscle signals for accelerating and decelerating the eye are first programmed, then the program is run to make the eye movement. The movement cannot be adjusted in mid-saccade. During the course of a saccadic eye movement, we are less sensitive to visual input than we normally are. This is called *saccadic suppression* (Riggs et al., 1974). The implication is that certain kinds of events can easily be missed if they occur while we happen to be moving our eyes. This is important when we consider the problem of alerting a computer operator to an event.

Another implication of saccadic suppression is that it is reasonable to think of information coming into the visual system as a series of discrete snapshots. The brain is often processing rapid sequences of discrete images. This capacity is being increasingly exploited in television advertising, in which several cuts per second of video have become commonplace.

Accommodation

When the eye moves to a new target at a different distance from the observer, it must refocus, or *accommodate*, so that the target is clearly imaged on the retina. An accommodation response typically takes about 200 msec. The mechanisms controlling accommodation and convergent eye movements are neurologically coupled, and this can cause problems with virtual-reality displays. This problem is discussed in Chapter 8.

Eye Movements, Search, and Monitoring

How does the brain plan a sequence of eye movements to interpret a visual scene? A simple heuristic strategy appears to be employed according to the theory of Wolfe and Gancarz (1996). First, the feature map of the entire visual field is processed in parallel (see Chapter 5) to generate a map weighted according to the current task. For example, if we are scanning a crowd to look for people we know, the feature set will be highly correlated with human faces. Next, eye movements are executed in sequence, visiting the strongest possible target first and proceeding to the weakest. Finally once each area has been processed, it is cognitively flagged as visited. This has the effect of inhibiting that area of the weighted feature map.

A searchlight is a useful metaphor for describing the interrelationships among visual attention, eye movements, and the useful field of view. In this metaphor, visual attention is like a searchlight used to seek information. We point our eyes at the things we want to attend to. The diameter of the searchlight beam, measured as a visual angle, describes the useful field of view (UFOV). The central two degrees of visual angle is the most useful, but it can be broader, depending on such factors as stress level and task. The direction of the searchlight beam is controlled by eye movements. Figure 11.9 illustrates the searchlight model of attention.

Supervisory Control

The searchlight model of attention has been developed mainly in the context of supervisory control systems to account for the way people scan instrument panels. *Supervisory control* is a term used for complex, semiautonomous systems that are only indirectly controlled by human operators.

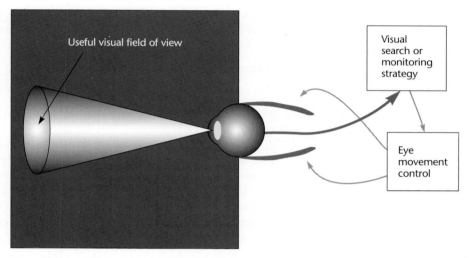

Figure 11.9   The searchlight model of attention. A visual search strategy is used to determine eye movements that bring different parts of the visual field into the useful visual field of view.

Examples are sophisticated aircraft and power stations. In these systems, the human operator has both a monitoring and a controlling role. Because the consequences of making an error during an emergency can be truly catastrophic, a good interface design is critical. Two Airbus passenger jets have crashed for reasons that are attributed to mistaken assumptions about the behavior of supervisory control systems (Casey, 1993). There are also stories of pilots in fighter aircraft turning warning lights off because they are unable to concentrate in a tense situation.

A number of aspects of visual attention are important when considering supervisory control. One is creating effective ways for a computer to gain the attention of a human—a user-interrupt signal. Sometimes, a computer must alert the operator with a warning of some kind, or it must draw the operator's attention to a routine change of status. In other cases, it is important for an operator to become aware of *patterns* of events. For example, on a power grid, certain combinations of component failures can indicate a wider problem. Because display panels for power grids can be very large, this may require the synthesis of widely separated visual information.

In many ways, the ordinary human–computer interface is becoming more like a supervisory control system. The user is typically involved in some foreground task, such as preparing a report, but at the same time monitoring activities occurring in other parts of the screen.

Visual Monitoring Strategies

In many supervisory control systems, operators must monitor a set of instruments in a semi-repetitive pattern. Models developed to account for operators' visual scanning strategies generally have the following elements (Wickens, 1992):

Channels: These are the different ways in which the operator can receive information. Channels can be display windows, dials on an instrument panel, or nonvisual outputs, such as loudspeakers (used for auditory warnings).

Events: These are the signals occurring on channels that provide useful information.

Expected cost: This is the cost of *missing* an event.

System operators base their monitoring of different channels on a mental model of system event probabilities and the expected costs of these (Moray and Rotenberg, 1989; Wickens, 1992). Charbonnell et al. (1968) and Sheridan (1972) proposed that monitoring behavior is controlled by two factors: the growth of uncertainty in the state of a channel (between samples) and the cost of sampling a channel. *Sampling* a channel involves fixating part of a display and extracting the useful information. The cost of sampling is inversely proportional to the ease with which the display can be interpreted. This model has been successfully applied by Charbonnell et al. (1968) to the fixation patterns of pilots making an instrument landing. A number of other factors may influence visual scanning patterns:

- Operators may minimize eye movements. The cost of sampling is reduced if the points to be sampled are spatially close. Russo and Rosen (1975) found that subjects tended to make comparisons most often between spatially adjacent data. If two indicators are within the same effective field of view, this tendency will be especially advantageous.

- There can be oversampling of channels on which infrequent information appears (Moray, 1981). This can be accounted for by short-term memory limitations. Human working memory has very limited capacity, and it requires significant cognitive effort to keep a particular task in mind. People can reliably monitor an information channel every minute or so, but they are much less reliable when asked to monitor an event every 20 minutes. One design solution is to build in visual or auditory reminders at appropriate intervals.

- Sometimes operators exhibit dysfunctional behaviors in high-stress situations. Moray and Rotenberg (1989) suggested that under crisis conditions, operators cease monitoring some channels altogether. In an examination of control-room emergency behavior, he found that under certain circumstances, an operator's fixation became locked on a feedback indicator, waiting for a system response at the expense of taking other, more pressing actions.

- Sometimes, operators exhibit systematic scan patterns, such as the left-to-right, top-to-bottom one found in reading, even if these have no functional relevance to the task (Megaw and Richardson, 1979).

Long-Term Memory

We now turn away from strictly visual processing to consider the structure of information in verbal-propositional memory. We will need this background information to understand how visualizations can function as memory aids by rapidly activating structured nonvisual information.

Long-term memory contains the information that we build up over a lifetime. We tend to associate long-term memory with events we can consciously recall—this is called *episodic memory* (Tulving, 1983). However, long-term memory also includes motor skills, such as the finger movements involved in typing and the perceptual skills, integral to our visual systems, that enable us to rapidly identify words and thousands of visual objects. Nonvisual information that is not closely associated with concepts currently in verbal working memory can take minutes, hours, or days to retrieve from long-term memory.

There is a common myth that we remember everything we experience but we lose the indexing information; in fact, we remember only what gets encoded in the first 24 hours or so after an event occurs. The best estimates suggest that we do not actually store very much information in long-term memory. Using a reasonable set of assumptions, Landauer (1986) estimated that only about 10^9 bits of information are stored over a 35-year period. This is what can currently be found in the solid-state main memory of a personal computer. The power of human long-term memory is not in its capacity but in its remarkable flexibility. The same information can be combined in many different ways and through many different kinds of cognitive operations.

Human long-term memory can be usefully characterized as a network of linked concepts (Collins and Loftus, 1975; Yufic and Sheridan, 1996). Our intuition supports this model. If we think of a particular concept—for example, data visualization—we can easily bring to mind a set of related concepts: computer graphics, perception, data analysis, potential applications. Each of these concepts is linked to many others. Figure 11.10 shows some of the concepts relating to information visualization.

The network model makes it clear why some ideas are harder to recall than others. Concepts and ideas that are distantly related naturally take longer to find; it can be difficult to trace a path to them and easy to take wrong turns in traversing the concept net, because no map exists. For this reason, it can take minutes, hours, or even days to retrieve some ideas. A study by Williams and Hollan (1981) investigated how people recalled names of classmates from their high school graduating class, seven years later. They continued to recall names for at least 10 hours, although the number of falsely remembered names also increased over time. The forgetting of information from long-term memory is thought to be more of a loss of access than an erasure of the memory trace (Tulving and Madigan, 1970). Memory connections can easily become corrupted or misdirected; as a result, people often misremember events with a strong feeling of subjective certainty (Loftus and Hoffman, 1989).

Chunks of information are continuously being prioritized, and to some extent reorganized, based on the current cognitive requirements (Anderson and Milson, 1989). It is much easier to recall something that we have recently had in working memory. Seeing an image from the past will prime subsequent recognition so that we can identify it more rapidly (Bichot and Schall, 1999).

Long-term memory and working memory appear to be overlapping, distributed, and specialized. Long-term visual memory involves parts of the visual cortex, and long-term verbal memory involves parts of the temporal cortex specialized for speech. More abstract and linking concepts may be represented in areas such as the prefrontal cortex. Working memory is better

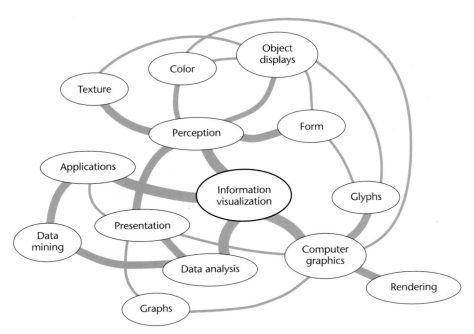

Figure 11.10   A concept map showing a set of linked concepts surrounding the idea of information visualization.

thought of as existing within the context of long-term memory than as a distinct processing module. As visual information is processed through the visual system, it activates the long-term memory of visual objects that have previously been processed by the same system. This explains why visual recognition is much faster and more efficient than visual recall. In recognition, a visual memory trace is being reawakened, so that we know that we have seen a particular pattern. In recall, it is necessary for us actually to describe some pattern, by drawing or in words, but we may not have access to the memory trace. In any case, the memory trace will not generally contain sufficient information for reconstructing an object, which would be required for recognition but not for recall. The memory trace also explains priming effects: If a particular neural circuit has recently been activated, it becomes primed for reactivation.

Chunks and Concepts

Human memory is much more than a simple repository like a telephone book; information is highly structured in overlapping and interconnected ways. The term *chunk* and the term *concept* are both used in cognitive psychology to denote important units of stored information. The two terms are used interchangeably here. The process of grouping simple concepts into more complex ones is called *chunking*. A chunk can be almost anything: a mental representation of an object, a plan, a group of objects, or a method for achieving some goal. The process of becoming an expert in a particular domain is largely one of creating effective high-level concepts or chunks.

It is generally thought that concepts are formed by a kind of hypothesis-testing process (Levine, 1975). According to this view, multiple tentative hypotheses about the structure of the world are constantly being evaluated based on sensory evidence and evidence from internal long-term memory. In many cases, the initial hypotheses start with some existing concept: a mental model or metaphor. New concepts are distinguished from the prototype by means of transformations (Posner and Keele, 1968). For example, the concept of a zebra can be formed from the concept of a horse by adding a new node to a concept net containing a reference to a horse and distinguishing information, such as the addition of stripes.

What about purely visual long-term memory? It does not appear to contain the same kind of network of abstract concepts that characterizes verbal long-term memory. However, there may be some rather specialized structures in visual scene memory. Evidence for this comes from studies showing that we identify objects more rapidly in the right context, such as bread in a kitchen (Palmer, 1975). The power of images is that they rapidly evoke verbal-propositional memory traces; we see a cat and a whole host of concepts associated with cats becomes activated. Images provide rapid evocation of the semantic network, rather then forming their own net (Intraub and Hoffman, 1992). To identify all of the objects in our visual environment requires a great store of visual appearance information. Biederman (1987) estimated that we may have about 30,000 categories of visual information. The way visual objects are cognitively constructed is discussed more extensively in Chapter 8.

Visual imagery is the basis for a well-known mnemonic technique called the *method of loci* (Yates, 1966). This was known to Greek and Roman orators and can be found in many self-help books on how to improve your memory. To use the method of loci, you must identify a path that you know well, such as the walk from your house to the corner store. To remember a series of words—for example, mouse, bowl, fork, box, scissors—place each object at specific locations along the path in your mind's eye. You might put one at the end of your driveway next to the mailbox, the next by a particular lamppost, and so on. Now, to recall the sequence, you simply take an imaginary walk—magically, the objects are where you have placed them. The fact that this rather strange technique actually works suggests that there is something special about associating concepts to be remembered with images in particular locations that helps us remember information.

The Data Mountain was an experimental computer interface designed to take advantage of the apparent mnemonic value of spatial layout (Robertson et al., 1998). The Data Mountain allowed users to lay out thumbnails of Web pages on the slope of an inclined plane, as illustrated in Figure 8.4. A study by Czerwinski et al. (1999) found that even six months later, subjects who had previously set up information in this way could find particular items as rapidly as they could shortly after the initial layout. It should be noted, however, that before retesting subjects were given a practice session that allowed them to relearn at least some of the layout; it is possible to scan a lot of information in the two minutes or so that they were given.

Using a setup very similar to the Data Mountain, Cockburn and Mackenzie (2001) showed that removing the perspective distortion, as shown in Figure 8.4, had no detrimental impact on performance. Thus, although spatial layout may aid memory, it does not, apparently, have to be a 3D layout. On balance, there does appear to be support for the mnemonic value of spatial layout, because a lot of items (i.e., 100 items) were used in the memory test and the review period was brief, but there is little evidence that the space must be three-dimensional.

One important aspect of the Data Mountain study was that subjects were required to organize the material into categories. This presumably caused a deeper level of cognitive processing. Depth of processing is considered a primary factor in the formation of long-term memories (Craik and Lockhart, 1972). To learn new information, it is not sufficient to be exposed to it over an over again, the information must be integrated cognitively with existing information. Tying verbal and visual concepts together may be especially effective. Indeed, this is a central premise in the use of multimedia in education.

Problem Solving with Visualizations

We are now in a position to outline a theory of how thinking can be augmented by visual queries on visualizations of data. Figure 11.11 provides an overview of the various components. This

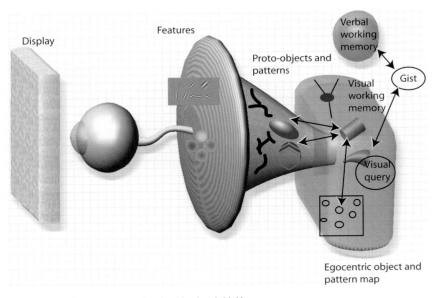

Figure 11.11   The cognitive components involved in visual thinking.

borrows a great deal from Rensink (2000, 2002) and earlier theorists, such as Baddeley and Hitch (1974), Kahneman et al. (1992) and Triesman (1985). It is based on the three-stage model developed throughout this book, but with the third stage now elaborated as an active process. At the lowest stage is the massively parallel processing of the visual scene into the elements of form, opponent colors, and the elements of texture and motion. In the middle stage is pattern formation, providing the basis for object and pattern perception. At the highest level, the mechanism of attention pulls out objects and critical patterns from the pattern analysis subsystem to execute a visual query.

The content of visual working memory consists of "object files," to use the term of Kahneman et al., a visual spatial map in egocentric coordinates that contains residual information about a small number of recently attended objects. Also present is a visual query pattern that forms the basis for active visual search through the direction of attention.

We tend to think of objects as relatively compact entities, but objects of attention can be extended patterns, as well. For example, when we perceive a major highway on a map winding though a number of towns, that highway representation is also a visual object. So, too, is the V shape of a flight of geese, the pattern of notes on a musical score that characterize an arpeggio, or the spiral shape of a developing hurricane.

Following is a list of the key features of the visual thinking process:

1. Problem components are identified that have potential solutions based on visual pattern discovery. These are formulated into visual queries consisting of simple patterns.

2. Eye-movement scanning strategies are used to search the display for the query patterns.

3. Within each fixation, the query determines which patterns are pulled from the flux of pattern-analysis subsystems.

   a. Patterns and objects are formed as transitory object files from proto-object and proto-pattern space.

   b. Only a small number of objects or pattern components are retained from one fixation to the next. These object files also provide links to verbal-propositional information in verbal working memory.

   c. A small number of cognitive markers are placed in a spatial map of the problem space to hold partial solutions where necessary. Fixation and deeper processing are necessary for these markers to be constructed.

4. Links to verbal-propositional information are activated by icons or familiar patterns, bringing in other kinds of information.

Visual Problem Solving Processes

The actual process of problem solving can be represented as a set of embedded processes. They are outlined in Figure 11.12. At the highest level is problem formulation and the setting of high-level goals—this is likely to occur mostly using verbal-propositional resources.

Problem-solving strategy
Set up problem context and provisional steps for solving it (much of this may be nonvisual).
▲ **Visual query construction**
Parts of the problem are formulated so as to afford visual solution.
Pattern-finding loop
Set up the search for elementary visual patterns important to the task.
Eye movement control loop
Make eye movements to areas of interest defined by the current query pattern.
Intrasaccadic image-scanning loop
Load object from proto-object flux.

Test object structure pattern against visual query pattern.
Determine next most interesting region of the visual field.

Save result as necessary. Advance to next visual subpattern required.
Flag problem component solutions. Advance to next step.

Move to next step in overall problem strategy. Redefine subtasks as necessary.

Figure 11.12   Visually aided problem solving can be considered a set of embedded processes. Interactive techniques, such as brushing, zooming, or dynamic queries, can be substituted for the eye movement control loop.

To give substance to this rather abstract description, let us consider how the model deals with a fairly common problem—planning a trip aided by a map. Suppose that we are planning a trip through France from Port-Bou in Spain, near the French border, to Calais in the northeast corner of France. The visualization that we have at our disposal is the map shown in Figure 11.13.

The Problem-Solving Strategy

The initial step in our trip planning is to formulate a set of requirements, which may be precise or quite vague. Let us suppose that for our road trip through France we have five days at our disposal and we will travel by car. We wish to stop at two or three interesting cities along the way, but we do not have strong preferences. We wish to minimize driving time, but this will be weighted by the degree of interest in different destinations. We might use the Internet as part of the process to research the attractions of various cities; such knowledge will become an important weighting factor on the alternate routes. We begin planning our route: a problem-solving strategy involving visualization.

Visual Query Construction

We establish the locations of various cities through a series of preliminary visual queries to the map. Fixating each city icon and reading its label helps to establish a connection to the verbal-

Figure 11.13   Planning a trip from Port-Bou to Calais involves finding the major routes that are not excessively long and then choosing among them. This process can be understood as a visual search for patterns.

propositional knowledge we have about that city. Little, if any, of this will be retained in working memory, but the locations will be primed for later reactivation.

Once this has been done, path planning can begin by identifying the major alternative routes between Port-Bou and Calais. The visual query we construct for this will probably not be very precise. Roughly, we are seeking to minimize driving time and maximize time at the stopover cities. Our initial query might be to find the set of alternative routes that are within 20% of the shortest route, using mostly major highways. From the map, we determine that major roads are represented as wide orange lines and incorporate this fact into the query.

The Pattern-Finding Loop

The task of the pattern-finding loop is to find all acceptable routes as defined by the previous step. The patterns to be discovered are continuous contours, mostly orange (for highways) and not overly long, connecting the start city icon with the end city icon. Two or three acceptable solutions may be stored in visual working memory, or a single route may use the entire capacity of this limited resource.

Once a complete path has been identified, it must be retained in some way while alternate solutions are found. If a route is complex, part of the task can be held in verbal-propositional form (e.g., the western route or the Bordeaux route), and this label can be used later as the starting point for a rapid visual reconstruction. An interactive computer-based map can support this loop by allowing a user to highlight a potential solution, as illustrated for the Bordeaux, Poitiers, Paris path in Figure 11.13. This will free up more capacity in searching for alternative paths.

As a result of this process, three alternative solutions are identified. A western route goes through Toulouse, Bordeaux, Nantes, Caen, and Rouen. A central route shares a path to Bordeaux but then goes via Poitiers, Orleans, and Paris. An eastern route would get us to Paris via Montpellier, Avignon, Lyon, and Dijon.

The Eye Movement Control Loop

The detailed execution of the pattern-finding process is carried out through a series of eye movements to capture each of the major continuous paths meeting the criteria. The eye movements are planned using the task-weighted spatial map of proto-patterns. Those patterns most likely to be relevant to the current task are scheduled for attention, starting with the one weighted most significant. As part of this process, partial solutions are marked in visual working memory by setting placeholders in the egocentric spatial map. For example, the part of the route that goes to Bordeaux might be marked while the alternatives for the rest of the trip are explored. Once an entire path has been identified, it may be checked with a set of rapid eye movements.

This stage may be supported in an interactive system by some form of both spatial and semantic scaling (Furnas 1986). At the early planning stage, only major highways and good secondary roads are required, so it will be easier to carry out this task if the map is simplified to show only these. A smaller map may also be easier to parse with eye movements. Later planning stages will require more detail and zoomed-in map views.

The Intrasaccadic Scanning Loop

This is the innermost loop of the visual query system, where the information available from a single fixation is processed. Sections of lines representing roads are successively formed through selective tuning of the pattern-finding mechanism (Dickinson et al., 1997). Those representing minor roads going in the wrong direction will be rejected, whereas those representing connected major roads going in the right direction will be held in visual working memory up to a limit of three or four road segments. City names will also be processed, causing information about them to be loaded into verbal-propositional memory.

Implications for Interactive Visualization Design

The model presented here has a number of implications for data display systems. The following are perhaps the three most important:

1. Data should be presented in such a way that informative patterns are easy to perceive, allowing us to take advantage of the pattern-finding capabilities of the middle stage of visual processing.

2. The cognitive impact of the interface should be minimized, so that thinking is about the problem, not the interface.

3. The interface should be optimized for low-cost, rapid information seeking.

In the following sections, we consider these implications in more detail, first speculating on the nature of visual queries and then in the context of interactive data navigation techniques, both in isolation and as they are encapsulated in various experimental applications.

Visual Query Patterns

The patterns that can be part of visual problem solving are infinitely diverse: path finding in graphs, quantity estimation, magnitude estimation, trend estimation, cluster identification, correlation identification, outlier detection and characterization, target detection, identification of structural patterns (e.g., hierarchy, degree of coupling), to name a few.

For a visual query to be performed rapidly and with a low error rate, it should consist of a simple pattern or object that can be held in visual working memory. Three elementary queries, or one more complex query, can be held in visual working memory. Other cognitive strategies are required when a query is more than the capacity of visual working memory. Figure 11.14

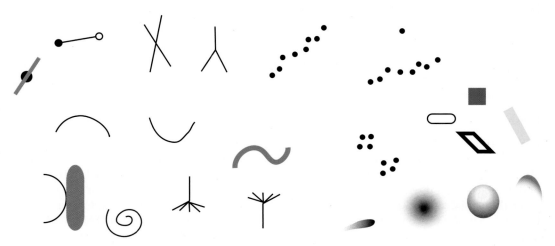

Figure 11.14   Any simple pattern can form the basis for a visual query. Expertise with a particular kind of visual display will allow for more complex queries.

gives some suggestions of patterns that might constitute simple queries. The number of possible patterns is astronomical. Knowledge from vision research about pattern perception and pre-attentive vision can provide a good understanding of the kinds of visual queries that can be processed rapidly. After all, most studies of perception take the form of having subjects make repeated visual queries of a display.

We may be able to query patterns of considerably greater complexity as we become expert in a particular set of graphical conventions, such as a circuit diagram. A chess master can presumably make visual queries consisting of patterns that would not be possible for a novice. Nevertheless, even for the expert, the laws of preattentive processing and elementary pattern perception will make certain patterns much easier to see than others.

Costs of Navigation

In the previous chapter, we discussed various methods for navigating through information spaces. Now we briefly reconsider these in the light of the current theory. The benchmark point of comparison for all navigation techniques should be saccadic eye movement. This allows us to acquire a new set of informative visual objects in 100–200 msec. Moreover, information acquired in this way will be integrated readily with other information that we have recently acquired from the same space. Thus, the ideal visualization is one in which all the information for visualization is available on a single high-resolution screen. Even if the information is in different windows, the cost of navigating there is only a single eye movement, or in the worst case, an eye movement plus a head movement if the angle is large. Consider some of the computer-based alternatives to eye movements.

Hypertext Link

Clicking a hypertext link involves a 1–2 sec guided hand movement and a mouse click. This can generate an entirely new screenful of information. However, the cognitive cost is that the entire information context typically has changed, and the new information may be presented using a different visual symbol set and different layout conventions. Several seconds of cognitive re-orientation may be required.

Brushing, Dynamic Queries, and Hover Queries

Both brushing (Ahlberg et al., 1992) and dynamic queries (Becker and Cleaveland, 1987) allow information to be revealed on some data dimension by making a continuous mouse movement. Hover queries cause extra information to pop up rapidly as the mouse is dragged over a series of data objects. All three of these require a mouse movement typically taking about two seconds. After this initial setup time, the mouse can allow rapid scanning in a tight, exploratory visual feedback. The data is continuously modified according to the mouse movement. This may enable an effective query rate of several per second, similar to the rate for eye movements. However, this rate is only possible for quite specific kinds of query trajectory; we cannot jump from point to point in the data space as we can by moving our eyes.

Walking or Flying in Virtual Reality

Compared to eye movements or rapid exploration techniques like hyperlink following or brushing, navigating a virtual information space by walking or flying is likely to be both considerably slower and cognitively more demanding. In virtual reality, as in the real world, walking times are measured in minutes at best. Even with virtual flying interfaces (which do not attempt to simulate real flying and are therefore much faster), it is likely to take tens of seconds to navigate from one vantage point to another. In addition, the cognitive cost of manipulating the flying interface is likely to be high without extensive training. And although walking in virtual reality simulates walking in the world, it cannot be the same, so the cognitive load is higher.

Table 11.1 gives a set of rough estimates of the times and cognitive costs associated with different navigation techniques. When simple pattern finding is needed, the importance of having a fast, highly interactive interface cannot be emphasized enough. If a navigation technique is slow, then the cognitive costs can be much greater than just the amount of time lost, because an entire train of thought can become disrupted by the loss of the contents of both visual and nonvisual working memories.

The figures in Table 11.1 should be taken as ballpark estimates; they have not been empirically validated.

Magnifying Windows vs. Zooming

As an example of how visual working memory capacity can be used to make substantial design decisions, we now consider the problem of when extra windows are needed in a visualization interface. Consider the task of finding similar or identical patterns spaced far apart in a large geographical space, as illustrated in Figure 11.15. With a zooming interface, it is necessary to

Navigation Technique	Time	Cognitive Effort
Attentional object switch within a fixation	50 msec	Minimal
Saccadic eye movement	150 msec	Minimal
Hypertext jump	2 sec	Medium
Brushing	2 sec setup, 250 sec/query	Medium
Dynamic queries	2 sec setup, 250 sec/query	Medium
Floating queries	2 sec setup, 250 sec/query	Medium
Zooming	2 sec setup + log spatial change	High
Flying	30 sec–3 min	High
Walking	30 sec–10 min	High

Table 11.1 Approximated times for navigation in information spaces

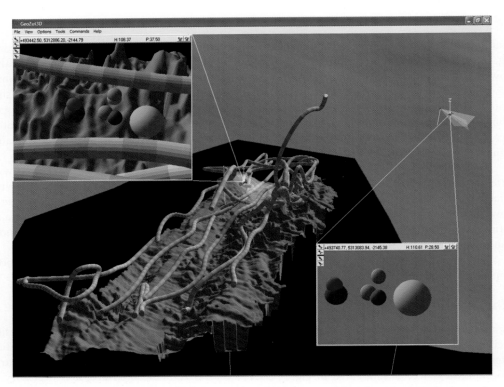

Figure 11.15   Subwindows show a magnified view together with the source of the information in the background overview.

zoom in to and look at one pattern, then hold that pattern in visual working memory while zooming out to seek other patterns. The pattern in visual working memory is then compared to new patterns seen during the search process. If a possible match is found, it may be necessary to zoom back and forth to confirm details of the match. An alternative method is to use extra windows to magnify parts of the main display. When two such windows are in position, it is possible simply to make eye movements between them to assess the match more rapidly.

The critical resource here is visual working memory capacity, because this determines how many visits are required to make the comparison. If the target pattern is simple enough to be held in visual working memory, then zooming will often be more efficient, because it avoids the overhead of setting up multiple windows. If more than three items are in the target pattern, then it will be necessary to zoom back and forth between them, and the multiwindow solution will be faster.

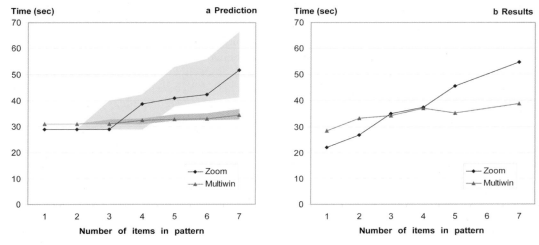

Figure 11.16 Model predictions are shown on the left. Measured task performance is shown on the right. Multiple windows speed performance relative to the use of a zooming interface when the number of objects to be compared is five or more.

We have modeled two user interfaces—simple zooming vs. multiple windows—considering visual working memory capacity as a critical resource and estimating the number of zooms vs. window movements necessary to complete the task of finding identical groups of simple shapes clustered but widely separated in a geographical space (Plumlee and Ware, 2002). The predictions of the model are shown in Figure 11.16(a), modeled for capacities of visual working memory at two, three, and four items, leading to a range of predictions as shown by the broad colored wedges. As can be seen, the model predicts that zooming will have an initial benefit because extra windows take more time to set up. However, as the number of objects increases, the extra window interface will be beneficial. The measured results, as shown Figure 11.16(b), closely matched the prediction.

Interfaces to Knowledge Structures

Although a visual icon or object can activate logical verbal information rapidly and effectively, it can do so only if this information has a strong, previously learned association between the image and the meaning. This is why advertisers spend millions promoting logos. It is also why the design of symbol sets is so critical. Once a symbol set has been learned by a wide group of users, the cost of changing it can be huge.

Concept Maps and Mind Maps

A more complex way to map out knowledge structures is to use some form of node–link diagram, with nodes representing concepts and the links representing the relationships between them. The technique of sketching out links between concepts, as shown in Figure 11.10, has received considerable attention from educational theorists. These *concept maps* (or *mind maps* as they are sometimes called) are often recommended as study aids for students (Jonassen et al., 1993). Usually, such maps are constructed informally by sketching them on paper, but computer-based tools also exist. Essentially, a concept map is a type of node–link diagram in which the nodes represent concepts and the links represent relationships between concepts. It can be used to make the structure of a cognitive concept network explicitly available. An individual can use a concept map as a tool for organizing his or her own personal concept structure, and it may reveal patterns of relationships between ideas that had not been evident when the concepts were stored internally. A concept map can also be constructed in a group exercise, in which case it becomes a tool for building a common understanding.

Constellation

The Constellation system of Munzner et al. (1999) provides an example of how a highly interactive node–link visualization can provide views into very a complex semantic network, far larger than can be displayed on a static concept map. Figure 11.17 shows a screen shot, but this static image does not do justice to the system. Constellation uses hover queries to allow for rapid highlighting of subsets of the graph. Links attached to a node became highlighted as the cursor passes over the node. In addition, when the user clicks on a particular node, Constellation uses intelligent zoom, causing the graph to rearrange itself partially so that closely related semantic concepts are allocated more screen space and larger fonts. By using these techniques, a large amount of semantic information can be accessed very quickly.

Note that the rapid query techniques get around the usual problems of graph layout. Most of the work in graph layout is aimed at producing aesthetically pleasing drawings of graph structures, by paying particular attention to minimizing edge crossings of nodes (Di Battista et al., 1998). A good, clear static graph drawing of the information in Figure 11.17 by the conventional criteria, is probably impossible, because there are simply too many links. In Constellation, Munzer abandoned the usual criteria, allowing edges to cross each other and to cross nodes. Using interactive techniques to reveal information as needed allowed visual access to much larger structures.

The node–link diagram is a method for looking at networks of concepts, but a common way of organizing knowledge is through a hierarchy, and the most common visualization of a hierarchy is a tree. A degree-of-interest tree (Card and Nation, 2002) is a tree visualization that uses a *degree-of-interest function* (Furnas, 1986) to show or hide interactively parts of the tree structure based on their estimated relevance to a selected node. It enables a large tree structure to be interactively explored.

Linking Computer-Based Analysis with Visualization

The greatest power in information visualization arises when the power of computers to sample and condense very large amounts of information is combined with a visual interface. If the computer contains a model of a knowledge domain, then this model can form the basis for inter-

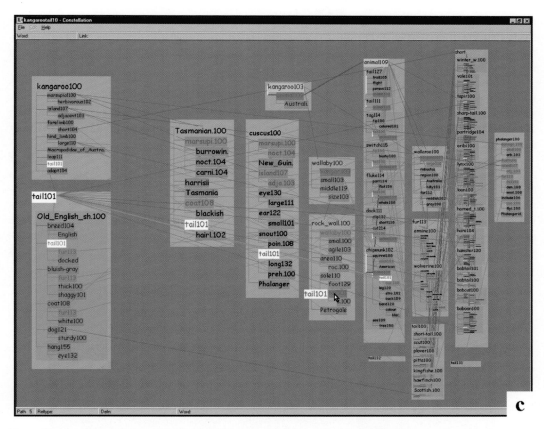

Figure 11.17 A screen image of the Constellation system showing a view into the MindNet semantic network database.

active applications that visually hide and show information based on the estimated relevance to some task. Only the most relevant information is being displayed to the user.

Psychologists have developed a number of other tools for mapping the cognitive structure of concepts, besides simple sketching. One is based on multidimensional scaling (Shepard, 1962). The technique involves giving participants pairs of examples of the ideas or objects to be mapped and asking them to rate the similarity. For example, if the goal is to find out how someone conceptualizes different kinds of animals, that person is given pairs of cat–dog, mouse–cow, cat–elephant, and so on, and asked to give each pair a similarity rating. Once all pair ratings for the entire set have been obtained, the multidimensional scaling technique is used to compute a mathematical space in which similar animals are close together. This technique can sometimes reveal the nature of the most significant dimensions of this space, but often the mathematical dimensions that are found have little intuitive meaning. The multidimensional scaling technique does not show links between concepts; it only shows proximity. Concepts that are close together in the space are assumed to be related.

Multidimensional scaling can be used as a tool in visualizing concept spaces, but it suffers from the problem that the space created can have a high dimensionality. However, the dimensionality can be reduced by simply showing the two or three most significant dimensions as a 2D or 3D scatter plot. More dimensions can be added by color-coding or changing the shape of each data glyph, as discussed in Chapters 4 and 5.

The analysis of large text databases is an application area where it is useful to get a view of a large number of points in a multidimensional conceptual space. The SPIRE system creates a classification of documents with respect to a keyword query and can be applied to databases consisting of hundreds of thousands of documents (Wise et al., 1995). The result is a set of vectors in an n-dimensional space. To help people understand the resulting clusters of documents, Wise et al. created a visualization called a *ThemeScape*, which shows the two most important dimensions as a kind of data landscape. This is illustrated in Figure 11.18. Flags on the tops of hills

Figure 11.18   An entire week of CNN news stories is summarized in a ThemeScape visualization (Wise et al., 1995).

label and identify the largest clusters of documents in this space. Essentially, a ThemeScape uses the two most significant dimensions of the space to create a smoothed two-dimensional histogram. This can be regarded as a different kind of concept map—one that does not show the links but uses spatial proximity and salience to show the major concentrations of information and, to some extent, their relationships. This kind of display will be useful when two dimensions really do capture most of the variability in the data. If more dimensions are significantly involved, then color-coding and more interactive exploratory techniques may be necessary.

Trajectory Mapping

Trajectory mapping is a recent psychological method for mapping out the structure of concept spaces (Richards and Koenderink, 1995). Unlike multidimensional scaling, trajectory mapping explicitly finds links between concepts. In trajectory mapping, a participant is also given pairs of examples from the set of objects (or concepts) to be organized. However, in this case the person is asked to look at the objects that make up the pair and extrapolate on the basis of some difference between them, then select another sample concept that represents the result of that extrapolation. For example, someone given a mouse and a dog as exemplars might extrapolate to a cow if they thought size was a critical variable, or might extrapolate to a monkey based on a concept of animal intelligence. Participants are also allowed to say that there is no meaningful extrapolation, in which case one of the exemplars becomes a terminator in the resulting concept graph. This exercise is designed to produce a set of cognitive pathways linking concepts. Strong pathways can be distinguished from weak ones.

Lokuge et al. (1996) used a combination of trajectory mapping and multidimensional scaling to create different visual maps linking various tourist attractions in the Boston area, such as museums and open-air markets. The results were based both on conceptual similarity between the different items and the pathways between them. One of the results is shown in Figure 11.19. This technique could be used to generate customized tours automatically. The tourist would enter a set of interests, and the system would combine this with the database information to create a walking tour of suitable attractions.

It should be recognized that no matter how they are generated, concept maps are somewhat crude instruments for making knowledge explicit. All of them reveal only that there is a relationship between ideas, not the nature of that relationship.

Creative Problem Solving

We commonly divide problem-solving activities into the routine and the creative. The essential difference is that in creative thinking, the emphasis is on novelty. Theories of creative thinking generally break the process into three states: preparation, production, and judgment (Matlin, 1994). Visualization can help with all three.

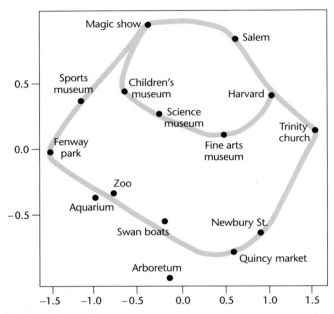

Figure 11.19   A trajectory map of tourist destinations in the Boston area, laid out according to the results of a multidimensional scaling experiment (Lokuge et al., 1996).

In the *preparation* stage, the problem-solver acquires the background information needed to build a solution. Sometimes, preparation will involve a stage of exploratory data analysis. Visualization can help through pattern discovery (discussed especially in Chapter 6). In this process, the visual queries may initially be a loosely defined search for any significant pattern, becoming more focused as the issues become better defined.

In the *production* stage, the problem-solver generates a set of potential solutions. A solution often starts with a tentative suggestion, which is either rejected or later refined. Early theorists proposed that the quantity of ideas, rather than the quality, was the overriding consideration in the production of candidate solutions. However, experimental studies fail to support this (Gilhooly, 1988). Generating ideas irrespective of their value is probably not useful.

Possibly the most challenging problem posed in data visualization systems is to support the way sketchy diagrams are used by scientists and engineers in the production stage. Discoveries and inventions made using table-napkin sketches are legendary. Here is a description of the role of a diagram by an architectural theorist (Alexander, 1964):

> *Each constructive diagram is a tentative assumption about the nature of the context. Like a hypothesis, it relates an unclear set of forces to one another conceptually; like a hypothesis, it is usually improved by clarity and economy of notation. Like a hypothesis,*

it cannot be obtained by deductive methods, but only by abstraction and invention. Like a hypothesis, it is rejected when a discrepancy turns up and shows that it fails to account for some new force in the context.

If creativity is to be supported, the medium must afford tentative interactions. The lack of precision in quick, loose sketches actually allows for multiple interpretations. The fact that a line can be interpreted in many different ways, as discussed in Chapter 6, can be a distinct benefit in enabling a diagram to support multiple tentative hypotheses. The sketches people construct as part of the creative process are rapid, not refined, and readily discarded. Giving a child high-quality watercolor paper and paints is likely to inhibit creativity if the child is made aware of the expense and cautioned not to "waste" the materials. Schumann et al. (1996) carried out an empirical study of architectural perspective drawings executed in three different styles: a precise line drawing, a realistically shaded image, and a sketch. All the drawings contained the same features and level of detail. The sketch version was rated substantially higher on measures of ability to stimulate creativity, changes in design, and discussions.

In the *judgment* stage, the problem-solver analyzes the potential solutions. This stage is an exercise in quality control; as fast as hypotheses are created and patterns are discovered, most must be rejected. In a visualization system used for data mining, the user may discover large numbers of patterns but will also be willing to reject them almost as rapidly as they are discovered. Some will already be known, some will be irrelevant to the task at hand, only a few will be novel, and even fewer will lead to a practical solution. Many judgment aids are not visual; for example, statistical tools can be used to test hypotheses formally. But when visualization is part of the process, it should not be misleading or hide important information.

The challenge for problem-solving interfaces is to support the rapid creation of loose sketches, the ability to modify them, and the ability to discard all or some of them. All this must be done with an interface so simple that it does not intrude on the visual thinking process.

Conclusion

The best visualizations are not static images to be printed in books, but fluid, dynamic artifacts that respond to the need for a different view or for more detailed information. In some cases, the visualization can be an interface to a simulation of a complex system; the visualization, combined with the simulation, can create a powerful cognitive augmentation. An emerging view of human–computer interaction considers the human and the computer together as a problem-solving system. The visualization is a two-way interface, although highly asymmetric, with far higher bandwidth communication from the machine to the human than in the other direction. Because of this asymmetry in data rates, cognitive support systems must be constructed that are semiautomatic, with only occasional nudges required from users to steer them in a desired direction. The high-bandwidth visualization channel is then used to deliver the results of modeling exercises and database searches.

At the interface, the distinction between input and output becomes blurred. We are accustomed to regarding a display screen as a passive output device and a mouse as an input device. This is not how it is in the real world, where many things work both ways. A sheet of paper or a piece of clay can both record ideas (input) and display them (output). The coupling of input and output can also be achieved in interactive visualization. Each visual object in an interactive application can potentially provide output as a representation of data and also potentially receive input. Someone may click on it with a mouse to retrieve information or may use it as an interface to change the parameters of a computer model. The ultimate challenge for this kind of highly interactive information visualization is to create an interface that supports creative sketching of ideas, affording interactive sketching that is as fluid and inconsequential as the proverbial paper-napkin sketch.

The person who wishes to design a visualization must contend with two sets of conflicting forces. On the one hand, there is the requirement for the best possible visual representation, tailored exactly to the problem to be solved. On the other hand, there is the need for consistency in representation any time that two or more people work on a problem. This need is even greater when large, international organizations have a common set of goals that demand industrywide visualization standards. At the stage of new discoveries in information visualizations, standardization is the enemy of innovation and innovation is the enemy of standardization. Thus it is important to get the research done before the standards are formed, otherwise it will be too late.

These are exciting times for information visualization, because we are still in the discovery phase, although this phase will not last for long. In the next few years, the wild inventions that are now being implemented will become standardized. Like clay sculptures that have been baked and hardened, the novel data visualization systems of today's laboratory will become cultural artifacts, everyday tools of the information professional.

Changing Primaries

This appendix describes the operation of transforming one set of primaries into another. The mathematical name for this operation is a *change of basis*.

To convert a color from one set of primary lights to another, it is first necessary to define a conversion between the primaries themselves. We can think of this as matching each of the new primary lights using the old primary system. Suppose we designate our original set of primaries P_1, P_2, and P_3 and the new set of primaries Q_1, Q_2, and Q_3. We now use our original primaries to create matches with each of the new primaries in turn. Let us call the amount of each of the P primaries c_{ij}.

Thus,

$$Q_1 \equiv c_{11}P_1 + c_{12}P_2 + c_{13}P_3$$
$$Q_2 \equiv c_{21}P_1 + c_{22}P_2 + c_{23}P_3$$
$$Q_3 \equiv c_{31}P_1 + c_{32}P_2 + c_{33}P_3 \tag{A.1}$$

If we denote the matrix of c_{ij} values C, then

$$P = CQ \tag{A.2}$$

To reverse the transformation, invert the matrix:

$$P \equiv C^{-1}Q \tag{A.3}$$

This same matrix can now be used to convert any set of values expressed in one set of primaries to the other set of primaries. Thus, the values p_1, p_2, and p_3 represent the amounts of the lights in primary system P needed to make a match.

$$\text{Sample} \equiv p_1 P_1 + p_2 P_2 + p_3 P_3 \tag{A.4}$$

Then we can calculate the values q in primary system Q simply by solving

$$q = Cp \tag{A.5}$$

CIE Color Measurement System

To determine a standard observer, a set of red, green, and blue lamps is used by a number of representative subjects to match all the pure colors of the spectrum. The result is called a set of *color-matching functions*. The set of color-matching functions for the Commission Internationale de l'Éclairage (CIE) standard observer is illustrated in Figure B.1. They were obtained with red, green, and blue pure spectral hues at 700, 546, and 436 nanometers, respectively, using a number of trained observers. Notice that there are negative values in these functions. These exist for the reasons discussed in Chapter 4. It is not possible to match directly all spectral lights with these, or any other, primaries.

For a number of reasons, the CIE chose not to use the standard-observer color-matching functions directly as the color standard, although it would have been perfectly legitimate to do so. Instead, they chose a set of abstract primaries called the *XYZ tristimulus values* and transformed the original color-matching functions into this new coordinate system. The process is the transformation from one coordinate system to another, as described in Appendix A. The transformed color-matching functions are illustrated in Figure B.2.

The CIE *XYZ* tristimulus values have the following properties:

1. All tristimulus values are positive for all colors. To achieve this, it was necessary to create primaries that do not correspond to any real lights. The *XYZ* primary axes are purely abstract concepts. However, this model has the advantage that all perceivable colors fall within the CIE gamut. They are, in effect, a set of virtual primaries.

2. The *X* and *Z* tristimulus values have zero luminance. Only the *Y* tristimulus value contains luminance information, and the color-matching function ($\bar{y}$) is the same as the $V(\lambda)$ function, discussed in Chapter 3.

To determine the *XYZ* tristimulus values for a given patch of light, we integrate the energy distribution with the three $\bar{x}, \bar{y}, \bar{z}$ color-matching functions that define the CIE standard. Note that

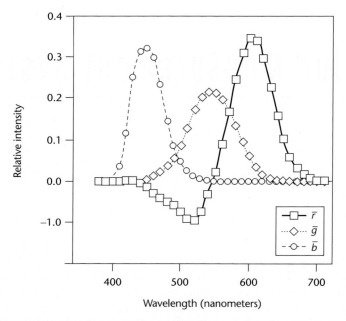

Figure B.1 The color-matching functions that define the CIE 1931 standard observer. To obtain these, each pure spectral wavelength was matched by a mixture of three primary lights.

this is a generalization of the process of obtaining luminance described in Chapter 3—only here, we obtain three values to fully specify a color:

$$X = K_m \int_\lambda E(\lambda)\bar{x}_\lambda d\lambda$$
$$Y = K_m \int_\lambda E(\lambda)\bar{y}_\lambda d\lambda$$
$$Z = K_m \int_\lambda E(\lambda)\bar{z}_\lambda d\lambda \qquad \textbf{(B1.1)}$$

If $K_m = 680$ lumens/watt and $E(\lambda)$ is measured in watts per unit area solid angle (steradians), then Y gives luminance.

This appendix provides only a very brief introduction to the complex and technical subject of colorimetry. Many important issues have been neglected that must be taken into account in serious color measurement. One issue is whether the light to be measured is an extended source,

Figure B.2   The CIE tristimulus functions used to define the color of a light in *XYZ* tristimulus coordinates.

such as a monitor, in which case we measure in light emitted per unit area (candelas per square meter), or a lamp, in which case we measure total light output in all directions.

The subject becomes still more complex when we consider the measurement of surface colors; the color of the illuminating source must be taken into account, and we can no longer use a trichromatic system. Fortunately, computer monitors, because they emit light, do allow us to use a trichromatic system. The reader who intends to get involved in serious color measurement should obtain one of the standard textbooks, such as Wyszecki and Stiles (1982) or Judd and Wyszecki (1975).

Wavelength

Figure 6.2

The Perceptual Evaluation of Visualization Techniques and Systems

There is a hierarchy of value in research. The ultimate goal of the scientist is to discover an immutable truth that will form the foundation for a new way of understanding the world. Applied researchers must often be satisfied with more humble objectives; sometimes it may be necessary to show that soon-to-be-obsolete interface *A* is better in some small way than soon-to-be-obsolete interface *B*. Between these two scenarios are many graduations. A research-based design guideline is something that can be of enduring value. A rough continuum of value exists, depending on the research goals. The following list starts with those goals that are most valuable.

Research Goals

Uncover fundamental truths and test theories. This is the holy grail of research—a fundamental truth that forever changes how we think of the world. Even small truths are to be prized. Because visualization techniques often produce patterns that do not exist in nature, or rarely do, studies of such techniques can be part of the new discipline of *information psychophysics*. Cognitive modeling of the way people interact with the interfaces to information systems is an important part of cognitive systems theory; and because all human intellectual achievements are ultimately the products of cognitive systems, not individuals alone, lasting truths may be achieved.

Discover the nature of the world. The early stages of science can be like butterfly collecting. It is necessary to get a feeling for the range of phenomena to be encompassed before developing theories. Some areas of perception are still like this. For example, the perception of patterns in motion is still at an early stage. The application of motion in visualization similarly lags.

Ascertain if an existing theory generalizes to practice. Many phenomena that are studied by vision researchers in the simplified conditions of the laboratory may not apply to a more complex data visualization. It can be a useful contribution simply to show that a well known laboratory result generalizes to a common visualization problem.

Make an objective comparison between two or more display methods. Directly comparing two display methods can show which is the more effective. Ideally, the two methods should be tested with a variety of test data to provide some degree of generality.

Make an objective comparison between two or more display systems. Directly comparing two interfaces to an information system has obvious value to someone intending to choose one or the other. However, because system interfaces are typically complex, with usually dozens of differences between them, it is rarely possible to make valid generalizations from such studies.

Measure task performance. Simply measuring the time to perform a task with a particular interface is useful; it is even more useful if the task is elementary and frequently used. Error rates and error magnitudes are other common measurements providing useful guidelines for the designer of information systems.

Ascertain user preferences for different display methods. Occasionally, factors such as the "cool appearance" of a particular interface can be decisive in its adoption. Naturally, the techniques used for research should be suited to the goals of the research. Finding the balance between an attractive display, and an optimal display for the task, should be the goal.

This appendix is intended to provide a preliminary acquaintance with the kinds of empirical research methods that can be applied to visualization. It is not possible in a few thousand words to give a complete cookbook of experimental designs. When studies are looked at in detail, there are almost as many designs as there are research questions, but a number of broad classes stand out. It is generally the case that the methods used for evaluating visualization are borrowed from some other discipline, such as psychophysics or cognitive psychology. Such methods have been continually refined through the mill of peer review. For introductory texts on experimental design and data analysis, see Elmes et al. (1999) or Goodwin (2001). What follows is an introduction to some of the more common methodologies and measurement techniques.

Psychophysics

Psychophysics is a set of techniques based on applying the methods of physics to measurements of human sensation. These techniques have been extremely successful in defining the basic set of limits of the visual system. For example, how rapidly must a light flicker before it is perceived as steady, or what is the smallest relative brightness change that can be detected? Psychophysical techniques are ideal for discovering the important sensory dimensions of color, visual texture, sound, and so on, and more than a century of work already exists. Psychophysicists insist on a precise physical definition of the stimulus pattern. Light levels, temporal characteristics, and spatial characteristics must all be measured and controlled.

Psychophysical techniques are normally used for studies intended to reveal early sensory processes, and it is usually assumed (sometimes wrongly) that instructional biases are not significant in these experiments. Extensive studies are often carried out using only one or two observers, frequently the principal investigator and a lab assistant or student. These results are then generalized to the entire human race, with a presumption that can infuriate social scientists. Nevertheless, for the most part, scientific results—even those obtained with few subjects or as early as the 19th century—have withstood the test of time and dozens of replications. Indeed, because some of the experiments require hundreds of hours of careful observation, experiments with large subject populations are usually out of the question.

If a measured effect is easily altered because of instructional bias, we must question whether psychophysical methods are appropriate. The sensitivity of a measurement to how instructions are given can be used as a method for teasing out what is sensory and what is arbitrary. If a psychophysical measurement is highly sensitive to changes in the instructions given to the subject, it is likely to be measuring something that has higher-level cognitive or cultural involvement.

A few of the studies that have been published in recent years can be understood as a new variant on psychophysics, namely *information psychophysics*. The essence of information psychophysics is to apply methods of classical psychophysics to common information structures, such as elementary flow patterns, surface shapes, or paths in graphs.

When designing studies in information psychophysics, it is important to use meaningful units. For specifying the size of graphical objects there are three possibilities: pixels, centimeters, and visual angle. Each of these can be important. For larger objects, the size in centimeters and the visual angle should be determined. For small objects, pixel size can also be an important variable, and this should be specified. If you want to get really serious about color, then the monitor should be calibrated in some standard way, such as the CIE *XYZ* standard (Wyszecki, 1982). For moving objects, it is also important to know both the refresh rate (the frame rate of the monitor) and how fast your computer graphics are actually changing (update rate). It is worth thinking about how a graphics system actually works to get a better idea of the true precision of measurement. For example, if the update rate and refresh rate of the display are 60 Hz, then the granularity of measurement cannot be better than 16 msec.

Following are some of the common psychophysical methods that may also be applied to information psychophysics.

Detection Methods

There is a range of techniques that rely on how many errors people make when performing a certain task. Sometimes, determining an *error rate* is the goal of the experiment. If, for example,

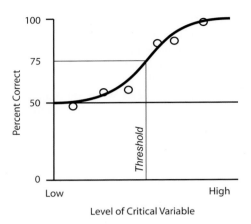

Figure C.1   The threshold in this particular example is defined as a 75% correct rate of responding. Errors are determined at many levels of a critical variable. A curve is fit through the points (heavy line) and this is used to define the threshold.

a visualization is used as part of an aircraft inspection process, then the expected error rate of the inspector is a critical issue.

More commonly, error rates are used as a rigorous way of finding thresholds. The idea is to keep showing subjects a display with some parameter at a range of levels. The percentage of correct detections is measured at each level, and a plot like Figure C.1 is generated. We define the threshold by some error rate; for example, if the chance error rate is 50%, then we might define the threshold as 75%. A problem with this process is that it requires a large number of trials to get a percent error rate for each level of our test parameter, and this can be especially difficult if the region of the threshold is not known. Hundreds of trials can be wasted making measurements that are well above, or below, threshold.

The *staircase procedure* is a technique for speeding up the determination of thresholds using error rates. The subject's responses are used to home in on the region of the threshold. If the subject makes a correct response to a target, the stimulus level is lowered for the next trial. If a subject fails to see a target, the stimulus level is raised. In this way, the program homes in on the threshold (Wetherill and Levitt, 1965).

The most sophisticated way of using error rates in determining thresholds for pattern detection is based on *signal detection theory*. A target pattern is assumed to produce a neural signal with a normal distribution, in the presence of neural noise caused by other factors. A parameter in the model determines whether observers are biased toward positive responses (producing false positives) or negative responses (producing false negatives). One way to represent the results of a study using signal detection theory is the *receiver operating characteristics* (ROC) *curve* (Swets, 1996; Irwin and McCarthy, 1998).

Method of Adjustment

A useful technique for tuning up a visualization is to give application domain experts control over some variable and ask them to adjust it so that it is optimal in some way for them. This is called the *method of adjustment*. Get a population of users to do this, and a useful default setting can be derived from the mean or median setting.

The method of adjustment can also be used to answer questions about perceptual distortion. For example, if we are interested in simultaneous lightness contrast, we can ask subjects to adjust a patch of gray until it matches some other gray and use the difference to estimate the magnitude of the distortion due to contrast.

There are biases associated with method of adjustment. If we are interested in the threshold for just seeing a target, we might turn up the contrast until it is visible or turn down the contrast until it disappears. The threshold will be lower in the latter case. Once we can see something, it is easier to perceive at a lower contrast.

Cognitive Psychology

In cognitive psychology, the brain is treated as a set of interlinked processing modules. A classic example of a cognitive model is the separation of short-term and long-term memory. Short-term memory, also called *working memory*, is the temporary buffer where we hold concepts, recent percepts, and plans for action. Long-term memory is a more or less permanent store of information that we have accumulated over a lifetime.

Methods in cognitive psychology commonly involve *measuring reaction time* or *measuring errors*, always with the goal of testing a hypothesis about a cognitive model. Typical experiments involve very simple, but ideally important tasks, such as determining whether or not a particular object is present in a display. The subject is asked to respond by hitting a key as fast as possible. The resulting time measurement can be used to estimate the time to perform simple cognitive operations, once the time taken to physically move the hand or depress a key is subtracted.

Another common kind of experiment measures *interference* between visual patterns. The increase in errors that results is used as evidence that different channels of information processing converge at some point. For example, if the task of mentally counting down in sevens from 100 were to interfere with short-term memory for the locations of objects in space, it would be taken as evidence that these skills share some common cognitive processing. The fact that there is little or no interference suggests that visual short-term memory and verbal short-term memory are separate (Postma and De Haan, 1996).

Recently, some cognitive theories have gained a tremendous boost because of advances in brain imaging. Functional MRI techniques have been developed that allow researchers actually to see which parts of the brain are active when subjects perform certain tasks. In this way, functional units that had only been previously inferred have actually been pinpointed (Zeki, 1993).

Structural Analysis

In structural analysis, theories of cognitive processing are constructed using direct observation as evidence. Structuralist researchers conduct studies that are more like interviews than formal experiments. Often the subjects are required to carry out certain simple tasks and report at the same time on their understanding and their perceptions. Using these techniques, researchers such as Piaget have been able to open up large areas of knowledge very rapidly and to establish the basic framework of our scientific understanding. However, in some cases, the insights obtained have not been confirmed by subsequent, more careful experiments. In structuralism, emphasis is given to hypothesis formation, which at times may seem more like the description and classification of behavior than a true explanation.

A structural analysis is often especially appropriate to the study of computer interfaces, because it is fast-moving and can take a variety of factors into account. We can quantify judgments to some extent through the use of rating scales. By asking observers to assign numbers to subjective effectiveness, clarity, and so on, we can obtain useful numerical data that compares one representation to another. There are several tools of structural analysis. We can ask domain experts what they need in a visualization (*requirements analysis*). We can try to understand what they are attempting to accomplish at a more elementary level (*task analysis*). Research tools also include testbench applications, *semistructured interviews*, and rating scales.

Testbench Applications for Discovery

At the early, butterfly-collecting stage of science, the goal is to map out the range of phenomena that exist. In visualization research, the goal is to gain an intuitive understanding of diversity, notable phenomena, and what works and does not work from an applied perspective.

The primary early-stage tool for the visualization researcher is the *testbench application*. It gives the researcher the flexibly to try out different ways of mapping the data into a visual representation. Of course, there is no such thing as a universal testbench. The goal should be to build a flexible tool capable of producing a range of visual mappings of the data and a range of interaction possibilities. For example, if the problem is to find the best way to represent the shape of a surface, the testbench application should be able to load different surface shapes, change lighting, change surface texture properties, turn stereoscopic viewing on and off, and provide motion parallax cues.

There is a tendency for programmers to make the user interface for a testbench too sophisticated. This can be self defeating, because it limits flexibility. The objective should be to explore, not to build a polished application for scientists. If the easiest way to explore is to change a constant in the code and recompile, then this is what should be done. Often a good testbench interface is a text file of parameters, setting various aspects of the display. This can be modified in a word processor and reloaded. Sometimes a panel of sliders is useful, allowing a researcher to adjust parameters interactively. For the most part, the quality of the code does not matter for a testbench application, although it is essential that the parts of the program dealing with display parameters are correct.

There are many ways to play with testbenches, and *play* is definitely the operative word. This is a time for creative exploration, forming hypotheses quickly and discarding them easily. Interesting possibilities can be shown to domain experts. It is especially useful to show them the best solutions you have. You may only get one chance to have a physicist, an oceanographer, or a surgeon to take you seriously. Asking their opinions about something that actually looks better than whatever they are currently using is one way to get their interest. Phenomena that may be significant can be shown to other vision researchers.

Once something interesting has been identified with a testbench, a rigorous study can be carried out using the methods of psychophysics or cognitive psychology.

Structured Interviews

One of the most useful tools, both for initial requirements and task analysis and for the evaluation of problem solutions, is the *structured* or *semistructured* interview. The method is to construct an interview with a structured set of questions to elicit information about specific task requirements. It is structured to make sure that the important questions are asked and that the answers come in a somewhat coherent form.

Structured interviews can be excellent tools to evaluate what aspects of a visualization actually are important to potential users. They can also be used to evaluate a number of different solutions for strengths and weaknesses. In many cases, it is useful for structured interviews to be built around the performance of particular tasks. The participant is asked to perform particular tasks with the system or with more than one system and is then asked to comment on suitability, ease of use, clarity of presentation, and so on. The great advantage of structured interviews is that they make it possible to gain information about a wide range of issues with relatively little effort, in comparison with more objective methods, such as reaction time or error rate measurements. Also, you might learn something you did not ask about.

Rating Scales

The Likert scale (also called a *rating scale*) is a method for turning opinions into numbers. Subjects are simply asked to rate some phenomenon by choosing a number on some range, such as the following:

(GOOD) 1   2   3   4   5 (BAD)

For example, if we have six different visual representations of a flow pattern, we might ask subjects to rate how well they can see each pattern on a scale of 1 to 5.

Subjects tend to use rating scales in their own idiosyncratic ways. Some will be biased to the low end of the scale and others to the upper end, but generally they will tend to try to use most to the scale for whatever set of samples they are shown. Because of this, no absolute meaning should ever be given to rating scale data. If 10 inferior visual representations are shown to subjects, they will still differentiate them into good and bad; the same will be true for 10 very good ones. However, rating scales are an excellent tool for measuring relative preferences.

Rating scales can be used to answer broad questions about preferences for two or more different solutions to a problem. Quite often, users will prefer one solution to another, even though no objective differences are measured. In some cases, one interface might even be objectively superior, but another preferred.

Statistical Exploration

Sometimes it may be useful to use statistical discovery techniques to learn about some class of visualization methods. Suppose we wish to carry out an investigation into how many data dimensions can be conveyed by visual texture. The first obvious question is: How many perceptually distinct texture dimensions are there? The next question is: How can we effectively map data dimensions to them? If the answer cannot be found in the research literature, one way to proceed is to use a kind of statistical data-mining strategy to find the answer. First, we might ask people to classify textures in as many different ways as we can think of (e.g., roughness, regularity, elongation, fuzziness). The next step is to apply a statistical method to discover how many dimensions there really are in the subjects' responses. The following sections list the major techniques.

Principal Components Analysis

The goal of *principal components analysis* is to take a set of variables and find a new set of variables (the principal components) that are uncorrelated with each other (Young et al., 1978; Tabachnick and Fidell, 2001; Hotelling, 1933). This might be used to reduce a high-dimensional data set to lower dimensions. In many data sets (think of multiple measurements on the dimensions of parts of beetles, for example), many of the variables are highly correlated, and the first two or three principal components contain most of the variability in the data. If this is the case, then one immediate advantage of the data reduction resulting from PCA is that the data can be mapped into a two- or three-dimensional space and thereby visualized as a scatter plot.

Multidimensional Scaling

Multidimensional scaling (MDS) is a method explicitly designed to reduce the dimensionality of a set of data points to two or three, so that these dimensions can be displayed visually. The method is designed to preserve, as far as possible, metric distances between data points (Young et al., 1978; Wong and Bergeron, 1997).

Clustering

Cluster analysis is a statistical technique designed to find clusters of points in a data space of any dimensionality (Romesburg, 1984). There are two basic kinds: hierarchical and k-means. In *hierarchical clustering*, a tree structure is built, with individual data points at the leaves. These points are combined recursively, most similar first. Hierarchical clustering can provide the basis for hierarchical taxonomy.

K-means clustering requires the user to input a number of clusters (k). A set of k clusters is generated by finding the cluster means that minimize the sum of squared distances between each set of data points and its nearest mean.

Either kind of clustering can be used as a method for data reduction in visualization, because a tight cluster of points can be reduced to a single data glyph.

Multiple Regression

In visualization, *multiple regression* is a statistical technique that can be used to discover whether it is possible to predict some response variable from display properties. For example, the time required to judge the shortest path in a node–link diagram might be predicted from the number of link crossings in the diagram and the bendiness of the path (Ware et al., 2002).

Cross-Cultural Studies

If sensory codes are indeed interpreted easily by all humans, this proposition should be testable by means of *cross-cultural studies*. In a famous study by Berlin and Kay (1969), color naming was compared across more than 100 languages. In this way, the researchers established the universality of certain color terms, equivalent to our red, green, yellow, and blue. This study is supported by neurophysiological and psychophysical evidence that suggests these basic colors are hard-wired into the human brain. Such studies are rare, for obvious reasons, and with the globalization of world culture, meaningful studies of this type are rapidly becoming impossible. Television is bringing about an explosive growth in universal symbols. In the near future, cross-cultural studies aimed at basic questions relating to innate mechanisms in perception may be impossible.

Child Studies

By using the techniques of *behaviorism*, it is possible to discover things about a child's sensory processing even before the child is capable of speech. Presumably, very young children have only minimal exposure to the graphic conventions used in visualization. Thus, the way they respond to simple patterns can reveal basic processing mechanisms. This, of course, is the basis for the Hochberg and Brooks' (1978) study discussed in Chapter 1.

It is also possible to gain useful data from somewhat older children, such as five-year-olds. They presumably have all the basics of sensory processing in place, but they still have a long way to go in learning the graphic conventions of our culture, particularly in those obscure areas that deal with data visualization.

Practical Problems in Conducting User Studies

Experimenter Bias

Researchers' careers depend on what they publish, and it is much easier to publish results that confirm a hypothesis than results showing no effects. There are many opportunities for experimenter bias in both the gathering and the interpretation of results.

As a rule of thumb, if the data being measured relates to some low-level, fundamental aspect of vision, then it will be less subject to bias. For example, if a subject is given a control that allows the setting of what seems to be a "pure" yellow, neither reddish nor greenish, the setting is likely to be extremely consistent and will be relatively robust even if the experimenter makes comments like "Are you sure that's not a little tinged with green?" On the other hand, if the experimenter says, "I want you to rate this system, developed by me to obtain my PhD, in comparison with this other system, developed at the University of Blob," then experimenter bias effects can be extreme.

When considering your own work or that of others, be critical. The great advantage of science is that it is incremental and always open to reasoned criticism. Applied science tends to adopt somewhat looser standards, and replications of experiments are rare. Many of the studies we read are biased. In evaluating a published result, always look to see whether the data actually supports what is being claimed. It is common for claims to be made that go far beyond the results. Often the abstract and title suggest that some method or other has clearly been demonstrated to be superior. An examination of the method may show otherwise. A common example is when a difference that is not statistically significant is claimed to support a hypothesis. Some of most important questions to ask are:

What is the task?

Does the experiment really address the intended problem?

Are the control conditions appropriate?

Does the experiment actually test the stated hypothesis?

Are the results significant?

Are there possible confounding variables?

Confounding variables are variables that change in the different experimental conditions, although they are not the variables that the researchers claim to be responsible for the measured effect.

How Many Subjects to Use?

In vision research, some kinds of studies are run with only two, three, or four subjects. These are studies that purport to be looking at the low-level machinery of vision. It makes sense; humans all have the same visual system, and to measure its properties you do not need a large sample of the population. On the other hand, if you are interested in how color terms are used in the general population, then the general population must be sampled in some way.

Statistically, the number of subjects and the number of observations required depend on the variability of responses with a single subject and the variability from one subject to another.

Most experiments are run with between 12 and 20 subjects, where all of the experimental conditions can be carried out on the same subjects (a *within subjects* design). In some cases, because of learning effects, different subjects must be assigned to different conditions. Such experiments will require more subjects.

Research is always an optimization problem—how to get the most information with the least effort. One reason there have been so many simple reaching experiments presented at the Association for Computing Machinery (ACM) Computer-Human Interaction (CHI) conferences is that a Fitts' law experiment (the standard experimental method) is very easy to carry out; it is possible to gather a data point every two or three seconds. A substantial amount of data can be gathered in half an hour of subject time, making it possible to run large numbers of subjects.

Combinatorial Explosion

One of the major problems in designing a visualization study is deciding on the *independent variables*. Independent variables are set by the experimenter in the design stage. In a study of the effectiveness of flow visualization, independent variables might be line width and line spacing of streamlines. The *dependent variables* are the measured user responses, such as the amount of error in judging the flow direction.

In visualization design problems, there are often many possible independent variables. Let us take the example of flow visualization consisting of streaklets–small, curved line segments showing the direction of flow. Streaklet length, streaklet start width, streaklet end width, streaklet start color, streaklet end color, and background color may all be important. Supposing we would like to have four levels of each variable and we wish to study all possible combinations. The result is $4^6 = 2048$ different conditions. Normally, we would like at least 10 measurements of user performance in each condition. We will require over 20,000 measurements. If it were to take 30 seconds to make each measurement, the result would be more than 160 hours of observation for each subject. We might decide to have 15 subjects in our experiment. This means over a year of work, running subjects 40 hours per week. For most researchers, such a study would be impossibly large.

The brute force approach experimental design is to include all variables of interest at all meaningful levels. Because of the combinatorial explosion that results, this cannot work. The way to obtain more from studies, with less effort, is to develop either theories or descriptive models that can be applied to a range of design problems. Empirical studies can be much simpler and focus on specific aspects of the theory.

Task Identification

A critical element in experimental design is deciding on the *task* the subject is to perform. Ideally, this will be something that is both theoretically interesting and very commonly used in real applications. Even if the exact task is not common, it should be representative of activities that are common in visualization interfaces. For example, if the application domain involves visualizing node–link diagrams, the subject might be asked if there is a path between two highlighted nodes. This task is good, because perceiving links between nodes is likely to be important for almost all of the great variety of node–link diagrams that exist.

In order to provide a useful measure of performance, it is also important that the task can be set up to have a clear and simple user response. For example, the subject might push the right mouse button to indicate *yes* and the left mouse button to indicate *no*.

Controls

In an experimental design, a *control* is a condition that is used to provide some basis for comparison. In a theoretical study, the control is usually some condition that provides a reference for theory testing. A theory might predict that a contrast effect will bias a judgment by 30%; the control measurement would be made without the contrast-causing factor to provide a baseline for comparison.

In evaluating a new visualization method, the most reasonable control is the current best practice display method. Some studies employ the somewhat dishonest practice of using a very poor alternative method as a control, thereby exaggerating the value of their own method. This is one of the reasons that the research literature should be read with a measure of skepticism.

Getting Help

Studies in information visualization are fundamentally multidisciplinary. Usually knowledge of computer science, human visual perception, and some application domain is necessary. Often, the best way to do research is to be part of a collaborative team—a computer scientist who can design and build novel interactive visualization systems, a psychologist who understands the perceptual issues and has experience in perception and cognition research, and a domain expert who understands the potential application. Naturally, everyone has his or her own area of interest, and finding compatible collaborators can be difficult, but it can also be very rewarding.

In reality, a single researcher must take on several roles, although getting help and advice is usually worth the effort. Most academics are willing to provide a certain amount of free advice for no more reward than a line in the acknowledgments section of a published paper.

Finally, many universities operate a statistical consulting service that can provide help in experimental design or data analysis.

Bibliography

Accot, J. and Zhai., S. (1997). Beyond Fitts' law: Models for trajectory-based HCI tasks. *Proceedings of CHI '97,* ACM, 295–302.

Ahlberg, C. and Shneiderman, B.N. (1994). Visual information seeking using the FilmFinder. *Proceedings of CHI '94, Conference Companion,* 433.

Ahlberg, C., Williamson, C., and Shneiderman, B. (1992). Dynamic queries for information exploration. *Proceedings of CHI '92,* ACM, 619–626.

Alexander, C. (1964). *Notes on the Synthesis of Form.* Harvard University Press, Cambridge, MA.

Amaya, K., Bruderlin, A., and Calvert, T. (1996). Emotion from motion. *Proceedings of Graphics Interface '96,* 222–229.

Anderson, J.R., Matessa, M., and Lebiere, C. (1997). ACT-R: A theory of higher-level cognition and its relation to visual attention. *Human-Computer Interaction* 12: 439–462.

Anderson, J.R. and Milson, R. (1989). Human memory: An adaptive perspective. *Psychological Review* 96(4): 703–719.

Anderson, S.J., Mullen, K.T., and Hess, R.F. (1991). Human peripheral spatial resolution for achromatic and chromatic stimuli: Limits imposed by optical and retinal factors. *Journal of Physiology* 442: 47–64.

Anstis, S.M. (1974). A chart demonstrating variations in acuity with retinal position. *Vision Research* 14: 589–592.

Anstis, S.M. and Cavanaugh, P. (1983). A minimum motion technique for judging equiluminance in color vision. In *Physiology and Psychophysics*, ed. J.D. Mollon and L.T. Sharpe, 156–166. Academic Press, London.

Arditi, A. (1987). Binocular vision. In *Handbook of Perception and Human Performance*, ed. K.R. Boff, L. Kaufman, and J.P. Thomas, 23–41. Wiley, New York.

Aretz, A.J. (1991). The design of electronic map displays. *Human Factors* 33(1): 85–101.

Armstrong, D.F., Stokoe, W.C., and Wilcox, S.E. (1994). Signs of the origin of syntax. *Current Anthropology* 35(4): 349–368.

Arsenault, R. and Ware, C. (1994, in press). The importance of stereo, eye coupled perspective and touch for eye-hand coordination. In *Presence: Teleoperators and Virtual Environments*. MIT Press, Cambridge.

Arthur, K.W., Booth, K.S., and Ware, C. (1993). Evaluating task performance for fish-tank virtual worlds. *ACM Transactions on Information Systems* 11(3): 239–265.

Baddeley, A.D. and Hitch, G.J. (1974). Working memory. In *The Psychology of Learning and Motivation: Advances in Research and Theory*, ed. G.H. Bower, 647–667. Erlbaum, Hillsdale, NJ.

Baddeley, A.D. and Logie, R.H. (1999). Working memory: The multiple-component model. In *Models of Working Memory*, ed. A. Miyake and P. Shah, 28–61. Cambridge University Press, Cambridge.

Badler, N.I., Manoocherhri, K.H., and Baraff, D. (1986). Multi-dimensional interface techniques and articulated figure positioning by multiple constraints. *Proceedings Workshop on Interactive 3D Graphics*, ACM, October, 151–169.

Baecker, R.M. (1981). *Sorting out Sorting*. Presented at ACM SIGGRAPH Conference, Dallas, TX, 1981. Film and video versions available from Morgan Kaufmann, San Francisco.

Baecker, R.M. and Small, I. (1990). Animation at the Interface. In *The Art of Human-Computer Interface Design*, ed. B. Laurel, 251–267. Addison-Wesley, Reading, MA.

Baecker, R.M., Small, I., and Mander, R. (1991). Bringing icons to life. *Proceedings CHI '91*, ACM, 1–12.

Balakrishnan, R. and MacKenzie, I.S. (1997). Performance differences in the fingers, wrist and forearm in computer input control. *CHI '97 Proceedings,* ACM, 303–310.

Ballesteros, S. (1989). Some determinants of perceived structure: Effects of stimulus and tasks. In *Object Perception: Structure and Process,* ed. B.E. Shepp and S. Ballesteros, 235–266. Lawrence Erlbaum Associates, Hillsdale, NJ.

Bar, M. and Biederman, I. (1998). Subliminal visual priming. *Psychological Science* 9: 464–469.

Barfield, W., Hendrix, C., Bjorneseth, O., Kaczmarek, K.A., and Lotens, W. (1995). Comparison of human sensory capabilities with technical specifications of virtual environment equipment. *Presence* 4(4): 329–356.

Barlow, H. (1972). Single units and sensation: A neuron doctrine for perceptual psychology? *Perception* 1: 371–394.

Bartram, D.J. (1980). Comprehending spatial information: The relative efficiencies of different methods for presenting information about bus routes. *Journal of Applied Psychology* 65: 103–110.

Bartram, L. (1998). Perceptual and interpretative properties of motion for information visualization. *Proceedings of the Workshop on New Paradigms in Information Visualization and Manipulation,* ACM, 3–7.

Bartram, L., Ho, A., Dill, J., and Henigman, F. (1995). The continuous zoom: A constrained fisheye technique for viewing and navigating large information spaces. *Proceedings of UIST '95,* ACM, 207–215.

Bartram, L., Ovans, R., Dill, J., Dyck, M., Ho, A., and Harens, W.S. (1994). Contextual assistance in user interfaces to complex, time-critical systems: The intelligent zoom. *Graphics Interface '94,* 216–224.

Bartram, L. and Ware, C. (2002). Filtering and brushing with motion. *Information Visualization* 1(1): 66–79.

Bartram, L., Ware, C., and Calvert, T. (2003). Moticons: Detection, distraction and task. *International Journal of Human-Computer Studies* 58(5): 515–545.

Bassili, J.N. (1978). Facial motion in the perception of faces and of emotional expressions. *Journal of Experimental Psychology: Human Perception and Performance* 4: 373–379.

Bassili, J.N. (1979). Emotion recognition. *Journal of Personality and Social Psychology* 37: 2049–2058.

Baudisch, P., Good, N., and Stewart, P. (2001). Focus plus context screens: Combining display technology with visualization techniques. *Proceedings of UIST '01*, 31–34, Orlando.

Bauer, B., Jolicoeur, P., and Cowan, W.B. (1996). Distractor heterogeneity versus linear separability in colour visual search. *Perception* 25: 1281–1294.

Beardsley, T. (1997). The machinery of thought. *Scientific American*, August, 78–83.

Beck, J. (1966). Effect of orientation and of shape similarity on perceptual grouping. *Perception and Psychophysics* 1: 300–302.

Beck, J. and Ivry, R. (1988). On the role of figural organization in perceptual transparency. *Perception and Psychophysics* 44: 585–594.

Becker, R.A. and Cleaveland, W.S. (1987). Brushing scatterplots. *Technometrics* 29(2): 127–142.

Bederson, B. and Hollan, J. (1994). Pad++: A zooming graphical interface for exploring alternate interface physics. *Proceedings of UIST '94*, ACM, 17–36.

Bellugi, U. and Klima, E.S. (1976). Two faces of sign: Iconic and abstract. *Annals of the New York Academy of Sciences* 280: 514–538.

Benedikt, M. (1991). Cyberspace: Some proposals. In *Cyberspace: First Steps*, 119–224. MIT Press, Cambridge, MA.

Bennett, A. and Rabbetts, R.B. (1989). *Clinical Visual Optics*, 2d ed., 31. Butterworth Heinemann, Oxford.

Berlin, B. and Kay, P. (1969). *Basic Color Terms: Their Universality and Evolution*. University of California Press, Berkeley.

Berry, R.N. (1948). Quantitative relations among vernier, real depth and stereoscopic depth acuities. *Journal of Experimental Psychology* 38: 708–721.

Bertin, J. (1977). *Graphics and Graphic Information Processing*. de Gruyter Press, Berlin.

Bertin, J. (1983). *Semiology of Graphics* (W.J. Berg, trans.). University of Wisconsin Press, Madison.

Bichot, N.P. and Schall, J.D. (1999). Effects of similarity and history on neural mechanisms of visual selection. *Nature Neuroscience* 2(6): 549–554.

Bickerton, D. (1990). *Language and Species*. University of Chicago Press, Chicago.

Biederman, I. (1987). Recognition-by-components: A theory of human image understanding. *Psychological Review* 94(2): 115–117.

Biederman, I. and Cooper, E. (1992). Size invariance in visual object priming. *Journal of Experimental Psychology: Human Perception and Performance* 18: 121–133.

Bier, E.A., Stone, M.C., Pier, K., Buxton, W., and DeRose, T.D. (1993). Tool glasses and magic lenses: The see-through interface. *Proceedings SIGGRAPH '93*, ACM, 73–80.

Bieusheuvel, S. (1947). Psychological tests and their application to non-European peoples. In *Yearbook of Education*, ed. G.B. Jeffrey, 185–207. University of London Press, London.

Bingham, G.P., Bradley, A., Bailey, M., and Vinner, R. (2001). Accommodation, occlusion, and disparity matching are used to guide reaching: A comparison of actual versus virtual environments. *Journal of Experimental Psychology: Human Perception and Performance* 27(6): 1314–1334.

Blake, R. and Holopigan, K. (1985). Orientation selectivity in cats and humans assessed by masking. *Vision Research* 23(1): 1459–1467.

Booher, H.R. (1975). Comprehensibility of pictorial information and printed word in proceduralized instructions. *Human Factors* 17(3): 266–277.

Boritz, J. and Booth, K.S. (1998). A study of interactive 6 DOF docking in a computerised virtual environment. *Proceedings of the IEEE Virtual Reality Annual International Symposium*, 139–146, Atlanta, GA.

Bovik, A.C., Clark, M., and Geisler, W.S. (1990). Multichannel texture analysis using localized spatial filters. *IEEE Transactions on Pattern Analysis and Machine Intelligence* 12: 55–73.

Bower, G.H., Karlin, M.B., and Dueck, A. (1975). Comprehension and memory for pictures. *Memory and Cognition* 3(2): 216–220.

Bradshaw, M.F., Parton, A.D., and Glennister, A. (2000). The task-dependent use of binocular disparity and motion parallax information. *Vision Research* 4: 3725–3734.

Bray, T. (1996). Measuring the Web. *Computer Networks and ISDN Systems* 28: 993–1005.

Bremmer, F., Schlack, A., Duhamel, J.R., Graf, W., and Fink, G.R. (2001). Spaced coding in primate posterior parietal cortex. *Neuroimage* 14: S46–S51.

Brewer. C.A. (1996a). Guidelines for selecting colors for diverging schemes on maps, *Cartographic Journal* 33(2): 79–86.

Brewer, C.A. (1996b). Prediction of simultaneous contrast between map colors with Hunt's model of color appearance, *Color Research and Application* 21(3): 221–235.

Bridgeman, B. (1991). Separate visual representations for perception and visually guided behavior. In *Pictorial Communications in Virtual and Real Environments*, ed. S.R. Ellis, 316–327. Taylor and Francis, London.

Brooks, F.P. (1988). Grasping reality through illusion: Interactive graphics serving science. *Proceedings of CHI '88*, ACM, 1–11.

Bruce, V. and Morgan, M.J. (1975). Violations of symmetry and repetition in visual principles. *Perception* 4: 239–249.

Bruce, V. and Young, A. (1986). Understanding face recognition. *British Journal of Psychology* 77: 305–327.

Bruce, V. and Young, A. (1998). *In the Eye of the Beholder: The Science of Face Perception.* Oxford University Press, Oxford.

Bruno, N. and Cutting, J.E. (1988). Minimodality and the perception of layout. *Journal of Experimental Psychology: General* 117: 161–170.

Bull, P. (1990). What does gesture add to the spoken word? In *Images and Understanding*, ed. H. Barlow, C. Blakemore, and M. Weston-Smith, 108–121. Cambridge University Press, Cambridge.

Burr, D.C. and Ross, J. (1982). Contrast sensitivity at high velocities. *Vision Research* 22(4): 479–558.

Bushnell, I.W.R., Sai, F., and Mullin, J.T. (1989). Neonatal recognition of the mother's face. *British Journal of Developmental Psychology* 7: 3–15.

Buxton, W. and Myers, B. (1986). A study in two-handed input. *Proceedings of CHI '86*, ACM, 321–326.

Cabral, B. and Leedom, L.C. (1993). Imaging vector fields using line integral convolution. *SIGGRAPH '93, ACM*, 263–272.

Caelli, T. and Bevan, P. (1983). Probing the spatial frequency spectrum for orientation sensitivity with stochastic textures. *Vision Research* 23(1): 39–45.

Caelli, T., Brettel, H., Rentschler, I., and Hilz, R. (1983). Discrimination thresholds in the two-dimensional spatial frequency domain. *Vision Research* 23(2): 129–133.

Caelli, T., Manning, M., and Finlay, D. (1993). A general correspondence approach to apparent motion. *Perception* 22: 185–192.

Caelli, T. and Moraglia G. (1985). On the detection of Gabor signals and discrimination of Gabor textures. *Vision Research* 25(5): 671–684.

Callaghan, T.C. (1989). Interference and dominance in texture segmentation: Hue, geometric form and line orientation. *Perception and Psychophysics* 46(4): 299–311.

Campbell, F.W. and Green, D.G. (1965). Monocular versus binocular visual acuity. *Nature* 208: 191–192.

Card, S.K., Moran, T.P., and Newell, A. (1983). *The Psychology of Human-Computer Interaction.* Lawrence Erlbaum Associates, Hillsdale, NJ.

Card, S.K. and Nation, D. (2002). Degree-of-interest trees: A component of an attention-reactive user interface. *Proceedings of Advanced Visual Interfaces,* 231–245, Trento, Italy.

Card, S.K., Pirolli, P., and Mackinlay, J.D. (1994). The cost-of-knowledge characteristic function: Display evaluation of direct-walk dynamic information visualizations. *CHI '94, ACM*, 238–244.

Card, S.K., Robertson, G.G., and York, W. (1996). The WebBook and the Web Forager: An information workspace for the World Wide Web. *SIGCHI '96 Proceedings, ACM*, 111–117.

Carroll, J.M. and Kellogg, W.A. (1989). Artifact as theory-nexus: Hermeneutics meets theory-based design. *Proceedings of SIGCHI '89. ACM*, 7–14.

Casey, S. (1993). *Set Phasers on Stun and Other True Tales of Design, Technology and Human Error.* Aegean Publishing, Santa Barbara, CA.

Cataliotti, J. and Gilchrist, A.L. (1995). Local and global processes in lightness perception. *Perception and Psychophysics* 57(2): 125–135.

Chambers, J.M., Cleveland, W.S., Kleiner, B., and Tukey, P.A. (1983). *Graphical Methods for Data Analysis*. Wadsworth, Belmont, CA.

Chandler, P. and Sweller, J. (1991). Cognitive load theory and the format of instruction. *Cognition and Instruction* 8: 293–332.

Charbonnell, J.R., Ware, J.L., and Senders, J.W. (1968). A queuing model of visual sampling: Experimental validation. *IEEE Transactions on Man-Machine Systems*, MMS-9, 82–87.

Chau, A.W. and Yeh, Y.Y. (1995). Segregation by color and stereoscopic depth in three-dimensional visual space. *Perception and Psychophysics* 57(7): 1032–1044.

Chen, P.P.S. (1976). The entity-relationship model—toward a unified view of data. *ACM Transactions on Database Systems* 1: 1–22.

Chernoff, H. (1973). Using faces to represent points in k-dimensional space. *Journal of the American Statistical Association* 68: 361–368.

Chomsky, N. (1965). *Aspects of the Theory of Syntax*. MIT Press, Cambridge, MA.

CIE subcommittee E-1.3.1. (1971.) *Recommendations on Uniform Color Spaces*. Commission Internationale de l'Éclariage (CIE), Supplement #2 to CIE Publication #15, Paris.

Cleveland, W.S. and McGill, R.A. (1983). A color-caused optical illusion on a statistical graph. *American Statistician* 37(2): 101–105.

Cockburn, A. and McKenzie, B. (2001). 3D or not 3D? Evaluating the effect of the third dimension in a document management system. *Proceedings of SIGCHI '99*, ACM, 434–441.

Cohen, M.F. and Greenberg, D.P. (1985). The hemi-cube: A radiosity solution for complex environments. *SIGGRAPH '85*, ACM, 31–40.

Colby, C.L. (1998). Action-oriented spatial reference frames in cortex. *Neuron* 20: 15–24.

Cole, J. (1995). *Pride and a Daily Marathon*. MIT Press, Cambridge, MA.

Colle, H.A. and Reid, G.B. (1998). The room effect: Metric spatial knowledge of local and separated regions. *Presence* 7(2): 116–128.

Collins, A.M. and Loftus, E.F. (1975). A spreading activation theory of semantic processing. *Psychological Review* 82: 407–428.

Coltheart, V. (1999). *Fleeting Memories: Cognition of Brief Visual Stimuli.* MIT Press, Cambridge, MA.

Coren, S. and Ward, L.M. (1989). *Sensation and Perception,* 3d ed. Harcourt Brace Jovanovich, New York.

Cornsweet, T.N. (1970). *Visual Perception,* Academic Press, New York.

Cowan, W.B. (1983). An inexpensive scheme for calibration of a colour monitor in terms of CIE standard coordinates. *SIGGRAPH '83 Proceedings,* ACM, 315–322.

Craik, F. and Lockhart, R. (1972). Levels of processing: A framework for memory research. *Journal of Verbal Learning and Behavior* 11: 671–684.

Cross, A.R., Armstrong, R.L., Gobrecht, C., Paton, M., and Ware, C. (1997). Three-dimensional imaging of the Belousov-Zhabotinsky reaction using magnetic resonance. *Magnetic Resonance Imaging* 15(6): 719–728.

Cruz-Neira, C., Sandin, D.J., DeFanti, T.A., Kenyon, R.V., and Hart, J.C. (1992). The CAVE: Audio visual experience automatic virtual environment. *Communications of the ACM* 35(6): 65–72.

Cutrell, E.B., Czerwinski, M., and Horvitz, E. (2000). Effects of instant messaging interruptions on computing tasks. *Proceedings of the CHI 2000 Conference on Human Factors in Computing Systems, Extended Abstracts,* 99–100. ACM Press, New York.

Cutting, J.E. (1986). *Perception with an Eye for Motion.* MIT Press, Cambridge, MA.

Cutting, J.E. (1991). On the efficacy of cinema, or what the visual systems did not evolve to do: Visual enhancements in pick-and-place tasks. In *Pictorial Communication in Virtual and Real Environments,* ed. S.R. Ellis, 486–495. Taylor and Francis, London.

Cutting, J.E., Springer, K., Braren, P.A., and Johnson, S.H. (1992). Wayfinding on foot from information in retinal, not optical flow. *Journal of Experimental Psychology: General* 121: 41–72.

Cypher, A. and Smyth, D. (1995). KidSim: End user programming of simulations. *CHI '95 Proceedings,* ACM, 27–34.

Czerwinski, M., van Dantzich, M., Robertson, G.G., and Hoffman, H. (1999). The contribution of thumbnail image, mouse-over text and spatial location memory to Web page retrieval in 3D. *Proceedings of Interact '99,* Edinburgh, Scotland, 163–170.

Darken, R.P., Allard, T., and Achille, L.B. (1998). Spatial orientation and wayfinding in large-scale virtual spaces: An introduction. *Presence* 7(2): 101–107.

Darken, R.P. and Banker, W.P. (1998). Navigating in natural environments: A virtual environment training transfer study. *Proceedings of VRAIS '98*, 12–19.

Darken, R.P. and Sibert, J.L. (1996). Wayfinding strategies and behaviors in large virtual worlds, *CHI '96, Proceedings*, 142–149.

Daugman, J.G. (1984). Spatial visual channels in the Fourier plane. *Vision Research* 24: 891–910.

Daugman, J.G. (1985). Uncertainty relation for resolution in space, spatial frequency, and orientation optimized by two-dimensional visual cortical filters. *Journal of the Optical Society of America* A/2: 1160–1169.

Davies, D.R. and Parasuraman, R. (1980). *The Psychology of Vigilance*. Academic Press, London.

Deering, M. (1992). High-resolution virtual reality. In *Proceedings of SIGGRAPH '92. Computer Graphics* 26(2): 195–202.

Dehaene, S. (1997). *The Number Sense: How the Mind Creates Mathematics*. Oxford University Press, Oxford.

Deregowski, J.B. (1968). Picture recognition in subjects from a relatively pictureless environment. *African Social Research* 5: 356–364.

Deuchar, M. (1990). Are the signs of language arbitrary? In *Images and Understanding*, ed. H. Barlow, C. Blakemore, and M. Weston Smith, 168–179. Cambridge University Press, Cambridge.

De Bruijn, O., Spence, R., and Tong, C.H. (2000). Rapid serial visual presentation: A space-time trade-off in information presentation. *Proceedings, Advance Visual Interfaces (AVI '2000)*, Palermo, Italy, 189–192. ACM Press: New York.

De Valois, R.L. and De Valois, K.K. (1975). Neural coding of color. In *Handbook of Perception*, ed. E.C. Carterette and M.P. Friedman, vol. 5, *Seeing*, ch. 5, 117–166. Academic Press, New York.

Di Battista, G., Eades, P., Tamassia, R., and Tollis, I.G. (1998). *Graph Drawing: Algorithms for the Visualization of Graphs*. Prentice Hall, Upper Saddle River, NJ.

Dickinson, S., Christensen, H., Tsotsos, J., and Olofsson, G. (1997), Active object recognition integrating attention and viewpoint control. *Computer Vision and Image Understanding* 6(3): 239–260.

Distler, C., Boussaoud, D., Desmone, R., and Ungerleider, L.G. (1993). Cortical connections of inferior temporal area REO in Macaque monkeys. *Journal of Comparative Neurology* 334: 125–150.

DiZio, P. and Lackner, J.R. (1992). Spatial orientation, adaptation and motion sickness in real and virtual environments. *Presence* 1(3): 319–328.

Donoho, A.W., Donoho, D.L., and Gasko, M. (1988). MacSpin: Dynamic graphics on a desktop computer. *IEEE Computer Graphics and Applications,* July, 51–58.

Dosher, B.A., Sperling, G., and Wurst, S.A. (1986). Trade-offs between stereopsis and proximity luminance covariance as determinants of perceived 3D structure. *Vision Research* 26(6): 973–990.

Douglas, S. and Kirkpatrick, T. (1996). Do color models really make a difference? *ACM CHI '96 Proceedings,* 399–405.

Drasdo, N. (1977). The neural representation of visual space. *Nature* 266: 554–556.

Drasic, D. and Milgram, P. (1991). Positioning accuracy of a virtual stereoscopic pointer in a real stereoscopic video world. *SPIE vol. 1457—Stereoscopic Displays and Applications II,* 58–69.

Driver, J., McLeod, P., and Dienes, Z. (1992). Motion coherence and conjunction search. *Perception and Psychophysics* 51(1): 79–85.

Drucker, S.M. and Zeltzer, D. (1995). CamDroid: A system for implementing intelligent camera control. *Proceedings of the 1995 Symposium on Interactive 3D Graphics,* 139–144.

Drury, C.G. and Clement, N.R. (1978). The effect of area, density, and number of background characters on visual search. *Human Factors* 20: 597–603.

Duda, R. and Hart, P.E. (1973). *Pattern Classification and Scene Analysis.* Wiley, New York.

Duncan, J. and Humphreys, G. (1989) Visual search and stimulus similarity. *Psychological Review* 96: 433–458.

Durgin, F.H., Proffitt, D.R., Olson, T.J., and Reinke, K.S. (1995). Comparing depth from motion with depth from binocular disparity. *Journal of Experimental Psychology: Human Perception and Performance* 21(3): 679–699.

Dwyer, F.M. (1967). The effect of varying the amount of realistic detail in visual illustrations. *Journal of Experimental Education* 36: 34–42.

D'Zmura, M., Lennie, P., and Tiana, C. (1997). Color search and visual field segregation. *Perception and Psychophysics* 59(3): 381–388.

Edelman, S. (1995). Representation of similarity in 3D object discrimination. *Neural Computation* 7: 407–422.

Edelman, S. and Buelthoff, H.H. (1992). Orientation dependence in the recognition of familiar and novel views of 3D objects. *Vision Research* 32: 2385–2400.

Edwards, B. (1979). *Drawing on the Right Side of the Brain.* J.P. Tarcher, Los Angeles.

Ekman, P. (2003). *Emotions Revealed: Recognizing Faces and Feelings to Improve Communication and Emotional Life.* Times Books, New York.

Ekman, P. and Friesen, W. (1975). *Unmasking the Face: A Guide to Recognizing Emotions from Facial Expressions.* Prentice Hall, Upper Saddle River, New Jersey.

Ekman, P. and Friesen, W. (1978). *The Facial Action Coding System.* Consulting Psychologists Press, Palo Alto, CA.

Ekman, P., Friesen, W., and O'Sullivan, M. (1988). Smiles when lying. *Journal of Personality and Social Psychology* 54: 414–420.

Eley, M.G. (1988). Determining the shapes of land surfaces from topographical maps. *Ergonomics* 31: 355–376.

Elmes, D., Kantowitz, B.H., and Roedinger, H.L. (1999). *Research Methods in Psychology,* 6th ed. Brooks/Cole, Pacific Grove, CA.

Elvins, T.T., Nadeau, D.R., and Kirsh, D. (1997). Worldlets—3D thumbnails for wayfinding in virtual environments. *UIST '97 Proceedings,* 21–30.

Elvins, T.T., Nadeau, D.R., Schul, R., and Kirsh, D. (1998). Worldlets: 3D thumbnails for 3D browsing. *Proceedings of CHI '98,* ACM, 163–170.

Englehardt, Y., de Bruin, J., Janssen, T., and Scha, R. (1996). The visual grammar of information graphics. *Artificial Intelligence in Design (AID '96)* in the Workshop on Visual Representation, Reasoning and Interaction in Design, 24–27, June.

Enns, J.T., Austin, E.L., Di Lollo, V., Rauchenberger, R., and Yantis, S. (2001). New objects dominate luminance transients in setting attentional priority. *Journal of Experimental Psychology: Human Perception and Performance* 27(6): 1287–1302.

Fach, P.W. and Strothotte, T. (1994). Cognitive maps: A basis for designing user manuals for direct manipulation interfaces. In *Cognitive Aspects of Visual Languages and Visual Interfaces*, ed. M.J. Tauber, D.E. Mahling, and F. Arefi., 89–117. Elsevier Science Inc., New York.

Faraday, P. (1998). Theory-based design and evaluation of multimedia presentation interfaces. Ph.D. thesis. School of Informatics, City University, London.

Faraday, P. and Sutcliffe, A. (1997). Designing effective multimedia presentations. *Proceedings of CHI '97*, ACM, 272–279.

Faraday, P. and Sutcliffe, A. (1999). Authoring animated Web pages using "contact points." *Proceedings of CHI '99*, ACM, 458–465.

Farah, M.J., Soso, M.J., and Dashieff, R.M. (1992). Visual angle of the mind's eye before and after unilateral occipital lobectomy. *Journal of Experimental Psychology: Human Perception and Performance* 18: 214–246.

Feiner, S., MacIntyre, B., Haupt, M., and Solomon, E. (1993). Windows on the world, 2D windows for 3D augmented reality. *Proceedings UIST '93*, ACM Atlanta, GA, Nov.: 145–155.

Feldman, J.A. (1985). Four frames suffice: A provisional model of vision and space. *Behavioural and Brain Sciences* 8: 265–289.

Field, D.J., Hayes, A., and Hess, R.F. (1993). Contour integration by the human visual system: Evidence for a local "association field." *Vision Research* 33(2): 173–193.

Field G. and Spence R. (1994). Now, where was I? *New Zealand Journal of Computing* 5(1): 35–43.

Fine, I. and Jacobs, R.A. (2000). Perceptual learning for a pattern discrimination task. *Vision Research* 41: 449–461.

Fine, I. and Jacobs, R.A. (2002). Comparing perceptual learning across tasks: A review. *Journal of Vision* 2: 190–203.

Fisher, S.K. and Cuiffreda, K.J. (1990). Adaptation to optically increased interocular separation under naturalistic viewing conditions. *Perception* 19: 171–180.

Fitts, P.M. (1954). The information capacity of the human motor system in controlling the amplitude of movements. *Journal of Experimental Psychology* 47: 381–391.

Fleet, D. (1998). *Visualization of Communications in 3D*. Unpublished master's thesis. Faculty of Computer Science, University of New Brunswick.

Foley, J.D., van Dam, A., Feiner, S.K., and Hughes, J.F. (1990). *Computer Graphics: Principles and Practice*, 2d ed. Addison-Wesley, Reading, MA.

Fowler, D. and Ware, C. (1989). Strokes for representing univariate vector field maps. *Graphics Interface '89 Proceedings*, 249–253.

Fowler, R.H. and Dearholt, D.W. (1990). Information retrieval using pathfinder networks. In *Pathfinder Associative Networks: Studies in Knowledge Organization*, ed. R.W. Schvaneveldt, 165–178. Ablex, Norwood, NJ.

Frisby, J.P. (1979). *Seeing, Illusion, Brain and Mind*. Oxford University Press, Oxford.

Frisby, J.P., Buckley, D., and Duke, P.A. (1996). Evidence for good recovery of lengths of real objects seen with natural stereo viewing. *Perception* 25: 129–154.

Furnas, G. (1991). New graphical reasoning models for understanding graphical interfaces. *Proceedings of CHI '91*, ACM, 71–78.

Furnas, G.W. (1986). Generalized fisheye views. *Proceedings of CHI '86*, ACM, 17–26.

Garner, W.R. (1974). *The Processing of Information and Structure*. Lawrence Erlbaum Associates, Hillsdale, NJ.

Geertz, C. (1973). *The Interpretation of Cultures*. Basic Books, New York.

Gibson, J.J. (1979). *The Ecological Approach to Visual Perception*. Houghton Mifflin, Boston. (Currently published by Lawrence Erlbaum, Hillsdale, NJ.)

Gibson, J.J. (1986). *The Ecological Approach to Visual Perception.* Lawrence Erlbaum Associates, Hillsdale, NJ.

Gilbert, S.A. (1997). Mapping mental spaces: How we organize perceptual and cognitive information. Ph.D. thesis. MIT.

Gilchrist, A.L. (1979). The perception of surface blacks and whites. *Scientific American,* March, 88–96.

Gilchrist, A.L. (1980). When does perceived lightness depend on perceived spatial arrangement? *Perception and Psychophysics* 28: 527–538.

Gilhooly, K.J. (1988). *Thinking: Directed, Undirected and Creative.* Academic Press, London.

Ginsburg, A.P., Evans, D.W., Sekuler, R., and Harp, S.A. (1982). Contrast sensitivity predicts pilots' performance in aircraft simulators. *American Journal of Optometry and Physiological Optics* 59: 105–108.

Goldin-Meadow, S. and Mylander, C. (1998). Spontaneous sign systems created by deaf children in two cultures. *Nature* 391: 279–281.

Goldstein, D.A. and Lamb, J.C. (1967). Visual coding using flashing lights. *Human Factors* 9: 405–408.

Gonzalez, R.C. and Woods, P. (1993). *Digital Image Processing,* 2d ed. Addison-Wesley, Reading, MA.

Goodman, N. (1968). *Language of Art.* Bobbs Merrill, New York.

Goodwin, C.J. (2001). *Research in Psychology: Methods and Design.* Wiley, New York.

Gray, C.M., Konig, P., Engel, A.K., and Singer, W. (1989). Oscillatory responses in cat visual cortex exhibit intercolumnar synchronisation which reflects global stimulus properties. *Nature* 388: 334–337.

Gray, W.G.D., Mayer, L.A., and Hughes Clarke, J.E. (1997). Geomorphological applications of multibeam sonar and high-resolution DEM data from Passamaquoddy Bay. Geological Association of Canada, Ottawa, '97 *Proceedings Abstracts 57.*

Gregory, R.L. (1977). Vision with isoluminance color contrast: A projection technique and observations. *Perception* 6(1): 113–119.

Guiard, Y. (1987). Asymmetric division of labor in skilled bimanual action: The kinematic chain as a model. *Journal of Motor Behavior* 19: 486–517.

Guitard, R. and Ware, C. (1990). A color sequence editor. *ACM Transactions on Graphics* 9(3): 338–341.

Gutwin, C., Greenberg, S., and Roseman, M. (1996). Workspace awareness support with radar views. *CHI '96 Conference Companion,* ACM, 210–211.

Hagen, M.A. (1974). Picture perception: Toward a theoretical model. *Psychology Bulletin* 81: 471–497.

Hagen, M.A. and Elliott, H.B. (1976). An investigation of the relationship between viewing conditions and preference for true and modified perspective with adults. *Journal of Experimental Psychology: Human Perception and Performance* 5: 479–490.

Hallett, P.E. (1986). Eye movements. In *Handbook of Perception and Human Performance,* ed. K.R. Boff, L. Kaufman, and J.P. Thomas. vol. 1, ch. 10: 25–28. Wiley, New York.

Halverston, J. (1992). The first pictures: Perceptual foundations of paleolithic art. *Perception* 21: 389–404.

Hammond, N. (1987). Principles from the psychology of skill acquisition. In *Applying Cognitive Psychology to User Interface Design,* ed. M.M. Gardener and B. Christie, 163–188. Wiley, Chichester.

Haring, M.J. and Fry, M.A. (1979). Effect of pictures on children's comprehension of written text. *Educational Communication and Technology Journal* 27(3): 185–190.

Harris, C.S. (1965). Perceptual adaptation to inverted, reversed and displaced vision. *Psychological Review* 72(6): 419–444.

Harrison, B. and Vincente, K.J. (1996). An experimental evaluation of transparent menu usage. *CHI Conference Proceedings,* ACM, 391–398.

Healey, C.G. (1996). Choosing effective colors for data visualization. *IEEE Visualization '96 Proceedings,* 263–270.

Healey, C.G., Booth, K.S., and Enns, J.T. (1998). High-speed visual estimation using pre-attentive processing. *ACM Transactions on Human-Computer Interaction* 3(2): 107–135.

Heider, F. and Simmel, M. (1944). An experimental study of apparent behavior. *American Journal of Psychology* 57: 243–259.

Held, R., Efstanthiou, A., and Green, M. (1966). Adaptation to displaced and delayed visual feedback from the hand. *Journal of Experimental Psychology* 72: 887–891.

Hendrix, C. and Barfield, W. (1996). Presence within virtual environments as a function of visual display parameters. *Presence* 5(3): 272–289.

Hering, E. (1920). *Grundzuge der Lehr vom Lichtsinn.* Springer-Verlag, Berlin. (*Outlines of a Theory of Light Sense.* Translated by L.M. Hurvich and D. Jameson. Harvard University Press, Cambridge, MA, 1964.)

Herndon, K.P., Zelenik, R.C., Robbins, D.C., Conner, D.B., Snibbe, S.S., and van Dam, A. (1992). Interactive shadows. In *Proceedings of the ACM Symposium on User Interface Software and Technology, UIST '92,* ACM, 1–6.

Herskovits, M.J. (1948). *Man and His Works.* Knopf, New York.

Hill, B., Roger, T., and Vorhagen, F.W. (1997). Comparative analysis of the quantization of color spaces on the basis of the CIELAB color-difference formula. *ACM Transactions on Graphics,* 16(2): 109–154.

Hillstrom, A.P. and Yantis, S. (1994). Visual attention and motion capture. *Perception and Psychophysics* 55(4): 399–411.

Hochberg, J. (1968). In the mind's eye. In *Contemporary Theory and Research in Visual Perception,* ed. R.N. Haber, 309–331. Holt, Rinehart, and Winston, New York.

Hochberg, J. (1971). Perception: Space and movement. In *Experimental Psychology,* ed. J.W. Klink and L.A. Riggs, 475–550. Holt, Rinehart and Winston, New York.

Hochberg, J. (1986). Representation of motion and space in video and cinematic display. In *Handbook of Perception and Human Performance,* ed. K.R. Boff, L. Kaufman, and J.P. Thomas, 1–64. Wiley, New York.

Hochberg, J. and Brooks, V. (1978). Film cutting and visual momentum. In *Eye Movements and the Higher Psychological Functions,* ed. J.W. Senders, D.F. Fisher, and R.A. Mony, 293–313. Lawrence Erlbaum Associates, Hillsdale, NJ.

Hochberg, J.E. and Brooks, V. (1962). Pictorial recognition as an unlearned ability. *American Journal of Psychology* 75: 624–628.

Hollingworth, A. and Henderson, J.M. (2002). Accurate visual memory for previously attended objects in natural scenes. *Journal of Experimental Psychology: Human Perception and Performance* 28(1): 113–136.

Horgan, J. (1997) *The End of Science: Facing the Limits of Knowledge in the Twilight of the Scientific Age.* Helix Books, Reading, MA.

Hotelling, H. (1933). Analysis of a complex of statistical variables into principal components. *Journal of Educational Psychology* 24: 498–520.

Houde, S. (1992). Iterative design of an interface for easy 3-D direct manipulation. *CHI '92, ACM, Monterey, May Proceedings.* 135–142.

Howard, I.P. (1991). Spatial vision within egocentric and exocentric frames of reference. In *Pictorial Communication in Virtual and Real Environments,* ed. S.R. Ellis, M.K. Kaiser, and A.J. Grunwald, 338–358. Taylor and Francis, London.

Howard, I.P. and Childerson, L. (1994). The contributions of motion, the visual frame, and visual polarity to sensations of body tilt. *Perception* 23: 753–762.

Howard, I.P. and Heckman, T. (1989). Circular vection as a function of the relative sizes, distances and positions of two competing visual displays. *Perception* 18(5): 657–667.

Howard, J.H. and Kerst, S.M. (1981). Memory and perception of cartographic information for familiar and unfamiliar environments. *Human Factors* 23(4): 495–504.

Huber, D.E. and O'Reilly, R.C. (2003). Persistence and accommodation in short-term priming and other perceptual paradigms: Temporal segregation through synaptic depression. *Cognitive Science* 27: 403–430.

Hummel, J.E. and Biederman, I. (1992). Dynamic binding in a neural network for shape recognition. *Psychological Review* 99(3): 480–517.

Humphreys, G.W. and Bruce, V. (1989). *Visual Cognition: Computational, Experimental and Neurological Perspectives.* Lawrence Erlbaum Associates, Hillsdale, NJ.

Hurvich, L.M. (1981). *Color Vision.* Sinauer Associates, Sunderland, MA.

Hutchins, E. (1995). *Distributed Cognition.* MIT Press, Cambridge, MA.

Hyman, R. (1953). Stimulus information as a determinant of reaction time. *Journal of Experimental Psychology* 45: 423–432.

Iavecchia, J.H., Iavecchia, H.P., and Roscoe, S.N. (1988). Eye accommodation to head-up virtual images. *Human Factors* 30(6): 689–702.

Immel, D.S. and Brock, P.J. (1986). An effecient radiosity aproach for realistic image synthesis. *IEEE Computer Graphics and Applications* 6(2): January, 26–35.

Inselberg, A. and Dimsdale, B. (1990). Parallel coordinates: A tool for visualizing multidimensional geometry. In *Proceedings of IEEE Conference on Visualization,* Los Angeles, 361–378.

Interrante, V., Fuchs, H., and Pizer, S.M. (1997). Conveying 3D shape of smoothly curving transparent surfaces via texture. *IEEE Transactions on Visualization and Computer Graphics* 3(2): 98–117.

Intraub, H. and Hoffman, J. E. (1992). Reading and visual memory: Remembering scenes that were never seen. *American Journal of Psychology* 105: 101–114.

Irani, P., Tingley, M., and Ware, C. (2001). Using perceptual syntax to enhance semantic content in diagrams. *IEEE Computer Graphics and Applications,* September, 76–84.

Irani, P. and Ware, C. (2003). Diagramming information structures using 3D perceptual primitives. *ACM Transactions on Computer-Human Interaction* 10(1): 1–19.

Irwin, D.E. (1992). Memory for position or identity across eye movements. *Journal of Experimental Psychology: Learning, Memory and Cognition* 18: 307–317.

Irwin, R.J. and McCarthy, D. (1998). Psychophysics: Methods and analyses of signal detection. In *Handbook of Research Methods in Human Operant Behavior*, ed. K.A. Lattal, M. Perone, et al., 291–321. Plenum Press, New York.

Ishii, H. and Kobayashi, M. (1992). ClearBoard: a seamless medium of shared drawing and conversation with eye contact. *Proceedings of CHI '92,* ACM, 525–532.

Jackson, R., MacDonald, L., and Freeman, K. (1994). *Computer-Generated Color: A Practical Guide to Presentation and Display.* Wiley, New York.

Jackson, R., MacDonald, L., and Freeman, K. (1998). *Computer-Generated Color.* Wiley Professional Computing, Chichester.

Jacob, R.J.K. (1991). The use of eye movements in human-computer interaction techniques: What you look at is what you get. *ACM Transactions on Information Systems* 9(3): 152–169.

Jacob, R.J.K., Egeth, H.E., and Bevon, W. (1976). The face as a data display. *Human Factors* 18: 189–200.

Johansson, G. (1973). Visual perception of biological motion and a model for its analysis. *Perception and Psychophysics* 14(2): 201–211.

Johansson, G. (1975). Visual motion perception. *Scientific American* (232): June, 76–98.

Johnson, B. and Shneiderman, B. (1991). Treemaps: A space-filling approach to the visualization of hierarchical information structures. *Proceedings IEEE Information Visualization '95,* 43–50.

Johnson, S.H. (2001). Seeing two sides at once: Effects of viewpoint and object structure on recognizing three-dimensional objects. *Journal of Experimental Psychology: Human Perception and Performance* 27(6): 1468–1484.

Jonassen, D.H., Beissner, K., and Yacci, M.A. (1993). Structural knowledge: Techniques for conveying, assessing, and acquiring structural knowledge. Lawrence Erlbaum Associates, Hillsdale, NJ.

Jonides, J. (1981). Voluntary versus automatic control over the mind's eye. In *Attention and Performance*, vol. 9, ed. J. Long and A.D. Baddeley, 187–203. Erlbaum, Hillsdale, NJ.

Jorg, S. and Hormann, H. (1978). The influence of general and specific labels on the recognition of labelled and unlabelled parts of pictures. *Journal of Verbal Learning and Verbal Behaviour* 17: 445–454.

Judd, D.B. and Wyszecki, G.W. (1975). *Color in Business, Science and Industry,* 3d ed. Wiley, New York.

Kabbash, P., Buxton, W., and Sellen, A. (1994). Two-handed input in a compound task. *Proceedings of CHI '94,* ACM, 417–423.

Kahn, K. (1996a). Drawings on napkins, video-game animation and other ways to program computers. *Communications of the ACM* 39(8): 49–59.

Kahn, K. (1996b). ToonTalk—an animated programming environment for children. *Journal of Visual Languages and Computing* 7(2): 197–217.

Kahneman, D. and Henik, A. (1981). Perceptual organization and attention. In *Perceptual Organization*, ed. M. Kubovy and J.R. Pomerantz, 181–209. Lawrence Erlbaum Associates, Hillsdale, NJ.

Kahneman, D., Triesman, A., and Gibbs, B.J. (1992). The reviewing of object files: Object-specific integration of information. *Cognitive Psychology* 24: 175–219.

Kaiser, M., Proffitt, D., Whelan, S., and Hecht, H. (1992). Influence of animation on dynamic judgments. *Journal of Experimental Psychology: Human Perception and Performance* 18(34): 669–690.

Kalaugher, P.G. (1985). Visual effects with a miniature Leonardo's window: Photographs and real scenes fused stereoscopically. *Perception* 14: 553–561.

Kalra, P., Gobbetti, E., Magnenat-Thalmann, N., and Thalmann, D. (1993). A multimedia testbed for facial animation control. In *International Conference of Multi-Media Modeling, MMM '93*, ed. T.S. Chua and T.L. Kunii, Singapore, 59–72.

Kanizsa, G. (1976). Subjective contours. *Scientific American* (234): April, 48–64.

Kanwisher, N., McDermott, J., and Chun, M. (1997). The fusiform face area: A module in human extrastriate cortex specialized for the perception of faces. *Journal of Neuroscience* 17: 4302–4311.

Kanwisher, N., Stanley, D., and Harris, A. (1999). The fusiform face area is selective for faces, not animals. *NeuroReport* 10(1): 183–187.

Kawai, M., Uchikawa, K., and Ujike, H. (1995). Influence of color category on visual search. *Annual Meeting of the Association for Research in Vision and Ophthalmology, Paper #2991*, Fort Lauderdale, FL.

Kelly, D.H. (1979). Motion and vision II: Stabilized spatio-temporal threshold surface. *Journal of the Optical Society of America* 69: 1340–1349.

Kennedy, J.M. (1974). *A Psychology of Picture Perception*. Jossey-Bass, San Francisco.

Kennedy, R.S., Lilienthal, M.G., Berbaum, K.S., Baltzley, D.R., and McCauley, M.E. (1989). Simulator sickness in U.S. Navy flight simulators. *Aviation, Space and Environmental Medicine* 15: 10–16.

Kersten, D., Mamassian, P., and Knill, D.C. (1997). Moving cast shadows induce apparent motion in depth. *Perception* 26: 171–192.

Kersten, D., Mamassian, P., Knill, D.C., and Bulthoff, I. (1996). Illusory motion from shadows, *Nature* 351: 228–230.

Kieras, D.E. and Meyer, D.E. (1997). An overview of the EPIC architecture for cognition and performance with application to human-computer interaction. *Human-Computer Interaction* 12: 391–438.

Kim, S., Hagh-Shenas, H., and Interrante, V. (1993). Showing shape with texture: Two directions are better than one. *Human Vision and Electronic Imaging VIII, SPIE 5007*, 332–339.

Kim, W.S., Tendick, F., and Stark, L. (1991). Visual enhancements in pick-and-place tasks. In *Pictorial Communication in Virtual and Real Environments*, ed. S.R. Ellis, 265–282. Taylor and Francis, London.

Kirby, R.M., Marmanis, H., and Laidlaw, D.H. (1999). Visualizing multivalued data from 2D incompressible flows using concepts from painting. *Proceedings of Visualization'99*, IEEE, 333–340.

Kirsh, D. and Maglio, P. (1994). On distinguishing epistemic from pragmatic action. *Cognitive Science* 18: 513–549.

Koffka, K. (1935). *Principles of Gestalt Psychology.* Harcourt-Brace, New York.

Kohlberg, D.L. (1971). Simple reaction time as a function of stimulus intensity in decibels of light and sound. *Journal of Experimental Psychology* 54: 757–764.

Kolers, P.A. (1975). Memorial consequences of automatized encoding. *Journal of Experimental Psychology: Human Learning and Memory* 1: 689–701.

Komerska, R. and Ware, C. (2003). Haptic task constraints for 3D interaction. *Proceedings, IEEE Haptic Interfaces for Virtual Environments and Teleoperator Systems Symposium*, 270–277.

Kosara, R., Miksch, S., Hauser, H., (2002). Focus+context taken literally. *IEEE Computer Graphics and Appplications* 22(1): 22–29.

Kosslyn, S.M. (1987). Seeing and imagining in the cerebral hemispheres: A computational approach. *Psychological Review* 94: 148–175.

Kosslyn, S.M. (1994). *Image and Brain: The Resolution of the Imagery Debate*. MIT Press, Cambridge, MA.

Kosslyn, S.M., Alpert, N.M., Thompson, W.L., Maljkovic, S.B., Weise, C.F., Chabreis, S., Hamilton, E., Rauch, S.L., and Buonanno, F.S. (1993). Visual mental imagery activates topographically organized visual context: PET investigations. *Journal of Cognitive Neuroscience* 5: 263–287.

Kroll, J.F. and Potter, M.C. (1984). Recognizing words, pictures and concepts: A comparison of lexical, object and reality decisions. *Journal of Verbal Learning and Verbal Behaviour* 23: 39–66.

Kubovy, M. (1986). *The Psychology of Linear Perspective and Renaissance Art*. Cambridge University Press, Cambridge.

Kurtenbach, G., Fitzmaurice, G., Baudel, T., and Buxton, B. (1997). The design and evaluation of a GUI paradigm based on two-hands, tablets and transparency. *Proceedings of CHI '97*, ACM, 35–42.

Laidlaw, D.H., Ahrens, E.T., Kramers, D., Avalos, M.J., Readhead, C., and Jacobs, R.E. (1998). Visualizing diffusion tensor images of the mouse spinal cord. *Proceedings of IEEE Visualization Conference*, 127–134.

Laidlaw, D.H., Kirby, R.M., Davidson, J.S., Miller, T.S., da Silva, M., Warren, W.H., and Tarr, M. (2001). Quantitative comparative evaluation of 2D vector field visualization methods. *Proceedings of IEEE Visualization 2001*, 143–150. San Diego, CA, October.

Lamping, J., Rao, R., and Pirolli, P. (1995). A focus + content technique based on hyperbolic geometry for viewing large hierarchies. *Proceedings CHI '95*, ACM, 401–408.

Landauer, T.K. (1986). How much do people remember? Some estimates of the quantity of learned information in long-term memory. *Cognitive Science* 10: 477–493.

Laramee, R.S. and Ware, C. (2002). Rivalry and interference with a head-mounted display. *ACM Transactions on Human-Computer Interaction* 9(3): 1–14.

Larkin, J.H. and Simon, H.A. (1987). Why a diagram is (sometimes) worth ten thousand words. *Cognitive Science* 11: 65–99.

Lawson, R., Humphreys, G.W., and Watson, D. (1994). Object recognition under sequential viewing conditions: Evidence for viewpoint-specific recognition procedures. *Perception* 23: 595–614.

Lennie, P. (1998). Single units and cortical organization. *Perception* 27: 889–935.

Leslie, A.M. and Keeble, S. (1987). Do six-month-old infants perceive causality? *Cognition* 25: 265–288.

Levelt, W., Richardson, G., and Heu, W. (1985). Pointing and voicing in deictic expressions. *Journal of Memory and Language* 24: 133–164.

Levine, M. (1975). *A Cognitive Theory of Learning.* Lawrence Erlbaum Associates, Hillsdale, NJ.

Levkowitz, H. and Herman, G.T. (1992). Color scales for image data. *IEEE Computer Graphics and Applications,* 12: 72–80.

Levoy, M. and Whitaker, R. (1990). Gaze-directed volume rendering. *Proceedings of ACM Symposium on Interactive 3D Graphics, Computer Graphics* 24(2): 217–224.

Li, Y. (1997). Oriented particles for scientific visualization. M.S. thesis. Computer Science, University of New Brunswick.

Liang, J., Shaw, C., and Green, M. (1991). On temporal-spatial realism in the virtual reality environment. *Proceedings of UIST '91,* ACM, 19–25.

Limoges, S., Ware, C., and Knight, W. (1989). Displaying correlation using position, motion, point size, or point color. *Proceedings, Graphics Interface '89,* 262–265.

Linos, P.K., Aubet, P., Dumas, L., Helleboid, Y., Lejeune, D., and Tulula, P. (1994). Visualizing program dependencies: An experimental study. *Software Practice and Experience* 24(4): 387–403.

Linstrom, C.J., Silverman, C.A., and Susman, W.M. (2000). Facial motion analysis with a video and computer system: A preliminary report. *American Journal of Otology* 21: 123–129.

Liu, F. and Picard, R.W. (1994). Periodicity, directionality, and randomness: World features for perceptual pattern recognition. *Proceedings of the 12th International Conference on Pattern Recognition,* vol. II, 184–189, Jerusalem, October 9–13.

Livingston, M.S. and Hubel, D.H. (1988). Segregation of form, movement and depth: Anatomy, physiology and perception. *Science* 240: 740–749.

Lloyd, R. (1997). Visual search processes used in map reading. *Cartographica* 34(1): 11–32.

Loftus, E.F. and Hoffman, H.G. (1989). Misinformation and memory: The creation of new memories. *Journal of Experimental Psychology: General* 118: 100–104.

Logan, G.D. (1994). Spatial attention and the apprehension of spatial relations. *Journal of Experimental Psychology: Human Perception and Performance* 20: 1015–1036.

Lokuge, I., Glibert, S.A., and Richards, W. (1996). Structuring information with mental models: A tour of Boston. *CHI '96 Proceedings*, ACM, 413–419.

Lowther, K. and Ware, C. (1996). Vection with large-screen 3D imagery. *CHI '96 Conference Companion*, ACM, 233–234.

Lu, C. and Fender, D.H. (1972). The interaction of color and luminance in stereoscopic vision. *Investigative Opthalmology* 11: 482–490.

Luck, S.J. and Vogel, E.K. (1997). The capacity of visual working memory for features and conjunctions. *Nature* 390: 279–280.

Lynch, K. (1960). *The Image of the City.* MIT Press, Cambridge, MA.

Mack, A. and Rock, I. (1998). *Inattentional Blindness.* MIT Press, Cambridge MA.

Mackenzie, C.L. and Iberall, T. (1994). *The Grasping Hand.* Advances in Psychology Series, 104. North-Holland, Amsterdam.

MacKenzie, I.S. (1992). Fitts' law as a research and design tool in human-computer interaction. *Human-Computer Interaction* 7: 91–139.

Mackinlay, J.D., Card, S.K., and Robertson, G.G. (1990). Rapid controlled movement through a virtual 3D workspace. *Proceedings SIGGRAPH '90*, ACM, 24: 171–176.

MacLeod, C.M. (1991). Half a century of research on the Stroop effect: An integrative review. *Psychological Bulletin* 109(2): 163–203.

Mackworth, N.H. (1976). Ways of recording line of sight. In *Eye Movements and Psychological Processing*, ed. R.A. Monty and J.W. Senders, 173–178. Erlbaum, Hillsdale, NJ.

Madison, C., Thompson, W., Kersen, D., Shirley, P., and Smits, B. (2001). Use of interreflection and shadow for surface contact. *Perception and Psychophysics* 63: 187–193.

Malik, J. and Perona, P. (1990). Preattentive texture discrimination with early vision mechanisms. *Journal of the Optical Society of America* A 7(5): 923–932.

Mark, D.M. and Franck, A.U. (1996). Experiential and formal models of geographical space. *Environment and Planning*, B. 23: 3–24.

Marr, D. (1982). *Vision*. W.H. Freeeman and Company, New York.

Marr, D. and Nishihara, H.K. (1978). Representation and recognition of the spatial organization of three-dimensional shapes. *Proceedings of the Royal Society of London*, B. 207: 269–294.

Masin, S.C. (1997). The luminance conditions of transparency. *Perception* 26: 39–50.

Massie, T.H. and Salisbury, J.K. (1994). The phantom haptic interface: A device for probing virtual objects, ASME haptic interfaces for virtual environments and teleoperator systems. *Dynamic Systems and Control* 1 (Nov.): 295–301.

Matlin, M.W. (1994). *Cognition*, 3d ed. Harcourt Brace, Fort Worth.

Mayer, L.A., Dijkstra, S., Hughes Clarke, J., Paton, M., and Ware, C. (1997). High-frequency acoustics in shallow water. *SACLANT Conference Proceedings Series*, CP-45, ed. N.G. Pace, E. Pouliquen, O. Bergem, and J. Lyons.

Mayer, R.E., Moreno, R., Boire, M., and Vagge, S. (1999). Maximizing constructivist learning from multimedia communications by minimizing cognitive load. *Journal of Educational Psychology* 91(4): 638–643.

Mayer, R.E. and Sims, V.K. (1994). For whom is a picture worth a thousand words? Extensions of a dual-coding theory of multimedia learning. *Journal of Educational Psychology* 86: 389–401.

McCauley, M.E. and Sharkey, T.J. (1992). Cybersickness: Perception of self-motion in virtual environments. *Presence* 1(3): 311–318.

McCormick, E., Wickens, C.D., Banks, R., and Yeh, M. (1998). Frame of reference effects on scientific visualization subtasks. *Human Factors* 40: 443–451.

McGreevy, M.W. (1992). The presence of field geologists in Mars-like terrain. *Presence* 1(4): 375–403.

McManus, I.C. (1977). Note: Half a million basic color words: Berlin and Kay and the usage of color words in literature and science. *Perception* 26: 367–370.

McNeill, D. (1992). *Hand and Mind: What Gestures Reveal about Thought.* University of Chicago Press, Chicago.

Megaw, E.D. and Richardson, J. (1979). Target uncertainty and visual scanning strategies. *Human Factors* 21(3): 303–316.

Melcher, D. (2001). Persistence of visual memory for scenes: A medium-term memory may help us keep track of objects during visual tasks. *Nature* 412: 401.

Metelli, F. (1974). The perception of transparency. *Scientific American* 230 (April): 91–98.

Meyer, G.W. and Greenberg, D.P. (1988). Color-defective vision and computer graphics displays. *IEEE Computer Graphics and Applications* September: 28–40.

Michotte, A. (1963). *The Perception of Causality.* (Translated by T. Miles and E. Miles.) Methuen, London.

Milner, A.D. and Goodale, M.A. (1995). *The Visual Brain in Action.* Oxford Psychology Series 27. Oxford University Press, Oxford.

Miyake, A. and Shah, P. (1999). Toward unified theories of working memory: Emerging general consensus, unresolved theoretical issues, and future research directions. In *Models of Working Memory*, ed. A. Miyake and P. Shah, 442–481. Cambridge University Press, Cambridge.

Mon-Williams, M. and Wann, J.P. (1998). Binocular virtual reality displays: When problems do and don't occur. *Human Factors* 40(1): 42–49.

Moray, N. (1981). Monitoring behavior and supervising control. In *Handbook of Perception and Human Performance*, Vol. 2, ed. K.R. Boff, L. Kaufman, and J.P. Thomas, 40–46. Wiley, New York.

Moray, N. and Rotenberg, I. (1989). Fault management in process control: Eye movements and action. *Ergonomics* 32(11): 1319–1342.

Morton, J. and Johnson, M.H. (1991). CONSPEC and CONLEARN: A two-process theory of infant face recognition. *Psychological Review* 98: 164–181.

Mousavi, S.Y., Low, R., and Sweller, J. (1995). Reducing cognitive load by mixing auditory and visual presentation modes. *Journal of Educational Psychology* 87: 319–334.

Mullen, K.Y. (1985). The contrast sensitivity of human color vision to red–green and blue–yellow chromatic gratings. *American Journal of Optometry and Physiological Optics* 359: 381–400.

Munzner, T., Guimbretière, F., and Robertson, G. (1999). Constellation: A visualization tool for linguistic queries from MindNet. *Proceedings of the 1999 IEEE Symposium on Information Visualization*, 132–135, San Francisco, CA, October 25–26, 1999.

Najjar, L.J. (1998). Principles of educational multimedia user interface design. *Human Factors* 40(2): 311–323.

Nakayama, K., Shimono, S., and Silverman, G.H. (1989). Stereoscopic depth: Its relation to image segmentation, grouping and the recognition of occluding objects. *Perception* 18: 55–68.

Nakayama, K. and Silverman, G.H. (1986). Serial and parallel processing of visual feature conjunctions. *Nature* 320: 264–265.

Nemire, K., Jacoby, R.H., and Ellis, S.R. (1994). Simulation fidelity of a virtual environment display. *Human Factors* 36(1): 79–93.

Neveau, C.F. and Stark, L.W. (1998). The virtual lens. *Presence* 7(4): 370–381.

Newell, A. (1990). *Unified Theories of Cognition.* Harvard University Press, Cambridge, MA.

Newell, A. and Rosenbloom, P. (1981). Mechanisms of skill acquisition and the law of practice. In *Cognitive Skills and Their Acquisition*, ed. J.R. Anderson, 1–55. Lawrence Erlbaum Associates, Hillsdale, N.J.

Norman, D.A. (1988). *The Psychology of Everyday Things.* Basic Books, New York.

Norman, J.F., Todd, J.T., and Phillips, F. (1995). The perception of surface orientation from multiple sources of optical information. *Perception and Psychophysics* 57(5): 629–636.

Noro, K. (1993). Industrial application of virtual reality and possible health problems. *Japan. Journal Ergonomica* 29: 126–129.

North, M.N., North, S.M., and Coble, J.R. (1996). Effectiveness of virtual environment desensitization in the treatment of agoraphobia. *Presence* 5(3): 346–352.

Novak, J.D. (1991). Clarify with concept maps: A tool for students and teachers alike. *The Science Teacher* 58(7): 45–49.

O'Regan, J.K. (1992). Solving the "real" mysteries of visual perception: The world as an outside memory. *Canadian Journal of Psychology* 46: 461–488.

Oakes, L.M. (1994). Development of infants' use of continuity cues in their perception of causality. *Developmental Psychology* 30: 869–879.

Ogle, K.N. (1962). The visual space sense. *Science* 135: 763–771.

Oliva, A. and Schyns, P. (1997). Coarse blobs or fine edges? Evidence that information diagnosticity changes the perception of complex visual stimuli. *Cognitive Psychology* 34: 72–107.

Oviatt, S. (1999). Mutual disambiguation of recognition errors in a multimodal architecture. *Proceedings of CHI '99*, ACM, 576–583.

Oviatt, S., DeAngeli, A., and Kuhn, K. (1997). Integration and synchronization of input modes during multimodal human-computer interaction. *Proceedings of CHI '97*, ACM, 415–422.

Owlsley, C.J., Sekuler, R., and Siemensne, D. (1983). Contrast sensitivity through adulthood. *Vision Research* 23: 689–699.

Paivio, A. (1987). *Mental Representations: A Dual Coding Approach*. Oxford Psychology Series. Oxford University Press, Oxford.

Paivio, A. and Csapo, K. (1969). Concrete image and verbal memory codes. *Journal of Experimental Psychology* 80: 279–285.

Palmer, S.E. (1975). The effect of contextual scenes on the identification of objects. *Memory and Cognition* 3(5): 519–526.

Palmer, S.E. (1992). Common region: A new principle of perceptual grouping. *Cognitive Psychology* 24: 436–447.

Palmer, S.E. and Rock, I. (1994). Rethinking perceptual organization: The role of uniform connectedness. *Psychonomic Bulletin and Review* 1(1): 29–55.

Palmer, S.E., Rosh, E., and Chase, P. (1981). Canonical perspective and perception of objects. *Attention and Performance IX*, ed. J. Long and A. Baddeley, 135–151. Lawerence Erlbaum Associates, Hillsdale, N.J.

Palmiter, S., Elkerton, J., and Paggett, P. (1991). Animated demonstrations vs. written instructions for learning procedural tasks: A preliminary investigation. *International Journal of Man-Machine Studies* 34: 687–701.

Parker, G., Franck, G., and Ware, C. (1998). Visualizing of large nested graphs in 3D: Navigation and interaction. *Journal of Visual Languages* 9: 299–317.

Pashler, H. (1995). Attention and visual perception: Analyzing divided attention. In *An Invitation to Cognitive Science: Visual Cognition*, vol. 2, ed. S. Kosslyn and D. Osherson, 71–100. MIT Press, Cambridge, MA.

Patterson, R. and Martin, W.L. (1992). Human stereopsis. *Human Factors* 34(6): 669–692.

Pausch, R., Snoddy, J., Taylor, R., Watson, S., and Haseltine, E. (1996). Disney's Aladdin: First steps towards storytelling in virtual reality. *SIGGRAPH '96 Proceedings*, 193–203.

Pearson, D., Hanna, E., and Martinez, K. (1990). Computer-generated cartoons. In *Images and Understanding*, ed. H. Barlow, C. Blakemore, and M. Weston Smith, 46–60. Cambridge University Press, Cambridge.

Peli, E. (1999). Optometric and perceptual issues with head-mounted display (HMD). In *Optical Design for Visual Instrumentation*, ed. P. Mouroulis, 205–276. McGraw-Hill, New York.

Perrett, D.I., Oram, M.W., Harries, M.H., Bevan, R., Hietanen, J.K., Benson, P.J., and Thomas, S. (1991). Viewer-centered and object-centered coding of heads in the Macaque temporal cortex. *Experimental Brain Research* 86: 159–173.

Perry, M. (2003). Distributed cognition. In *HCI Models, Theories, and Frameworks: Toward a Multidisciplinary Science*, ed. John M. Carroll, 193–223. Morgan Kaufmann, San Francisco.

Peterson, H.E. and Dugas, D.J. (1972). The relative importance of contrast and motion in visual detection. *Human Factors* 14: 207–216.

Phillips, W.A. (1974). On the distinction between sensory storage and short-term visual memory. *Perception and Psychophysics* 16: 283–290.

Pickett, R.M. and Grinstein, G.G. (1988). Iconograhic displays for visualizing multidimensional data. *Proceedings of the 1988 IEEE Conference on Systems, Man and Cybernetics*, vol. I, 514–519.

Pickett, R.M., Grinstein, G.G., Levkowitz, H., and Smith, S. (1995). Harnessing pre-attentive perceptual processes in visualization. In *Perceptual Issues in Visualization*, ed. G. Grinstein and H. Levkowitz. 33–45. Springer, New York.

Pirolli, P. (2003). Exploring and Finding Information. In *HCI Models, Theories and Frameworks: Toward a Multidisciplinary Science*, ed. John M. Caroll. Morgan Kaufmann, San Francisco.

Pirolli, P. and Card, S.K. (1995). Information foraging in information access environments. *Proceedings of CHI '95*, ACM, 51–58.

Plumlee, M. and Ware, C. (2002). Modeling performance for zooming vs multi-window interfaces based on visual working memory. *Advanced Visual Interfaces*, Trento, Italy, May Proceedings, 59–68.

Plumlee, M. and Ware, C. (2003). An evaluation of methods for linking 3D views. *Proceedings of the ACM SIGGRAPH 2003 Symposium on Interactive 3D Graphics*, Monterey, CA, 193–201.

Posner, M.I. and Keele, S. (1968). On the generation of abstract ideas. *Journal of Experimental Psychology* 77: 353–363.

Post, D.L. and Greene, F.A. (1986). Color name boundaries for equally bright stimuli on a CRT: Phase I. *Society for Information Display, Digest of Technical Papers* 86: 70–73.

Postma, A. and De Haan, E.H.F. (1996). What was where? Memory for object locations. *Quarterly Journal of Experimental Psychology* 49A(1): 178–199.

Postma, A., Izendoorn, R., and De Haan, E.H.F. (1998). Sex differences in object location memory. *Brain and Cognition* 36: 334–345.

Potter, M.C. (1976). Short-term conceptual memory for pictures. *Journal of Experimental Psychology: Human Learning and Memory* 2: 509–522.

Potter, M.C. (2002). Recognition memory for briefly presented pictures: The time course of rapidly forgetting. *Journal of Experimental Psychology: Human Perception and Performance* 28(5): 1163–1175.

Potter, M.C. and Levy, E.I. (1969). Recognition memory for a rapid sequence of pictures. *Journal of Experimental Psychology* 81: 10–15.

Poupyrev, I., Billinghurst, M., Weghorst, S., and Ichikawa, T. (1996). The Go-Go interaction technique: Non-linear mapping for direct manipulation in VR. *Proceedings of UIST '96*, Seattle, WA, November 6–8, 1996.

Price, C.J. and Humphreys, G.W. (1989). The effects of surface detail on object categorization and naming. *Quarterly Journal of Experimental Psychology* 41A: 797–828.

Puce, A., Allison, T., Gore, J.C., and McCarthy, G. (1995). Face-sensitive regions in human extra-striated cortex studied by functional MRI. *Journal of Neurophysiology* 74: 1192–1199.

Pylyshyn, Z.W. and Storm, R.W. (1988). Tracking multiple independent targets: Evidence for a parallel tracking mechanism. *Spatial Vision* 3: 179–197.

Quinlan, P. and Humphreys, G. (1987). Visual search for targets defined by combinations of color, shape and size: An examination of task constraints on feature and conjunction searches. *Perception and Psychophysics* 41(5): 455–472.

Rader, C., Brand, C., and Lewis, C. (1997). Degrees of comprehension: Children's understanding of a visual programming environment. *Proceedings of CHI '97*, ACM, 351–358.

Ramachandran, V.S. (1988). Perception of shape from shading. *Nature* 331: 163–166.

Ramachandran, V.S. (1999). *Phantoms in the Brain: Probing the Mysteries of the Human Mind*. Quill Press, New York.

Rao, R. and Card, S.K. (1994). The table lens: Merging graphical and symbolic representations in an interactive focus + context visualization for tabular information. *Proceedings of CHI '94*, ACM, 318–322.

Raymond, J.E., Shapiro, K.L., and Arnell, K.M. (1992). Temporary suppression of visual processing in an RSVP task: An attentional blink? *Journal of Experimental Psychology: Human Perception and Performance* 18: 849–860.

Regan, D. (1989). Orientation discrimination for objects defined by relative motion and objects defined by luminance contrasts. *Vision Research* 18: 1389–1400.

Regan, D. and Hamstra, S. (1991). Shape discrimination for motion and contrast defined contours: Squareness is special. *Perception* 20: 315–336.

Rensink, R.A. (2000). The dynamic representation of scenes. *Visual Cognition* 7: 17–42.

Rensink, R.A. (2002). Change detection. *Annual Review of Psychology* 53: 245–277.

Rensink, R.A., O'Reagan, J.K., and Clark, J.J. (1997). To see or not to see: The need for attention to perceive changes in scenes. *Psychological Science* 8(5): 368–373.

Rheingans, P. (1999). Task-based color scale design: 3D visualization for data exploration and decision making. *28th Applied Image and Pattern Recognition Workshop*, October 1999, Washington D.C., SPIE, 35–43.

Rhodes, G. (1995). Face recognition and configurational coding. In *Cognitive and Computational Aspects of Face Recognition*, ed. T. Valentine. Routledge, New York.

Rhodes, P.A. and Luo, M.R. (1996). A system of WYSIWYG colour communication. *Displays*, Elsevier Science 16(4): 213–221.

Richards, W. (1967). Differences among color normals: Classes I and II. *Journal of the Optical Society of America* 57: 1047–1055.

Richards, W. and Koenderink, J.J. (1995). Trajectory mapping: A new non-metric scaling technique. *Perception* 24: 1315–1331.

Riggs, L.A., Merton, P.A., and Mortion, H.B. (1974). Suppression of visual phosphenes during saccadic eye movements. *Vision Research* 14: 997–1010.

Rimé, B., Boulanger, B., Laubin, P., Richants, M., and Stroobants, K. (1985). The perception of interpersonal emotions originated by patterns of movements. *Motivation and Emotion* 9: 241–260.

Robertson, G., Czerwinski, M., Larson, K., Robbins, D., Thiel, D., and van Dantzich, M. (1998). Data Mountain: Using spatial memory for document management. *Proceedings of UIST '89*, ACM, 153–162.

Robertson, G., Mackinlay, J.D., and Card, S.W. (1993). Information Visualization Using 3D Interactive Animation. *Communications of the ACM* 36(4), 57–71.

Robertson, P.K. and O'Callaghan, J.F. (1986). The generation of color sequences for univariate and bivariate mapping. *IEEE Computer Graphics and Applications* 6(2): 24–32.

Robertson, P.K. and O'Callaghan, J.F. (1988). The application of perceptual colour spaces to the display of remotely sensed data. *IEEE Transactions on Geoscience and Remote Sensing* 26(1): 49–59.

Rock, I. and Gutman, D. (1981). The effect of inattention on form perception. *Journal of Experimental Psychology: Human Perception and Performance* 7(2): 275–285.

Rogers, B. and Cagnello, R. (1989). Disparity curvature and the perception of three-dimensional surfaces. *Nature* 339: 137–139.

Rogers, B. and Graham, M. (1979). Similarities between motion parallax and stereopsis in human depth perception. *Vision Research* 22: 261–270.

Rogers, E. (1995). A cognitive theory of visual interaction. In *Diagrammatic Reasoning: Cognitive and Computational Perspectives*, ed. J. Glasgos, N.H. Narayanan, and B. Chandraseekaran, 481–500. AAAI Press/MIT Press, Cambridge, MA.

Rogowitz, B.E. and Treinish, L.A. (1996). How not to lie with visualization. *Computers in Physics* 10(3): 268–273.

Romesburg, C.H. (1984). *Cluster Analysis for Researchers*. Lifetime Learning Publications, Belmont, CA.

Rood, O.N. (1897). *Modern Chromatics*. Reprinted in facsimile, 1973, Van Nostrand Reinhold, New York.

Roscoe, S.R. (1991). The eyes prefer real images. *Pictoral Communication in Virtual and Real Environments*, ed. S.R. Ellis, M. Kaiser, and A.J. Grunwald, 577–585. Taylor and Francis, London.

Rosenthal, N.E. (1993). Diagnosis and treatment of seasonal affective disorder. *Journal of the American Medical Association* 270: 2717–2720.

Rosetti, Y., Koga, K., and Mano, T. (1993). Prismatic displacement of vision induces transient changes in the timing of eye-hand coordination. *Perception and Psychophysics* 54(3): 355–364.

Rumbaugh, J., Booch, G., and Jacobson, I. (1999). *Unified Modeling Language Reference Manual*. Addison-Wesley Object Technology Series, Reading, MA.

Russo, J.E. and Rosen, L.D. (1975). An eye fixation analysis of multi-alternative choice. *Memory and Cognition* 3: 267–276.

Rutkowski, C. (1982). An introduction to the Human Applications Standard Computer Interface, Part 1: Theory and principles. *BYTE* 7(11): 291–310.

Ruttkay, Z., Noot, H., and Hagen, P. (2003). Emotion disc and emotion squares: Tools to explore the facial expression space. *Computer Graphics Forum* 22(1): 49–53.

Ryan, T.A. and Schwartz, C.B. (1956). Speed of perception as a function of mode of representation. *American Journal of Psychology* 69: 60–69.

Sadr, J., Jarudi, F., and Sinha, P. (2003). The role of the eyebrows in face recognition. *Perception* 32(3): 285–293.

Saito, T. and Takahashi, T. (1990). Comprehensible rendering of 3-D shapes. *SIGGRAPH '90 Proceedings, Computer Graphics* 24(4): 197–206.

Sarkar, M. and Brown, M.H. (1994). Graphical fisheye views. *Communications of the ACM* 37(12): 73–83.

Saussure, F. de. (1959). *Course in General Linguistics.* Reprinted by Fontana/Collins, New York. (Published posthumously based on lectures given at the University of Geneva between 1906 and 1911.)

Scanlan, L.A. (1975). Visual time compression: Spatial and temporal cues. *Human Factors* 17: 337–345.

Schroeder, W., Martin, K., and Lorenson, B. (1997). *The Visualization Toolkit.* Prentice Hall, Upper Saddle River, NJ.

Schumann, J., Strotthotte, T., Raab, A., and Laser, S. (1996). Assessing the effect of non-photorealistic rendered images in CAD. *CHI '96 Proceedings,* ACM, 35–41.

Schwarz, M., Cowan, W., and Beatty, J. (1987). An experimental comparison of RGB, YIQ, LAB, HSV and opponent color models. *ACM Transactions on Graphics* 6(2): 123–158.

Seigel, A.W. and White, S.H. (1975). The development of spatial representations of large-scale environments. In *Advances in Child Development and Behaviour,* ed. H.W. Reese, 9–55. Academic Press, London.

Sekuler, R. and Blake, R. (1990). *Perception,* 2d ed. McGraw-Hill, New York.

Selker, T. and Koved, L. (1988). Elements of visual language. *IEEE Conference of Visual Languages, Proceedings,* 38–44.

Sellen, A., Buxton, B., and Arnott, J. (1992). Using spatial cues to improve videoconferencing. *CHI '92 Proceedings*, ACM, 651–652. Also, CHI video proceedings, same year.

Serra, L., Hern, N., Choon, C.B., and Poston, T. (1997). Interactive vessel tracing in volume data. *1997 Symposium on Interactive 3D Graphics, Proceedings*, 131–137.

Shelton, A.L. and McNamara, T.P. (2001). Systems of spatial reference in human memory. *Cognitive Psychology* 43: 274–310.

Shenker, M. (1987). Optical design criteria for binocular helmet-mounted display. *Display System Optics, SPIE Proceedings* 778: 173–185.

Shepard, R.N. (1962). The analysis of proximities: Multidimensional scaling with unknown distance function, Part I. *Psychometrika* 27(2): 125–140.

Sheridan, T. (1972). On how often the supervisor should sample. *IEEE Transactions on Systems Man and Cybernetics* 6: 140–145.

Shneiderman, B. (1987). *Designing the User Interface*. Addison-Wesley, Reading, MA.

Shneiderman, B. (1998). *Designing the User Interface*, 3d ed. Addison-Wesley, Reading, MA.

Shorter Oxford English Dictionary, Volume II. (1972). Prepared by Little, W., Fowler, H.W., and Coulson, J. Revised by C.T. Onions. N–Z, 3d ed, 2364. Oxford University Press, Oxford, U.K.

Sigman, M. and Gilbert, C.D. (2000). Learning to find a shape. *Nature Neuroscience* 3: 264–269.

Simons, D.J. and Levin, D.T. (1998). Failure to detect changes to people during a real-world interaction. *Psychonomic Bulletin and Review* 5: 644–669.

Singer, W. and Gray, C.M. (1995). Visual feature integration and the temporal correlation hypothesis. *Annual Review of Neuroscience* 18: 555–586.

Slater, A. and Kirby, R. (1998). Innate and learned perceptual abilities in the newborn infant. *Experimental Brain Research* 123: 90–94.

Slater, M., Usoh, M., and Steed, A. (1995). Taking steps, the influence of walking technique on presence in virtual reality. *ACM Transactions on CHI* 2(3): 201–219.

Slocum, T.S. (1983). Predicting visual clusters on graduated circle maps. *American Cartographer* 10(1): 59–72.

Smith, A.R. (1978). Color gamut transform pairs. *Computer Graphics* 12: 12–19.

Smith, G. and Atchison, D.A. (1997). *The Eye and Visual Optical Instruments.* Cambridge University Press, Cambridge.

Snyder, F.W. and Pronko, N.H. (1952). *Vision with Spatial Inversion.* University of Wichita Press: Wichita, KS.

Sollenberger, R.L. and Milgram, P. (1993). The effects of stereoscopic and rotational displays in the three-dimensional path tracing task. *Human Factors* 35(3): 483–500.

Spangenberg, R.W. (1973). The motion variable in procedural learning. *AV Communications Review* 21(4): 419–436.

Spence, I. and Efendov, A. (2001). Target detection in scientific visualization. *Journal of Experimental Psychology: Applied* 7(1): 13–26.

Spence, I., Kutlesa, N., and Rose, D.L. (1999). Using color to code quantity in spatial displays. *Journal of Experimental Psychology: Applied* 5(4): 393–412.

Spence, R. (2002). Rapid, serial and visual: A presentation technique with potential. *Information Visualization* 1: 13–19.

Sperling, G. (1960). The information available in brief visual presentations. *Psychological Monographs: General and Applied* 74(11).

Standing, L., Conezio, I., and Haber, R.N. (1970). Perception and memory for pictures: Single trial learning of 2560 visual stimuli. *Psychonomic Science* 19: 73–74.

Stankiewicz, B.J., Hummerl, J.E., and Cooper, E.E. (1998). The role of attention in priming for left–right reflections of object images: Evidence for a dual representation of object shape. *Journal of Experimental Psychology: Human Perception and Performance* 24: 732–744.

Stasko, J.T. (1990). Tango: A framework and system for algorithm animation. *IEEE Computer* 23(9): 27–39.

State, A., Livingston, M.A., Garrett, W.F., Hirotal, G., Whitton, M.C., and Pisano, E.D. (1996). Technologies for augmented reality systems: Realizing ultrasound-guided needle biopsies. *SIGGRAPH '96 Proceedings*, ACM, 439–446.

Stenning, K. and Oberlander, J. (1994). A cognitive theory of graphical and linguistic reasoning: Logic and implementation. *Cognitive Science* 19: 97–140.

Stevens, S.S. (1946). On the theory of scales of measurement. *Science* 103: 677–680.

Stevens, S.S. (1961). The psychophysics of sensory function. In *Sensory Communication*, ed. W.A. Rosenblith, 1–33. MIT Press, Cambridge, MA.

Stone, M.C., Cowan, W.B., and Beatty, J.C. (1988). Color gamut mapping and the printing of digital color images. *ACM Transactions on Graphics* 7(4): 249–292.

Stone, M.C., Fishkin, K., and Bier, E.A. (1994). The movable filter as a user interface tool. *Proceedings of CHI '94*, ACM, 306–312.

Stroop, J.R. (1935). Studies of interference in serial verbal reactions. *Journal of Experimental Psychology* 18: 643–662.

Strothotte, C. and Strothotte, T. (1997). *Seeing between the Pixels*. Springer-Verlag, Berlin.

Sun, F., Staerk, L., Nguyen, A., Wong, J., Lakshminarayanan, V., and Mueller, E. (1988). Changes in accommodation with age: Static and dynamic. *American Journal of Optometry and Physiological Optics* 65(6): 492–498.

Sweller, J., Chandler, P., Tierner, P., and Cooper, G. (1990). Cognitive load as a factor in the structuring of technical material. *Journal of Experimental Psychology* 119(2): 176–192.

Swets, J.A. (1996). *Signal Detection Theory and ROC Analysis in Psychology and Diagnostics: Collected Papers*. Erlbaum, Mahwah, NJ.

Tabachnick, B.G. and Fidell, L.S. (2001). *Using Multivariate Statistics*, 4th ed. HarperCollins, New York.

Thomas, K.M., King, S.W., Franzen, P.L., Welsh, T.F., Berkowitz, A.L., Noll, D.C., Birmaher, V., and Casey , B.J. (1999). A developmental functional MRI study of spatial working memory. *NeuroImage* 10: 327–338.

Thorisson, K., Koons, D., and Bolt, R. (1992). Multi-modal natural dialogue, *CHI '92 Video Proceedings*, ACM, 653.

Thorndyke, P.W. and Hayes-Roth, B. (1982). Differences in spatial knowledge acquired from maps and navigation. *Cognitive Psychology* 14: 560–589.

Tittle, J.S., Todd, J.T., Perotti, V.J., and Norman, J.F. (1995). Systematic distortion of perceived three-dimensional structure from motion and binocular stereopsis. *Journal of Experimental Psychology: Human Perception and Performance* 21(3): 663–687.

Todd, J.T. and Mingolla, E. (1983). Perception of surface curvature and direction of illumination from patterns of shading. *Journal of Experimental Psychology: Human Perception and Performance* 9(4): 583–595.

Treisman, A. (1985). Preattentive processing in vision. *Computer Vision, Graphics and Image Processing* 31: 156–177.

Treisman, A. and Gelade, G. (1980). A feature integration theory of attention. *Cognitive Psychology* 12: 97–136.

Treisman, A. and Gormican, S. (1988). Feature analysis in early vision: Evidence from search asymmetries. *Psychological Review* 95(1): 15–48.

Trumbo, B.E. (1981). A theory for coloring bivariate statistical maps. *American Statistician* 35: 220–226.

Tufte, E.R. (1983). *The Visual Display of Quantitative Information.* Graphics Press, Cheshire, CT.

Tufte, E.R. (1990). *Envisioning Information.* Graphics Press, Cheshire, CT.

Tulving, E. (1983). *Elements of Episodic Memory.* Oxford University Press, New York.

Tulving, E. and Madigan, S.A. (1970). Memory and verbal learning. *Annual Review of Psychology* 21: 437–484.

Turk, G. and Banks, D. (1996). Image-guided streamline placement. *SIGGRAPH '96 Proceedings*, ACM, 453–460.

Tweedie, L. (1997). Characterizing interactive externalizations. *CHI '97, ACM, Atlanta Proceedings*, 375–382.

Tweedie, L., Spence, R., Dawkes, H., and Su, H. (1996). Externalizing abstract mathematical models. *CHI '96 Proceedings*, 406–412.

Uomori, K. and Nishida, S. (1994). The dynamics of the visual system in combining conflicting KDE and binocular stereopsis cues. *Perception and Psychophysics* 55(5): 526–536.

Valyus, N.A. (1966). *Stereoscopy.* (Translated from the original). Focal Press, London.

Venturino, M. and Gagnon, D. (1992). Information trade-offs in complex stimulus structures: Local and global levels in naturalistic scenes. *Perception and Psychophysics* 52(4): 425–436.

Veron, H., Southard, D.A., Leger, J.R., and Conway, J.L. (1990). Stereoscopic displays of terrain database visualization. *Proceedings of the 1992 ACM Symposium on Interactive 3D Graphics*, 39–42.

Viguier, A., Clement, G., and Trotter, Y. (2001). Distance perception within near visual space. *Perception* 30: 115–124.

Vinson, N.G. (1999). Design guidelines for landmarks to support navigation in virtual environments. *Proceedings of CHI '99*, ACM, 278–285.

Vishton, P.M. and Cutting, J.E. (1995). Wayfinding, displacements, and mental maps: Velocity fields are not typically used to determine one's aimpoint. *Journal of Experimental Psychology: Human Perception and Performance* 21(5): 978–995.

Vogel, E.K., Woodman, G.F., and Luck, S.J. (2001). Storage of features, conjunctions and objects in visual working memory. *Journal of Experimental Psychology: Human Perception and Performance* 27(1): 92–114.

Wade, N.J. and Swanston, M.T. (1966). A general model for the perception of space and motion. *Perception* 25: 187–194.

Wadill, P. and McDaniel, M. (1992). Pictorial enhancement of text memory: Limitations imposed by picture type and comprehension skill. *Memory and Cognition* 20(5): 472–482.

Wainer, H. and Francolini, C.M. (1980). An empirical enquiry concerning human understanding of two variable maps. *American Statistician* 34(2): 81–93.

Wallach, H. (1959). The perception of motion. *Scientific American* 201 (July): 56–60.

Wallach, H. and Floor, L. (1971). The use of size matching to demonstrate the effectiveness of accommodation and convergence as cues for distance. *Perception and Psychophysics* 10: 423–428.

Wallach, H. and Karsh, E. (1963). The modification of stereoscopic depth perception based on oculomotor cues. *Perception and Psychophysics* 11: 110–116.

Wallach, H. and O'Connell, D.N. (1953). The kinetic depth effect. *Journal of Experimental Psychology* 45: 205–217.

Wang, W. and Milgram, P. (2001). Dynamic viewpoint tethering for navigation in large-scale virtual environments. *Proceedings of the Human Factor and Ergonomics Society*, 1862–1866.

Wang, Y. and Frost, B.J. (1992). Time to collision is signaled by neurons in the nucleus rotundus of pigeons. *Nature* 356: 236–238.

Wang, Y., and MacKenzie, C.L. (1999). Object manipulation in virtual environments: Relative size matters. *Proceedings of CHI '99*, ACM, 48–55.

Wanger, L. (1992). The effect of shadow quality on the perception of spatial relationships in computer-generated images. *Proceedings of the 1992 ACM Symposium on Interactive 3D Graphics*, 39–42.

Wanger, L.R., Ferwander, J.A., and Greenberg, D.A. (1992). Perceiving spatial relationships in computer-generated images. *IEEE Computer Graphics and Applications*, 12(3): 44–58.

Wann, J.P., Rushton, S., and Mon-Williams, M. (1995). Natural problems for stereoscopic depth perception in virtual environments. *Vision Research* 35(19): 2731–2736.

Wann, J.P., Rushton, S.K., and Lee, D.N. (1995). Can you control where you are heading when you are looking at where you want to go? In *Studies in Perception and Action III*, ed. B.G. Bardy, R.J. Bootsmal, and Y. Guiard, 201–210. Lawrence Erlbaum Associates, Hillsdale, NJ.

Ware, C. (1988). Color sequences for univariate maps: Theory, experiments, and principles. *IEEE Computer Graphics and Applications*, Sept., 41–49.

Ware, C. (1989). Fast hill shading with specular reflection and cast shadows. *Computers and Geosciences* 15: 1327–1334.

Ware, C., Arthur, K.W., and Booth, K.S. (1993). Fish-tank virtual reality. In *Proceedings of INTERCHI '93 Conference on Human Factors in Computing Systems*, ACM, New York, 37–42.

Ware, C. and Balakrishnan, R. (1994). Object acquisition in VR displays: Lag and frame rate. *ACM Transactions on Computer Human Interaction* 1(4): 331–357.

Ware, C. and Beatty, J.C. (1988). Using color dimensions to display data dimensions. *Human Factors* 30(2): 127–142.

Ware, C., Bonner, J., Knight, W., and Cater, R. (1992). Moving icons as a human interrupt. *International Journal of Human-Computer Interaction* 4(4): 341–348.

Ware, C. and Cowan, W.B. (1982). Changes in perceived color due to chromatic interactions. *Vision Research* 22: 1353–1362.

Ware, C. and Cowan, W.B. (1987). Chromatic mach bands: Behavioral evidence of lateral inhibition in color vision. *Perception and Psychophysics* 41: 173–178.

Ware, C. and Cowan, W.B. (1990). The RGYB color geometry. *ACM Transactions on Graphics* 9(2): 226–232.

Ware, C. and Franck, G. (1996). Evaluating stereo and motion cues for visualizing information nets in three dimensions. *ACM Transactions on Graphics* 15(2): 121–140.

Ware, C., Gobrecht, C., and Paton, M. (1998). Dynamic adjustment of stereo display parameters. *IEEE Transactions on Systems, Man and Cybernetics* 28(1): 56–65.

Ware, C. and Knight, W. (1995). Using visual texture for information display. *ACM Transactions on Graphics* 14(1): 3–20.

Ware, C. and Lewis, M. (1995). The DragMag image magnifier. *CHI '95 Conference Companion* and *Conference Video Proceedings*, ACM, 407–408.

Ware, C. and Mikaelian, H. (1987). An evaluation of an eye tracker as a device for computer input. *Proceedings of CHI '87*, ACM, 183–188.

Ware, C. and Osborne, S. (1990). Explorations and virtual camera control in virtual three-dimensional environments. *Computer Graphics* 24(2): 175–183.

Ware, C., Plumlee, M., Arsenault, R., Mayer, L.A., Smith, S., and House, D. (2001). GeoZui3D: Data fusion for interpreting oceanographic data. *Oceans 2001 Proceedings*, Hawaii, 1960–1964.

Ware, C., Purchase, H., Colpoys, L., and McGill, M. (2002). Cognitive measurements of graph aesthetics. *Information Visualization* 1: 103–110.

Ware, C. and Rose, J. (1999). Rotating virtual objects with real handles, *ACM Transactions on CHI* 6(2): 162–180.

Warren, W.H. (1984). Perceiving affordances: Visual guidance of stair climbing. *Journal of Experimental Psychology: Human Perception and Performance* 10: 683–703.

Warrick, M.S., Kibler, A., Topmiller, D.H., and Bates, C. (1964). Response time to unexpected stimuli. *American Psychologist* 19: 528.

Watanabe, T. and Cavanaugh, P. (1996). Texture laciness: The texture equivalent of transparency. *Perception* 25: 293–303.

Weigle, C., Emigh, W., Liu, G., Taylor, R., Enns, J., Healey, C. (2000). Oriented texture slivers: A technique for local value estimation of multiple scalar fields *Proceedings of Graphics Interface2000*, 163–170.

Welch, R.B. (1978). *Perceptual Modification: Adapting to Altered Sensory Environments.* Academic Press, New York.

Welch, R.B. and Cohen, M.M. (1991). Adaptation to variable prismatic displacement. In *Pictorial Communication in Virtual and Real Environments*, ed. S.R. Ellis, 295–304. Taylor and Francis, London.

Wetherill, G.B. and Levitt, H. (1965). Sequential estimation of points on a psychometric function. *British Journal of Mathematical and Statistical Psychology* 18: 1–10.

Wickens, C.D. (1992). *Engineering Psychology and Human Performance*, 2d ed. HarperCollins, New York.

Wickens, C.D., Haskell I., and Harte, K. (1989). Ergonomic design for perspective flight path displays. *IEEE Control Systems Magazine* 9(4): 3–8.

Wijk, J.J. van, Wetering, H. van de. (1999). Cushion treemaps. In *Proceedings 1999 IEEE Symposium on Information Visualization (InfoVis '99)*, ed. G. Wills, D. Keim, 73–78, IEEE Computer Society, October 25–26, 1999.

Wilkins, A. (1995). *Visual Stress.* Oxford Psychology Series #24. Oxford University Press, Oxford.

Williams, A.J. and Harris, R.L. (1985). Factors affecting dwell times on digital displays. *NASA Technical Memorandum 86406.* NASA Langley Research Center.

Williams, L.J. (1985). Tunnel vision induced by a foveal load manipulation. *Human Factors* 27(2): 221–227.

Williams, M.D. and Hollan, J.D. (1981). The process of retrieval from very long-term memory. *Cognitive Science* 5: 87–119.

Williams, S.P. and Parrish, R.V. (1990). New computational control techniques and increased understanding for stereo 3-D displays. *Proc. SPIE Stereoscopic Display Applications*, Santa Clara, CA, 73–82.

Wilson, H.R. and Bergen, J.R. (1979). A four mechanism model for threshold spatial vision. *Vision Research* 19: 19–32.

Wise, J.A., Thomas, J.J., Pennock, K., Lantrip, D., Pottier, M., Schur, A., and Crow, V. (1995). Visualizing the non-visual: Spatial analysis and interaction with information and text documents. *Proceedings of IEEE Information Visualization '95*, 51–58.

Witkin, A. and Kass, M. (1991). Reaction diffusion textures. *SIGGRAPH '91 Proceedings: Computer Graphics*, 25(4): 299–308.

Wittenburg, K., Ali-Ahmad, W., LaLiberte, D., Lanning, T. (1998). Rapid-fire image previews for information navigation. *Proceedings, Advance Visual Interfaces (AVI '98)*, 76–82, Aquila, Italy ACM Press, New York.

Wolfe, J.M. and Gancarz, G.G. (1996). Guided Search 3.0. A model of visual search catches up with Jay Enoch 40 Years Later. In *Basic and Clinical Application of Visual Science*, ed. V. Lakshminarayanan, 189–192. Kluwer Academic, Dordrecht, Netherlands.

Wong, P.C. and Bergeron, R.D. (1997). Multivariate visualization using metric scaling. *Proceedings IEEE Visualization*, 111–118.

Wyszecki, G. and Stiles, W.S. (1982). *Color Science Concepts and Methods, Quantitative Data and Formulae*, 2d ed. Wiley Interscience, New York.

Xu, Y. (2002). Limitations of object-based features encoding in visual short-term memory. *Journal of Experimental Psychology: Human Perception and Performance* 28(2): 458–468.

Yaniv, I. and Mayer, D.E. Activation and metacognition of inaccessible stored information: Potential basis for incubation effects in problem solving. *Journal of Experimental Psychology: Learning, Memory and Cognition* 13: 187–205.

Yantis, S. (1992). Multielement visual tracking: Attention and perceptual organization. *Cognitive Psychology* 24: 295–340.

Yates, F.A. (1966). *The Art of Memory.* University of Chicago Press, Chicago.

Yeh, Y. and Silverstein, L.D. (1990). Limits of fusion and depth judgment in stereoscopic color displays. *Human Factors* 32(1): 45–60.

Yoshimura, T., Nakamura, Y., and Sugiura, M. (1994). 3D direct manipulation interface: Development of the Zashiki-Warashi system. *Computers and Graphics* 18(2): 201–207.

Young, F.W., Takane, Y., and de Leeuw, J. (1978). The principal components of mixed measurement level multivariate data: An alternating least squares method with optimal scaling features. *Psychometrika* 43: 279–281.

Young, M.J., Landy, M.S., and Maloney, L.T. (1993). A perturbation analysis of depth perception from combinations of texture and motion cues. *Vision Research* 33: 2685–2696.

Yufic, Y.M. and Sheridan, T.B. (1996). Virtual networks: New framework for operator modeling and interface optimization in complex supervisory control systems. *Annual Review of Control* 20: 179–195.

Zeki, S. (1992). The visual image in mind and brain. *Scientific American* (Sept.): 69–76.

Zeki, S. (1993). *A vision of the brain.* Blackwell, Oxford.

Zhai, S., Buxton, W., and Milgram, P. (1994). The "silk cursor": Investigating transparency for 3D target acquisition. *CHI '94 Proceedings*, ACM, 459–464.

Zhang, J. (1997). The nature of external representations in problem solving. *Cognitive Science* 21(2): 179–217.

SUBJECT INDEX

2D flow visualization techniques, 201, 203–205

2D positioning and selection, 319–320

2-handed interaction, 321–322

2–1/2D sketch processing, 22

3D displays. *See* stereoscopic displays; task-based space perception; virtual-reality (VR) displays

1976 uniform chromaticity scale (UCS) diagram (CIE), 109, 110

"action system" of pattern perception, 22

acuities. *See* visual acuities

adaptation, lightness constancy and, 85

advection trajectories, 204

aesthetic impression of 3D space (presence), 293–294

affordance theory
    direct perception of affordances, 18
    interface design and, 18–20
    top-down approach of, 18

affordances
    computer monitor deficiencies, 68

    constraints on navigation metaphors and, 327
    defined, 18
    design using, 20
    physical vs. graphical, 19–20, 323–324
    surfaces and, 31
    visual representation of, 18–19

aliasing
    antialiasing techniques, 64–65
    Nyquist limit and, 63–64
    temporal, 67
    useful effects, 65

ambient optical array
    computer graphics and, 31–32
    defined, 31, 32
    dynamic flow patterns, 32–33

ambient shading, 36, 245–246

amodal control memory, 353

analytic processing, separable dimensions and, 177

angular disparity for stereoscopic depth, 271–272

animated visual languages, 312–315

animation. *See also* motion
    animated images vs. words, 305–306
    animated visual languages, 312–315

correspondence problem, 218–219
    for diagram enrichment, 224–225
    moving frames, 221
    perception of animate motion, 223–224
    visual momentum in, 311–312
    wagon-wheel effect, 219

antialiasing techniques
    overview, 64–65
    temporal, 67
    vernier acuity and, 65–66

arbitrary representations
    characteristics, 15–17
    defined, 10
    hybrids with sensory representations, 13
    methodologies for studying, 15, 16
    Saussure's arbitrariness principle, 6
    sensory representations vs., 10, 27

artifacts (cultural), 1–2, 17

artifacts (graphical)
    aliasing, 63–65
    visualization and perception of, 3

artificial spatial cues, 279–280

atmospheric depth, 280

attention
    as both low-level and high-level property of vision, 146

AUTHOR INDEX

ABOUT THE AUTHOR

Colin Ware, PhD, had an early interest in both art and science, which eventually led to a fascination with the effective display of information. He grew up in England and obtained a Bachelor of Science degree in psychology from Durham University. He moved to Canada to attend Dalhousie University, where he studied stereoscopic depth perception and completed a Master's degree in psychology. At this point, he left the academic world in an attempt to become an artist. But he continued to study on his own, pursuing the idea of applying the science of visual perception to the study of art.

After three years, he returned to academia to study picture perception under John Kennedy at the University of Toronto. This turned into a study of form perception, and he received his doctorate in psychology in 1980. He moved to Ottawa to work at the National Research Council with William Cowan and Gunter Wyszecki on problems of color perception. With Cowan, he conducted a series of applied color tutorials at SIGGRAPH. These fueled an emerging interest in computing and information display, which led him to the University of Waterloo to do an MMath (Master's degree in mathematics) in computer science, investigating the use of color for discrete information display. At the age of 35 he obtained his first "real" job at the University of New Brunswick, where for 14 years he concentrated his research on interactive display techniques.

Dr. Ware has published over 100 articles in scientific and technical journals and at leading conferences. Many of these relate to the use of color, texture, motion, and interactive 3D displays for information visualization. His approach is always to combine theory with practice, and his publications range from rigorously scientific contributions to the *Journal of Physiology* and *Vision Research* to applications-oriented articles in *ACM Transactions on Graphics* and *IEEE Transactions on Systems, Man and Cybernetics*.

Ware also takes pride in building useful visualization systems. While at the University of New Brunswick, he was instrumental in the creation of two spin-off visualization companies based initially on his research. Interactive Visualization Systems Inc. makes Fledermaus, a visualization software for advanced ocean-mapping applications. NVision Software Systems Inc. provided visualization tools to enhance the understanding of large, highly interconnected datasets.

Professor Ware currently directs the Data Visualization Research Lab, which is part of the Center for Coastal and Ocean Mapping at the University of New Hampshire. Among other projects, his team is developing GeoZui3D, an experimental zooming 3D geographical data visualization system, and a very high–resolution stereoscopic display system.